Stimulating Creativity

VOLUME 1

Individual Procedures

STIMULATING CREATIVITY

VOLUME 1
Individual Procedures

MORRIS I. STEIN

Department of Psychology
New York University

ACADEMIC PRESS   New York   San Francisco   London

A Subsidiary of Harcourt Brace Jovanovich, Publishers

ACADEMIC PRESS, INC.
111 Fifth Avenue, New York, New York 10003

BF
408
.S747
V. 1

United Kingdom Edition published by
ACADEMIC PRESS, INC. (LONDON) LTD.
24/28 Oval Road, London NW1

Library of Congress Cataloging in Publication Data

Stein, Morris Isaac, Date
     Stimulating creativity.

     Bibliography: v. 1, p.   ; v. 2, p.
     CONTENTS: v. 1.   Individual procedures.–v. 2.   Group
procedures.
     1.   Creation (Literary, artistics, etc.)
2.   Problem solving.   I.   Title.
BF408.S747   153.3′5   72-77340
ISBN 0–12–664201–X (v. 1)

To
J S G
and
S J G

Contents

Preface

This book is an outgrowth of one of the earliest creativity studies in post-World War II United States concerned with the psychological and social factors affecting creativity. After the results were presented to various lecture and seminar audiences, on nearly each occasion there were one or more persons who would ask: Can creativity be stimulated? If yes, what are the techniques for doing so? What assumptions underlie them? How effective are they?

To find the answers to these questions I became involved in a search of the literature (primarily research) and this led to the present two-volume work. The first volume presents procedures designed primarily to help individuals who can then work alone or in groups. The second volume contains procedures for groups of individuals. That procedures are divided in this manner should not deter any one reader or group from selecting what they think they can use, regardless of the section in which it appears.

The first volume also contains my theoretical orientation to creativity. I used it in my empirical research and it also served in organizing the material presented here. This orientation, succinctly stated, is: Creativity is a process that results in a novel work that is accepted as useful, tenable, or satisfying by a significant group of people at some point in time. As a process it consists of overlapping stages—hypothesis formation, hypothesis testing, and the communication of results—all of which follow a preparatory or educational stage which is not always uniquely part of the creative process. In each stage one may see the effects of *intra*personal and *inter*personal factors. All these factors reflect the fact that

creativity occurs in a social context and is a function of the transactional relationships between the individual and his environment—the creating individual is
both affected by and affects his environment.

This statement and other related matters, such as criteria of creativity, set the
stage for discussion of the aforementioned individual and group procedures, and
also prepare the reader for a presentation of procedures specially suited for each
stage in the creative process.

The relevance of procedures for stimulating creativity to the stages of hypothesis formation and hypothesis testing will be immediately evident. On other
occasions, however, especially when we discuss the communication stage of the
creative process, the relevance of the procedures to creativity may not be so
readily apparent. The reason for this may well be that when many persons think
about creativity, they limit themselves to the creating individual, whereas in my
approach, while the creating individual is the center of attention, he is not all
there is. He is seen as creating in a social context and thus as affecting and being
affected by the persons and social forces in his environment. Stimulating creativity, therefore, involves not only stimulating the individual but also affecting
his social milieu and the people in it. If those around the creating person do not
value creativity, if they do not provide the necessary supportive environment, if
they do not accept the creative work when it is completed, then it is likely that
the creative individual's efforts will encounter serious if not insurmountable
obstacles. Since creativity is a process, it is necessary to keep in mind not only
the creating individual but also the direct and indirect forces in the social environment that affect him. Knowledge of such forces, in addition to what it can
do to help the creating individual, can also be used to stimulate creativity further.

In addition to the statement about the creative process there are other background statements such as the effects of an individual's cognitive and personality
characterisitics on his behavior. This discussion is intended to provide additional
theoretical background and rationale for the individual procedures. By the same
token, the discussion of some of the characteristics of groups is intended to
highlight for the reader some of the problems in group behavior with which
techniques for stimulating creativity have to cope as well as to indicate some
assets of groups that can be built upon.

The aim in selecting the procedures discussed in this two-volume work was to
be as thorough and as diversified as possible in the hope of maximizing their
usefulness for readers concerned with the sciences, arts, engineering, humanities,
business management, and everyday aspects of living. But at least two shortcomings need to be noted at the outset. No work such as this can hope to be up
to date on publication. There is always some creative person, somewhere, who is
developing a technique for stimulating creativity, and his work came to our
attention after the manuscript was completed.

Further, this book contains a larger proportion of techniques for technological and consumer-related product areas than it does of techniques for the arts and humanities. Such a disproportion reflects the status of the field. There is less information available on the deliberately designed techniques in the arts and humanities, other than those involved in good teaching, than in the areas mentioned.

In presenting the various individual and group procedures for stimulating creativity, we have tried to include sufficient detail so that readers who become curious enough to try the procedures will have a basis on which to proceed. We would also like to encourage these persons to consult the original descriptions of the procedures, for although there may be some redundancy in such reading it may frequently add some piece of information or detail that would be beneficial for a successful experience.

While the material presented here is intended for use, it is not intended to be a guide to the perplexed who seek instant creativity. By presenting the theoretical rationale underlying the various techniques and the research on their assumptions and effectiveness, we do hope to provide readers with a more solid basis than is currently available for making their various choices. Where systematic research was not available we do cite available anecdotal evidence and are careful to point out that it is anecdotal. And when we have felt that research findings needed further substantiation, as occurred on numerous occasions, we asked for further replication.

Hopefully those who try the various procedures described here will make their experiences, their failures as well as their successes, known in appropriate publications. Such information together with the efforts of future investigators in this area will help us come closer to learning more about what kinds of procedures for stimulating creativity should be used by what kinds of individuals under what kinds of conditions to achieve creative results. If these two volumes also turn out to be a step in this direction, then their purpose will have been fulfilled.

Acknowledgments

There are a number of persons who have been most helpful in the various stages of development of these volumes. Chief among them is my colleague Professor Joseph Weitz of the Psychology Department at New York University who read an early version of the manuscript and parts of the later one. To him I am indebted for his insightful criticisms. To Alexander Biel, of Ogilvy and Mather, I am indebted for numerous discussions. To Professor Harold Basowitz, with whom I have been associated at the Research Center for Human Relations in the Psychology Department of New York University, I am most indebted for his help in coping with countless administrative details. To Barbara Fried I am grateful for many a beneficial dialog, in which she brought to bear her own knowledge of creativity. To Myron A. Coler, Professor of Continuing Education and Director of the Creative Science Program at New York University, I am most grateful for the many opportunities he gave me to discuss ideas contained here. And to the Lewis and Eugenia Van Weazel Foundation I want to convey my appreciation for their support of The Creative Science Program which provided me with data and information.

There is another large group of persons whom I am grateful, those whose work is cited at length in these volumes and to whom I sent my descriptions of their work for comments and criticism. While I followed their suggestions in correcting my description of their work, when it came to the matter of evaluation and interpretation the final word had to be mine.

I am also indebted to all those unnamed seminar participants who gave me the opportunity to test out my meterial with them. And, of course I am thankful for all the inputs accumulated during the years from my co-workers and students with whom I worked on research designed to understand the creative process.

I am grateful to Mrs. Eleanor Cunningham for her secretarial efforts throughout much of the time this work was in preparation, and to Mary Insinna, Sue Ellen York and Stephanie Meketansky for the secretarial aid they gave me in the final stages of the two volumes. I am most appreciative of the ever-present patience, guidance, and helpfulness of the Academic Press production staff. Finally, I want to express my appreciation to the Public Health Service for its support through a Career Award (5K06-MH18679) to me from the National Institutes of Health.

Excerpts on p. 21 from H. Poincaré, Mathematical creation, in B. Ghiselin (Ed.), _The creative process_. Originally published by the University of California Press (1952); reprinted by permission of The Regents of the University of California.

Excerpt on p. 25 from _The basic writings of Sigmund Freud_, translated and edited by Dr. A.A. Brill, copyright © 1938 by Random House, Inc. Copyright renewed 1965 by Gioia Bernheim and Edmund R. Brill. Reprinted by permission.

Excerpt on p. 55 from M.I. Stein and S.J. Heinze, _Creativity and the individual_, © 1960 by The Free Press.

Excerpts on pp. 58-60, 98 from M.I. Stein, Creativity, in E.F. Borgatta and W.W. Lambert (Eds.), _Handbook of personality theory and research_, © 1968 by Rand McNally and Co., Chicago.

Excerpts on pp. 70-71 from P.G. Bowers, Effect of hypnosis and suggestions of reduced defensiveness on creativity test performance, _Journal of Personality_, **35**, 311-322, copyright 1967 by the Duke University Press.

Excerpts on pp. 78-79 from E.T. Gendlin _et al._, Focusing ability in psychotherapy, personality, and creativity, in J.M. Shlien (Ed.), _Research in psychotherapy, Vol. 3_, copyright 1968 by the American Psychological Association and reproduced by permission.

Excerpts on p. 81 from L.G. Wispé and M.B. Parloff, Impact of psychotherapy on the productivity of psychologists, _Journal of Abnormal Psychology_, **70**, 188-193. Copyright 1965 by the American Psychological Association and reproduced by permission.

Excerpts on pp. 94, 99 from J.P. Guilford, _The nature of human intelligence_, copyright 1967 by McGraw-Hill Book Co. Used by permission.

Excerpts on pp. 110-111 from H. Nash, _Alcohol and caffeine_, 1962. Courtesy of Charles C. Thomas, Publisher, Springfield, Illinois.

Excerpts on pp. 122, 127-128 from J.C. Grossman _et al._, Openness to experience and marijuana use: An initial investigation, in _Proceedings 79th Annual Convention_, copyright 1971 by the American Psychological Association and reproduced by permission.

Excerpts on pp. 173-174 from E.P. Torrance, The creative teacher and the school team: Problems and pleasures of the principal, in _Professional growth for principals_, copyright 1961, Croft Educational Services, Inc., New London, Connecticut. Reprinted by permission of the publisher, Croft Educational Services, Inc.

Excerpts on pp. 173-177 from E. Paul Torrance, *Guiding creative talent*, © 1962. Reprinted by permission of Prentice-Hall, Inc., Englewood Cliffs, New Jersey.

Excerpt on p. 195 from p. 246, *The life and work of Sigmund Freud, Vol. I*, by Ernest Jones. Basic Books, Inc., Publishers, New York, 1953.

Excerpts on pp. 211-212, 214, 216-221 from C.S. Whiting, *Creative thinking,* © 1958 by Litton Educational Publishing, Inc. Reprinted by permission of Van Nostrand-Reinhold Co.

Excerpts on pp. 212-213 from *Morphological creativity* and *The Allen Morphologizer*, both by M.S. Allen, © 1962. Reprinted by permission of Prentice-Hall, Inc., Englewood Cliffs, New Jersey.

Excerpts on pp. 257, 271 from H.G. Barnett, *Innovation: The Basis of cultural change*, copyright 1953 by McGraw-Hill Book Co. Used by permission.

Excerpt on pp. 264-265 from p. 60, *The origins of psycho-analysis: Letters to Wilhelm Fliess, drafts and notes: 1887-1902*; edited by Marie Bonaparte, Anna Freud, Ernst Kris; translated by Eric Mosbacher and James Strachey. Basic Books, Inc., Publishers, New York 1954.

Excerpt on p. 267 from G.M. Prince, *The practice of creativity*, copyright © 1970 by George M. Prince. Reprinted by permission of Harper and Row, Publishers, Inc., New York.

Excerpts on p. 272 from R. Strother, The concentrations of Isaac Newton, *Saturday Review*, July 23, 1955; and pp. 273-274 from J. Steinbeck, From a writer's viewpoint, *Saturday Review*, August 27, 1955. Copyright 1955, The Saturday Review Associates, Inc.

Excerpt on p. 273 from J. Barzun, Each age picks its literary greats, *New York Times Book Review*, March 6, 1955, © 1955 by The New York Times Co. Reprinted by permission.

CONTENTS OF VOLUME 2: Group Procedures

PART I

PLAN OF THE WORK

This work consists of two volumes divided into seven parts. This first part contains both the introduction to the work and some of the basic assumptions underlying the techniques that will be presented for stimulating creativity.

Part II contains a discussion of the theory of creativity that is central to this work. The orientation here is that creativity is a process consisting of three overlapping stages—hypothesis formation, hypothesis testing, and the communication of results. (All of these are preceded by a preparatory or educational phase. Since this phase may be used for purposes other than creativity, it is not regarded here as part of the creative process. Nevertheless some of the ways in which this phase may affect creativity are discussed later.)

The second major section of Part II concerns itself with criteria of creativity that have been used in research studies to differentiate between levels of creativity. These studies have brought to light some of the social and psychological characteristics that differentiate more creative persons from their less creative peers. These characteristics are regarded as intimately involved in and related to the creative person's capacity to fulfill the requirements of the creative process. The different techniques for stimulating creativity that are presented in this book are oriented to helping an individual achieve these characteristics.

1

Part III is devoted to a consideration of procedures that an individual himself might use to overcome blocks to creativity or to stimulate his creativity. Attention here is focused on the individual and procedures he might use as differing from those procedures that are designed for use by groups of persons. The latter are discussed in Part V.

It should be noted that the separation of individual and group procedures is only one of several arbitrary separations in this book that are necessary for heuristic purposes. It is assumed, however, that the reader will not allow the arbitrariness of the separations to deter him from using whatever he wishes, needs, and finds useful, regardless of the part of the book in which it appears.

Procedures for use by an individual are further divided into two major categories of a person's psychological characteristics—his personality characteristics and his cognitive characteristics. Both of these are involved in all parts of the creative process, hence, as in separating individual and group procedures, this separation is also arbitrary but again necessary for heuristic purposes. The procedures discussed in this section that may affect personality or cognitive characteristics are those which are most general and which may have the broadest effects. This is what differentiates the procedures discussed in this part of the book from those discussed later which also focus upon either personality or cognitive characteristics.

Part IV considers each of the stages of the creative process in turn and each is followed by a discussion of the techniques for stimulating creativity that are most appropriate to that stage. This is still another arbitrary matter. Hopefully, readers will select again those techniques and procedures they need regardless of the stage they are associated with here.

We do not consider the preparatory or educational phase as part of the creative process, for education and training may be used for a variety of purposes other than creativity. Nevertheless, we devote a chapter to this phase in this section pointing out how some very important aspects of the educational process can affect the creativity of younger persons who have already manifested their creativity or have yet to do so. In addition, new teaching techniques including programmed instruction procedures are presented which serve as techniques for stimulating creativity in and of themselves or they may stimulate the reader to think of additional ideas that may facilitate the course of the creative process during the preparatory stage.

A comment is in order about our discussion of the communication stage in this part of the book. Our theoretical orientation is that the creative process, even though it occurs in the mind of one person, takes place in a social context. All stages of the creative process may be affected by this. In the systematic approach followed here, the role played by the social context is most manifest in the communication stage. Our approach to the techniques for stimulating creativity in this stage is different from that in the other stages. In the other stages, attention is focused on specific techniques that may be of help but the communication stage has so many parts and so many participants that it is impossible to follow this procedure. In addition there has not been enough work done to date on the techniques that may be of help in coping with the different problems that arise at each of the parts of the communication stage. Hence, wherever possible, techniques that are appropriate to this stage are presented but the major approach is to make salient the various significant characteristics of this part of the creative process. In so doing, it is hoped that the creative individual would not be surprised when they appear, and also both he and we by knowing of their existence might be better able to develop appropriately effective procedures to cope with them when they obstruct or impede the creative process.

Part V devotes itself to a consideration of four group procedures for stimulating creativity. Three of them, brainstorming, creative problem-solving, and synectics, are systematically used with groups of persons. The fourth approach, a personality-insight approach, is a report of a research study of two procedures for stimulating a group's creativity. Although it is a research study, it is presented here because its results are quite intriguing and if replicated in future research might prove very valuable for efforts in this area.

In view of the fact that many readers may not be acquainted with group processes and group behavior, the group procedures are introduced with some theoretical material about groups. Needless to say, it is beyond our scope to present a full treatment of group behavior. What we have done is select from available literature what appeared to be most relevant to the techniques for stimulating creativity that are to follow.

The group procedures are then followed in Part VI with a presentation of programs for stimulating creativity that have been used in various companies and organizations. While data are lacking on the effectiveness of these programs, as well as on other related matters, they are presented nevertheless for the reader's interests and for the possibility that they may be of potential value in serving as a springboard for the development of newer programs.

Finally, Part VII is devoted to a summary of the essential points made and a discussion of guidelines to be followed in selecting a course of action designed to stimulate creativity and the need for future work.

Chapter I

Introduction

Can a person who has never manifested creativity be taught or stimulated to be creative? Can an individual who has been creative, but who is currently blocked, be helped to overcome his difficulties? Are certain educational procedures better than others for laying a fertile ground for creativity so that students are better prepared to make significant creative contributions in the future? How "good" are such techniques as brainstorming and synectics for stimulating the creativity of advertising personnel, salesmen, scientists, engineers, and executives?

These are some of the questions I have been asked during professional, educational, and industrial seminars on creativity over the past several years. The attempt to answer them has led me to this practical, theoretical, and evaluative study of the different procedures for stimulating creativity and their effectiveness.

ASSUMPTIONS UNDERLYING THE DISCUSSION

In order to set the groundwork, I will set down here the assumptions that underlie my discussion.

First, we know enough about what creativity is to be able to stimulate its development. Second, the artists, scientists, philosophers, psychologists, psychoanalysts, and communications specialists who have told us about their own creativity generally agree with the idea that creativity is a process as a result of which novelty is achieved. Third, the creative process takes time, and it also takes time to learn what it is, how it works, and how to use it productively. There is no quick and easy shortcut to the development of creativity. All the techniques presented here will be effective only in conjunction with sincere motivation and persevering application.

Furthermore, like every process, creativity occurs not all at once, but in stages. Insofar as creativity is concerned, each of these stages has its own characteristics, and tends to overlap the stages that precede and follow. No single technique for stimulating creativity fulfills the conditions or requirements for all stages in the creative process, which means that a variety of techniques exist that are valid for certain stages and not others. In general, I will discuss the techniques in terms of the stage for which they have greatest effectiveness.

The most important stages of the creative process are referred to here as (1) hypothesis formation; (2) hypothesis testing; and (3) the communication of results.* As these terms imply, the first two stages occur within the individual, and the final stage involves both the creative individual and those with whom he wishes to communicate.

Individuals vary in their ability to meet the requirements for the different stages of the creative process. Some individuals can fulfill all aspects of the creative process, but most seem to be able to handle certain aspects better than others, which is why under certain conditions, a group may be more capable of reaching a creative solution to a problem than its individual members working alone.

The concept of novelty—novelty that is useful (Stein, 1967) (practically, aesthetically, theoretically) or, in general terms, is adaptive (MacKinnon, 1964)—is central to all definitions of creativity. Novelty can be achieved in a variety of ways including trial and error, serendipity, and problem solving; and it can be regarded as a measure of the "distance" between that which is developed and that which existed. Some novel things depart only very little from that which existed (the "new and improved products" or modifications of the old), while others, advances like Einstein's theory, depart a great deal. Both kinds of jumps, of course, subsume knowledge that came before.

Because novelty differs in the way in which it can be achieved, and because it differs in terms of its distance from the already known, it is by definition not precise to call novelty that is achieved "creative." Novelty may be achieved

---

*In the text, a preparation stage is also considered. This stage is not part of the creative process *per se* but is part of the groundwork out of which creative works develop.

without going through the stages of the creative process as we or others have described it, which involves both a specific set of stages, plus a *qualitative* evaluation of the novelty of the final product produced. By definition, novelty achieved through processes other than the creative process might be better referred to with some such term as "innovation." Such distinctions are probably more important as fine points for researchers or others very deeply involved in working in and furthering our understanding of creativity but for most persons the distinction is not too important. To avoid confusion with much of current usage of the term creative or creativity, we shall use these terms to conform with current usage and not seek to make here very fine distinctions.*

In addition to the assumption that we know enough about the creative process to use it as a springboard for fostering creativity, other assumptions that underlie the present techniques for stimulating creativity have to do with the psychological characteristics associated with creativity; the potential for change within an individual; the possibility of developing valid techniques for stimulating creativity; and the value of doing so.

Judging from the vast amount of work that has been done in the psychology of creativity and the number of studies that have appeared in the literature, it is very reasonable to assume that we understand which psychological characteristics are necessary for the creative process. Guilford (1962), for instance, pointed out that the number of publications on creativity between 1940 and 1960 about equals all the articles that appeared on this topic since Galton first published his book *Hereditary Genius* in 1870. It is doubtful that since 1962 the rate of publications dealing with the psychological characteristics of creative individuals has decreased. Our knowledge may not be complete in all respects, but we do know a good deal about the motivational and personality characteristics of creative individuals as well as their cognitive characteristics—perception, thought processes, and problem-solving behavior (Stein & Heinze, 1960). Consequently, it seems reasonable to assume that creativity can be stimulated if individuals are helped to become more like those persons who are known to be creative. For example, we have learned that creative individuals are self-confident†; if we can develop techniques that will stimulate or foster self-confidence, we can expect that to the extent to which this goal is attained, the probability of

---

*In defining creativity in terms of a process through which novelty is achieved, I am aware that few research studies exist based on individuals selected because they followed these process characteristics. Our knowledge of the creative process is derived almost wholly from studies of creative individuals selected by many different criteria. These criteria, the reasons they are used in research, and their advantages and shortcomings are described in Chapter III.

† Single characteristics are used so as not to complicate the examples. It is obvious however, that it would be a rare situation in which only one characteristic required changing. It is more common that a combination of characteristics, both personality and

an individual becoming creative is enhanced. We know that flexibility of thought processes is characteristic of creative individuals; we can expect, therefore, that if an individual can be helped to achieve more flexible thought processes, then he can also be expected to be more creative.

On the other hand, these apparently reasonable assumptions must still be regarded with some measure of caution for we do not yet know whether the psychological characteristics of individuals who have manifested creativity were changed by the mere act of having been creative. Self-confidence may be characteristic of *manifestly* creative persons, but that does not necessarily mean they were similarly self-confident before their creativity was manifest. It is conceivable that their self-confidence may originally have been weak, and improved only after their creativity was accepted and rewarded. There is a story about Einstein, who talked one day to a young physicist. Einstein was very impressed with the boy and asked, "How is it I haven't heard about you or your ideas until now?" The young man said, "Professor Einstein, I am a humble man." To which Einstein's response was, "My boy, you aren't great enough to feel humble yet."

Another and closely related assumption I have made in writing this book is that it is possible for people to change and become more creative. Change occurs naturally in all of us as a result of maturation and aging; in response to external, environmental pressures; as a result of psychotherapy; and whenever we are motivated to achieve new patterns of behavior. The question to be asked here is that assuming there are techniques that do foster changes in the direction of creativity, what groups of people are most likely to find these techniques valuable? Executives, managers, supervisors, teachers, all those who have and are responsible for subordinates would probably fall into this category. Also, creative individuals who have become blocked in their creative work should find the techniques presented here useful in overcoming their obstacles. Individuals who have never ventured into creative work may be helped by these techniques to embark on their first experience. And finally, people who are manifestly creative may find new techniques to help them develop their creativity further.

Of course, those who are already creative have the least need to change. As for the other three groups, change in the direction of creativity is possible; it does, however, demand a great deal of motivation and energy, and the capacity to acquire new ways of thinking, feeling, and behaving. Much perseverance is needed to become involved in the creative process, and much tolerance for the ambiguities and the frequent lack of social support. Being or becoming creative is hard work, but not impossible.

---

cognitive, require change. And, if one major central characteristic is changed, the change usually brings with it changes in other characteristics because of how an individual's psychological characteristics are interrelated and organized.

Still another assumption that is sometimes made for the techniques to be discussed is that each of us has the potential for creativity. This assumption takes us into the area of personality theory; the theory that is most useful here is that of self-actualization (Maslow, 1959). Those who are involved in stimulating creativity generally cannot say with certainty that any one individual does indeed have a potential for creativity, or how much potential he does have. Instead, they must wait until after an individual has been trained and has (or has not) manifested his creativity, at which point they infer that he did (or did not) have a creative potential originally. Personality theorists however, implicitly or explicitly, make assumptions about the nature of man. Those that follow self-actualization theory, which focuses on the idea that man is oriented to fulfilling himself, would also adhere to the idea that each of us has the potential for creativity. Indeed, without such an assumption, it would be untenable to think that techniques for stimulating creativity could be of any use at all.

The individual interested in improving his creativity need not concern himself with theoretical matters, however; for him, the proof of the pudding will be whether or not he can and does change to become more creative. Someday a diagnostic technique may be developed that will allow an individual to tell ahead of time which of the various ways to stimulate creativity would be most effective for him, but at present, he simply has to pick and choose from what is available, and develop the techniques or combinations of techniques himself that will help him most.

Environmental factors also play a critical role in blocking or facilitating the creative process. It is possible that some individuals would manifest more creativity if they were in environments that valued and supported creativity. Such people may already be aware of techniques for stimulating creativity, but lack the opportunity to put what they already know into practice. All too often, for instance, individuals who have attended seminars or meetings where they have learned how to improve their creativity, and have in fact done so, return to working environments where their new knowledge is not considered valuable. Only if the environment is supportive and congenial can the effects of a training program be maximized.

Another assumption that underlies the techniques to be presented is that it is a worthwhile goal to train or to help people become creative or more creative. Of course, this assumption is also a value statement, and, as with many value statements, it is apt to provoke emotional rather than purely rational responses. It may therefore be necessary for an individual reader to decide where he would place creativity in the hierarchy of his own values. Some may put it at the very top of the list; others would put *success* or *happiness* not achieved through creativity before it. The point is that being creative and learning how to be creative require time and energy, of which we all have only limited amounts. Each of us therefore ought to be aware of his own feelings about the value of creativity, so that he will not spend more psychic energy on working toward the goal of being creative than he can tolerate.

Furthermore, there are social implications attached to increasing an individual's capacity to think of new ideas. Society must be geared to any increase in creativity, otherwise it means there will only be an increasingly large number of ideas placed on shelves. In other words, we cannot expect to use our creativity techniques to solve scientific, technological, and social problems, unless we also remember that using creativity techniques for such purposes implies a set of social values.

Underlying all these assumptions is one basic assumption: *It is possible to develop techniques to train for and to stimulate creativity*. And this assumption, with the evidence for and against it, is what this book is all about. I am concerned with presenting the techniques for stimulating creativity; and I am interested in marshaling evidence about the effectiveness of these techniques, hence, I focus on research studies. I am aware that there is much anecdotal material on the effectiveness of the various techniques, but I have generally avoided including it because this material cannot be evaluated scientifically. This, of course, does not mean that the anecdotal material is not accurate; it is simply beyond the scope of this book.

Because, in limiting myself to research evidence, I have not been able to find data on all aspects of creativity, I have had to supplement studies in this area with related kinds of material. There are two places, especially, where this is the case. One of these is the section on psychotherapy. The fact of the matter is that there is very little research on how much, if at all, psychotherapy helps creativity, and certainly no good systematic study involving a large number of individuals. Therefore, I have included a study of the relationship between psychotherapy and productivity. This study may not be directly relevant— creative behavior may be productive, but productive people are not necessarily creative—but it does include data and information of considerable interest for our purposes.

The other place I have had to digress is in my discussion of the relationships between drugs and creativity, an area that is too new to have much pertinent material to cite. Although some studies of drugs and creativity are presented, the discussion focuses primarily on the relationships between drugs and certain psychological functions that may bear some relationship to creativity.

PART II

THEORY AND CRITERIA

This part of the book contains two chapters. The first, entitled "The Creative Process," contains a theoretical orientation based on both the research and nonresearch literature. It involves a presentation of three overlapping stages in the creative process—hypothesis formation, hypothesis testing, and the communication of results, all of which follow a stage of preparation—that form a rubric for discussing the techniques to stimulate creativity.

The second chapter in this section contains a discussion of the criteria used to select those individuals who are studied to learn more about the characteristics associated with creativity. These characteristics, as we shall see later, become those that some procedures seek to attain for those persons whose creativity they try to stimulate.

Chapter II

The Creative Process

Creativity is a process. Our fascination with the emotional experience stirred in us by a poem; our awestruck regard for the insights that follow from understanding an integrative theory; our gratitude for the development of new drugs are all attitudes that focus on the novelty of the final product that is produced. Often, these attitudes do not reflect adequate understanding and appreciation either of the processes that went on within the creative individual (intrapersonal processes) or those that occurred between the individual and his environment (interpersonal processes). Within both these sets of processes there are factors that might have stimulated and facilitated or blocked and inhibited the course of the creative process and the development of the creative product.

VARIOUS DESCRIPTIONS OF THE CREATIVE PROCESS

The creative process has been described in a variety of ways. One of the first to talk about it was Helmholtz (Whiting, 1958), who described it as consisting of saturation, incubation, and illumination. Saturation consisted of the gathering of data, facts, and sensations to serve for the development of new ideas. Incubation occurred without conscious effort and involved shifting the material about and making new combinations. Illumination occurred when the solution or some concept of the end state came to mind. Whiting (1958) also tells us that Henri Poincaré, in a famous lecture before the Société de Psychologie in Paris, described the creative process in approximately the same way as Helmholtz, with the addition of a fourth step called *verification*. His first step was called *preparation* rather than *saturation*.

In 1926 Wallas presented his systematic description in terms that are now rather well known—preparation, incubation, illumination, and verification. Preparation is the stage during which the problem is investigated from all directions. Incubation is the stage during which no conscious thought is devoted to the problem, but "work" still continues on nonconscious levels. Illumination is the stage during which the "happy idea" occurs together with the psychological factors that immediately preceded and accompanied its appearance. And verification is the stage during which the validity of the idea is tested and reduced to exact form.

Reichenbach (1938), the scientist-philosopher, in studying the creative process, differentiated the "context of discovery" from the "context of justification" to distinguish between "the thinker's way of finding [his] theorem and his way of presenting it before a public [p. 6]." Three phases in creativity were differentiated by the psychoanalyst Kris (1953): inspiration, elaboration, and communication. During the inspiration phase the creative individual is "driven; he is in an exceptional state. Thoughts or images tend to flow, things appear in his mind of which he never seemed to have known [p. 343]." Elaboration is characterized by labor, concentration, and endeavor. And the communication phase contains those factors involved in presenting the final product to others.

I (Stein, 1967) also prefer to describe the creative process as consisting of three stages: hypothesis formation, which starts after preparation and ends with the formation of a tentative idea or plan; hypothesis testing, which involves determining whether or not the idea will stand up under careful scrutiny and testing; and communication, which involves presenting the final product so that others may react to and possibly accept it.

Characteristics Common to All Descriptions

Having presented various different descriptions of the creative process, it is well to repeat that although the terms and emphases may vary, there is a great deal of agreement among them and there are, as we pointed out previously (Chapter I), numerous characteristics common to all of them.

The different descriptions agree that the stages of the creative process do not occur in a systematic and orderly manner. Only at certain times during the total process will one of its aspects become more salient than others. Indeed, it is also likely that the different characteristics of the process stand out most markedly only when the process is halted, blocked, or inhibited for some reason or other, only to continue again when the course of a new stage with its attendant characteristics makes itself manifest.

All descriptions of the creative process agree that the creative man has spent a great deal of time or smaller amounts of time used intensively in formal or informal preparation, training, or education in the field in which he works. The creative individual also makes a selection of a problem or a project on which he will work and, in all likelihood, the original statement of the problem and/or the initial ideas about the solution undergo change.

The process does not run off smoothly from start to finish. Work may be halted from boredom, fatigue, not knowing how to proceed, etc. Nevertheless, it continues or incubates on unconscious or nonconscious levels and from this work or from a test of this work there is a growing conscious awareness of a new possibility that illuminates and "lights up" a new direction, another approach, a different pathway to the solution, which the individual did not see before or which he could not think of before. Attendant upon this experience there is also the feeling of excitement or exhilaration that has also been called inspiration. And, finally, there is a sense of knowing, a combination of affective feeling and cognitive awareness, or an aesthetic sensitivity that signals the completion of the work. These very same feelings and awareness no doubt alerted him to the presence of one idea among several which was then selected for further test. From this kind of sorting and testing procedure, finally one is hit upon that becomes crucial to the completion of the final work. And then, these very same feelings, awarenesses, or aesthetic responses play a significant role once again as the creative individual comes to the completion of his work. They, in effect, "tell" him when the work is done.

Those of us who assign communication a critical role in the creative process, place the whole process within a social context and call attention to the numerous factors that may affect the process. Whether or not a critical role is given to the communication stage, various approaches agree that the resultant of the creative process is something novel. The novelty that is produced is of some significance, for novelty in some insignificant detail, while no doubt of worth, does not merit being called creative. The novel result is also useful, tenable, or satisfying (Stein, 1967) or adaptive (MacKinnon, 1964). For the result to be called creative, it needs also to represent a "leap." To use a spatial analogy, the novelty that has been achieved must not be a mere "step" away from that which has existed but a "good distance" away. The final novel product that is called creative changes the course of future actions and behavior. It alters our way of looking at things and it opens up new vistas that stimulate still further creativity.

In Anticipation of Some Communication Problems

My previous experiences in lectures and seminars on creativity suggest that at about this point in our discussion of the creative process there are several questions that are likely to occur to the readers, and it is best to deal with them now or else our discussion will be impeded. Unless several points are clarified at this stage, difficulties may arise in continuing with or following the material to be presented.

The questions that have been asked overlap to some extent. Nevertheless, it is probably wise to separate them and treat each of them separately. (1) Why is it that your presentation of the creative process makes it sound so much like problem solving rather that what one generally has come to think of as creativity? (2) From some of the things you say about the creative process, you make it sound as if there were no differences between artistic and scientific creativity? Is this so? (3) Are there not works that were recognized at one time but which have not survived as creative? And, are there not works that were not recognized as creative when they were first produced only to be recognized as creative at some later point in time? How does what you have said about the creative process account for this? (4) Do you really mean that the techniques you will discuss will help an individual be creative as you have discussed the term creative?

Let us consider the first question, "Why is it that your presentation of the creative process makes it sound so much like problem solving rather than what one generally has come to think of as creativity?" It is understandable that the use of such words as "problem," "solution," "hypothesis," and the like, could give the reader the impression that I am talking about problem solving only, since these terms appear quite "rational," as the problem-solving process may be for some persons. The fact of the matter is, though, that it would be in error to think of my presentation of the creative process as the same as problem solving. The terms I selected for my discussion I thought would be quite neutral and could be applied in a variety of ways. Needless to say, for those individuals who come to regard them as referring to problem solving, I have failed in some way and hope that the explicit statements just made will serve to clarify what I mean. At this juncture it is also wise to point out that the kinds of terms selected in describing the creative process no doubt vary by fields and by individuals within fields. Thus, scientists may well refer to the "problem" or "experiments" they are working on. On the other hand, writers may refer to their "projects" and painters to their "work." To establish some sort of communality among all the terms, I would say that I have used the term "problem" in the same way these others have used "project" and "work," and I have also used the word "problem" to refer to some stopping of the ongoing flow of the creative process. Any attempt to continue with the work or project I have called a *hypothesis* in an effort to underscore its tentative quality and the fact that the whole effort is still in process of development. Finally, the term "solution" has been used in my discussion in a manner to indicate the end state or goal of the creative process.

It would be more helpful for some if a more objective language were available, and in one of my papers (Stein, 1967) I have made use of the phrase "lack of closure," that is part of Gestalt psychology, as another way of referring to "problem." In other words, where there is closure or where an individual experiences it, there is no problem and there is no need for resolution. It is only when there is lack of closure or where it has been demonstrated that there is lack of closure that a series of processes, one of which is creativity, is set in motion.

Finally, if there is still any doubt, I would say that among other characteristics, the creative process is distinguished from problem solving in that the former results in greater leaps, in giving things more of a twist, and the final result is regarded as much more novel than the result of problem solving. Also there is more of the irrational or more of what I later refer to as the mystiques in the creative process than there is in the problem-solving process.

(2) "From some of the things you say about the creative process, you make it sound as if there were no differences between artistic and scientific creativity. Is this so?" To a great extent this is true. I do believe that the same variables are involved in both artistic and scientific creativity. The variables may vary in how they are "mixed" in each of these areas, but the presence of each of them can be discerned. For example, given my definitions of the terms hypothesis formation, hypothesis testing, communication, and such terms as "problem" and "solution," I would say that they are equally applicable to the arts as well as the sciences. Many would feel that these terms are applicable only to the sciences. By the same token, they might feel that what I have referred to as the mystique aspects of creativity—inspiration, intuition, aesthetic feeling either for a potentially creative response or the final end state—are limited only to artistic creativity. Some people think this way because they have been affected by a romantic tradition about creativity; and since writings and communications about artistic creativity have a longer history than do those that concern themselves with scientific creativity, we still maintain this tradition and hence think that the terms should be limited to the artistic world. Another kind of orientation differentiates between scientific creativity and artistic creativity in that the former is said to be produced as a result of stimulation from the outside—that is, from the environment. Artistic creativity, on the other hand, is said to occur from ideas or stimuli from within oneself. This, too, is an arbitrary distinction that does not hold. The creative landscape artist and the creative portrait painter have models which they paint (unless we are then going to say that only elements that came from within the painter are the truly creative ones, but then we will have a problem determining what is really within the person and what is outside) and the theoretical physicist works with concepts that exist only within his own mind.

I have found it of value in answer to the question to suggest that one watch a mathematician present the derivation of a formula. On occasion when I have done so, I have been impressed with the fact that as the mathematician works on the blackboard and communicates with his audience he bounces around very much like a ballet dancer, and in this very juxtaposition of mathematics and ballet one sees the relationship between science and art. Another illustration, again from mathematics, is that it has been said that two mathematicians can solve the same problem and come up with the same solution but that one is the more creative mathematician who comes up with the elegant solution. And it is this elegance of solution, coherence of feeling, form in a painting, parsimony of explanation of an experimental finding, that is another outstanding point of similarity in the creative process in the arts and the sciences.

These are some of the marked similarities, but I would submit that there are similarities all along the line and that the differences in the creative process in the arts and sciences would, by and large, be a function of how much of some of the variables we have mentioned are present in one area and how much some of them are present in the other area.

Some might then ask, if this is so, if the creative process in the arts and sciences is the same, then can an individual who has been creative in one area apply the process to the other? At one point in history, in what has been referred to as Renaissance Man, it might well have been possible to be creative in more than one area, but with increasing specialization, with increasing growth of knowledge and technique, it is unlikely that this will continue to be the case on any significant scale. Furthermore, while the creative process may be similar in both areas, it needs to be borne in mind that the process is applied to different contents, and the individuals involved, the artists and scientists, were attracted to different contents for a variety of historical and developmental reasons. Thus, the scientist and artist go into their respective fields because of their unique life experiences, including the models they were exposed to, the opportunities in their environments, the kinds of education they received, the values they were exposed to (especially the value on creativity), and the like. In addition to all this, we must consider the individual's abilities, not only those he learned but also those that stem from his hereditary potential and which are generally referred to as *talent*. In other words, while the creative process is a process through which novelty may be achieved, where, how, and to what it may be applied—the arts, the sciences, interpersonal relations, etc.—is determined by a host of other factors.

(3) The third question was: "Are there not works that were recognized at one time but which have not survived as creative? And, are there not works that were not recognized as creative when they were first produced only to be recognized as creative at some later point in time? How does what you have said about the creative process account for this?" Nothing I have said about the process itself actually accounts for this. Indeed, I personally believe that in defining creativity as I have done here, I need to add a historical variable. Thus, in another context I said, "The creative work is a novel work that is accepted as tenable or useful or satisfying by a group at some point in time [Stein, 1967, p. 109]." It is the phrase, "at some point in time," that is critical here. Some persons feel quite

uncomfortable with this phrase. They would like some kind of absolute statement in the definition so that that which is regarded as creative is immediately recognized as such on its presentation and then still recognized as such forevermore. There may well be instances of such works but, more often than not, works that come to be regarded as creative are recognized as such only with the passage of time and even then changes may occur in the future. There are some individuals who may regard a work as creative immediately on seeing it, but this small group may be even too small for any significant determination. It might take some time and even some changes in presentation before a significant number (but still less than the people at large) regard it as creative. One of the best examples in this regard is Stravinsky's *Rites of Spring* which was greeted with much negative response when it was first produced but has come to be regarded as an important factor in the development of contemporary music. Instances where a work came to be regarded as creative only late in its history, and instances where a work which was first regarded as creative was later lost sight of, compel us to add a historical qualification to the definition of creativity.

(4) The fourth and final question was: "Do you really mean that the techniques you will discuss will help an individual be creative as you have discussed the term creative?" I would hope so. It would indeed be most gratifying to learn that someone, as a result of reading this book, has come up with something that would be regarded as creative either in terms of the definitions presented here or in terms of the definitions others have developed. What I have tried to do is present techniques which we believe creative persons have used in coming to their creative results. The techniques have been used in combination with all other sorts of information, knowledge, and behavior as well as by individuals with all kinds of abilities and talents. Hopefully, those who use the techniques to be presented here will have these same combinations so that creative works will be produced, and if they do not result in major leaps into the unknown, then at least they will result in bigger steps than might have been possible without them.

Hopefully by answering these questions we have cleared the way for a more detailed discussion of our conceptualization of the creative process as consisting of three overlapping stages—hypothesis formation, hypothesis testing, and the communication of results.

STAGE I—HYPOTHESIS FORMATION

No creative man thinks, feels, or behaves in a rigid manner. Einstein, in working on his theory of relativity, did not start thinking of axioms. It was only after the idea occurred to him that the solution lay in the concept of time and specifically simultaneity that the axioms followed. "No really productive man thinks in such a paper fashion [p. 183], " said Einstein in an interview with the psychologist Wertheimer (1945).

In the creative process the idea which culminates in the creative product or theory does not arise through a purposeful or willed act. Purpose, intention, and the desire to be creative set the groundwork for the creative idea, but the individual cannot intentionally pluck it out from wherever it is. A thinker may maximize the probability that he will be creative by purposefully, consciously, and conscientiously learning what there is to know about his specific endeavor—provided also that he does not overlearn or become intimidated by what he has learned—but having done so there is no absolute assurance that he will be inspired to come up with the critical idea.

Individualized Conditions Favoring Creativity

Frequently the creative individual is aware of the circumstances and conditions under which he can be most creative and will utilize them to best advantage. There are some who can begin their work only after all the pencils are sharpened; others work best on typewriters. There are some who can work only when the desk is "cleared for action," but there are others who prefer a disorderly room or studio. While some prefer quiet, others prefer music and even noise. Some will insist upon carrying out their rituals; others may know rituals they prefer but may not always indulge in them for fear of what others around them may think.

Creative individuals have always utilized to advantage a variety of techniques that, no doubt, suited their individual personalities. One investigator in this field reports that Emile Zola avoided daylight and pulled the shades at midday to work in artificial light. Kipling wrote only with the blackest ink he could find, and "Ben Jonson . . . believed that he performed best while drinking great quantities of tea, and while stimulated by the purring of a cat and the strong odor of orange peel [Parloff, 1967, pp. 22-23] ." And another investigator reports:

> Schiller kept rotten apples in his desk; Shelly [sic] and Rousseau remained bareheaded in the sunshine; Bousseut [sic] worked in a cold room with his head wrapped in furs; Milton, Descartes, Leibniz and Rossini lay stretched out; Tycho-Brahe [sic] and Leibniz secluded themselves for very long periods, Thoreau built his hermitage, Proust worked in a cork-lined room, Carlyle in a noise-proof chamber, and Balzac* wore a monkish working garb; Gretry and Schiller immersed their feet in ice-cold water; Guido Reni could paint, and de Musset could write poetry, only when dressed in magnificent

*Balzac also liked to work at night with the help of much strong black coffee (Parloff, 1967).

style; Mozart, following exercise; Lammenais, in a room of shadowy darkness, and D'Annunzio, Farnol and Frost only at night. The aesthetician, Baumgarten, advised poets seeking inspiration to ride on horseback, to drink wine in moderation, and, provided they were chaste, to look at beautiful women [Levey, 1940, p. 286].

The precise circumstances that are conducive to inspiration or to the generation of ideas are varied. Nevertheless, they characteristically make the individual feel safe and secure. That is, they provide him with an environment in which he does not feel threatened or under pressure. He is relaxed but alert.

Relaxation and the Lull in the Creative Process

Another period during which creative ideas may arise is the lull—essentially a state of watchful waiting—that follows an intense period of fruitless study and work. During such a lull, the individual is not consciously preoccupied with his problem, but work on it still continues on nonconscious levels. Simultaneously, he is prepared to recognize and seize any valuable idea, and is alert enough to utilize whatever ideas he may have.

To be capable of using this period productively requires the ability to relax after a period of intense activity and the courage to rise above disappointment when an initial idea has not worked out. Poincaré (1952), in describing his own creative behavior, says he tried for 15 days

> to prove that there could not be any functions like those I have since called Fuchsian functions. I was then very ignorant; every day I seated myself at my work table, stayed an hour or two, tried a great number of combinations and reached no results. One evening, contrary to my custom, I drank black coffee and could not sleep. Ideas rose in crowds; I felt them collide until pairs interlocked, so to speak, making a stable combination. By the next morning, I had established the existence of a class of Fuchsian functions, those which come from the hypergeometric series; I had only to write out the results, which took but a few hours [p. 25].

Poincaré also tells us that once while on a geologic excursion

> the changes of travel made me forget my mathematical work. Having reached Coutances, we entered an omnibus to go some place or other. At the moment when I put my foot on the step the idea came to me, without anything in my former thoughts seeming to have paved the way for it, that the transformations I had used to define the Fuchsian functions were identical with those of non-Euclidean geometry. I did not verify the idea; I should not have had time, as, upon taking my seat in the omnibus, I went on with a conversation already commenced, but I felt a

perfect certainty. On my return to Caen, for conscience' sake I verified the result at my leisure [p. 26].

Not all interruptions have such happy endings. Sometimes there is "the man from Porlock" who so interrupts Coleridge's meanderings and thought processes that much is lost. Coleridge had fallen asleep in a lonely farmhouse after taking an anodyne and after reading a sentence in "Purchas's Pilgrimage." This sentence stimulated a composition of two to three hundred lines "without any sensation or consciousness of effort [pp. 83, 84]." On waking he began to write out the lines of "Kubla Khan" but was interrupted for about an hour by a man who came from Porlock on business and when he returned to his work he found that he had forgotten almost all of what he had not written down before the interruption (Coleridge, 1952).

Inspiration

At the time the individual has the idea, or the insight, which in the final analysis guides him to his goal, he is said to be inspired. This aspect of the creative process, which we later refer to as one of its mystiques, when it occurs, is so fantastic, so incomprehensible, so awe-inspiring, and so defying of description to the individual who experiences it or to the observer of it in another, that its origin has been attributed to a muse, a deity, God, to the "beyond," and, in the terms of contemporary psychoanalytic theory, to man's preconscious and unconscious.

Note should be taken of how our attribution of these sources of inspiration has varied over the course of history and what it was at any one point in time. The word or concept used is congruent with significant aspects of the *Zeitgeist*. When muses were regarded as the source of truth, the creative individual was said to "have his muse." When God was regarded to be the inspirational source; the creative individual was *chosen* for *His* work. With the growth of psychological sophistication, these sources have been attributed to the preconscious and unconscious.

These are not merely variations in semantic usage. Over time, the locus for creativity did in fact shift from outside man to man himself. This shift in locus signaled two major developments. The first was that man himself can create; and the other was the shift in the locus of responsibility for creative developments. Prior to these developments it was only God or the muse that was creative. Man was the instrument through which their creativity was manifest. In the Old Testament there is a separate word in Hebrew that is used for God's creating the world, but in that text man only "makes" things.

Later, man was regarded as imitative. Then uniqueness and individuality were denied, for they could only lead to distortions in what was copied or imitated. It was only much later that the idea developed that man could be inventive and still later that he could be creative.

The Creative Individual and Responsibility

In this conceptualization of the creative process, man, who fulfilled the ways of God or who carried out the will of his muse, carried no responsibility for novel developments. This responsibility belonged to God or the muses. When the locus of creativity shifted to man himself, he bore the responsibility for his creation, both implicitly and explicitly. When the creative man had a muse, he could blame his muse for ideas, thoughts, actions, and behavior (man was only the passive recipient of inspiration; he was simply carrying out God's or the muse's will). In so doing, the individual could avoid being regarded as one who was out of line, challenging the status quo, or confronting the powers that be with novel thoughts and ideas. By definition, novelty involves difference, which may be perceived as questioning and challenging. When questioned, the creative individual could always point to God or his muse who "made" him speak the way he did.

With the shift in the locus of creativity and in the responsibility for it, it is now the creative individual himself who has gone off into the unknown; it is *he* who has deviated from the traditional and the status quo; and it is *he* who must stand by what *he* has done and be prepared to defend it.

Intuition and the "Aesthetic Feel" for a Hypothesis

Inspiration has been referred to previously as one of the mystiques of the creative process. Indeed, as we have said, it is quite awe-inspiring, etc., as well as quite mystifying. Its characteristics are such and it is valued so highly that some creative persons will refuse to be studied by psychologists or others interested in the creative process for fear of destroying their inspirational sources or of "putting a hex" on them. Other creative individuals present the idea of inspiration as a challenge to the investigator, insisting that while his investigational techniques may reveal characteristics of thought processes, or unconscious factors in motivation, etc., they will never reveal anything about the mystique aspects of creativity and especially about inspiration. They may be right, but meanwhile as a psychologist one tries to understand the phenomenon referred to and possibly to describe it more clearly, or to present the conditions under which it appears, and also to devise experiments to clarify further the nature of these conditions or even of the phenomenon itself. For some of the mystique aspects of creativity, either a discussion of the conditions associated with them or experiments devised to clarify them will be presented.

There are two other mystiques of the creative process during the hypothesis formation stage. One of these is intuition and the other is an "aesthetic feel" for a hypothesis. There are some creative individuals who behave quite intuitively. When confronted with a problem they may come up with an answer and it will be the correct one, although they may not be able to give any reasons or rational bases for their answer. Observers can find this quite mystifying.

Still other creative persons are not intuitive in the sense in which we have just used the term. They, as distinguished from their intuitive-creative colleagues, come up with what appear to be several equally reasonable alternative solutions to a problem. An observer might see each of these solutions as equally good, but the creative person somehow makes his selection on some kind of "aesthetic feeling" about one of the solutions, and then on later reflection, usually after the creative person has demonstrated the value of his choice, does one realize that not all of the solutions were equally good, parsimonious, or elegant. Creative persons in forming hypotheses frequently manifest intuitive or "aesthetic feel" characteristics. Less creative persons might arrive at the same solutions but through more circuitous and tortured ways.

With this discussion of the characteristics of the hypothesis formation stage of the creative process, which might then be regarded as the demands or requirements of this stage, let us now turn to a discussion of the psychological characteristics that could result in fulfilling these demands or requirements.

Psychological Characteristics That Facilitate Hypothesis Formation

Personality Factors

To embark on the hypothesis formation stage in the creative process frequently takes much courage and self-confidence, for it may involve a confrontation with the status quo as to the significance of progress and that which is novel. It may involve differing from and deviating from the here and now. These kinds of behavior cannot occur in tradition-bound, conforming, rigid, and anxious individuals.

To be inspired, to have access to his unconscious, the individual requires freedom to explore, to be himself, to entertain ideas no matter how wild, and to express that which is within him without fear of censure and concern with evaluation.

> [Picasso's] "only wish has been desperately to be himself; in fact he acts according to suggestions which come to him from beyond his own limits. He sees descending upon him a superior order of exigencies, he has a very clear impression that something compels him imperiously to empty his spirit of all that he has only just discovered, even before he has been able to control it, so that he can admit other suggestions. Hence his torturing doubts. But his anguish is not a misfortune for Picasso. It is just this which enables him to break down all his barriers, leaving the field of the possible free to him, and opening up to him the perspectives of the unknown" [Zervos quoted in Read, 1948, p. 109].

The adult in our society who complains about his own lack of creativity or who complains about the lack of creativity in others is often incapable of emptying his spirit of what he has learned. He is intolerant of ambiguities and doubts and fearful of the unknown. Rigidities, fears, and doubts are replaced with premature evaluations and parental "don'ts" and "shouldn'ts" that serve only to inhibit curiosity and exploration that might result in inspired and creative ideas.

A friend once complained to Schiller about his lack of creative power; Schiller replied:

> "The reason for your complaint lies, it seems to me, in the constraint which your intellect imposes upon your imagination. Here I will make an observation, and illustrate it by an allegory. Apparently it is not good—and indeed it hinders the creative work of the mind—if the intellect examines too closely the ideas already pouring in, as it were, at the gates. Regarded in isolation, an idea may by quite insignificant, and venturesome in the extreme, but it may acquire importance from an idea which follows it; perhaps, in a certain collocation with other ideas, which may seem equally absurd, it may be capable of furnishing a very serviceable link. The intellect cannot judge all these ideas unless it can retain them until it has considered them in connection with these other ideas. In the case of a creative mind, it seems to me, the intellect has withdrawn its watchers from the gates, and the ideas rush in pell-mell, and only then does it review and inspect the multitude. You worthy critics, or whatever you may call yourselves, are ashamed or afraid of the momentary and passing madness which is found in all creators, the longer or shorter duration of which distinguishes the thinking artist from the dreamer. Hence your complaints of unfruitfulness, for you reject too soon and discriminate too severely [Brill, 1938, p. 193]."

Another characteristic of that phase of the creative process in which the individual has an idea is that the phase is often experienced as having a goal without a charted pathway leading to it. Nevertheless, there is a sense of direction, a feeling of orientation, and of a possible end state but no necessarily definite awareness of the intermediate steps or actual knowledge of how to achieve the goal.

In discussing his experiences during the development of the theory of relativity, Einstein said he always had "a feeling of direction, of going straight toward something concrete." Einstein found it difficult to characterize this feeling but felt that in this feeling of direction "there is always something logical; but I have it in a kind of survey, in a way visually [Wertheimer, 1945, p. 184]."

During this phase of the creative process, the creative individual may appear as if he is no longer in contact with reality as we know it, for indeed, he is probing the unknown, charting the uncharted, creating his own reality—a reality which we may only later come to accept as a new and better reality.

These are some of the characteristics of that phase of the creative process which has been called "inspiration," "hypothesis formation," and the "context of discovery." Even if we allow for much romanticizing about this aspect of the process, it possesses many idiosyncratic features. It is during this part of the process that the creative individual is said to be his most individual and unique self.

The creative person's individuality and uniqueness is manifest in at least three different ways. He works in an environment in which he feels psychologically and even physically unthreatened and comfortable so that he can relax the barriers that exist between himself and the outside world, as well as the barriers that may exist within him. This individuality and uniqueness is also manifest in his self-confidence, courage, tolerance of ambiguity, capacity to move forward in the face of anxiety, etc.

Cognitive Factors

Coexisting with the aforementioned personality characteristics are character-istic thought and perceptual processes. When presented with a stimulus for associations, the thought processes of the creative individual are such that he is likely to come up with more ideas or associations than do other people. When he comes forth with a series of alternatives, he does not lose himself obsessively in trying to choose among them, but selects from them in terms of some kind of priority system he has developed. And, if what he has selected does not satisfy the demands of the situation, he can come up with another series of alternatives to which he devotes himself with sincerity and perseverance. He is not stimulus-bound in his thinking. His thought processes are not fixed on the functions he once learned that the objects in his environment manifest. He can adapt things in his environment to meet his needs, for he realizes that the functions that had been assigned to them in the past had been so assigned by other men, and he can therefore alter them to suit his will and needs.

In the process of solving a problem, it is not characteristic of creative individuals to jump impulsively to conclusions. This is not to say that they will not check different possible solutions and conclusions, nor that they will not be impulsive on occasion, but it is more likely that they will "feel out" a problem and its elements before suggesting a conclusion or solution.

On the perceptual level, creative individuals perceive objects and other stimuli in their environment as brighter, more precise, and even less form-bound than others do. They are capable of physiognomic perceptions—they attribute human-like characteristics to stimuli in the environment so that what is there is not dead but enlivened. When they are so enlivened, so animated, so physiognomic, they have a less form-bound quality. When the boundaries of form have been broken down, then what exists in the environment as separate entities can be combined with other less form-bound elements into newer and more novel and creative combinations. For example, Kandinsky in discussing his work says:

"On my palette sit high, round rain drops, puckishly flirting with each other, swaying and trembling. Unexpectedly they unite and suddenly become thin, sly threads which disappear in amongst the colors and roguishly skip about . . . ! [quoted in Werner, 1957, p. 71]."

What the creative adult does in what has just been described is different from what other adults do, but it is not likely to be different from what many other persons might have been capable of at one time in their lives. Developmental psychologists tell us that in the course of perceptual development, children are capable of and do manifest physiognomic perception. But, with development, with "growing up," with socialization, and with aging, the frequency of physiognomic perception disappears in many people.

The creative individual perceives his environment, in the sense of seeing and learning about it, not only with his eyes but with his whole body. He senses, feels with, and follows the lead of the stimuli in his problem or in his environment through bodily or kinesthetic sensations. It is even likely that this capacity of attending to kinesthetic sensations, his "aesthetic feel" or hedonic response (Gordon, 1961), is also what enables the creative individual to select from among the alternatives that have presented themselves that one which will lead him in the direction of the solution to his problem.

The creative individual is capable of what psychoanalysts refer to as *regression in service of the ego*, of allowing himself to perceive, think, and feel about the external world in terms that others would regard as primitive. The creative individual is not afraid of such primitive processes and behavior. Others, when they have such experiences, become anxious and upset. Their emotional and mental stability depends on their perceptual stability and on their belief that what is in the environment will always be there in the form they have always known it to have. For the creative individual, there is no such demand for sameness, and he will even make his world or immediate environment disorderly just so that he can make a new and more creative order out of it.

Transactional Relationships between Personality and Cognitive Characteristics

At this point, having discussed the first phase of the creative process—inspiration, or the context of discovery, or hypothesis formation—it is important to digress for a moment and make explicit the conceptualization of the person that is at the root of what has just been presented.

For our purposes here, the individual has been conceptualized as composed of two transacting systems. One system is composed of his drives, feelings, attitudes, values, etc., which we have loosely termed *personality* factors. The second system is composed of the individual's manner of dealing with information, his perceptual processes, his associations, thought processes, and problem-solving behavior, which we have assembled under the heading *cognitive* factors. As we have seen, both systems are in operation as the creative individual embarks upon the first phase of the creative process. But they are not separate systems, each going its own way. They are involved in transactional relationships, i.e., they affect one another. The anxious individual may become constricted and rigid in his behavior and may not develop very many ideas for coping with the problem at hand. The self-confident individual may persevere with one idea that others deemed unworthy of consideration and come up with a creative solution. And just as personality factors affect cognitive factors, so cognitive factors affect personality factors. The individual who has not had an idea to solve a problem can become depressed, not only because he is still confronted with the problem but because he may begin to feel impotent about the possibility of having any ideas. By the same token, an individual who has begun to doubt his creative capacity may become elated and more hopeful once he gets the idea that sets him on his way to the solution.

The Functions of Creativity Programs for Hypothesis Formation

The techniques and methods discussed later that are designed to help facilitate the creative process generally focus primarily on personality *or* cognitive factors. Sometimes they assume that training that leads to effectiveness in one domain will have a positive effect on the other. If this assumption is correct, then we will usually not need to test for both effects. A technique that does try to deal with both personality and cognitive factors will be discussed later.

Those techniques that concentrate on personality variables may try to help the individual become less anxious about what is in his unconscious so that he can make more positive use of the constructive ideas that it contains. They also help him to be more confident of his ideas and less upset when he encounters ambiguity and not be inclined to accept premature answers which might lead him to be satisfied with the fact that he has *an* answer, although it is not necessarily *the creative* answer.

Other techniques are not necessarily concerned with *direct* attempts to cope with personality problems and difficulties whose resolution might facilitate and foster an individual's creativity. Instead of direct work these techniques try to create environments with an atmosphere of acceptance and nonevaluation so that the individual feels more free. Instead of pointing out to the individual the reasons for his lack of freedom, these technqiues provide the individual with freedom and encourage him to make use of it. And should he have difficulty they may limit themselves solely to encouragement or they may try to foster some understanding of why he is having trouble taking advantage of the freedom and acceptance with which his environment provides him.

Just as there are methods of coping with personality problems that may interfere with the creative process, so there are training procedures that try to make the individual more flexible cognitively. Some of these involve learning information in a flexible manner; others provide questions to stimulate thought; still others provide guidelines for how to proceed in the development of an idea or help the individual by providing a description of the creative process in easy-to-follow steps. In this manner, part of this process can be mastered more easily. These are only a sample of the techniques for stimulating cognitive factors that will be discussed later.

STAGE II—HYPOTHESIS TESTING

Having discussed our conceptualization of the individual, let us now return to the creative process. An idea, when it occurs to an individual, still leaves open the question whether it will or will not yield or lead to a creative result. Simply stated, the question is: "Is the idea 'crazy' or is it potentially creative?" A partial answer is obtained during the "elaboration" stage, the time devoted to "hypothesis testing" or to what has also been called the "context of justification." Characteristic of this stage are attempts to determine whether ideas which vary in degree of tentativeness can be implemented and whether they do or do not check out in reality. After the artist conceives of an idea for a painting, he takes brush in hand and works away at his easel. The composer, hearing a tune in his head, goes to the piano and listens to how the notes combine realistically. The scientist goes to his laboratory to test whether his formulas are consistent with experimental data. The theoretician may have to wait years before instruments are developed with which he can test his ideas.

Variability in Criticism and Evaluation

Regardless of the techniques involved in the testing phase, a shift of attitude and behavior is involved which is different from that which was characteristic of the inspiration phase in the creative process. Initially, criticism and evaluation were ruled out so that ideas could rush in and be viewed in their various combinations. But as the creative process proceeds, care and judgment play more significant roles, and evaluation and criticism of the work make their appearance. They give the important ingredients, control and discipline, to the work. They give form and substance to ideas. In this context we agree with Kaplan (1957) that, to become art, fantasy has to be "externalized and controlled by the responsible realistic and logical ego." The artistry exists in both the quality of criticism as well as the quality of the creative materials that are criticized. "Without both," says Kaplan, "the work is either as formless and unintelligible as the so-called 'art' of the insane, or as mechanical and superficial as the formulas of the skillful hack [Kaplan, 1957, p. 215]."

From a Private to a Public Experience

As the creative individual moves from the inspiration phase in which he has been his most unique self to the testing and justification phases when he gives his idea palpable meaning and existence, he proceeds from a private experience to a state of expression in which he will make his work manifest and public. He has moved from a laissez-faire attitude and a state of anarchy to one in which he will bring order out of chaos. In so doing he presents others with a new way of perceiving some facet of the world; he establishes new freedom for himself and others.

Both Creator and Audience

In working out his inspiration, the creative individual plays two finely balanced roles—he is both creator and audience. He communicates with himself and his work. "While the artist creates, in the state of inspiration," says the psychoanalyst Kris (1952), "he and his work are one; when he looks upon the product of his creative urge, he sees it from the outside, and as his own first audience, he participates in 'what the voice has done '[p. 61]." There is thus a dialog between the creator and his work. As it has been said of Goethe, "It is not Goethe who creates *Faust* but Faust who creates Goethe." Goethe's own statement was, "I did not make my songs, my songs made me." In the field of painting we find Picasso saying,

> I see ... for others; that is to say, so that I can put on canvas the sudden apparitions which force themselves on me. I don't know in advance what I am going to put on the canvas, any more than I decide in advance what colours to use. Whilst I work, I take no stock of what I am painting on the canvas. Every time I begin a picture, I feel as though I were throwing myself into the void. I never know if I shall fall on my feet again. It is only later that I begin to evaluate more exactly the result of my work [Read, 1948, p. 107].

From Passivity to Activity

During the inspiration phase the individual was the passive recipient of stimuli and ideas, the *re*active observer who stood by as ideas rushed in. When he tests, he becomes more active and more critical. With the entrance of the critic role, the creative process not only begins to shift from a private to a public experience but the creative individual also starts to become object rather than subject. Later, when the efforts are viewed and evaluated by others, he is primarily objective.

Discipline and Control

The creative process, therefore, has its own built-in controls. In the creative individual the freedom needed for inspiration and for toying with ideas does not go out of control. The energy is harnessed, and only out of this control—the discipline of his field and his self-discipline—does the creative product result. Creativity training programs cannot do very much to provide the individual with the *discipline of his field*, but they can give him an awareness of the factors that might impede his creativity, which stem from his approach to the data and information of his field.

Feeling with the Stresses and Strains of the Problem

Just as the first stage of the creative process—hypothesis formation—has its mystique as manifested in inspiration, intuition, and the aesthetic feeling for the potentially correct response, so the second stage, hypothesis testing, also has its mystique. This is manifested in the creative individual's capacity to move with the stresses and strains in his work as he brings it to a conclusion. Again, as he tests or works out an idea, he may not be able to verbalize or present a rational case for what he is doing but he knows it is the correct way to proceed. He allows the problem to lead him to the solution. Because the creative person cannot verbalize what he is up to, others are frequently mystified by his behavior.

The creative individual also has the capacity to sense and feel and then acknowledge that a work is complete. When it feels right to him, he knows he has achieved his goal and can stop. Other persons who lack this aesthetic feeling either stop with uncompleted works or continue their efforts with a work that is in fact completed only to "mess it up" or do it an injustice in some way.

The Function of Creativity Programs for Hypothesis Testing

Theoretically, creativity programs that cope with personality problems can indeed help the individual with his self-discipline. Through supportive, insight, or other psychotherapies, the individual can learn how to satisfy growing needs and drives so that massive amounts of energy need not be expended to control, suppress, or repress them. Energy that is not needed for such purposes can then be used for constructive control purposes in the creative process.

Techniques for stimulating creativity through the cognitive processes do not place as much emphasis on this discipline or control aspect of the creative process as they do on the inspiration or hypothesis-formation phase. Their orientation emphasizes so much the need to relax controls for getting ideas that they appear to underemphasize the need to reinstitute controls later in the creative process. A possible antidote to this shortcoming appears in group techniques for stimulating creativity, since one of the functions of the leader or of the other members is to keep the individuals in the group focused upon the task at hand.

STAGE III–COMMUNICATION OF RESULTS

Communication with the self alone is insufficient for the creative process. Like the neologisms of the schizophrenic, such communication may be too idiosyncratic to have significance for other persons.

"The hysteric [Freud said] is undoubtedly a poet, [who] represents his phantasies essentially by mimicry, without considering whether other people understand them or not. The ceremonials and prohibitions of obsessional patients" represent their personal religions, and the paranoids' delusions are similar to the philosophers' systems. All this to Freud suggested the possibility that these patients were trying in some "asocial manner" to cope with their conflicts and desires in ways "which, when carried out in a manner acceptable to a large number of persons are called poetry, religion and philosophy [Freud, 1931, pp. 7-8]."

In the process of communication with others the creative person must eliminate some of the difficulties he experienced in the course of arriving at his final product. This does not mean that the final product may not be complex but only that the audience is not expected to re-experience all the problems and difficulties involved in the process. Wertheimer (1945) says that Einstein tells us that how he presented material concerning the two triple sets of axioms in the Einstein-Infeld book is not how it occurred to him in thinking through the problems involved. His manner of presentation was a function of how he felt he could best present his material. And furthermore, Einstein also reported that after coming upon the solutions there is a joy in formulating them properly.

To be able to communicate with others in this manner requires flexibility in thought processes and the capacity to shift roles, which is probably more apparent in the scientist than in the artist. " 'We have a paradox in the method of science. The research man may often think and work like an artist, but he has to talk like a bookkeeper, in terms of facts, figures, and logical sequence of thought' [Smyth quoted in Holton, 1953, p. 93]."

Elegance of Solution

The creative person may present his work so well to others that they may regard it as "obvious," "simple," and wonder why they never thought of it. John Milton put it well, as Holton (1953, p. 94) tells us, when he said, "so easy it seemed/ Once found, which yet unfound most would have thought/ Impossible!" And, as Holton has also pointed out in considering the scientist's work, to get something elegantly stated may take months of hard work and the final form is not necessarily consistent with the order in which the findings or ideas occurred. Those who come later and who try to reconstruct the sequence of events may only be confused by the order that they find (Holton, 1953).

The "elegance" and integrated quality of the solution makes for overlooking the fact that creativity is a process. It is sometimes difficult for individuals looking at the coherent quality of a final solution to imagine that the solution was developed through a process and that the product did not appear full-blown. The "obviousness" of the solution and its simplicity is frequently seductive for some individuals, who think, "I could easily have done *that*." And finally, the manner in which the product is produced and the circumstances in which it is admired do not prepare the individual who is learning how to be creative for the difficulties he will have to undergo along the way. He frequently cannot *imagine* that creative individuals did in fact experience any problems at all.

"Eureka"—and the Good Gestalt

On completing the creative product, the creative individual often experiences a feeling of exhilaration. He is ready to shout, "This is it!" "Eureka!" Part of this exhilarated feeling is related to the release of previously pent up emotions which had to be controlled so that they would not interfere with the progress of the work, and part of it is related to the aesthetic experience, in scientists as well as artists, of having developed the *good gestalt*, the good form in the final product—but it is more than just form, it is the combination of feeling and form. The creative individual's experience at this time reflects the goodness of fit, the "oneness" of the creative individual and that which he has created. The same aesthetic factor that was previously involved in selecting from the various possibilities that one which led to the correct path to the solution is now again involved in deciding when the work is completed and when enough has been accomplished. When the capacity to make this judgment is lacking or inhibited, the artist is unable to put the finishing touches on his work or he is unable to part with his painting or sculpture, and the scientist has that additional experiment or "only one more revision" of his final paper.

It would not be at all surprising if this aesthetic factor, or, as Gordon (1961) calls it, a "hedonic response," when and if we learn how to study and measure it appropriately, were to turn out to be one of the most important differentiators between the creative individual and less creative persons. It will probably also turn out to be one of the most difficult characteristics for which to provide training.

The creative individual has the aesthetic sensitivity that enables him to select from the myriad existing possibilities or stimuli that one which is most critical for his work. The creative individual is frequently incapable of verbalizing just what it was that made him "feel" that something was "right" and, while his "feelings" may lead him to errors and blind alleys, they also lead him to the correct goal. Possibly, as more individuals become involved in the creative process and as more information about their experiences becomes available, we may gain better insight into the nature of these feelings.

Novelty

The aspect of the final product that marks it as creative is its novelty. Novelty arises from a reintegration of already existing materials or knowledge. When this integration is completed, it contains one or more elements that are new in terms of their specific characteristics or the integration has resulted in a completely new organization. The product never existed previously in its new form. It deviates in some critical or significant manner from that which existed. There is *distance* between it and the status quo or the traditional. *Distance* alone is a necessary but insufficient condition for creativity. That which is produced must also be "useful, tenable, or satisfying (Stein, 1967)"; it should be "adaptive (MacKinnon, 1964)" and contain an element of "effective surprise (Bruner, 1962)."

Ways of Arriving at Novelty

Novelty, while it is the most critical outcome of creativity, can, however, be produced in a variety of ways other than the creative process. Novelty may also be an outcome of trial and error, serendipity, inventiveness, discovery, and the like. There are several characteristics that distinguish creativity from these other processes. In the creative process the individual draws more heavily on his own resources. It is more of an internal process than the others mentioned, and it involves a greater leap into the unknown, a leap that results in a high degree of meaning and significance.

Some investigators differentiate between degrees of creativity. Lacklen defines creativity in terms of the *breadth of applicability* of a man's work and provides a 15-point scale for rating it (Lacklen & Harmon, 1958). For Ghiselin (1963) there is a distinction between creative action of the *higher sort* which he says "alters the universe of meaning itself, by introducing into it some new element of meaning or some new order of significance, . . . [p. 42] ." It occurs more commonly when someone feels that the old universe of meaning is inadequate. Creative action of the *lower sort* "gives further development to an established body of meaning through initiating some advance in its use . . . [p. 42] ."

One of the reasons that the *creative process* has been described here rather than the other processes that also result in novelty is because these other processes can be regarded as subcases of the more general case of creativity. Trial and error, discovery, serendipity, or problem solving can all occur in the creative process, but inspiration and the leap into the unknown that occur in the creative process do not occur in and are not characteristic of these other processes. From a psychological point of view, the characteristics of the individual who produces novelty through trial and error should be different in certain respects from the one who produces novelty through creativity. Both individuals may share characteristics in common, but just as these individuals are different from other noncreative persons in certain respects, so they are theoretically different from each other in other characteristics.

Throughout this book the term "creative" has been used to refer to all of the processes through which novelty can be achieved. This is consistent with current usage of the term in speaking of stimulating creativity. But, as just pointed out, it is not completely accurate. The term "creative" should be reserved for those processes and those individuals whose behavior follows the *creative process* and not the other processes of achieving novelty.

Novelty and Cultural Values

Statements of what is novel are culture bound, and the kinds of persons who are valued for creating novelty also vary as a function of cultural characteristics. At the height of Greek culture it was the philosopher-thinker who was most highly regarded. But when the Romans achieved prominence, it was the man of action, the doer, and the practical man who was most valued. In contemporary Western society, one of the most coveted prizes for creative accomplishments in the physical sciences, the Nobel Prize, is given to individuals who have produced tangible and workable models of their ideas and not simply theory.

In contemporary society also there is a strong tendency to use the term "creativity" for a wide range of phenomena, from creative playthings to the theory of relativity; from the child who fingerpaints to the adult theoretician and scientist. Such a wide range of uses for the word not only devalues its significance but is also a reflection of the spread of democratic values and ideology. In a society such as ours with the opportunity it provides for upward mobility, with its attempts to overcome the limitations and restrictions of hereditary and traditional societies, there is at times the tendency to use the word indiscriminately. Such indiscriminate use is reminiscent of the advertiser's penchant for superlatives. Objects and products are not just "good" or "very good" but "super" or "super, super."

The Significant Others

That an individual has achieved novelty and has completed his work to his own satisfaction does not mean that the creative process, in terms of the thesis presented here, is at an end. For completion, the final product must be presented to and accepted by a group of *significant others* as tenable, useful, or satisfying. The "significant others" may be a formally or informally organized group of persons that has the ability and expertise to evaluate developments in its own field. The size and composition of the group may vary, and the degree of recognition it receives from the broader society as expert in its own field may also vary. At times it may consist only of a small "psyche" group on the Left Bank in Paris, or in New York's Greenwich Village, or of the small number of persons who first gathered around Freud, or of those who first understood

Einstein. On other occasions it may be the larger group of authorities and experts who attend exhibitions or professional and scientific meetings.

Intermediaries

In a complex society such as ours, the persons just referred to serve in the role of intermediaries. They carry out and fulfill significant functions between the creative individual and the audience or members of the broader society. Among these intermediaries, and usually counted among the significant others, are the *supporters*—the psyche group, the patron, the entrepreneur, the executive, and the expert—all of whom provide the creative individual with emotional, financial, and even technical support for his undertaking. The second group, whom I have called *judges and evaluators*—the specialists and authorities, the foundation staffs, gallery owners and museum administrators, the critics and reviewers—evaluate and pass judgment on the final work.

For the public or for the society these intermediaries serve as selective filters, since their decisions and evaluations provide some individuals with support and recognition for their work, whereas they deprive others of these advantages. Consequently, their decisions are most critical for the society that it presumably protects from being inundated with noncreative works. Its decisions are also most critical for the person involved in creative work since intermediaries' judgments will not only affect how his past work is regarded but how much opportunity he may have for future creative work.

Intermediaries are rather powerful figures in the interpersonal aspects of the creative process. In some fields the creative individual can avoid dealing with them directly by working through an agent, but in most instances he has to deal with them directly, and to do this effectively involves a set of personal characteristics that are different from those involved in the intrapersonal aspects of the creative process. It may require the ability to socialize, persuade, convince, communicate clearly, etc., all of which did not come into play when the individual was at his work.

Acceptance by intermediaries and significant others is important to the creative individual not only because it marks his work as creative but also because, from a psychological point of view, it provides the creative individual with important feedback and reinforcement. By accepting the final product and by regarding it as creative, the group indirectly indicates that it accepts and approves of the psychological needs that initially motivated the creative person to deviate from the status quo and move off into the unknown. In the process of accepting the creative product the group identifies with the creative individual and, in a sense, has joined him as "cocreator." For the group, then, the creative product fulfills or gives expression to certain psychological needs, just as it does for the creative individual. For the group the creative product "says" things that it may have wanted to but was unable to say. Just as this holds true for the significant others among the intermediaries so does it hold true for groups of individuals in the broader society or public.

The creative person's supporters and judge-evaluators are only two groups of intermediaries. Their orientation is usually with the creative person in that they are usually more concerned with him than with others. But there are other groups of intermediaries whose orientation is toward the public or audience. These are the *change agents*—the farm extension agents, the salesmen and advertising people—who either present information about innovations or try to sell innovations. And then, too, there are the opinion leaders and tastemakers who also shape and direct the public's attitudes to creative developments.

The intermediaries' effectiveness in fulfilling their role in the creative process may be a function of their personalities, their knowledge of their field, their persuasive capacity, etc. But it may also be a function of certain characteristics of the creative product or innovation. Some creative products or innovations more readily find acceptance than do others, and knowledge of these characteristics are important to facilitate the creative process.

By the same token, it is important that intermediaries be aware of the characteristics of the media through which they communicate with the public about a creative product. Some media have certain requirements that need to be understood and followed or else the message will be confused or lost sight of.

The public is the final target and recipient of creative work. It is important to bear in mind, however, that the public does not behave, react or move as a single unit or body. It is composed of subgroups, some of whom are much more ready to accept and appreciate creative works than are others. Much time and effort can be saved, and the creative process can run more smoothly and effectively when there is available knowledge of these subgroups' characteristics and the processes through which they go in the adoption process. Similarly, it is advantageous to know about ways of overcoming resistances to change, for then there is an alternative available to persuasion and "selling" which can be quite effective in achieving acceptance of creative works.

All of what has just been said will be considered and discussed later. There are, however, additional factors that affect the public's readiness to accept creative work which we can do little more than mention. These factors include: the nature of the geographical environment, not only as a source of sense impressions but also as a factor affecting communications between persons from different backgrounds and countries, for experience with such diversity stimulates curiosity. If it occurs with tolerance, then the public is more amenable to and aware of the variety and range of existing differences from which selections can be made for new creative integrations. Mention would also have to be made of the philosophical orientation of the culture and its relationship to the culture's value system. The values placed on different areas of activity (technology or the humanities, pure or applied science, abstract or representational art) and even on creativity itself require consideration. The culture's attitudes toward tradition and change and, if the latter is more prized, the way it is fostered, are significant. Is change valued for its own sake, and when it occurs, is it re-incorporated into the matrix of the existing culture? Language as a guide to reality (Mandelbaum, 1962) has to be mentioned, for it reflects the concepts available to the people for understanding and appreciating that which is presented to them. Not all societies possess the same concepts and, by the same token, neither do all of the subgroups within the society.

In addition, consideration needs to be given to the society's child-rearing practices and educational opportunities. These would be related to the individuals' attitudes to both new and old information and how flexibly they would deal with such information. They would also be related to the individuals' tolerance and respect for differences between people, ideas, customs, etc., and their confidence and courage when coping with complexity and diversity and integrating it creatively.

These are some of the additional variables that require further discussion to understand more completely the public's receptivity to creativity. They are also necessary for a further understanding of the cultural context of creativity that is central to the work of the creative individual, for it is the matrix in which the creative process is embedded.

The Functions of Creativity Programs for the Communication Stage

The communication stage of the creative process has not received as much attention as the hypothesis formation and hypothesis testing stages of the creative process. In part, this is a function of the fact that most persons regard the creative process from an intrapersonal point of view, in terms of what goes on in the individual, and therefore much more has been thought about and done about the cognitive and personality factors that have to do with creativity. The other reason why creativity stimulating programs have had relatively little to do with the communication stage is that in our society a variety of separate professional groups have developed and exist to deal with its different aspects. To be sure, an individual involved in the creative process can attend seminars to learn how to improve his report-writing technique and such, but it is unlikely that he would have the time, inclination, or ability also to become involved in learning how to communicate with intermediaries, learn more about the public's adoption processes or how one utilizes different media effectively to communicate with the public, etc. It is best to leave all of these to persons trained and expert in these areas.

These different areas are part of the total creative process. And, if we are not aware of them in the histories of creative works that have passed through the process successfully, then we become painfully aware of them through the histories of the failures—not just the negligible failures but those that have to go through another process of rediscovery, not because the intrapersonal processes were not carried out well but because the ball was dropped when the interpersonal aspects of the creative process came into play. Hopefully, by explicating and clarifying the various aspects of the communication stage, even though fewer suggestions for stimulating creativity may appear in this than in the other sections, more persons will become aware of the total creative process so that the frequency of creative work will increase and the failures will diminish.

SUMMARY

Creativity is a process of hypothesis formation, hypothesis testing, and the communication of results. Preparation, or education in the broad sense, precedes these stages. These stages are discrete but they overlap. At times one may be more salient than the other. It is only for heuristic purposes that they are presented separately here.

Each of these stages has distinct requirements and demands in terms of the cognitive, personality, and social characteristics of the creative individual. Various programs to stimulate creativity differentially emphasize one or more of the appropriate characteristics involved. The book has been organized in terms of stages of the creative process, and for each of these stages the techniques available to stimulate creativity at that point will be discussed.

Before turning to these various techniques we shall consider the criteria used in different studies of creativity and the creative individual. This information serves as important background material, for the studies in which it is involved are frequently the bases on which the techniques for stimulating creativity have been developed.

Chapter **III**

Criteria in Studies of Creativity

All the techniques for stimulating creativity, as well as our knowledge of the creative process as spelled out in the previous chapter, are based on studies of creative individuals. But who are these creative persons? And on what bases were they selected for study? These are the questions to which this chapter addresses itself. As will soon be obvious, none of the criteria is likely to satisfy everyone; each has both positive and negative characteristics.

GENERALLY ACKNOWLEDGED CREATIVITY

One of the most common criteria is *generally acknowledged creativity*. No one would deny that Michelangelo, da Vinci, Shakespeare, and Einstein were creative individuals and that their works have withstood the test of time. Where *generally acknowledged creativity* is the criterion, the investigator relies on secondary sources, or primary ones if the subject is living, for information about the creative individual and the factors affecting his creativity. The investigative technique is the case study. The investigator may concern himself with the creative individual's life history, his personality, his intellectual and perceptual characteristics as they might have been related to or involved in the creative work that was produced. The degree to which any single part of the creative person's life or work is emphasized depends on the particular interests of the investigator. For example, Freud (1948) concerned himself with the mother in the life history of da Vinci. Wertheimer (1945) was interested in Einstein's thought processes as he worked on the theory of relativity.

Such individual case studies are usually quite thorough and frequently provide many fruitful insights and hypotheses regarding the creative process and/or the psychological processes involved in it. Although we cannot generalize from a study of any single case, it is possible through the study of different single cases to begin to develop principles or ideas about the creative process that may have general application.

Along with the advantages of this approach, there are also disadvantages. Although we may feel secure when an outstandingly creative person has been selected for study, no new guideposts are provided for the selection of other individuals except that they too must have withstood the test of time. Another shortcoming in the case study approach is that the kind and extent of material obtained is dictated and limited by the investigator's interests. For example, psychoanalysts and some psychologists have stressed the importance of personality factors in their case studies, but omit considerations of the cognitive characteristics of their subjects. Similarly, investigators who specialize in the study of cognitive characteristics omit or underemphasize personality characteristics. Such case studies may lead the reader to believe that only the characteristics considered are significant for creativity. To compensate for such shortcomings, it would almost be necessary to ask for the impossible—to have some person studied by persons representing different orientations.

Case studies of dead persons may suffer from the further criticism that the investigator is limited to the use of secondary sources. With secondary sources, the investigator must be aware of the fact that the data have been filtered through the eyes of various people and probably do not contain all relevant data. Finally, the fact that an individual has been acknowledged as creative gives us no assurance that the factors involved while he demonstrated his creativity are the same as the characteristics he possessed before his creativity became manifest or the same as the characteristics he possesses after his creativity is generally acknowledged. That an individual has manifested his creativity and that his creativity is acknowledged by others may have a significant effect on the individual's personality and behavior. For example, if he did not do so previously, he may begin to behave like his image of a creative person. That these effects may be quite important is common knowledge among students of human behavior. Individuals who have positive self-concepts will behave differently from those with poor or negative self-concepts. The case study approach is often limited to descriptions of the subject by persons who are aware of his creativity after it has already been manifested. They are, therefore, describing persons who possibly have already been affected by having had feedback about their creativity. To learn what an individual was like before he was acknowledged for his creativity may require interviewing the creative person himself, as well as others, about his life. Both sources may be affected by memory lapses as well as by unconscious selective recall with the selectivity determined by their own liking or disliking of the individual. Or, there may be other distortions determined by trying to rationalize how the creative person's previous life history can be made consonant with his current creative behavior.

REPRESENTATION IN SECONDARY SOURCES

A second criterion used in the selection of creative men is one in which the investigator starts with some significant secondary source, such as an encyclopedia or book on the life history of famous people. To this might be added one or more criteria to make differentiations on the basis of which some person may be eliminated or to make further refined distinctions among the individuals selected for study.

One of the first major studies in this area was the work of Galton (1870), entitled *Heriditary Genius*, in which he was concerned with judges, statesmen, writers, scientists, divines, poets, musicians, and artists. The judges were selected from Foss's *Lives of the Judges*; the statesmen were premiers beginning with the reign of George III who were mentioned in Lord Broughman's *Statesmen of the Reign of George III*; literary men and scientists came from biographical dictionaries; the divines came from Middleton's *Biographica Evangelica*.

James McKeen Cattell (1903) and Cora Sutton Castle (1913) in their studies of eminent men and women also used biographical dictionaries for their initial sample and then retained those who appeared in three additional sources and had the greatest amount of space devoted to them. One of the most important contributions, which relates creative and productive achievements to age, is that by Lehman (1953), *Age and Achievement*, in which both secondary sources and opinions of experts were used. For example, for his sample of chemists Lehman (1953) selected persons from Hilditch's *A Concise History of Chemistry*, and then submitted their names to four university professors of chemistry for evaluation.

One of the main advantages in using dictionaries, biographies, encyclopedias, and other published secondary sources is that it is a reasonably economical and efficient manner of collecting data on a relatively large number of individuals. Not only are the names of these persons available but also a good deal of other information, which might be used for differentiating among individuals who are creative and those who are not. A second advantage of this technique is that the investigator has already had a major decision made for him when the people were included in these secondary sources. These individuals, it might be argued, have the potential to withstand the test of time or else they might not have been included in the first place, or they might have been deleted from later editions.

This method also has its shortcomings. Biographers might become so personally involved with the persons about whom they are writing that they might tend to gloss over some details while exaggerating others. Not all biographers utilize the same set of variables in writing their case studies. Hence, when one characteristic is mentioned in one instance and omitted in another, it cannot necessarily be said that its omission in the second instance was because of its absence, or its relative unimportance. That a particular trait does not appear in a write-up of an individual does not necessarily mean that the individual did not possess it or that he had some opposite characteristic. The biographer may think that the trait should be taken for granted in the person studied and therefore neither discusses the trait nor provides evidence to support it.

The same can be said about the amount of space given to an individual. First, investigators using encyclopedias, etc., do not indicate the criteria utilized by the encyclopedists and, while it might be tempting to regard the amount of space devoted to a given individual as a criterion of his creativity or importance, we also need to bear in mind the possibility that the author may simply have been carried away with some characteristics of the person he is describing or that the amount of space allotted to him may be due to some other reason. Should anyone in the future use the current *Who's Who* volumes for similar purposes, he might find himself in an odd position, since those pieces are written by the individuals themselves. Hence, while the amount of space devoted to any one person may indeed be a reflection of his accomplishments or the societies or associations to which he belongs, it cannot be denied that individuals vary in the emphasis they place on enumerating organizations, etc.

Finally, while individuals included in major works may be regarded as eminent, we may question whether they were also creative. Stating the problem differently, we may ask whether these individuals were simply "popular" or "visible" (and factors associated with popularity or visibility may or may not be associated with creativity).

EXPERT JUDGMENT

Although case histories and secondary sources have been traditional techniques in the field of creativity study, many contemporary researchers (especially those interested in learning about the psychological factors that differentiate among individuals who differ in creativity), use judgments of experts or other individuals deemed capable of evaluating the individuals in the study.

In one study of outstanding scientists J. McK. Cattell (1906) had the names and addresses of "all those known to have carried on research work of any consequence [p. 660]" sent to leading representatives in their fields. These representatives were then asked to rank-order the names they received on the basis of their contributions to the advancement of science. In her study of biologists Roe (1951) selected those who were members of the National Academy of Sciences and/or the American Philosophical Society and on the basis of ratings of six men chosen to represent all subdivisions of biology. In other words, two criteria were used. First, the individual had to be a member of an honorific society; second, he had to be rated high by the six raters.

In another group of studies, close observers of the individuals to be studied were asked for their judgments. In their study of "more" and "less" creative industrial research chemists, Stein *et al.* (1958) collected ratings on a number of variables related to the creative process from a research chemist's superiors, colleagues, and subordinates. Superiors were used as raters on the assumption that they had a broad overview of all their personnel, and much experience with research chemists and therefore were in a position to make comparative judgments. However, since superiors could be limited in the nature of their contacts with any individual researcher, judgments were obtained from a man's colleagues on the assumption that colleagues were closer to ongoing developments in their field, and if or because they were competitive they might be even more "hard-nosed" in their evaluations of their colleagues. Finally, judgments were also obtained from a man's subordinates on the assumption that they were probably closest to the work, knew how it originated and who was responsible for carrying it out. After judgments were obtained from all three groups of evaluators, their reliability was studied, and those on whom all three judges agreed were retained for further study.

One of the most thorough attempts to select a group for study according to the expert judgment approach was that used by MacKinnon (1961) and his group in their study of architects. The dean and four of his colleagues in the College of Architecture at the University of California at Berkeley were asked to nominate and rate the 40 most creative architects in the country in terms of a definition of creativity which included such variables as: original thought; a fresh approach to architecture; "constructive ingenuity; ability to set aside established conventions and procedures when appropriate; a flair for devising effective and original fulfillments of the major demands of architecture; the demands of technology, visual form, planning, human awareness and social purpose [Mac-Kinnon (1961) p. 8]." A total of 86 names was supplied. Using only the mean ratings and the summary of their work, the nominated architects were rank-ordered. MacKinnon wanted to study 40 individuals, and to do so required sending out 64 invitations, since 24 individuals did not accept. One of the questions that had to be answered was whether there was a difference in creativity ratings between those who did and those who did not accept. Analysis of the data indicated that there was no such difference. But MacKinnon checked further. Eleven editors of the major architectural journals in the United States were asked to rank the 64 architects. A comparison of the mean rankings of those who were studied and those who refused to come indicated that the latter did receive slightly higher ranks, but these were not statistically significantly different from rankings given to those architects who did come for study. As an aside, it is interesting to note that the evaluations of the 40 men obtained from the editors agreed rather well with the creativity ratings obtained from the architects themselves. They correlated .88.

Some investigators might have been satisfied to limit themselves to the group selected as described up to this point, but MacKinnon went further by selecting two control groups. Eighty-four architects were selected to match the experimental group ("Arch I") in terms of age and geographic location of practice. Their names were obtained from the 1955 *Directory of Architects*. This group was then divided into two subgroups. One of them, called "Arch II," was composed of 43 individuals and met an additional requirement in that they have at least 2 years of work experience in association with one of the originally nominated creative architects. The other control group, "Arch III," was composed of 41 men, none of whom had ever worked with any of the nominated architects.

Still not satisfied with the selection process and the control groups, MacKinnon then sought a measure that would be either directly or indirectly related to the creativity of his three groups, for there was the assumption that Arch I should be more creative than Arch II, and Arch II should be more creative than Arch III. Two indices of prominence were then established. One index was a weighted system of the number of articles by or about each architect and his work as referenced in the *Architectural Index* for the years 1950-1958. The other index was also a weighted index of the number of pages devoted to each architect for his work for the same period. This analysis indicated that Arch I was clearly superior to Arch II and Arch III. On both indices Arch II fell between Arch I and Arch III but they were closer to III than to I.

Finally, still in search of a better criterion, MacKinnon took the total list of 124 individuals [Arch I ($N = 40$), Arch II ($N = 43$), Arch III ($N = 41$)] and submitted it to six groups of architects and experts on architecture (including the professors who made the original ratings, editors of major architectural journals, the architects of I, II, and III groups, etc.). Each of the persons then rated, on a 9-point scale, the creativity of the people they felt they knew well enough to judge. Analysis of these data indicated that the average ratings for the individuals in each of the three groups were significantly different from each other—Arch I was rated higher than both Arch II and Arch III; Arch II was rated higher than Arch III. On the basis of all this, MacKinnon and his group were quite reassured that they had selected three groups that were adequately differentiated in terms of their creativity.

One of the most important advantages in using experts or close observers to evaluate and select individuals for studies of creativity is that they make it possible to conduct studies on individuals who are living and who might still be counted on to be involved in creative pursuits for some time to come. These raters have knowledge of the processes involved in the man's work—how much of it might have followed the creative process as it was discussed in the previous chapter, how much of it was due to trial and error, how much of it was due to serendipity, and the like. It should be emphasized that the fact that one uses experts does not mean that they will know all this, but the probability of their having such knowledge is increased over the possibility that biographers may have such knowledge. It is also assumed that experts and other close observers will be aware of developments in the total field of work, and therefore have the necessary background to make such judgments.

A third advantage is that if the investigator so desires, and if it is a function of his research when he is involved in a study of creativity, he is in a position to study the factors that might be involved in these experts' judgments. By giving the experts special rating forms with specific variables, it then becomes possible to determine how the raters weight specific factors in their ratings. For example, Harmon (1958) in a study of the ratings experts gave to the applications to the Atomic Energy Commission in 1949 for fellowships, found that the number of publications was essentially the primary factor. And, one of the findings of James *et al.* (1962) in their studies of innovative behavior among administrators in U. S. Government agencies was a significantly higher correlation between judgments of innovation and ratings of general effectiveness when raters also reported that they had a positive value for innovation than when they did not.

When the expert judgment approach is utilized, questions can be raised about the extent to which the raters are biased for or against the subject, the effects of interpersonal relationship, and other "halo phenomena" when ratings are used. These might result in over- as well as underestimates of a man's creativity. Using experts as judges does not necessarily mean that, because their status and prestige are not threatened, they are going to be unbiased. There are instances in the history of science, for example, where the scientific community itself was most vocal in its criticism of new developments. It was only after some time had passed that these developments were accepted as creative accomplishments.

People regard studies in which expert judgments are used for selecting creative individuals for study with a great deal of skepticism. This is probably the most subjective of the methods used. In responding to criticisms such as these, we might say, as Galton (1870) did when he was confronted with a similar problem, "I feel convinced that no man can achieve a very high reputation without being gifted with very high abilities; and I trust that reason has been given for the belief, that few who possess these very high abilities can fail in achieving eminence [p. 42]." J. McK. Cattell (1906) agreed that judges' evaluations were subject to a variety of errors but said, "there is, however, no other criterion of a man's work than the estimation in which it is held by those competent to judge [p. 661]." Furthermore, by using the judgments from several sources or several judges, it is felt that some of the systematic errors in this approach can be overcome.

QUANTITY OF PRODUCTS

A fourth criterion that has been used in studies of creativity is the quantity of novel products that an individual has produced. This criterion was used in Rossman's (1931) study of inventors. Obviously, quantity is not the sole criterion, for that which was patented had to satisfy the requirements of the patent office.

Quantity of patents, or even publications, may be a reasonable criterion in certain areas and with certain individuals, but it is not so in other instances. Thus, although number of patented inventions may be a reflection of an inventor's creativity, and although publications may be reasonable criteria for awarding fellowships or judging academicians of certain status, are they reasonable criteria in judging the creativity of scientists employed in industrial research organizations? In our study (Stein *et al.*, 1958) of individuals in such organizations, when we first considered the use of patents and publications, we were soon told by the men that these criteria were deficient in a variety of ways. In some instances, a company might refuse to have either a patent or publication appear for fear that the company's competitors would then learn what its personnel had been working on. On other occasions, to avoid problems of deciding who are the critical authors on a paper, the names of all persons (no matter how remotely involved) are listed, and they are not necessarily the names of all the people who did the work. On some occasions, they might include the names of individuals who made minimal contributions; on others the name of a research director has to appear on the paper. Furthermore, particularly with regard to patents, we need to be aware of the "patent hound"—the individual who studies published patents, develops some variation, and obtains a new patent for which he is rewarded by his company. Finally, when we concentrate solely on the quantity of works produced, we may sacrifice quality and thereby overlook an individual whose quantitative contributions were small but whose qualitative work may have been of tremendous significance, or vice versa.

PSYCHOMETRIC TESTS

Another criterion in the study of creativity is the *psychometric test*. The difference between this method and those described previously is that those who are regarded as creative in terms of the previous criteria have been manifestly creative in real-life situations. When the psychometric criterion is used, the individuals regarded as creative are those who have received scores on tests developed by psychologists or others that are presumed to be measures of aspects or factors involved in the creative process. As we conceive of them here, these tests have what has been called *face validity* among psychological test constructors, but have not, in terms of much of the work that has been done with them, been validated against an external criterion.

This approach is analogous to that followed by the chemist who synthesizes compounds in the laboratory. So, too, the psychologist tries to get increasingly pure measures of the factors he believes to be involved in creativity. When these measures are obtained, they may be utilized as independent variables, and their relationships to other psychological variables and judgments of creativity studied. They may also be used as dependent variables, in which case the first step is to obtain measures of the subject's creativity (in terms of other criteria discussed here) and then make a study of the manner in which his scores on the tests are related to his creativity rating.

The most important figure on the contemporary American scene involved in the psychometric approach is Guilford (1967). He and his researchers started with a group of subjects who were not distinguished or differentiated in terms of any independent criterion of creativity. Among the groups that were studied were Coast Guardsmen and "high-level" personnel. A battery of psychological tests, focusing on intellectual aspects of human behavior was administered to his groups. When the test results were obtained, their interrelationships were studied, and these results were then reduced to the smallest number of common denominators by using factor-analytic statistical procedures. Work continued until the purest possible factors were defined. New tests were then constructed to obtain better measures of these factors.

Guilford's work has had a tremendous impact on research in creativity. Investigators have used Guilford's tests or variations thereof as independent measures for selecting groups of subjects who are then studied to gather data on their personality and other characteristics. Other investigators have used a manifest criterion of creativity and then studied how the subjects scored on Guilford's or Guilford-like tests. However, more importantly for the purposes of this book, some people have regarded Guilford's tests as tests of creativity (which from our point of view is premature, since not all of the evidence is as strong as we would like for these purposes) and therefore used them to measure the effects of the training programs to be described later. Still other individuals try to develop training programs to stimulate or train for the mental operations involved in Guilford's tests. In our discussion of techniques for the stimulation of cognitive factors, we shall refer to Guilford's tests frequently. This will be especially true when such techniques as brainstorming are discussed.

One of the advantages of the psychometric approach is that the tests employed have been carefully developed. When these tests form the criteria, the method of differentiating among persons is clearly and carefully defined. This approach is not subject to the criticism of previous methods—i.e., that it is subjective. There are rather clearly defined scoring methods, and distinctions are made for when quality or quantity of response is to be used. These very characteristics make this approach appear to be very attractive.

In addition, because the tests developed by the psychometric approach have *face validity*—that is, because they appear to measure mental operations involved in the creative process—some investigators have been quick to label them tests of creativity or creativity tests. Thus, among these psychometric tests there might be one in which an individual is asked to give his associations (thoughts or responses to a stimulus word); then the individual who gives unusual or infrequent responses is regarded as being "on the creative side." Such a response is regarded as having face validity for a test of creativity because as it occurs infrequently so novelty in the creative process occurs infrequently. Aside from all the technical statistical questions involved in these tests, there is reason to exercise a good deal of caution in this regard, since there is as yet insufficient evidence to indicate for what individuals, for what areas of work, in what situations, and in what period of time scores on these tests may be related to manifest creativity.

In its relation to creativity, the psychometric approach has been limited generally to cognitive or intellective factors. Personality factors and social factors have not yet been subjected to the same kind of development. It is probably psychologically less threatening to some individuals if a test or an area of work is limited to intellectual factors. Personality and social factors are more personal and possibly too "subjective," but the very objectivity of the intellectual tests may be more apparent than real, for it overlooks the fact that these tests are based on psychologists' definitions and that it is psychologists who construct the test items.

Despite the criticism of the psychometric approach, we should not overlook the potential significance of the basic assumptions underlying it. As pointed out earlier, one of the ways of looking at this approach is that it is analogous to the activities carried out by the chemist as he tries to synthesize compounds. The chemist does this by studying and obtaining as much knowledge as possible about the compound he is working with; he then tries to purify the various elements and combine them so that they will be effective in coping with certain disease symptoms, let us say. In this approach, numerous compounds may need to be tried before the effective combination is found in actual field tests. Following this analogy, the behavioral scientist may well work in a similar fashion; he, too, tries to develop better and better tests of what he regards as components of creativity. These components can be tested against various criteria of creativity, and then, by a consistent process of checking and rechecking laboratory results against real situations, he may well develop precisely that combination of psychological characteristics and environmental factors that, when brought together at the proper time, result in the same or more creativity than is presently manifest. To be sure, this process is quite time consuming and requires a great deal of cooperation between behavioral scientists and persons involved in real-life situations. There is nothing we can do about the time involved, but if it will be possible to achieve greater cooperation between laboratory and real-life situation personnel, then it is conceivable that many valuable benefits may be reaped from this approach.

THE PROCESS AS A CRITERION

Creativity is a process, as was pointed out in the previous chapter. But none of the previous criteria has really been concerned with the process rather than with the product. Essentially, previous criteria were concerned with the number of products produced or their quality. However, within some of the criteria, rating scales composed of variables that purportedly get at some of the process aspects of creativity might be used. For example, we could ask experts to rate the subjects on number of ideas, quality of ideas, capacity to test ideas, capacity to communicate ideas, etc., which would reflect the three stages of the creative process. But it should be possible to get even "closer" to the process than that.

One possible way of getting closer to the process aspects of creativity is to observe individuals while at work and rate their behavior. From the variety of patterns that would emerge, we could probably differentiate between those that are congruent with the creative process and those that are not. The difficulty with this approach, however, is that any meaningful research study involving a reasonable number of subjects would require a tremendous amount of time from several investigators. The procedure would therefore be uneconomical. In addition, it is likely that the subjects of such a study would also object to being observed at work, for many of them have done so in the past.

A study by Ghiselin *et al.* (1964) suggests that it may be possible to overcome these objections and still get closer to the creative process. These investigators' work started with Ghiselin's (1963) definition of creativity, which emphasizes the first time that a "universe of meaning" is arrived at. In using this definition for criterion purposes, the authors "concentrated upon that crucial moment of performance, within the whole action, when a new configuration of insight is formed and brought into focal clarity [pp. 20-21]." They then concerned themselves with "what happens, in the configural field just before a new order is realized in it, and at the instant of realization, and immediately after [pp. 20-21]." To achieve this goal they then developed a *Creative Process Check List* that had two sublists, one concerned with "States of Attention" and the other with "States of Feeling." Both lists consist of a series of adjectives, and the subject has to choose that adjective which was "an appropriate description of his experience *before*, *during*, or *after* his act of grasping (or shaping) a new insight, solving a problem, or otherwise bringing a new order into being within the field of his consciousness [pp. 21-22]."

This technique is still in the process of development and consequently different methods of scoring and understanding the checklist are being tried. In the published report (Ghiselin *et al.*, 1964) referred to here, two techniques were tried. One consisted of a theoretical weighting system which did not yield very interesting or important results. Another scoring system, empirical in character, was tried, and yielded rather valuable material. These empirical scores yielded correlations that ranged from .34 to .69 with various criteria. But more important, from certain points of view, than the range of these correlations was the fact that the technique appears to be potentially valuable as a means of differentiating among scientists. Thus, the authors were able to differentiate between two types of scientists: the "creative scientists"—the scientists who were *"high in creativity and low in material success"*—and "materially successful scientists"—those who were *"low in creativity and high in material success"* (referred to later as the successful scientists). The states of feeling and attention for both types were studied before, during, and after some significant insight occurred. From the obtained results it was learned that the high creative scientists said on the checklist that in the early stage, their attention was "diffused" and "scanning," whereas the successful scientists said that their attention was "focused" and "sharp." The first is consistent with the reports in the literature of the disorder experienced by the creative individual. This disorder was not apparent in the materially successful scientist. Differences in their feelings after the moment of insight, also appeared. The creative scientists reported that they felt "delighted," while the successful scientists said that they felt "relieved," "satisfied," "exalted," "full," and "excited."

This technique requires further work, but it does appear a quite promising way to get closer to the process of creativity as a criterion. It might also help in differentiating among individuals who achieve novelty through the creative process and those who achieve it through trial and error, serendipity, problem solving, etc. Finally, it has potential usefulness in gathering data from an internal frame of reference and not only from an external frame of reference, as is evident in the other criteria. On this basis, then, it is conceivable that we may find individuals who are creative from their internal frames of reference but who are not acknowledged as such by other persons.

SUMMARY

To lay the groundwork for work to be discussed later, the following criteria utilized in studies of creativity were discussed: (1) Generally acknowledged creativity—persons who have been regarded as creative throughout history are selected for study. (2) Representation in secondary sources—dictionaries of famous people or histories written about specific areas of endeavor are consulted to compile a list of persons for further study. (3) Expert judgment—persons who are experts in their fields evaluate others in their field as to their creativity. (4) Quantity of products—persons are selected in terms of the number of products they have produced that presumably involve creativity as, for example, when we differentiate among individuals on the basis of the number of patents each has. (5) Psychometric tests—psychological tests that measure various psychological factors and characteristics that are presumably related to creativity. These tests are called by some "tests of creativity," although they have not necessarily been validated against criteria of manifest creativity in real-life situations. (6) The process as a criterion—the creative process itself is used as a criterion. Since novelty can be achieved in different ways, we observe individuals at work to determine whether they have achieved novelty through the creative process or through other processes.

These criteria have been used in studies of creative persons to learn which of their characteristics are associated with creativity. These characteristics are then utilized as standards or goals to be achieved by persons attending programs to stimulate creativity. Some of the criteria are also used to study and measure the effectiveness of programs that are designed to stimulate creativity. For example, after attending a creativity course it would be expected that if an individual's creativity did in fact increase, it should be manifest in how well he would do on psychometric tests after the creativity program as compared with his results before it. Similarly, we would expect that his superiors as experts in his field would give him higher ratings after the creativity course than before it.

PART III

INDIVIDUAL PROCEDURES

The individual procedures are divided into two parts. The first two chapters (Chapters IV and V) concern themselves with methods designed to help overcome blocks or obstacles due to personality characteristics or which try to engage constructive aspects of personality and so facilitate the creative process. Then, since more work has been undertaken with cognitive factors, there are six chapters (Chapters VI-XI) that focus on techniques that are designed to "loosen up" and make more effective the utilization of cognitive factors in the creative process. Chapters IX and X contain more of the self-help procedures than do the other chapters, while the other procedures generally require working with another person trained in the technique for stimulating creativity.

Techniques discussed in this section, although focusing directly on the individual may obviously be adopted in a number of instances for use by groups. Similarly some procedures discussed later that have been developed for use with groups may be utilized by individuals.

Chapter **IV**

Introduction to Personality Procedures

In their introduction to a review of the creativity literature, Stein and Heinze (1960) point out that

> Everything that might be regarded in one way or another as important in a study of any individual—his heredity, his childhood, his adolescence, his adult personality, his intelligence, his perceptual processes, his problem-solving behavior, etc.—has been considered in some study of the creative individual. As man has studied man, he has also sought to understand the creative individual, and he has applied the knowledge gained from a study of man in general to a study of the creative man in particular [p. 2].

There have been studies of the creative individual's life history, his personality and cognitive characteristics, the manner in which he interacts with others, and the way in which the environment in which he works may or may not affect his creative endeavors. In each of these areas, characteristic results for creative persons have been found; differences have also been found among individuals who are and are not regarded as creative. Before turning to a discussion of these results, it would be well to say something about the research designs and theories involved.

55

RESEARCH DESIGNS AND THEORIES INVOLVED

Several kinds of studies have been carried out to gather data on the relationships between personality and creativity. One is the case study, in which all that is learned about an individual is integrated and interpreted in some manner so as to cast light on his creativity. For these purposes both primary and secondary sources can be used. The second type of study uses survey procedures. A large questionnaire is developed that is sent out to the participants. And a third kind of study is one in which psychological tests are used. While we shall have more to say about these later, at this point the theoretical context of these studies should be mentioned.

In psychological research, a differentiation can be made between empirical and hypothetical-deductive research. In the latter there is a theoretical orientation from which certain deductions are made or hypotheses developed. Through appropriate means these are then tested. In empirical research no theory really plays a significant role at the beginning of the study, and it may or may not enter into the interpretation of the final results.

Both these kinds of research can use psychological tests to gather data. When the hypothetical-deductive method is used, a hypothesis is developed and test questions are related to the hypothesis. In empirical research, the tests can be constructed for purposes other than testing hypotheses about creativity. Indeed personality tests that have existed for some time may be used. But in empirical research such tests are administered to see if, for example, they differentiate between two groups who differ in creativity and if so, on what variables. Or, an extreme example may be a test in which a whole host of questions is developed without regard for how they might be related specifically to creativity. These questions are then studied in reference to the criterion to see which are and which are not related to it.

The vast majority of studies in the area of creativity are of the empirical research variety. Tests and questionnaires usually constructed and developed for a variety of purposes are used to learn more about creativity. When they are so applied they should be cross-validated—that is, they should be tried out on another similar group of subjects to ascertain whether the results are replicated. Experience in other research areas of psychology indicates that, in many situations, results are not confirmed at the correlational levels first obtained, and in most instances the cross-validated correlations drop a good deal from their original levels. Unfortunately, because of time and economic pressures, not all investigators cross-validate their results; they rely on others to check their findings. Although there is general agreement among different investigators' results, replications are not exact enough for us to say that a good check existed. The people studied are not usually very well matched and procedures used are not all the same. This shortcoming must be borne in mind in evaluating the results.

PERSONALITY THEORIES

Although, as just indicated, personality theories do not figure very much in the design of creativity research, it is nevertheless worthwhile to keep in mind at least those personality theories that do have something to say about creativity and that serve as the bases for case and group studies. For a more complete survey of personality theories, a reasonable source is the book by Hall and Lindzey (1970); although creativity is not considered within each theory presented in it, this book does supply a reasonable amount of information about the theories relevant to personality research.

For our purposes, personality theories might well be divided according to two of the models suggested by Maddi (1968). They are the *fulfillment* model and the *conflict* model. In creativity research, an example of the former is the *self-actualization theory* of Maslow (1959), according to which individuals seek to actualize or fulfill the potentialities they possess. The potentialities are treated as if they were forces seeking expression, and creativity is seen as one of man's potentialities. That it may be unexpressed or unfulfilled may be due to an inhibitory or deprived environment, which may be of short or long duration. Once these negative effects are removed, creative potential becomes manifest.

The second model, the *conflict model*, is best exemplified by that part of psychoanalytic theory which points to the development of a man's ego from his id. In this theoretical framework, man starts off in life with an id—the term given to a variety of psychological functions or factors, including man's impulses. These impulses constantly strive for expression. And if this expression were permitted at all times, the individual might obtain impulse-gratification, but he would never "grow up." Growing up takes place through resolution of conflicts and overcoming of obstacles or frustrations that arise between impulses and environments that do not readily satisfy the impulses. A number of the psychological functions so developed are regarded as "belonging" to (or as coming under the rubric called) the ego.

Just as it is important for other psychological functions, so conflict is necessary for creativity, according to some aspects of psychoanalytic theory. According to these formulations an individual sublimates an impulse from its more primitive goal to a goal of higher value in the society. In so doing, he will have to delay immediate gratification for later gratification.

It is beyond the scope of our effort to evaluate these theories here. What is important is that the reader who wishes to evaluate the findings to be presented later, will want to consider whether the data stem from characteristics that are "natural" (results of self-fulfillment) or results of conflicts. While such considerations may not be terribly important for the general reader of the material presented here, they are of importance for individuals doing research in this area and for individuals who try to understand the creative process and develop techniques to foster its further development.

PERSONALITY RESULTS

A review of the literature by Stein (1968) yielded the following list of personality characteristics that have been found associated with the creative individual.

The creative individual:

1. Is an achieving person. He scores higher on a Self-Description Test of need achievement (Stein *et al.*, unpublished) than in a projective (TAT) [Thematic Apperception Test] measure of the same variable (McClelland, 1962), possibly because his achievement is fulfilled in actuality and need not be converted into fantasy. Gough (1964), using the California Personality Inventory, found that creative individuals score below average on a scale measuring conformance motivation and the enhancement of form and structure but above average on achievement that stresses derivation of form and the modification of structure. Both scales are correlated in a student population but uncorrelated in creative individuals. This is also regarded as evidence for the complexity of the creative individual (Gough, 1964).

2. Is motivated by a need for order (Barron, 1958).

3. Has a need for curiosity (Maddi, 1963; Maddi & Berne, 1964; Maddi *et al.*, 1964, 1965).

4. Is self-assertive, dominant, aggressive, self-sufficient. He leads and possesses initiative (Barron, 1955, 1957; R. B. Cattell & Drevdahl, 1955; MacKinnon, 1959a; Shannon, 1947; Van Zelst & Kerr, 1951). He is high in need power as measured by TAT-like pictures (McClelland, 1962).

5. Rejects repression, is less inhibited, less formal, less conventional, is bohemianly unconcerned, is radical, and is low on measures of authoritarian values (Barron, 1955; Blatt & Stein, 1957; R. B. Cattell & Drevdahl, 1955; Drevdahl 1956; Van Zelst & Kerr, 1951). However, MacKinnon (1959a) finds that the creative individual is not "bohemian."

6. Has persistence of motive, liking and capacity for work, self-discipline, perseverance, high energy-output, is thorough (Blatt & Stein, 1957; Bloom, 1956; MacKinnon, 1959a; Peck, 1958; Roe, 1946a, 1949; Rossman, 1931; Shannon, 1947).

7. Is independent and autonomous (Barron, 1955; Blatt & Stein, 1957; Peck, 1958; Roe, 1953; Stein, 1962). Although independence has been an important factor in other groups studied, MacKinnon (1959a) did not find it to differentiate between groups of industrial engineers.

8. Is constructively critical, less contented, dissatisfied (Rossman, 1931; Shannon, 1947; Van Zelst & Kerr, 1951).

9. Is widely informed, has wide ranging interests, is versatile (Barron, 1957; MacKinnon, 1959b; R. K. White, 1931).

10. Is open to feelings and emotions. For him feeling is more important than thinking, he is more subjective, he possesses vitality and enthusiasm (MacKinnon, 1959a, 1959b; Peck, 1958; Shannon, 1947; Van Zelst & Kerr, 1951).

11. Is aesthetic in his judgment and value orientation (Blatt & Stein, 1957; Gough, 1964; MacKinnon, 1962; Roe, 1946a).

12. Is low in economic values (MacKinnon, 1962) or is a poor business man (Rossman, 1931). Blatt and Stein (1957), however, found with the Allport-Vernon-Lindzey Scale of Values that their more creative industrial research chemists did have higher economic values than their less creative colleagues. Using the same test but with a population of physicists, mathematicians, and electronic engineers, Gough (1961) did not find that any of the test's scales correlated with creativity.

13. Possesses freer expression of what has been described as feminine interests and lack of masculine aggressiveness (Blatt & Stein, 1957; Bloom, 1956; MacKinnon, 1959a, 1959b; Munsterberg & Mussen, 1953; Roe, 1946a, 1946b, 1946c).

14. Has little interest in interpersonal relationships, does not want much social interaction, is introverted, and is lower in social values, is reserved (Blatt & Stein, 1957; Bloom, 1956; MacKinnon, 1959a, 1959b; Munsterberg & Mussen, 1953; Roe, 1949). Nevertheless, Gough (1961, 1964) found in his study of industrial researchers that social sensitivity (as measured by the Chapin Social Insight Test) was correlated with creativity. In this study the predictive power of the the Chapin Social Insight Test was exceeded only by the Barron-Welsh Art Scale.

15. Is emotionally unstable but capable of using his instability effectively, not well adjusted by psychological definition but adjusted in the broader sense of being socially useful and happy in his work (R. B. Cattell & Drevdahl, 1955; Roe, 1953). That creative individuals are not unstable has been found by MacKinnon (1959a) and Stein *et al.* (unpublished). Blatt (1964), using a Self-Description Test developed by Stein (1965) found that the self-descriptions of industrial research chemists who were regarded as "more" creative were more congruent with psychologists' conceptions of mental health than were the descriptions of "less" creative chemists. Gough (1964) regards the variability found in the creative individual's personal adjustment as a reflection of his complexity.

16. Sees himself as creative (Stein *et al.*, unpublished; C. W. Taylor, 1963). He is also more likely to describe himself in terms that investigators

have found to be related to creativity than is true of less creative individuals. For example, MacKinnon in his study of architects (1962) found that his more creative group described themselves more frequently as "inventive, determined, independent, individualistic, enthusiastic, and industrious," while his less creative group described themselves more frequently as "responsible, sincere, reliable, dependable, clear thinking, tolerant, and understanding. In short, where creative architects more often stress their inventiveness, independence, and individuality, their enthusiasm, determination, and industry, less creative members of the profession are impressed by their virtue and good character and by their rationality and sympathetic concern for others." Considered in terms of their ideals, MacKinnon also found that the more creative group would like to be more sensitive, while the less creative groups would like to be more original and, at the same time, more self-controlled and disciplined.

17. Is intuitive and empathic. Test scales of "psychological-mindedness," intuitive preference, and need intraception correlate with creativity (Gough, 1964).

18. Is less critical of himself. He is less inclined to use negative and unfavorable adjectives and has a low self-criticality index on the Gough Adjective Check List (Gough, 1961).

19. Makes a greater impact on others. Gough (1961) found that assessment staff members who did not know criterion ratings of the subjects did differentiate between more highly and less highly rated research scientists. Some of the adjectives checked by assessors and which correlated positively with the criterion were: clear-thinking, interests wide, versatile, alert, and attractive. Among the adjectives that correlated negatively with the criterion were: undependable, pessimistic, commonplace, weak, and defensive [pp. 928-930].

These findings do not characterize any single individual. No creative individual has all these characteristics, but a creative person probably has more of them than does a less creative person. Evidence for personality factors characteristic of creative persons comes from studies of individuals in a wide variety of different scientific and professional fields: biology, psychology, chemistry, engineering, architecture. Just as these individuals differed from each other in field of endeavor, they also differed from each other in age, educational status, administrative status, etc. And in the studies in which they participated, there were also differences in the psychological tests and techniques used to gather data as to their creativity.

Psychological Tests

To gather the data on which our knowledge of creative persons' personality characteristics is based, a variety of psychological tests and procedures has been used. They include life history questionnaires (these were analyzed either as parts of case studies, or the data were tabulated as parts of larger group studies) and interviews and questionnaires. In addition, both objective and projective types of psychological tests were employed to study a variety of variables.

An objective test of personality consists of a series of questions that the individual answers with "yes," "no," "true," or "false," and the like. The positive and negative statements are generally summed, and the individual's score represents the extent to which he does or does not possess the personality characteristic for which the test was designed. Some objective personality tests provide scores on only one personality characteristic; others provide scores on several.

The projective personality test generally consists of unstructured stimuli—that is, stimuli that do not have the same immediate meaning to all people—such as inkblots (which are used in the Rorschach test) or pictures, usually of social situations [which are used in the Thematic Apperception Test (TAT)]. The individual's task is to say what he sees in the inkblots. These perceptions or responses are then analyzed in terms of such variables as how much of the blot was used for the response, what characteristics of the blot determined or played a role in the response (color, texture, shape, etc.), what was the content of the response (animal, human, etc.), and finally how original or popular was the response. When presented with the TAT pictures the individual is asked to make up stories about them. These are then analyzed, usually on the assumption that the hero in the story stands for the storyteller, to learn about the subject's needs, goals, energy level, behavior in interpersonal situations, etc.

In reviewing the results of personality research and before turning to other matters, we must once again emphasize that it is not certain whether these characteristics of personality are antecedent to or a consequence of having been creative. A correlation does not indicate any causal relationship. Is it really necessary for an individual to be self-confident and autonomous, for example, to be creative? Or, is there the possibility that some modicum of self-confidence may be necessary in getting started on the creative process and that after a person has completed it successfully self-confidence increases appreciably. Theoretically, the latter certainly can happen. It should also be pointed out that while the characteristics listed are separate and discrete, it may be the *pattern* of characteristics that is most critical.

Regardless of the temporal relationship between personality characteristics and creativity, they are used in at least two different ways in stimulating creativity: either as models to be adopted or as goals to be achieved by removing the forces or problems that inhibit or block their manifestation and operation. For example, the personality characteristics may be utilized as models to be adopted, as when in role playing the individual is asked to regard himself as creative and then to see whether he behaves more creatively.

Personality characteristics are also used as goals to be achieved by removing the forces or problems that inhibit or block their manifestation. Autonomy or independence may be related to creativity because an individual who deviates from the group and sees himself as different from others may actually think up different novel things. Individuals, however, may be concerned, insecure, and anxious about deviating from that which exists and about establishing their independence. Deference and submissiveness to custom and authority is more their pattern. Hypnosis and psychotherapy may help these individuals to gain insight into the nature of the problems that cause the inhibition or give them emotional support while they try to overcome their problems.

It should be apparent that these two uses to which personality data are put differ in terms of the amount of effort and labor an individual has to put forth to change in the desired direction. And by the same token, the two procedures differ in the extent to which we might expect major important, or what are called structural, changes in the individual. Although there are no major systematic studies of the long-term effects of these procedures, theoretically we would expect that the psychotherapies should result in deeper and more permanent changes and effects than might be obtained by the use of other procedures to be discussed. Yet what may appear to be a simple-minded technique that should produce only very transitory effects does in fact yield some interesting results.

SUMMARY

A wide variety of personality factors that characterize the creative individual and differentiate him from others has been presented. Knowledge of these characteristics comes from studies using various techniques, such as case study, surveys, biographical inventories, and both structured and unstructured psychological tests. These tests and techniques can be administered before and after a person attends a creativity stimulating program to determine whether his scores move in the direction of those found to be characteristic of creative persons.

With this information as background material, we now turn to several studies that focus on helping an individual overcome psychological blocks to creativity, where the problem apparently lies in the area of personality.

Chapter V

Affecting Personality Characteristics:
Role Playing, Hypnosis, and Psychotherapy

ROLE PLAYING

"Make Believe"

One of the oldest techniques for stimulating creativity in most people's lives is what we now call "role playing," which we as children did not have a specific word for but which usually started with, "Let's make believe that . . . ." The phrase would then be completed with a statement assigning each of the partici- pants a different *role*—"I'm the daddy, and you're the mommy"; "You're the patient and I'm the doctor"; "I'm the cop and you're the robber"; etc. When these roles were taken on, we had license to behave like daddy and mommy, and sometimes the role would "take over," it might run away with us, we would almost become the person, animal, or object whose role we took. When that happened, one of our friends would get us to keep our feet on the ground and let us know that we were not really daddy or mommy. And, on other occasions he would remind us, when we would innovate a bit, that daddy and mommy really do not behave that way.

When children get involved in these make-believe types of games, they know they are playing (that they are involved in unreal things) even if they momentarily allow the roles to "run away with them." But it is the very unreal, playful character of what they are doing, as well as the fact that they are someone else, that allows children to explore and learn about different ways of doing things and to try new behaviors that they had not experienced before.

During growing up or in the socialization process, the playful, role-playing kind of behavior just described diminishes and falls by the wayside. Most adults just do not make believe, and if they do, they make other people uncomfortable; they are told not to be childish or silly. An *adult*, by some people's definition, is someone who has outgrown forms of behavior, like wearing a pair of short pants, and has assumed behaviors that are very different and very proper and usually very constricting. Consequently, there are few occasions when adults engage in role playing except in more or less formal circumstances, as in job training or psychotherapy sessions.

Being Another Person or Object

Role playing is used in therapy for both diagnostic and therapeutic reasons. Diagnostically, the therapist might use it to try to find out how a patient thinks someone else feels or reacts toward him; by having the patient portray another person, the therapist can see what is going on. Role playing is also used for training purposes. For example, if we want a teacher to learn something more about how pupils feel about teachers we have him play the role of pupil; if we want a supervisor to learn more about how a subordinate feels about certain procedures in the company we have him act the part of subordinate, or if we want the subordinate to learn something more about how his supervisor sees the world, then the roles are reversed. There are countless training programs in which role playing has a more or less central place. In these situations a scene is developed in which a participant is told to take on the role of one person and another participant is told to take on the role of another person. The feelings and attitudes and thoughts of both participants in their respective roles are then discussed.

Role playing, the taking on and being or feeling like another (person, animal, or object), if an individual can allow himself the psychological freedom to engage in it, can prove of value in some aspects of the creative process. In fact, we find something akin to it later in the book in a group technique for stimulating creativity called *synectics*. One of the four operational mechanisms in synectics, described by Gordon (1961), is *personal analogy*, where the individual imagines himself to be the object or materials with which he is working. In so doing, he can learn more about the characteristics of these materials and hence more about the various uses to which they can be adapted for various purposes.

Research Evidence

It may appear odd that such a simple-minded procedure as telling oneself to behave like something or someone else can have a stimulating effect on what is produced, but there is, nevertheless, evidence in the literature that supports this. For example, Brown (1965) developed a "creativity symbol" for a creative subself and a "noncreativity symbol" for a noncreative subself in his subjects. These symbols were then used to "trigger" whichever self the experimenter wished the subject to assume. Under those conditions, when the creative subself was "operating," the individual performed significantly better than when the noncreative image was in operation.

A study by Bowers (1967), which we shall consider in the next section on the effects of hypnosis on creativity, indicates that originality, as measured by Guilford's tests, does improve after certain posthypnotic suggestions. Bowers also mentions an unpublished study (1965) in which she found that subjects who simulated or who made believe that they were hypnotized and gave themselves the same kind of suggestions as hypnotized subjects produced the same kind of originality scores as hypnotized subjects.

Barron and Leary (1961) studied the effect of role playing on changing creativity with students at the Rhode Island School of Design. Twenty pairs of juniors in the school were matched on faculty ratings for creativity. The groups were studied with a variety of tests, among which were the Barron tests for originality, independence, and preference for complexity; the Levinson revision of the Adorno *F* Scale (a measure of authoritarianism); the Guilford Plot Titles Test, etc.

The students were then divided into two groups. One was asked to "play the role of an extraordinarily original and creative person [p. 98]" and the other group was asked "to play the role of a highly intelligent (authoritarian) person [p. 98]" (Leary, 1964). Two tests were then administered to both groups. One, Barron's test of originality, had been given to them previously, and the other, Guilford's Unusual Uses Test, had not.

One result of this study was that the group that had assumed the creative set—played the role of the creative person—did better on thinking up ideas (as measured by the Unusual Uses Test) than did the group that did not assume this set. To Leary (1964) this "suggests that role playing, or set taking, is a specific mechanism for increasing creativity [p. 98]."

Another result of this study was that the group of students who were to assume the role of being intelligent-authoritarian obtained lower scores on the Barron tests of originality, independence of judgment, and preference for complexity than they had obtained on the same tests before assuming their assigned roles. The group with the creative role had higher scores.

One inference that might be drawn from the experience with role playing is that some people have more potential for creativity than they manifest. One of the possible reasons for this is that through much of their lives such people have been told that they are not creative and they then proceed to validate this statement by their behavior. If they were regarded more positively insofar as creativity is concerned, or if they were given license to behave like creative individuals through some method or other, like role playing, they could likely change into being more creative individuals.

Barron cites a related study by Brown (Leary, 1964) in which he worked with children. First, the children are asked to respond to the Barron-Welsh Art Scale. They then read a story of two characters—William Elephant and Mr. Owl: The two come upon clothing, which they have never seen before, lying on a beach. William Elephant makes some unusual uses of the clothes and Mr. Owl tells him he cannot do these things, but he does do them. Brown then instructs the students to " 'let that part of you which is William Elephant take over and take this art test again' [Leary, 1964, p. 106] ." Although Barron does not cite the data, he reports that apparently the scores on the test do improve.

On the adult level, in the previously mentioned study by Barron and Leary (1961) with the group of 40 juniors at the Rhode Island School of Design, the students' responses to the test measure of originality were discussed with them with a focus on how their responses compared with those creative people gave to the test. "In a sense, what we were doing," says Barron, "was educating them to behave in a way that would enable them to answer those questions or take those tests in the same way as the persons who had demonstrated creativity in what they did [Leary, 1964, p. 105] ." The discussion of these scores also involved a discussion of faculty ratings on creativity with which the test scores were found to be congruent.

Although actual data are cited neither by Leary nor by Barron (Leary, 1964), it is inferred that discussions with the students did result in higher test scores. Follow-up studies of these results would have been most desirable, for then we might know whether the effects of role playing are momentary, transitory, or lasting.

AFFECTING THE CREATIVE PROCESS

On the basis of what has just been presented, role playing can be quite helpful in generating more and new ideas. The research data appear congruent with what goes on in real-life creativity situations. For example, is not the author of a story role playing when he says to himself in the midst of his writing, "I wonder how this character will or will not behave or think under these circumstances." By the same token, the designer may ask himself, "How would an upper-class housewife want her appliances designed?" or the advertiser asks himself, "What would a middle-class suburbanite find appealing in a specific advertisement?" The possibilities are endless as to what characteristics or roles one would want to assume to generate ideas—fat man, thin man, beautiful woman, young woman— or what combination of characteristics—fat lower-class man, fat middle-class man, thin middle-class man, beautiful young lower-class woman, and beautiful older upper-class woman, etc. It is probably apparent, just from reading these statements, that different pictures come to mind. (Of course, there is a more systematic, and more expensive, way of getting the same information, and that is simply to have someone do a survey about how different individuals want or like certain things. Indeed, this would work best for consumers' activities, and it might someday be worthwhile to find out whether role playing is or is not predictive of such survey data.)

Most of what has been written about role playing as a technique for stimulating creativity discusses its potential usefulness for hypothesis formation. One can easily see how it would be helpful at that stage, for, in a sense, the individual is not himself, and by being someone else he has license to do things he might not otherwise do. This license, then, removes the censorship and rigidities that inhibit ideas.

It is also conceivable that role playing may be useful in the later phases of the creative process too. It could be useful in enabling an individual to think up ideas of how to sell others on the value or significance of his ideas. For example, one may ask, "If I were to sell an older person this object, how might I approach him?" or "If I were an older person to be sold this idea how might I be best approached?" And a still further possibility that would facilitate the communication stage would be what questions would I ask when presented with an idea, product, etc.? It is immediately apparent, both for the idea-generating stage of creativity as well as the communication phase or selling phase, that role playing may be most helpful and useful. Probably one of the most difficult phases of the creative process in which role playing may be of diminished value would be in trying to decide which of the various ideas generated were indeed valuable enough to be pursued and in trying to exert the discipline necessary to carry out testing of the idea.

Before leaving this section on the effectiveness of role playing, we note that when this technique works it does so primarily in the personality area, in the sense that it loosens blocks or inhibitions or allows the individual to assume more constructive personality characteristics. As these characteristics take over, there may well be consequent effects in the cognitive area too. Role playing does not affect technical or artistic know-how. If personality factors, such as self-concept, need to be changed, then role playing may be helpful. But change in that area alone without technical knowledge, artistic ability, etc. will obviously not result in creativity. A change in self-concept or motivation through role playing may, however, be of help in obtaining the necessary technical or artistic training and information.

HYPNOSIS

Man has known about hypnosis and how to hypnotize others for many years. Despite this, precise, well tested, and well supported knowledge of how hypnosis works is not yet available. Nevertheless, it has been used for a variety of purposes in the behavioral sciences—experimental, investigative, diagnostic, and therapeutic. It is also being used to further our understanding of the creative process by hypnotizing a person, suggesting that he dream about something, and then studying how that which was suggested is assimilated, elaborated upon, and distorted in the dream process (Barron, 1961).

Similarity between the Hypnotic State and the Creative Process

We cannot help but note much that is similar between some of what creative persons describe as what they experience during the creative process and descriptions of some aspects of the hypnotic state. Creative individuals frequently concentrate intensively and are oblivious to distraction. They behave in a monoideic manner. Having selected something to work on, their attention narrows to exclude all other things. All of these and other factors are some of the similarities between the hypnotic state and the creative process. Possibly, just as individuals under hypnosis are capable of carrying out suggestions that they are unable to under other conditions, so the creative individual, possibly because of the monoideic character of what he does, is also capable of doing more than most individuals believe he or they should or could be capable of.

Some of the behavior manifested by creative individuals during their experience in the creative process has been duplicated in hypnosis. The problem, then, is of trying to decide whether the observed similarities are indeed appropriate bases for saying that the dynamics of both processes are the same. Krippner (1969) presents several experiments and studies in which the psychedelic state, hypnotic trance, and creative act are compared. For illustrative purposes we report here several of the works he cites.

One of the experiences mentioned by individuals during the creative process is that when they feel inspired they can frequently get much more work accomplished than under usual or uninspired circumstances. A study by McCord and Sherrill (1961) indicates that the same result can be obtained with hypnosis. In their work, a mathematics professor was given the posthypnotic suggestion that he would be able to solve calculus problems at a faster rate and more accurately than he ever did before. When awakened, he was presented with a series of calculus problems and given 20 minutes to work on them. During this 20-minute period, he did as much work as it might usually have taken him to do in 2 hours. The professor did so much because he skipped several steps in the mathematical process; instead of writing things out, he did them in his head and he wrote very rapidly. All of this, it was reported, was accomplished without any loss in accuracy.

Another experience cited by persons who have experienced the creative process is coming up with sudden solutions and flashes of insight. To investigate this phenomenon Tinnin (1963) studied three male college students who could carry out posthypnotic suggestions and who had complete amnesia for the hypnotic experience.

The three men were put into a hypnotic trance and told that some time after they were awakened they would be given an algebraic equation (e.g., $y^2 + z^2 = ?$). The values for y and z would be supplied indirectly and they would come up with the answer. In supplying the values for y and z the subjects would be told, for example, that the y value would be the second digit in the left-hand column on a card and the z value would be the fifth digit in the right-hand column. The subjects did well in stating the correct answers but none of them remembered the instructions or the clues. Of the three subjects, one of them saw his answer as a momentary visual hallucination and the other two as a sudden flash of knowledge. Thus, as a result of hypnosis, subjects utilized cues without full conscious awareness of how they came to them. While this sounds very much like what people describe as occurring during the creative process, it is obviously not clear that the same dynamics are involved in both situations.

Other studies manipulated subjects' time sense. It is not uncommon for creative individuals, while they are carrying out their creative activities, to believe they are working much longer than is actually the case. Cooper and Erickson (1954) worked to slow the subjective time sense of their subjects. One of them was a girl with talent in dress designing. Six times she was given the task of designing a dress under hypnosis, and after each trance she was asked to draw a picture of the dress and to describe it. The subject experienced the hypnotic session as being an hour long; in actuality, it lasted 10 minutes. Cooper and Erickson saw their own work as exploratory and requiring further research. But they felt it might also be utilized for creative purpose by individuals who had talent in certain areas of work. While this may be true, the effects Cooper and Erickson found are still not to be regarded as quite well founded. Barber and Calverley (1964) repeated the Cooper and Erickson work, unfortunately with somewhat different techniques, and did not come up with the same findings. Because the same technique was not used it is best to delay final evaluation of the Cooper and Erickson results.

The use of time distortion in a practical situation is reported by Wollman (1965). Wollman worked with an actor who had only 1 week to learn the lead role in a Broadway play. He was seen twice a day and had additional sessions at home. By training him in time distortion, he was able to condense a great deal in the available time and so put on a rather successful performance. Thus we see that hypnosis can be used both to help elucidate aspects of the creative process and to facilitate the creative experience.

TO CHANGE PERSONALITY CHARACTERISTICS

In all likelihood, however, when most people think of hypnosis in relation to creativity, they tend to think of it in terms of its "therapeutic" aspects—in terms of its capacity to help the individual remove some of the blocks to creativity, such as defensiveness, which will be considered later, or to change in some way, by becoming more confident (also to be considered later), which would help the individual become more creative. It is to these effects of hypnosis that we now turn.

On the anecdotal level, or on the level of the single clinical case study, we have the case of Sergei Rachmaninoff who became depressed when his first piano concerto was not well received. He was persuaded to undertake hypnotic treatments with a Dr. Nikolai Dahl. These daily 1-hour treatments lasted for 3 months and Rachmaninoff improved to such a degree that he composed his *Concerto Number Two in C Minor for Piano and Orchestra*, and he recognized his debt to Dr. Dahl by dedicating this piece to him (Foley, 1963; Krippner, 1969).

Defensiveness

On the experimental level, there is also some work in which investigators selected some personality factors that might either block or facilitate the creative process and manipulated these in hypnosis to learn if the desired effects could be obtained. One of these studies was conducted by Bowers (1967), who selected defensiveness as one of the obstacles to creativity. For her, "Defensiveness implies the anxious avoidance of thoughts and feelings which might be unacceptable. It functions by tying the noncreative person more exclusively than his creative counterpart to the established categories and conventions, to conscious rather than preconscious thought [p. 311]." Hence she argues that "if the manifestation of creativity is contingent only upon its release from suppressing defenses, hypnosis should effect this release [pp. 312-313]." She then compared waking and hypnotized groups on several of Guilford's tests of creativity and predicted that hypnotized persons would do better on these tests than persons in the waking state, on the assumption that defenses would be relaxed during hypnosis. In addition, she also investigated the effect of suggestions, without hypnosis, of reduced defensiveness on creativity.

To gather her data, Bowers studied 80 female undergraduate students who were found to be rather susceptible to hypnosis. Each had obtained a score of seven or more on the Harvard Group Scale of Hypnotic Suggestibility. They were divided into four groups: two waking and two hypnotized groups. One of the waking groups and one of the hypnotized groups received *cognitive set* instructions, and the other two groups received *defense-reducing* instructions.

When a girl received the defense-reducing instruction, she was told that she had the ability to be creative and would allow herself to make use of all her relevant experience, to perceive in unconventional ways, and to notice aspects of the task overlooked previously. Blocks to creativity, especially those stemming from conformity through fear of criticism, were inappropriate in the experimental setting. The subjects were encouraged to recall previous moments of creative insight and the heightened emotional states that accompanied them. Finally, they were asked to be confident in their creative abilities.

Those of the groups that were instructed with the *cognitive set* "were told, essentially, to be clever, original, flexible, and fluent [p. 315] ." For both the cognitive set conditions and the defense-reducing conditions all subjects were told to produce relevant responses to the test stimuli. They were not asked, as in brainstorming, to suspend critical judgment. (It should be noted that the cognitive set instruction was essentially a control condition since it was impossible to give the defense-reducing instruction without also affecting cognitive factors.)

A total of five tests were administered. One of them was the *Minnesota Clerical Test*. Since it was possible that there were effects of hypnosis other than reduction in defensiveness that might result in increased creativity, this test was included to detect any such effects.

The remaining four tests were part of Guilford's tests of creativity. They all fall within the divergent thinking category and were utilized to yield eight scores, six of which were indices of creativity and two of which were derived to help study whether hypnosis increased the number of irrelevant responses.*

Half of each of the tests was administered before the experimental conditions, and half after the experimental conditions. Thus, the subjects who were to be hypnotized took half the tests before they were hypnotized and the other half afterward.

---

*The four Guilford tests were *Alternate Uses, Consequences, Plot Titles,* and *Simile Insertions.* The six creativity scores were (1) number of acceptable *alternate uses* (as a measure of spontaneous semantic flexibility); (2) number of acceptable *consequences* classes as "obvious" (as a measure of ideational fluency); (3) number of acceptable "remote" *consequences* (as a measure of originality); (4) number of acceptable responses to the *simile insertions* test (as a measure of associational fluency); (5) number of "clever" *plot titles* responses (as a measure of originality); and (6) number of "not clever" *plot titles* responses (as a measure of the factor of ideational fluency).

To aid in determining whether hypnosis operated by increasing the number of irrelevant rather than relevant responses, two additional scores were derived from the creativity battery. They were (1) number of unacceptable *alternate uses* responses and (2) number of unacceptable *simile insertions* responses.

The two groups of waking subjects also started by taking half of each of the tests, but then something new was added. After these subjects took the first halves of the test measures, they were instructed in a relaxation procedure. There were two reasons for this. First, it was necessary to control for the possible effects of relaxation that could be associated with the removal of defensiveness by hypnosis. The other reason was to equate the amount of *time* the waking and hypnotized subjects would spend with the experimenter. The girls in the relaxation procedure were told that there were similarities between hypnosis and relaxation. It was important that they be good hypnotic subjects, but they were not to become hypnotized. They were to close their eyes and relax while listening to a piece by Ralph Vaughan Williams for 35 minutes, which was the time needed to hypnotize the other subjects. The experimenter tapped her pencil at three intervals during the musical piece to get the subjects' estimates of how much time had elapsed. The purpose of these time estimations was to keep the subjects attentive and not allow them to fall asleep.

An analysis of the results of this experiment revealed that on only one test, *Remote Consequences*, part of Guilford's originality factor, was a significant difference found. Those groups that were in the hypnotized condition (regardless of whether they were given the defense-reducing or the cognitive set instructions) obtained higher scores on this test than did those in waking conditions (regardless of the instructions they received).

Although there were no significant differences between cognitive set and defense-reducing instructions, those subjects who were hypnotized and had the defense-reducing instruction did obtain the higher average score on the Remote Consequences test than the other three groups, but there was no significant interaction between instructions and experimental conditions in general. And no differences occurred on the clerical test. That no such differences occurred on this test especially for the hypnotized subjects who yielded the other significant differences suggests that these other differences were not due to increased motivation. Bowers included the clerical test because she hypothesized that reduced defensiveness could not affect the clerical scores; however, motivation could. If hypnosis increased motivation, then it would affect the clerical score. The fact that clerical scores did not improve suggests the possibility that motivation was not increased.

That there is no difference between cognitive set instructions and defense-reducing instructions is not surprising because it may be so difficult to separate the effects of the two through the instructions. If the subject took the requested cognitive set she might implicitly or explicitly remove the effects of defensiveness. If she removed the effects of defensiveness then she assumed the cognitive set. It is also not very surprising that in the hypnosis condition there should be no differential effect between the cognitive set and defense-reducing instructions. The subjects were told only to reduce their defenses, a general statement, but the specific reasons for or causes of their defenses and the specific defenses they used were not removed by the hypnosis. In hypnotherapy one would try to get at specific defenses and their causes to help a person overcome his problems with creativity. If the hypnotic suggestions had been directed more specifically, possibly the creativity of the subjects in this condition would have improved much more than the others.

What is surprising is that "the hypnotic condition, with no special training or instruction, should increase the expression of originality without appreciably affecting the total number of responses (fluency factor) . . . [Bowers, 1967, p. 319]." Unfortunately, Bowers' study does not provide us with a definitive answer to this question. She says, "the clinical literature which views hypnosis as a means of defense-reduction and of regression in the service of the ego continues to provide one of the more compelling hypotheses explaining the effect of hypnosis [pp. 320-321]." Unfortunately, this statement really does not add much new knowledge. We shall need more research to find out what did transpire to affect the results; otherwise we must view the results, as Bowers herself says, "simply as a demonstration of the effect of hypnosis on originality [p. 320]." But as we have seen previously (page 65), Bowers reported that subjects who *pretended* to be hypnotized did as well on creativity tests as the hypnotized subjects. Consequently, the obtained results are not necessarily a function of the hypnotic trance state but possibly of a change in the subject's attitude about responsibility, as Bowers suggests, which may have eased the censorship previously exercised.

Self-Confidence

Parloff (1972) studied the effects of hypnosis in the area of creativity by inducing in his subjects a feeling of heightened self-confidence in their ability to solve problems. He hypothesized that increased self-confidence would increase a subject's willingness to solve a problem, to persist in his problem-solving efforts and to evaluate seriously solutions that he might otherwise regard as trivial. The problems the subjects worked on were the usual Guilford cognitive problems that are frequently used as measures of creativity. Parloff's experiences in this work illustrate how careful one needs to be both in setting up laboratory studies of creativity and in evaluating the results obtained.

The subjects were college students each of whom was found to be a good hypnotic subject and each of whom was to be his own control for three experimental conditions: (1) normal waking state; (2) the hypnotic state; and (3) the hypnotic state plus the suggestion of increased self-confidence.

The tests used were seven of those devised by Guilford: Word Fluency, Associational Fluency, Ideational Fluency, Expressional Fluency, Alternate Uses, Sensitivity to Problems, and Explanations of Problems.

Because each subject served as his own control, "roughly equivalent forms" of each of the aforementioned tests were developed to avoid practice effects. Also, to cope with practice effects, amnesia was induced after each test condition and a restriction placed on how the experimental conditions were presented. For experimental design purposes it was felt that the hypnosis-plus-suggestion-of-self-confidence condition should come first. In this condition, the subject would be given the tests, and if he were to benefit from practice effects, they would benefit most the other two conditions and thus operate against the crucial experimental condition.

Six subjects were studied and five of them showed that they performed better when they were hypnotized and given the self-confidence instruction than when they were only hypnotized or in the waking state. The sixth subject, interestingly for some personal reason not stated in Parloff's paper, always awoke from the hypnotic state whenever the suggestion about self-confidence was given her.

The results obviously look very much in favor of hypnosis. But, Parloff (1972) in rethinking the design thought that, while he tried to develop an experimental design that would put the hypnosis-plus-suggestion to a severe test by having it come first, he had actually biased the study in favor of the hypnotized subjects not by helping them in the experimental condition but by inhibiting them in the control condition.

Parloff reasoned that a good hypnotic subject is one who tries to give the experimenter what he wants in terms of results. Consequently, he argues that, when the subjects were presented with the hypnosis-plus-increased-self-confidence suggestion first, each of them could have sensed or inferred from the investigator's behavior or something else that he was not to do as well under the other conditions. Having so reasoned, Parloff then repeated the experiment and randomized the experimental conditions allowing each of the three to appear in all possible positions. This time no positive effects for hypnosis were found.

It is not at all infrequent to find such contradictory findings in the hypnosis literature. They also occur in areas other than creativity. Krippner (1969), after citing the study reported previously (page 68) on how the mathematician's ability with calculus problems was increased, says that although there are such clinical instances of improved performance under hypnosis, he agrees with the evidence presented in two reviews in the hypnosis literature (Barber, 1965, Uhr, 1958) that there are no firm results because studies of the effects of hypnosis on problem solving have been poorly designed.

We can only hope that better experimental designs will be developed and, aside from all the factors that would need to be considered in controlling for the different aspects of hypnosis, it would also be important to consider person variables—the kinds of personality and cognitive characteristics the subjects possess. This is not to say that they be randomized to cancel out individual differences but rather to form different groups of individuals on the basis of characteristics that would be germane to the problem and then to investigate the effects of hypnosis on these diverse groups.

PSYCHOTHERAPY

Psychotherapy is a means of overcoming intrapsychic conflicts and problems and freeing the energy that an individual has tied up in these difficulties so that he has more energy and more capacity for living, loving, and working and, within that context, even creativity. The emphasis here is on intrapsychic problems, problems which have their primary locus within the individual rather than in the environment. Problems that are centered in the environment obviously have to be solved in other ways.

For Whom

There are at least three groups that may be interested in psychotherapy as a means of increasing their creativity. One is that group of individuals who may have been creative at one time in their lives and who for one reason or another are currently blocked in their creativity. They may have encountered problems in the work situation including possible difficulties with superiors, peers, or subordinates; they may have begun to think of themselves as uncreative because they have not come up with ideas very quickly, or they may have begun to encounter problems in other areas of living—spouse, children, parents, etc.— which spill over into the work area and which momentarily block creativity.

A second group of individuals may consist of individuals who have never manifested their creativity. Included in this group would be those persons who have always "felt they could be creative" but who were afraid to venture forth, to be different from others, to challenge the status quo, etc. Another subgroup of persons would include those who are frequently told by friends, "You could be creative, if you would only let yourself go." Or, they would be people who sense how close they come to manifesting their creativity and then, as if afraid of success, let the ball drop.

The third group could well consist of persons who are creative but who are having problems in other areas of living. The creative individual, because of the amount of time and effort he devotes to his work, may have difficulty in satisfying family needs; the creative individual, because he sees his work not immediately accepted or because he sees others promoted over him who are not as creative as he, may also have periods of anxiety and depression.

There are no sure-fire indices of how to determine which individuals will benefit from psychotherapy. And so, no specific recommendations can be made here. What can be said is that if psychotherapy is to have any positive effect, the individual needs to be unhappy (or anxious) with his present state of affairs and motivated to learn more about himself and to effect change in his personality and behavior.

We have been talking about psychotherapy in the singular, but actually we should have been using the plural—psychotherapies. There is no single form of psychotherapy. There is supportive psychotherapy in which essentially an individual will get support and encouragement to tide him over problem areas. There is nondirective psychotherapy in which the psychotherapist deals with helping the individual gain an appreciation of his immediate existential feelings and attitudes. There are the "deep" insight therapies, such as psychoanalysis, in which emotional insight is sought and structural changes are a goal.

Psychotherapies also vary along other dimensions. There are individual and group psychotherapies. There are other technical differences between them: the extent to which they will use transference, interpret dreams, use ancillary techniques, etc. The reader may wish to consult other sources (Stein, 1961) to learn about the kinds of psychotherapy that are available, since an extended discussion of this matter is beyond the scope of this book.

In general, the individual who seeks help through psychotherapy will likely make his decision as to what kind of psychotherapy to undertake or indeed whether psychotherapy is indicated by thinking the matter through by himself or on the basis of discussion with his physician, family, friends, company psychologist, etc. Then, in all likelihood, the final decision as to whether psychotherapy is indicated and the kind of therapy that will be used will no doubt be made by the psychotherapist after his diagnostic evaluation which is likely to be a continuing process.

In whatever manner the decision is made, the individual who undertakes this course of action need bear in mind that it can be a costly and time-consuming process. It is not intended for minor problems. Indeed, for our purposes, it is most likely indicated for individuals with deep-rooted problems (anxiety, inadequacy, etc.) that may interfere with their creativity. It is for individuals whose conflicts involve those personality characteristics that are related to the creative process. Theoretically, individuals who are afraid of manifesting their creativity because they fear challenging existing authorities; individuals who are too insecure to change or who are unable to concentrate on their work; individuals who are too angry to be creative; individuals who think of themselves as inferior and inadequate insofar as creativity is concerned are among those whose creativity might be augmented by psychotherapy. By the same token, those persons whose energies are tied up with problems of living in areas other than those directly related to creativity may also benefit from the fact that once these problem areas are cleared up, energy becomes available for creative pursuits to which they might have wanted to turn but simply did not have the "energy" available.

Expectations of Help

Psychotherapy can therefore be helpful in a variety of direct and indirect ways by "freeing" the person to think of new ventures and to implement them. Changes may be long term or short lived. Needless to say, psychotherapy is no panacea insofar as creativity is concerned. First, there is no certainty in any single case as to its effectiveness in resolving intrapsychic conflicts. Second, if intrapsychic conflicts are resolved, there is no certainty that the new psychological status of the individual will manifest itself in increased creativity, for the individual may be lacking in specific talent, knowledge, training, or opportunity for creativity. Individuals who have been manifestly creative but who are experiencing some emotional blocks to their creativity come into therapy expecting to overcome these blocks; few come expecting to sacrifice their creativity. But here and in other instances the possibility needs to be considered that psychotherapy may have an adverse effect on some people's creativity. This apparently negative evaluation of psychotherapy may seem unexpected or odd. It becomes clearer if the statement is considered in relation to what is regarded as Freud's briefest definition (Erikson, 1963) of normality—"to love and to work [p. 265]." Theoretically, creativity may be a symptom like any other symptom. A poet may select specific themes because of certain traumatic events in his life that sensitized him to these events. An architect who suffered a physical infirmity that he feels reflects on his personal adequacy may compensate for these feelings and seek, through his need for mastery, to demonstrate his superiority in the buildings he designs based on novel principles. An individual who finds interpersonal relationships difficult and anxiety provoking may devote his energies to the solution of critical problems in the laboratory where he finds sanctuary. Any of these persons could, during the course of therapy, gain insight into the sources of their anxieties and work them through successfully, at which time the creativity might continue conflict free or symptom free; or the manner in which the creativity is manifested might be changed; or now that his anxieties can be dealt with appropriately, the individual may turn to new lines of endeavor, even to the point of becoming less creative. At the same time, however, he may also become a psychologically happier and more effective person in areas in his life in which he dared not venture prior to therapy.

For those who regard creativity as the most important of all valued behaviors, this may sound like an indictment of psychotherapy. It is not. A therapist does not solicit patients. Patients come to him because they are unhappy or because they have experienced disturbing difficulties and conflicts in some areas of their lives. If at the same time their creativity was a neurotic symptom that stood in the way of their more complete growth and maturity, then they may be faced with the choice of whether they want to continue with the symptom or dissolve or diminish it by withdrawing energy from it for other purposes. If the latter decision is made, then the creativity may be diminished. This is, certainly not to say that all individuals entering therapy will have such experiences. There are creative persons whose creativity is conflict free and who come to therapy because of difficulties in life. These persons might have even more energy available for their future creative pursuits as they clear up their problems.

Research Evidence

What has just been said is derived from theory. There are no large-scale systematic investigations of the effects of therapy on creativity. Indeed, while there may be anecdotal reports and hearsay evidence on creative individuals who have been in therapy, there are no research reports. Lucy Freeman, the writer, wrote about her own psychotherapy (Freeman, 1969), and she has also written *Celebrities on the Couch* (Freeman, 1971) which contains brief case histories of the psychotherapy experiences of many celebrities, some of whom would also be regarded as creative. The best that the research literature on groups of persons can provide us with is a study of the effects of psychotherapy on productivity. Another study is one that investigates the relationship between a test of an ability that we would expect to improve with psychotherapy and a test that is presumed to measure creativity. While this study has errors, it is cited to indicate the care that needs to be taken in evaluating research reports.

On Focusing Ability

Gendlin *et al.* (1968), who are Rogerian or nondirective psychotherapists, became interested in *focusing ability*, which they define as "The ability to focus directly on preverbalized felt experiencing and to carry it forward concretely with attention, with words, and with actions . . . [p. 237]." This ability, for which the authors say they have a test, is expected to increase during the course of psychotherapy. They also believe that there is something similar between what they suspect goes on in the creative process and what is involved in focusing ability. For them, the creative individual turns his attention from the interpretation of well-articulated forms to those which are as yet unformulated. The creative person, they say, attends to conceptually vague impressions first, and from these develops meaningful statements. It is apparent therefore that these investigators see a similarity between the ability to focus on vague preverbalized experiences and what goes on in the creative process. To test whether this is indeed so they administered the focusing ability test, the *Hidden Figures Test* (in which the subject is to find which one of five geometrical figures is embedded in a complex design), and a series of pictures about which the subjects told as many stories as they could. This last was used as a measure of productivity. The implicit argument seems to be that if focusing ability is expected to improve with psychotherapy, and if it can also be related to a test that the authors regard as a measure of creativity, then apparently psychotherapy can improve creativity.

The tests were administered to 22 college sophomores and the results indicated that the productivity score was found to be correlated with the Hidden Figures Test but not with the focusing ability score. By the same token, focusing ability was correlated with scores on the Hidden Figures Test. The authors then proceed to argue on this basis that focusing ability is related to creativity because the Hidden Figures Test has been discussed in the literature as involving "the individual's ability to 'flexibly' adapt patterns, that is, to 'let go of' constructs or configurations when no longer appropriate to the situation [Gendlin *et al.*, 1968, p. 235]."

The problem with this study is that the authors err in what they think the Hidden Figures Test measures. This test is part of Guilford's (1967) test battery. While Guilford tells us that all of his factors may make a contribution to creativity, the *divergent* factors are counted upon primarily for these purposes. The Hidden Figures Test is not listed in Guilford's work (1967) as a measure of this factor but as a measure of the *convergent* factor.

That their focusing ability test is not necessarily related to creativity as indicated by its relationship to the Hidden Figures Test, is also evident in another part of the Gendlin *et al.* (1968) report. Later in their study, they report relationships between focusing ability and personality data (as measured by the Cattell High-School Personality Questionnaire) for high school students. Among the personality characteristics found to correlate positively with focusing ability were: intelligence, control, precision in social relationships, self-discipline, compulsiveness, etc. While some of these might be regarded as positively related to creativity, others are not.

On Productivity

The second study we turn to does not focus directly on creativity but on a related matter—productivity. Productivity is only indirectly related to our purposes, for while we would expect a creative individual to be productive we do not necessarily expect a productive person to be creative. However, because of the possible relationship between creativity and productivity and because there are no systematic studies using reasonable numbers of persons in a study of psychotherapy and creativity, this study is reported here.

Wispé and Parloff (1965) compared the productivity of 55 male psychologists who had 60 hours or more of psychotherapy over a period of from approximately 5 months to 95 months with a matched control group of 55 psychologists who had neither considered nor received therapy. They were matched in terms of publication productivity. Publications for the control group and for the experimental group before and after therapy were weighted as follows: A book written alone was given a weight of 36 points; a book with one collaborator, 18; a book with two collaborators, 12; a revision of a previously published book, 8; a book edited, 2; a chapter in a book, 2; an article written alone, 2; an article written in collaboration, 1; various reviews, notes, etc., 1. Although the productivity means and medians of the therapy sample were higher than those of the control group, the differences were not statistically significant. Those who had therapy were neither more nor less productive after therapy than before. And over an equivalent time period, the control group also showed no difference between earlier and later productivity. There was also no relationship between duration of therapy and productivity; between before-therapy productivity and duration of therapy in months; nor between productivity level and reasons for entering therapy. In other words, those who went into therapy did not appear to have done so because of their under- or over-productivity.

These objective measures do not support the idea that psychotherapy has a positive effect, but those based on more subjective evaluations do. Wispé and Parloff developed a *Therapy Satisfaction Index* based on the psychologists' own appraisal of their "objectivity," "insight," "comfort," and "competence." These ratings were then correlated with the psychologists' own ratings of the "effect of psychotherapy on quantity and quality" of their professional writing. The correlations were +.95. In other words, the psychologists' own perceptions of their satisfaction with their psychotherapy were related to their judgments of the effects of that psychotherapy on the quality and quantity of their professional writing. The more satisfied the man was with the therapy he received, the more favorably he felt it affected his publications. But the man's satisfaction with his therapy was not significantly related to the investigators' *weighting* system of his productivity.

In other words, we find a positive relationship between a subjective measure of satisfaction with psychotherapy and a subjective measure of the effects of psychotherapy. On the other hand, no significant relationship was found between the man's satisfaction with his own therapy and an objective measure of his productivity. This kind of discrepancy in results reflects almost exactly the kind of discussions that go on many times among creative individuals who have undergone psychotherapy and other persons. These creative persons on being questioned as to the effects of psychotherapy would, like Wispé and Parloff's (1965) subjects, probably say they were very satisfied with their psychotherapy and with the effects it had on their work. Creative individuals who were not satisfied with their creativity would probably downgrade its effects. Furthermore, the outsider with his own objective criteria, like prizes won, peers' acclaim, money or status earned, might feel that the individual was better or worse off before psychotherapy.

One of the questions is, why do the two subjective ratings agree? There is evidence (obtained through personal communication with Wispé and Parloff) that the several questions asked of the subjects on the effects of psychotherapy all intercorrelated in the .90's, suggesting either a halo effect—a response set—or dissonance effect. That is, the subjects might rate anything high that they would consider related to their therapy because of their global positive evaluation of it or because they have so much at stake in terms of time and money invested in therapy.

Indeed, these two factors may account for the results obtained between the two subjective ratings; moreover, it may be difficult, if not impossible, to separate these artifacts from the problem studied, but then there are those who would ask if this should ever be done. Is not the person who has had the therapy, they would argue, the best person to judge its effects? While there is much merit to this, we would also like to have supportive objective evidence. Better yet, both kinds of evidence are desirable.

Wispé and Parloff (1965) report another rather interesting analysis of their data that may relate to the lack of obtained statistical differences between their therapy and control samples. They report increased variability in the productivity of the therapy sample after therapy. The range of productivity for the middle 50% of the therapy sample was twice as great as the middle 50% of the control sample (those who did not have therapy). In the therapy group there were psychologists who were not productive before therapy or after therapy. And there were psychologists who were very productive before therapy who continued to be as productive, or more productive, after therapy. "This analysis also implies," say Wispé and Parloff (1965), "that 'having had therapy' is not a unitary variable [p. 193]." Hence they conclude:

> All of this suggests that psychotherapy may have had some effect, even if it failed to reach statistical significance. The impact of therapy upon productivity may have been different for different individuals, depending, for example, upon the importance of scientific publications in the adjustment of the individual. Further investigation is needed to test the hypothesis related to productivity, not that therapy frees creativity or reduces compulsivity, but that it enables those who are already productive to maintain their productivity when, for various reasons, their colleagues' output is declining [p. 193].

The very same statement should be made regarding the effects of therapy on creativity and, indeed, for the relationships among creativity and all of the other techniques and procedures designed to stimulate creativity. One of the major problems in discussing the value and effectiveness of all of these techniques for stimulating creativity through work on personality factors is that, at present, relatively little is known of under what conditions they will work and for what kind of person they will work.

SUMMARY

In summary, then, role playing is a technique that no doubt many have used to stimulate their creativity or to overcome their blocks or difficulties with the creative process. While there are no systematic studies of how role playing actually affected creativity in real-life situations, there is research evidence that it can have positive effects as measured by test criteria.

Hypnosis can be used as a technique to explore certain effects and relationships that occur in the creative process. It has been used as a psychotherapeutic technique to help persons overcome their intrapsychic blocks and difficulties. Since some of these blocks might also be related to a person's difficulties with creativity, it is assumed that under these conditions where the problems are cleared up, there will be indirect positive effects of hypnosis on creativity. At present, there is anecdotal material regarding the effects of hypnosis on creativity but there are no large-scale studies of such effects. Similarly, although hypnosis has been used to produce effects on the psychometric tests of creativity, these same effects have also been produced by role playing. More work is required before we can say with any certainty what the precise effects of hypnosis on creativity are. It is therefore to be hoped that research on the relationship of hypnosis to creativity will continue and that such research endeavors, in addition to controlling for the factors necessary for a better understanding of hypnosis, would also control for the personality and cognitive characteristics of the people, for hypnosis may be more effective with some types of persons than with others.

No systematic research effort has been carried out on the relationships between psychotherapy and creativity with numbers of people. The study that comes closest to our purposes is one of the relationship of psychotherapy to productivity. From it we learned that there is a positive relationship between an individual's satisfaction with his therapy and his judgment of the quality and quantity of his publications, but there is no significant relationship between satisfaction with therapy and an objective evaluation of publications. No doubt, readers will choose either the subjective or objective evaluations, as they wish, but for our purposes both are regarded as necessary. Finally, what the cited study on the relationship of psychotherapy to productivity did show was that psychotherapy probably helps those who are already productive to maintain their productivity, while for their colleagues (who have not had psychotherapy) productivity is on the decline. Would this also occur if creativity were involved? We can only hope that systematic studies of the effects of psychotherapy on creativity will be undertaken sometime in the future.

Chapter **VI**

Introduction to Cognitive Procedures

Cognitive processes are those psychological processes involved in knowing, understanding, perceiving, learning and problem solving, etc. They have to do with how the individual copes with stimuli from the outside world—how he senses and perceives them, how he stores them, how he transforms and combines them with previously stored data.

Cognitive processes are involved in all stages of the creative process. But at any one stage in the process one or more of them may be more salient than the others. Perception and learning figure primarily in the preparation stage. The capacity to form associations and develop ideas looms large during hypothesis formation. Problem solving stands out during hypothesis testing. And higher thought processes are involved in the communication stage. Again, it should be clear that it is only for heuristic purposes that any one cognitive process is said to be primary at any one stage of the creative process than another. All processes can and do occur in all stages of the creative process.

It also bears repeating that, although attention in the next several chapters is focused on cognitive factors, the person, considered from an intrapersonal viewpoint, consists of transactional relationships between cognitive and personality factors. That which occurs in the cognitive area can affect the personality and vice versa. Furthermore, since the individual is part of a social matrix with which

83

he also has transactional relationships, then social relationships and social forces can affect what goes on within the individual just as what goes on within the individual can affect his environment. Again, it is primarily for heuristic purposes that the cognitive and personality variables are treated separately. But another reason for their separation is that some techniques for stimulating creativity stress one more than the other.

We begin the discussion of the ways to stimulate creativity with a consideration of the effects of alcohol, caffeine (coffee), and the mind-expanding drugs. These are considered together since they are a group of stimulants or drugs that can affect all stages of the creative process. Also, although studies of their effects may be oriented primarily to the cognitive factors, several of them are excellent examples of the transactional factors just referred to. This is especially so when mind-expanding drugs are considered. The social atmosphere in which the drugs are taken can color their effects. Some persons may feel that the effects of these social factors diminish the significance of the drugs for creativity. However, a study will be presented in which the effects of the social factors were incorporated as part of the study, and rather impressive results of much potential interest were obtained.

The four chapters following the one on drugs consider, in turn, the preparatory stage and the stages of hypothesis formation, hypothesis testing, and the communication of results. The chapter on preparation, because of its very nature, has to be incomplete. It is concerned with education. If it were to be a more complete treatment of the topic it would have to consider, among other things, the education that takes place in the home; all that transpires in the school system including personal and social relationships among pupil, teacher, and peers; the effectiveness of various good teaching techniques, etc., since all of these will probably affect creativity. While all of this would certainly be relevant, it goes beyond our purposes. We have limited ourselves specifically to several recent studies concerned with stimulating or increasing creativity in the classroom through the use of rather interesting procedures.

Each of the chapters on hypothesis formation, hypothesis testing, and the communication of results focuses on techniques that, from our point of view, are concerned, respectively, with how to stimulate ideas, how to test them effectively, and how to cut down on the problems of disseminating and diffusing the creative product—be it an idea or something tangible. Hopefully, the reader will take from these chapters that which he can use for whatever stage of the creative process he needs them and not feel that he is limited to an area indicated by the chapter headings.

Chapter IX contains a variety of self-help techniques for hypothesis formation. These techniques require little, if any, training. While they are likely to be used most frequently during hypothesis formation, they may also prove useful in generating ideas for any stage in the creative process. In essence, what these techniques do is help a person avoid getting stuck with fixed notions and ideas.

They are designed to overcome *functional fixedness*, the perception of something and its use in some one fixed way. This goal is accomplished through procedures that externalize processes that go on in the minds of creative persons. Rather than keep numerous important variables in his head, the person is encouraged, for example, to write them down. Rather than toy with ideas mentally, the person is provided with questions he can ask about his variables, and he is also presented with a means of manipulating them so that they actually appear before him in combination with each other. Hopefully, as these different combinations turn up they strike significant chords, become part of a number of important associations, and are instrumental in the development of creative works.

Comparing the amount of material covered in discussing techniques for stimulating cognitive factors with that previously covered in discussing personality factors, it is apparent that there has been more activity in the cognitive than the personality area. There are several reasons for this. (1) It is more expensive in time and money to utilize personality techniques. (2) It takes longer and it is more expensive to accumulate data on large numbers of individuals for the systematic study of the effectiveness of changing or altering personality factors as a means of stimulating creativity. The number of persons affected by psychotherapy might be increased through the use of group therapy rather than individual therapy, but the number of persons in these sessions would still not be so large as that involved in cognitive training sessions. Moreover, the amount of time an individual would spend in group therapy would be a great deal more than that spent in a creativity session devoted to stimulating cognitive factors. (3) In general it is much easier to administer, score, and interpret cognitive tests for the evaluation of cognitive processes. (4) Our society and especially those persons primarily involved in the financial support of techniques for stimulating creativity have a different attitude toward cognitive factors than they have toward personality factors. They believe that to deal with an individual's personality, even with those of his personality problems that block his creativity, involves getting "too close" to him. Some among them fear that personality measures invade another's privacy. There is no such fear about training in such cognitive procedures as the development of more associations or better problem-solving techniques. If nothing else, these are regarded as educational procedures not too dissimilar from those experienced in school and therefore personally less threatening. All of the reasons just considered combine in some way to attract more work and support for programs designed to stimulate cognitive rather than personality factors.

SEVERAL THEORETICAL ISSUES

Several theoretical issues require consideration in this introductory section. Each is part of the theoretical background for a good deal that follows. In other words, a technique such as brainstorming is based on associationistic psychology; hence, that part of this theory will be discussed which relates to associations and their generation and formation. Other theories that may also have something to say about associations are not necessarily presented, because brainstorming is not based on them. We have tried to limit ourselves to a technique and its own theoretical framework. If the reader would like more information about the theory, he can consult additional references cited in the text.

The following issues will be considered in this introduction: (1) the theory of associationistic psychology for what it has to say about the formation of ideas. Several techniques for stimulating creativity are based on this theory, most notable among them brainstorming, as just mentioned. (2) The theory of Gestalt psychology will be considered for its position on problem solving and especially for its conceptualization of problems in terms of field forces. Individuals and the problems they work on constitute the same field. Those who sense the forces and follow their leads are in the best position to solve the problem. (3) Language is very much related to and affects thought processes. Some of these relationships and effects will be pointed out because the concepts and terms a person has available and uses may well determine how creatively he solves a problem. (4) Two interrelated processes will be discussed, one from the perceptual cognitive area called *physiognomic perception*, and another from the personality area called *regression in service of the ego*. Both these concepts play important roles in several techniques for stimulating creativity that are designed to help overcome (a) habitual and automatized ways of responding to environmental stimuli and (b) fixed perceptions of these stimuli. Furthermore, physiognomic perception relates very much to concepts in a group technique for stimulating creativity called *synectics* which may also be utilized by individuals. (5) Finally, throughout this book reference is made to Guilford's research. Because of its importance, it will be presented in this chapter.

Cognitive Theories

Associationistic Psychology

Elements of associationistic psychology go back at least as far as the Greek philosophers. According to this theory of psychology, associations, or thoughts, or ideas occur because of contiguity, similarity, or contrast. An association may occur because two stimuli occur together (contiguity); because in some way they are similar to each other (similarity); or in some way they are different from each other (contrast). Sequences of associations occur for the same reasons. While a chain or sequence of associations may be initiated by an external stimulus, each association in the sequence may serve as a stimulus for what follows. There may be characteristic differences between associations occurring early and those occurring later in a sequence. This is a basic assumption in a technique such as brainstorming where longer and longer chains of associations are encouraged, because those occurring early are regarded as the most habitual and most common and hence least valuable for creativity. Those occurring later are among the more unique and hence likely to be the most valuable for creativity. We shall present the research data on this assumption later.

In the 18th and 19th centuries, British empiricists took over the laws of association which

> were thought to be the basic principles which explained the way the mind functions. It was their belief that even the most complicated mental functions could be accounted for by the laws of association, or, to put it another way, that a thorough understanding of association could result in a complete understanding of thinking [Cramer, 1968, p. 3].

The British empiricists also undertook the development of secondary laws of association. (The primary laws involved contiguity, similarity, and contrast.) And they concerned themselves with such stimulus variables as intensity, duration, frequency, and recency of association. They also considered variables that had to do with the person—constitutional differences, differences in past experiences, etc. An excellent review and critical evaluation of these primary and secondary laws can be found in Cramer (1968).

If a stimulus can set off a chain of associations, and if these associations are necessary for creativity, then why does this process become ineffective? Why do some people insist that they do not have any ideas, that their minds are or become blank or that they become "stuck"? Needless to say, these questions are raised about individuals who, because of their training, backgrounds and experience, may be expected to be creative. Any one or a combination of the following reasons may be involved.

1. An individual may not be motivated to devote the energy necessary for the associative process. He may find it easier and less demanding to deal with stimuli through habitual and automatized responses.

2. The lack of environmental stimulation, the lack of environmental complexity, may put no challenge to the individual and make no demands on the person for new associations. Environments that are characterized by sameness provide no new informational inputs that can serve as building blocks for later associations.

3. The kinds of circumstances and experiences attendant upon the initial encounter with a stimulus may affect the association process. The experiences that an individual has when he first learns something new may well affect how or the extent to which he may be able to combine what he has learned with other ideas. For some persons, the initial learning experience may be fraught with

anxiety. Therefore, they do not really learn or understand what is presented to them but memorize it. Other persons learn only some outstanding characteristics of a stimulus situation but not in any manner that facilitates meaningful integration of the learned characteristics with prior knowledge. The experience may be such that what is learned is learned with a certain *functional fixedness* —the functions or characteristics of an object are regarded as immutable and irreversible. Objects so perceived do not serve well as stimuli for futher associations.

4. Affect-laden associations or "complexes" may be touched off or triggered, even though on a conscious level, the individual is dealing only with cognitive material. This may inhibit the associative process or keep it from moving along smoothly. (This is part of the rationale of using a word-association test for diagnostic purposes in clinical situations. By asking an individual for his associations to stimulus words, by watching for his reactions as well as the content of his responses, various "complexes" may be indicated.) When cognitive material hits upon an affect-laden complex we witness an instance of the transactional relationship between personality and cognitive factors. On an unconscious level the cognitive material sets off anxiety-laden complexes that interfere with or disrupt the associative process.

5. The associative process can be inhibited if the individual is given too much to evaluating his associations. The association process is slowed and affected when the individual takes the time to judge whether a response or association he is *about to give* is "correct," "worthy of him," "appropriate," etc. And, it is similarly slowed and affected when the individual deliberates whether a response he has *already given* meets certain critical criteria and standards he has set for himself. Finally, the process of judging may become so onerous and so painful because of the push-pull relationship between associating and judging that the individual gives up the whole process completely.

6. The earlier in life some of the inhibitory factors just mentioned occur, the more difficult it may be for the individual to overcome them. The younger child is more impressionable and he has a longer period in life during which reinforcements can "stamp in" patterns and attitudes that have negative effects on the association processes. By the same token, the individual who is too ego-involved, "too much on the line," due to factors in his life history may be unable to carry out the "natural" process of association because he has too much at stake.

Techniques presented later are designed to help restimulate the associative processes so that when the individual is confronted with a stimulus or a problem he will not be blocked but will come up with a number of ideas. The assumptions underlying these techniques and the research data supporting or negating the assumptions will also be discussed. Finally, just how effective these techniques are for achieving their goals will also be discussed.

Gestalt Psychology

About the latter part of the 19th century a conflict began between two psychological groups concerned with perception. One of these insisted that how we perceived the world depended on our past experiences. This was the theory of the *associationists* discussed above. And their theories were opposed by the *Gestalt* psychologists. While the associationists emphasized learning, the *Gestalt* psychologists emphasized the importance of innate factors in the nervous system. And herein we can see aspects of the much broader argument of the relative importance of the differences between hereditary and environmental factors in human behavior.

For the Gestalt psychologists, that which an individual perceives is partly the result of the organization of the stimulus as it falls on his visual receptors and brain. The stimulus, composed of forces that are organized into a *gestalt*, imposes itself upon the individual's nervous system, which has its own system of organization. If both of these mesh appropriately, then the individual has an accurate or *veridical* perception. This veridical perception is, for the Gestalt psychologists, not based on learning or prior experience. For the Gestalt psychologists, when an individual is shown a square, its squareness is given in the stimulus, while for the associationists the square is made up of its component lines and experience with the stimulus figure.

To further illustrate what the Gestalt psychologists are trying to get at in terms of field forces, let us take an example from one of their favorite areas of investigation, that of illusions. One oft-cited example is the Müller-Lyer illusion that consists of these two sets of stimuli,

Here, even though the center lines are exactly the same length in both, the organization and wholeness or *gestalt* created by the "forces" of the arrowheads in the total field composed also of the horizontal line is sufficiently different so that the left-hand figure is usually *seen* as shorter than the right-hand one. The Gestalt psychologists argue that this perception is *given* in the sense that it is not based on prior learning experience with the stimulus but on interaction between the organization of the field of the stimulus and the organization of the field of the individual's nervous system. They argue in favor of the importance of these factors for perception in general, while the associationists would argue in favor of sensory experience and learning behavior.

One of the important laws in Gestalt psychology is the law of Prägnanz. According to Kurt Koffka (1935), one of the major Gestalt psychologists, the law of Prägnanz "can briefly be formulated like this: psychological organization will always be as 'good' as the prevailing conditions allow. In this definition the term 'good' is undefined. It embraces such properties as regularity, symmetry, simplicity and others ... [p. 110] ." Thus, for Gestalt psychologists the more regular, symmetric and simple a form is, the better it is. For our purposes, we could say that this is what the creative individual strives for—the good gestalt—as he seeks a solution to a problem.

Subsumed under the law of Prägnanz is the *principle of closure* which says that if a figure is presented which has a small part missing from it or which has a gap in it, then the viewer will tend to see it with a closed boundary provided other forces permit this to happen. Here again, then, there are forces in the stimulus figure which work jointly with the innate organization of the nervous system. Taking this material one theoretical step further, we may say that for every stimulus that impinges on our receptors there is a physiological representation in the brain. The external stimulus is said to be isomorphic with the representation in the brain. Thus, for the square in the external environment there is a physiological representation that maintains its squareness in the brain; for every circle there is a circleness that is maintained in the brain. The form existing in the brain is in part determined by the stimulus transmitted by the receptors, but in part also by the pattern of excitation that is in the electrical fields provided by the brain tissue. Returning to the closure principle, then, it is the pattern of excitation in the brain that results in the closing of the gap. However, since the form in the brain is surrounded by other electrical stimuli and forces in the other parts of the brain, it can be affected by them, and it is possible that the gap may not be bridged if these other forces that are operating are of such a nature that they will interfere with the achieving of a good gestalt or a good form.

This is again an all-too-brief explanation of Gestalt theory. It is presented for the following reasons.

1. It contains the theoretical basis for a series of terms that are sometimes used both technically and metaphorically in discussions of creativity. It puts into theoretical context words that come up frequently in this area—closure, good gestalt, etc.

2. A study of problem-solving behavior will be presented later that illustrates how efficiency in problem solving is related to following the stresses and forces in a problem. Also, in techniques for stimulating creativity, such as synectics, it is frequently suggested that the participant should "feel" with the problem or with the forces of the problem as in Gestalt psychology. By sensing the forces in a problem and by allowing himself to follow its leads, an individual is more likely to perceive the real problem correctly and hence to arrive at a solution.

3. The field forces in the brain that represent the problem can be disrupted or interfered with by other field forces which may represent personality and emotional problems. Thus, as in the discussion of associationism, so here personality factors might either facilitate, inhibit, or distort perception and

problem-solving behavior. A study of such relationships will also be presented later.

LANGUAGE

Having mentioned thought processes and problem-solving behavior, it is appropriate to introduce the importance of language. Again, we cannot discuss all aspects of language and their relationships to the creative process, but we do wish to call attention to one concept—the Sapir-Whorf hypothesis (Hoijer, 1954)—which refers to the intimate relationship between language and thought. The vocabulary he has at his disposal affects what an individual thinks about, the characteristics of his thought processes, and the kinds of concepts he has available to deal with. These ideas are also basic to general semantics (Korzybski, 1941).

The layman is most likely to limit the importance of language to the communication stage of the creative process; its significance is most obvious there. But we should not overlook the importance of language during hypothesis formation and hypothesis testing. All stages of the creative process may be blocked or distorted if the individual does not possess a language with words for concepts necessary to the solution of the problem. For example, Whorf points out that, although it is possible to develop the idea of absolute spontaneity from our concept of time and use it for a variety of theoretical developments, it is impossible to do the same from the Hopi concept which is most appropriately translated as "duration." Our "time" is conceptualized as " 'a space of strictly limited dimensions, or sometimes as a motion upon such a space, and employed as an intellectual tool accordingly. Hopi 'duration' . . . [is] . . . the mode in which life differs from form, and consciousness *in toto* from the spatial elements of consciousness'[Fearing, 1954, p. 48] ."

Similarly, an individual whose vocabulary is composed largely of nouns may be limited to the "thing quality" of the objects he has to deal with and be unable to make new integrations out of them. When these same objects are seen in terms of what they do, when they are thought of in terms of actions and verbs, then the possibility of new integrations is fostered.

Techniques and programs designed to stimulate creativity do not necessarily stress these matters, but it is frequently quite implicit in what they do. We shall point these out as they occur.

PHYSIOGNOMIC PERCEPTION AND REGRESSION
IN SERVICE OF THE EGO

The two concepts—physiognomic perception and regression in service of the ego—that head this section come from two different fields of inquiry: perception and personality. Furthermore, physiognomic perception was elucidated by developmental psychologists, and regression in service of the ego has figured primarily in the writings of the psychoanalysts.

From a developmental point of view, as an individual grows from childhood to adulthood, there are characteristic processes through which he progresses. Not all of the processes need concern us here. We need only say that at one end of the progression, early in life, stimuli are perceived in terms of their animistic qualities, or they are perceived in terms of physiognomic (humanlike) characteristics. At the other end of the progression, in adulthood, as a result of the constricting effects of socialization, stimuli are perceived in terms of their formal, objective, or thinglike characteristics.

Physiognomic perception occurring earlier developmentally can be considered a more "primitive" kind of perception. Because it is not concerned with the objectlike quality of the stimuli, the boundaries of the formal aspects of percepts are less rigid and more flexible. Possessing such characteristics, the percepts are more likely to be combined with percepts of other environmental objects to yield newer or more novel objects and concepts. Perceptions that are concerned solely with the formal characteristics of objects and with their thinglike quality are more likely to be involved in the *functional fixedness* of the stimulus. And being so fixed, they are less likely to be used to develop newer combinations in conjunction with other stimuli in the environment.

As individuals progress from childhood to adulthood they vary in the experiences they have. Some of these experiences result in the repression or suppression in an individual of the capacity to have physiognomic perceptions, while in other individuals, other experiences may have allowed for a rather effective balance between physiognomic perceptions and the more formal or objectlike perceptions. An individual who is unable to perceive physiognomically may lose one possible way of seeing things flexibly and hence the opportunity to make use of his capability of making new combinations. The second type of person may be able to perceive environmental stimuli in terms of their object-like characteristics, but he may also be able to perceive them physiognomically. He perceives stimuli physiognomically and then makes new combinations with other stimuli. This process of utilizing a type of perception that is characteristic of an earlier stage of development but which also enables the individual to arrive at newer, better, and "higher" stages is referred to as regression in service of the ego.

The phrase "regression in service of the ego" was developed by psychoanalysts to differentiate between it and, say, "regression alone." The latter refers to the return to a previous stage of development as a reaction to some difficulty or anxiety, or as a defense mechanism. For example, a growing child may have stopped wetting the bed. However, after a new brother or sister appears on the scene the child begins to think that he is rejected or that some of the love over which he thought he had a monopoly is being shared with someone else and this results in the child beginning to wet the bed again. This is regression. In schizophrenia, for example, regression appears in various components of the individual's psyche—perception, thought process, affect, and social relationships. Here the regression is likely to be of much longer duration than in the case of the child just mentioned.

Regression in service of the ego shares with regression as a defense mechanism the regression aspects—that is, the return to a prior stage of development—but what differentiates the two is that in the former what is regressed to is utilized for constructive purposes. Hence, that regression is in *service* of the ego. Creative persons have this capacity.

ALTERED STATES OF CONSCIOUSNESS

The discussion of physiognomic perception and regression in service of the ego is preparatory and introductory to several matters that will be discussed later. But a knowledge of them also serves as a bridge to the consideration of a larger area known as altered states of consciousness.

One of these altered states of consciousness has already been considered: hypnosis with its hypnotic trance and posthypnotic suggestion. But there are others, such as the dream state, a state of deep reflection which, while presented here as a term used by Aldous Huxley to characterize an experience of his own, is no doubt also characteristic of the behavior of many individuals who engage in the creative process. In addition, there are the various mind-expanding drugs which also alter an individual's state of consciousness. When in such a state, an individual may perceive and think about the world and the environment around him in ways that are different from his usual ones. These newer perceptions and thoughts, if they can be retained, might well prove to be significant building blocks for later creativity.

It is implicit in what has been said that the usual state of consciousness can be quite limited (and limiting) because it operates in terms of habitual and automatized responses to stimuli that are perceived rigidly. The function of altering the state of consciousness is, obviously, to shake up this state of affairs. The goal is to achieve a state that the creative individual can bring about without the use of drugs or stimulants. The extent to which the stimulants and drugs achieve this goal will be the focus of our attention as will be some theoretical aspects of the state of consciousness and other states related to it.

GUILFORD'S INTELLECTIVE FACTORS*

One of the more important developments in the field of creativity has been Guilford's works on intellective factors. There will be numerous occasions

---

*Guilford's use of the term "intellective" is more similar to our use of the term "cognitive." He uses cognitive in a more restricted sense (Guilford, 1967) than we do.

throughout this book when Guilford's tests for these factors will be referred to. Sometimes, they are referred to in discussions of the characteristics of creative individuals, and, on other occasions, where the tests are regarded as measures of intellectual functions involved in the creative process, they are utilized to measure the effects of programs designed to stimulate creativity. In the latter situation, it is assumed that if the creativity stimulating procedure is effective, this should be reflected in significant increases in scores on Guilford's tests. Because of the important role that Guilford's tests have played in studies in this area, some of the background material for them is discussed in this introductory section.

Guilford's (1967) work began out of both theoretical and statistical considerations that led him to be critical of traditional intelligence testing procedures. It would take us too far afield to consider all the issues involved; hence we shall limit ourselves to what he has to say directly about the relationships between intelligence testing and creativity.

In 1950 Guilford said, "We must look well beyond the boundaries of the IQ if we are to fathom the domain of creativity [p. 448]," and he voiced the belief that the idea "that creative talent is to be accounted for in terms of high intelligence or IQ . . . is not only inadequate but has been largely responsible for lack of progress in the understanding of creative people [p. 454]."

Among the various faults that Guilford finds with the intelligence testing movement in the United States is that although there are many different tests, they do not test all of the intellectual abilities. In his most recent book, pulling together years of work, Guilford (1967) says,

> In spite of the fact that scales have included quite a variety of tests, for which we owe thanks to Binet, the variety has still not been wide enough to encompass the ranges of intellectual abilities as we know them today. The writer's inspection of the most recent revision of the Stanford-Binet, Form L–M, suggests that among the 140 single tests, including the alternates, some twenty-eight of the intellectual factors are represented, each by at least 1 test, as compared with about eighty that are regarded as known and more than one hundred that are probable when all are known. The most notable group of factors that have been missed in all intelligence scales consists of the divergent-production abilities, of which 24 are represented in the structure-of-intellect model and 16 have been demonstrated by means of tests. History shows many examples in which too restricted views of an area of investigations have hampered progress. It is doubtful that views that are too broad have ever done so [p. 37].

To arrive at a conceptualization of the different possible factors involved in the structure of the intellect Guilford used a technique called *morphological analysis* (to be considered later, page 211). This is a technique for stimulating creativity and therefore as an aside Guilford's work is a good illustration of this technique's use and value.

Guilford's morphological model consists of three dimensions or parameters—operations, contents, and products (cf. Table 1). Each of these dimensions consists of several categories. *Operations*, which as its name indicates, is the operation performed on material, consists of the following categories: cognition, memory, divergent production, convergent production, and evaluation. *Contents*, or the medium in which the thought occurs, consists of four categories: figural, symbolic, semantic, and behavioral. And *Products* consists of the results of the combinations of both operations and products and includes six categories: units, classes, relations, systems, transformations, and implications. All of these are more fully defined in Table 1.

Guilford regards the combination of any three categories from the three dimensions as consisting of a psychological factor. For example, cognition of figural systems is called spatial orientation; cognition of semantic implication is conceptual foresight; divergent production of symbolic units is called word fluency; and divergent production of semantic units is called ideational fluency, etc. For each of these factors tests have been developed.

Relating his own studies of intellect to creativity, Guilford (1963) says,

> Although the most obvious aspects of creative thinking appear to depend on the abilities to do divergent-productive thinking and the abilities to effect transformations of information, with the abilities of fluency, flexibility, elaboration, and redefinition playing significant roles, with creative thinking put in its larger context of problem solving, we see that any or all kinds of abilities represented in the structure of intellect can play their useful roles, directly or indirectly [p. 11].

To illustrate Guilford's factors and the tests used to get at them, let us consider the divergent production factors. A factor that Guilford (1967) calls *word fluency* (divergent symbolic units) consists of thinking up and writing out words containing a specified letter, e.g., the letter *g*; two of the tests for *ideational fluency* (divergent semantic units) are *Plot Titles* (nonclever) in which the subject is asked to list "possible titles for a given short story [p. 142]" and the score is the number of nonclever titles produced. And another is the *Utility Test* in which the subject is asked to list "uses he can think of for a common brick, or a wire coat hanger [p. 142]." The score is based on "the total number of relevant responses [p. 142]." When the uses for the common brick and lead pencil given by a person are scored for the number of *shifts* in classes in consecutive responses, it becomes a measure of semantic spontaneous flexibility

TABLE 1
DEFINITIONS OF CATEGORIES IN GUILFORD'S[a] STRUCTURE OF INTELLECT

Operations

Major kinds of intellectual activities or processes; things that the organism does with the raw materials of information, information being defined as "that which the organism discriminates."

Cognition. Immediate discovery, awareness, rediscovery, or recognition of information in various forms; comprehension or understanding.

Memory. Retention or storage, with some degree of availability, of information in the same form in which it was committed to storage and in response to the same cues in connection with which it was learned.

Divergent Production. Generation of information from given information, where the emphasis is upon variety and quantity of output from the same source. Likely to involve what has been called transfer. This operation is most clearly involved in aptitudes of creative potential.

Convergent Production. Generation of information from given information, where the emphasis is upon achieving unique or conventionally accepted best outcomes. It is likely the given (cue) information fully determines the response.

Evaluation. Reaching decisions or making judgments concerning criterion satisfaction (correctness, suitability, adequacy, desirability, etc.) of information.

Contents

Broad classes or types of information discriminable by the organism.

Figural. Information in concrete form, as perceived or as recalled possibly in the form of images. The term "figural" minimally implies figure–ground perceptual organization. Visual spatial information is figural. Different sense modalities may be involved, e.g., visual kinesthetic.

Symbolic. Information is the form of denotative signs, having no significance in and of themselves, such as letters, numbers, musical notations, codes, and words, when meanings and form are not considered.

Semantic. Information in the form of meanings to which words commonly become attached, hence most notable in verbal thinking and in verbal communication but not identical with words. Meaningful pictures also often convey semantic information.

Behavioral. Information, essentially nonverbal, involved in human interactions where the attitudes, needs, desires, moods, intentions, perceptions, thoughts, etc., of other people and of ourselves are involved.

Products

Forms that information takes in the organism's processing of it.

Units. Relatively segregated or circumscribed items of information having "thing" character. May be close to Gestalt psychology's "figure on a ground."

TABLE 1 (continued)

Classes. Conceptions underlying sets of items of information grouped by virtue of their common properties.

Relations. Connections between items of information based upon variables or points of contact that apply to them. Relational connections are more meaningful and definable than implications.

Systems. Organized or structured aggregates of items of information; complexes of inter-related or interacting parts.

Transformations. Changes of various kinds (redefinition, shifts, or modification) of existing information or in its function.

Implications. Extrapolations of information, in the form of expectancies, predictions, known or suspected antecedents, concomitants, or consequences. The connection between the given information and that extrapolated is more general and less definable than a relational connection.

[a]From Guilford and Hoepfner (1966).

(or divergent semantic class). And, when only *clever* titles are accepted from among the different titles given for a short short story, then the score is used as a measure of originality (divergent semantic relation).

Guilford's tests, especially those designed to measure divergent-production factors, have been used, as indicated previously, in various ways by researchers investigating creativity. Some have used the tests to study differences between creative persons, selected in terms of some criterion, and others who are less creative or who have not manifested any creativity. Other investigators have used Guilford's tests to differentiate between two groups of persons. One group scores significantly higher on these tests than does the other, and so the investigator has a psychometric criterion (cf. page 47) to differentiate between his groups. He then proceeds to study the groups with other psychological tests. Still another third group has used the tests to measure the effects of programs designed to stimulate creativity. And a fourth group has adapted or altered some of Guilford's original tests for specific purposes. These tests are referred to later as "Guilford-like" tests. Many of Guilford's tests and the Guilford-like tests are regarded as tests of creativity by some investigators, not because they have the evidence that the tests correlate with independent measures of manifest creativity, but because the tests appear to measure psychological functions that are assumed to be involved in the mental operations of creative persons during the creative process.

One of the unfortunate aspects of regarding these tests as tests of creativity is that some individuals have frequently pitted them against tests of intelligence and developed the issue of the existing or potential conflict between creativity and intelligence. This has unfortunately occupied many individuals. While their data may be interesting, the significance of it has been overemphasized, since Guilford has himself already pointed out that the divergent-production factors, those which are most likely to be related to creativity, are rarely to be found in some of the major tests of intelligence.

If the Guilford or Guilford-like tests are to be regarded as tests of creativity, then Stein (1968) suggests they should meet three criteria:

> First, the mental operations involved in them or the variables they purport to measure need to be of such a character that one would expect them to be related to creativity [i.e., have face validity]. And, by the same token, they must be meaningfully related to other psychological variables that one would also expect to be related to creativity. Secondly, the tests should relate to a criterion of creativity. And thirdly, since Guilford's tests are measures of the intellect, it has to be demonstrated that the former constitute a separate dimension that can be called creativity. In statistical terms, then, these tests should be highly correlated with each other and not significantly correlated with intelligence tests [pp. 911, 912].

The first condition, Stein says, has been met. The tests do seem to involve mental processes that one associates with creativity and they do relate in a meaningful way to other psychological variables. But, the research literature is at best ambiguous and at worst not supportive of the second and third conditions. The tests are not related as strongly as one would like to external criteria of creativity, and they are not necessarily independent of factors involved in traditional tests of intelligence.

That Guilford's tests do not meet all of the above criteria does cast some doubt on their being tests of creativity. Nevertheless, they cannot be brushed aside. It does make intuitive sense that the mental processes involved in these tests should also be involved in the creative process. It may be that further experimentation and study will reveal stronger relationships between Guilford's tests and criteria of manifest creativity. It would be interesting, for example, to select individuals on the basis of their scores on Guilford's tests and put them to work in real-life situations where data could be gathered on their consequent manifest creativity. Preselection of individuals in terms of Guilford's tests might yield better results for their relationships with creativity than existing studies which obtain their data from nonselected subjects. Nonselected subjects may not score as high on the different factors as might selected ones, and the former might not also have them in the proper combination for creativity as would be the case if they were selected. After such studies and further test development we might be in a better position to know just how well these tests do as tests of creativity.

When Guilford or Guilford-like tests are used as measures of the effectiveness of various programs to stimulate creativity, care needs to be exercised in evaluating the results. First, as we said previously, the tests have not as yet been as fully validated against creativity criteria as we would like. But there is another factor for which the reader must be on the alert. Obviously, what we want to know is the relationship between the tests and creativity. It is unlikely that any single measure among all of the divergent-production tests or among all of Guilford's tests is the one measure of creativity—no matter what the criterion. It is most likely that creativity is best measured by some combination of the different tests. Furthermore, if one single measure is used or regarded as the measure of creativity and it does improve, then before too much is made of this effect a check should be made of the training program, since possibly the training program focused directly or indirectly on stimulation of only this one factor. As Guilford (1967) says in his introduction to his major work on intellective factors:

> . . . if practice is in a test for a single factor, transfer is relatively limited within the area of performance related to that one factor. There is other scattered evidence that this principle applies. In a number of studies designed to increase the level of creative-thinking performance, where the emphasis is on cleverness or originality, there is likely to be improvement on tests of originality but not on tests of some other factors . . . [p. 44].

If there are in reality "other factors" related to creativity, then the effectiveness of the program has been rather limited. It is important that this caution be kept in mind.

It was the purpose of this chapter to provide necessary background material for what is to follow on the use of stimulants, altered states of consciousness, and various techniques for stimulating the effective use of cognitive processes. It is far beyond the scope of this book to provide all of the theoretical rationale for what follows, and more will be presented as separate issues come up. Hopefully, enough has been said so that the potential meaningfulness and usefulness of what follows will be increased.

SUMMARY

Knowing, understanding, perceiving, learning, and problem solving are among the cognitive processes involved in the creative process. For various reasons, more techniques have been developed to stimulate these processes than personality factors.

Associationistic psychology and Gestalt psychology concern themselves with cognitive processes and serve as the theoretical bases for many of the procedures and techniques to be presented later. To differentiate between the two schools of thought most succinctly, we may say that associationistic psychology maintains that a stimulus is made up of its different component parts, while Gestalt psychology maintains that the whole determines the parts.

By way of further introduction we concerned ourselves with three other matters:

(1) Since thought processes constitute a large part of the creative process, it was necessary to discuss language, since the verbal concepts available to a person will affect his thought processes.

(2) Just as we have stated previously that the individual is part of a larger social field and that the individual and the broader society or environment are involved in transactional relationships with each other, so we accept the conceptualization that within the individual there are transacting subfields. Consequently, attention is called to the fact that we should not consider cognitive factors as existing completely independently of personality factors and vice versa. To illustrate this transactional relationship we discussed the relationship between *physiognomic perception*, a cognitive factor, and *regression in service of the ego*, a personality factor.

(3) We then turned to a presentation of Guilford's work on intellective factors. These factors and the tests developed by Guilford and his co-workers have been of great significance to workers in the area of creativity. First, they have been among the most important cognitive factors studied by investigators for their presence or absence or for how they affected the creative process. Second, the tests developed by Guilford and his co-workers have been used as a criterion, or what we have called a psychometric criterion (page 47) of creativity. As such they have been used in a number of experiments and studies to investigate the effects of various training programs designed to stimulate creativity.

Chapter VII

Altering States of Consciousness

In his work the creative individual sees, approaches, thinks about, and deals with his materials differently than does the less creative person. Among other things, the creative person apparently has available to him more ideas and more energy; he is more persevering and less prone to the lasting negative effects of frustration than is the less creative individual.

Descriptions of the creative process focus on such experiences as the capacity to "transcend oneself," and to utilize inspirations that "come from the beyond." In psychological terminology the creative individual has easier and more ready access to his unconscious, greater sensitivity to and awareness of sense data, more flexibility in both his perceptual and thought processes. All these factors enable him to respond to and utilize what he finds and needs in his environment to achieve more novel and creative integrations.

With such descriptions as models to be emulated, the question therefore arises whether others could be helped to induce alterations in themselves so that they too could have available sense data, perceptions, flexible thought processes, etc., all of which would then culminate in creative works. Specifically, the question is whether, by reflection and a state of relaxation, by dreaming, by drinking liquor and/or coffee, or by taking drugs, the individual can induce in himself a state that could result in greater creativity. Each of these, taken alone, does bring about states that are apparently similar to those experienced by creative individuals. The question thus arises, if an individual did learn how to relax, did take the stimulants and the drugs, would his creativity be constructively affected?

In answer to this question we shall consider several varieties of data: the attitude of creative persons with regard to the various means of altering consciousness; the effects of caffeine, alcohol, and the mind-expanding drugs on both the cognitive and personality characteristics of the individuals involved; the short- and long-term effects of each of them and, where research evidence is available, their effects on creativity.

Before turning to these specific matters, it is necessary first to consider some of the characteristics of that mental state—consciousness—which is to be altered.

THE CONSCIOUSNESS THAT IS TO BE ALTERED

Different systems of thought have conceptualized the mind in different ways. In general, one part of it has been called the conscious mind and another part has been called unconscious or subconscious. In psychoanalysis there is still a third part that exists between the conscious and unconscious—the preconscious.

The conscious mind contains information of which one is aware. It is that part of the mind that is related to immediate knowing. It is involved with attention to objects and stimuli in the immediate environment but this span of attention is indeed limited. The conscious mind also tends to be logical in its considerations and thought processes.

The other part of the mind, the unconscious, is quite different. For our purposes this part of the mind serves as a storehouse of events that the conscious mind did not attend to, of experiences that occurred in an individual's past and that he suppressed or repressed. According to some theoretical formulations by Jung, the unconscious also contains data that make up the history of the race. Support for the idea that the unconscious mind is a storehouse of the aforementioned kinds of information comes from the fact that by hypnosis individuals can be helped to recall events that they consciously said they had forgotten, and by hypnosis individuals can be regressed to earlier states of their lives and behave as they did at that time. Stimulating exposed parts of the brain results in recalling events that have occurred. Evidence also comes from the study of memory, dreams, slips of the tongue, etc.

The "elements" that compose the unconscious mind do not exist or occur in any logical sequence. According to psychoanalytic theory, which has concerned itself a great deal with the workings of the unconscious mind, the information in the unconscious appears in sequences and forms that to the conscious mind are quite illogical. Elements in the unconscious mind are, again according to psychoanalysts, drive dominated. They constantly seek immediate satisfaction (i.e., they behave according to the pleasure principle). They are later to be controlled by the conscious mind which tries to delay their gratification until a proper place and time; this is the reality principle.

Neither the conscious nor the unconscious is in the best position to facilitate the creative process (Kubie, 1958). The conscious mind is much too logical and consequently too rigid to form new combinations of things and/or ideas. The unconscious, although illogical, is deceptive insofar as creativity is concerned for its very illogical character is a reflection of the *fluid* state in which its constituent elements exist. Fluidity, however, is constant change, and the very sameness of this state of affairs makes it as rigid as a condition that never changes. The critical area of the mind for creativity, therefore, is the preconscious—that area between the conscious and unconscious (Kubie, 1958).

The contents of the mind situated in the brain are "alive." They have electrical charges. While variations in specific mental content have not yet been associated with these electrical charges, variations in electroencephalographic (EEG) tracings (brain waves) have been found to accompany different mental states. The most recent work in this regard has been the study of the different dream states.

The material and data of the unconscious strive for expression. Avenues for such expression are not always readily available because some of that which strives for expression is quite threatening and anxiety provoking to the individual and his conscious mind. Other material that strives for expression also encounters obstructions because it would interfere with the individual's attention to and concentration on stimuli that impinge on him from the environment. If unconscious material spilled out, adjustment would be interfered with. Therefore, energy needs to be devoted to suppressing or repressing unconscious material. When this process continues for a period of time the individual becomes habituated to controlling himself, and potentially important resources in the unconscious are cut off or bound up so tightly that the individual is limited in the resources available to him for creativity. These resources consist both of cognitive and personality data, and because of the transactional relationships between the two a repression of one may result in the repression of the other. Thus, an individual's unconscious mind may contain necessary cognitive data for creative solution of a problem but he may not have access to this because he fears to allow a relaxation of internal controls for fear that anxiety-related material will also come to the fore.

Many of the techniques designed to stimulate creativity try to overcome some of the problems and obstructions just referred to. Psychotherapy tries by insight, understanding, and support to help the individual deal more effectively with unconscious material so that it is less threatening and can be used more constructively. There is then less need for excessive control and more unconscious data become available for use by the individual. Other techniques for stimulating creativity try to achieve the same goal by having the individual assume another role (as in role playing, considered in Chapter V) which gives him license to relax controls. In other methods (e.g., brainstorming, Chapter XIII) the individual is instructed not to prejudge or evaluate his thought processes and thus to give free rein to his associations.

There are also approaches that achieve the relaxation of controls through the use of "mind expanding" drugs. Using these stimulants both cognitive and personality effects are to be expected. After taking drugs, both internal (memories of previous events, current physiological reactions, current thoughts, etc.) and external stimuli could become more intense. Colors, for example, would be brighter and/or more saturated. Boundaries around objects and between objects could become less sharp and refined and more fluid so that they could run into each other and newer combinations could be formed. Sense of time and motoric behavior could be affected.

Some of these cognitive effects might be shortlived. Perceptions could be so fleeting that an individual is unable to retain them long enough to do much with them, to get them down on paper or canvas, or verbalize them to others. Or the drugs may have longer effects in motivating an individual to experience in the nondrugged condition that which he experienced while taking drugs. An individual who has once seen colors or shapes in some specific way might try very hard to see them that way once again and to utilize them in his work. Another individual for whom drugs resulted in a transcendental experience might become more abstract in his thought and work even without taking drugs.

On the personality side, drugs might be effective in developing the courage, self-assurance, and self-confidence necessary to carry out creative and novel ideas. Individuals might take a drink or drug to cope with their anxiety and bolster their courage so that they can "sell" an idea, or an individual might feel better when he confronts an empty canvas or blank sheet of paper in the typewriter. Alcohol, caffeine, and drugs can be used not only to cope with the anxiety and stress that occur before an individual embarks upon creative activity, but they may also serve as a means of loosening him up and relaxing him after creative work has been done. Creative work is usually carried out in isolation involving long hours of work. For some, working under these conditions involves much strain and discipline. For them, to work in an effective and organized manner, especially when there is also the possibility of an open schedule and freedom to do with one's time whatever one wants, can be very trying. The feeling engendered by such experiences may be dissipated by alcohol, drugs, etc.

The feeling of confidence and the air of assurance, if not bravado, may for some individuals be shortlived. These individuals return to their former selves after the effects of the drugs and stimulants wear off. Some of them may also feel guilty about the feelings and behavior experienced and/or expressed while on drugs.

Long-term positive effects might occur if, during or after taking drugs, the individual were to become aware of problems that inhibit or negatively affect his creative activity and were then to try to solve his problems. If, while taking the drug or stimulant, the individual also becomes aware for the first time of his potentialities and abilities in certain areas of creativity, he may then try to develop these further without the drugs or stimulants.

In addition to short- and long-term cognitive and personality effects, we must also consider the possibility of the cumulative effects that the use of the stimulants or drugs may have. We spoke previously of long-term effects. For many people the words "long-term" may connote a year or two, as distinguished from the short-term effects found during the course of an experiment or for a week, two weeks, or months thereafter. By cumulative effects we mean those effects that can occur after a decade or more of frequent or constant use, as in the case of the effects of smoking tobacco on the human lung. Another possible cumulative effect would be genetic effects that show up only in the next or later generations. Still another cumulative effect would be the possibility of individuals becoming increasingly dependent on the stimulants or drugs, a dependency which at its least may result in the individual's not being able to work when the stimulant is not available and at its worst may result in his refusing to work—the pleasure obtained from the stimulant, to enjoy passively what he experiences, would be more rewarding personally than going through the trials and tribulations of working to a final creative product.

These, then, are some of the concerns, thoughts, and hypotheses that serve as background introductory material to a consideration of the various means of altering consciousness and their possible effects on and relationships to creativity. We shall start with a description that in terms of their means of induction is closest to the natural state of affairs, move on to alcohol and caffeine, and conclude with the mind-expanding drugs.

RELAXATION-REFLECTION

On previous occasions during the course of this volume creative experiences were reported in which the individual came upon the creative idea after much work but while he was in a relaxed state. Other incidents were reported in which the individual was capable of such intense concentration and attention that what he was attending to had much more salience than it might have had under other conditions of attention. Also, such intense concentration was related to the creative person's concern with his inner thoughts and feelings, so that to all intents and purposes such a person was really oblivious to what was going on in the outside world.

Under usual conditions it is impossible for a researcher to be present while a creative individual has experiences like those just described. It is inconvenient;

there is no telling when the creative person will have these experiences; and creative persons usually do not like having anyone around while they are working or "creating."

Obviously, persons who are creative with a fair degree of consistency should experience the above states fairly regularly, and we might wonder if they can actually bring these states about "at will." That such is possible by at least one creative person is presented in a paper devoted to a study of Aldous Huxley (Erickson, 1969).

Huxley developed a procedure which he called "deep reflection." It was characterized by a state of physical relaxation, bowed head, closed eyes, a withdrawal from external stimulation but no loss of contact with reality. There was no amnesia but a complete involvement in what interested and concerned him at the moment. He could induce this state in himself in five minutes, and while in it ideas would occur to him freely and in an orderly manner, so that he could easily write them down.

Huxley had a special chair in which he carried out this technique of deep reflection. And while he was in this state he might respond to phone calls or other messages but would not recall doing so. When he was confronted with the fact that he had done so,

> He recalled merely that he had been working on a manuscript that after-noon, one that had been absorbing all of his interest. He explained that it was quite common for him to initiate a day's work by entering a state of Deep Reflection as a preliminary process of marshalling his thoughts and putting into order the thinking that would enter into his writing later that day [Erickson, 1969, p. 48].

Erickson explored with Huxley some of the characteristics of his deep reflection state. Two of these are repeated here. One has to do with the intensity of his experience while in the state of deep reflection, and the second involves responding to an external "significant stimulus" while concentrating on what-ever was going on in the state.

Huxley was asked to enter a state of deep reflection and to sense color. Upon awakening "His subjective report was simply that he had 'lost' himself in a 'sea of color,' of 'sensing,' 'feeling,' 'being' color, of being 'quite utterly involved in it with no identity of your own, you know' [p. 50]."

On one occasion, to test whether Huxley would indeed be aroused from his state of deep reflection only by a "significant stimulus," Erickson and Huxley agreed, before the latter entered this state, that he would be aroused from it when Erickson tapped on a chair three times in quick succession. While Huxley was in this state, Erickson tapped a table in various ways; he tapped once, paused, and then tapped twice in succession; he tapped four times in succession;

he tapped five times in succession; a chair was knocked over and four taps were given. It was only when the agreed-upon signal occurred that Huxley came out of his state. And when he was asked about his experiences during the course of this test, "He explained simply that they had been the same as previously with one exception, namely that several times he had a vague sensation that 'something was coming,' but he knew not what. He had no awareness of what had been done [p. 50]."

During the course of his work with Erickson, Huxley commented

I use Deep Reflection to summon my memories, to put into order all of my thinking, to explore the range, the extent of my mental existence, but I do it solely to let those realizations, the thinking, the understandings, the memories seep into the work I'm planning to do without my conscious awareness of them. Fascinating ... never stopped to realize that my deep reflection always preceded a period of intensive work wherein I was completely absorbed ... [p. 52].

To Erickson this state of deep reflection did not appear hypnotic in character.

Instead, it seemed to be a state of utterly intense concentration with much dissociation from external realities but with a full capacity to respond with varying degrees of readiness to externalities. It was entirely a personal experience serving apparently as an unrecognized foundation for conscious work activity enabling him to utilize freely all that had passed through his mind in Deep Reflection [p. 69].

Unfortunately, Erickson does not provide any instructions for how others might get into this state. We do know that Huxley always undertook his procedure in the same physical environment—the favorite chair mentioned earlier. So individuals are urged to find and to stay with the characteristics of the physical environment in which they can do their best work. It needs also to be stressed that Huxley no doubt practiced and learned this procedure over long periods of time. A person therefore should be patient in looking for and developing a satisfactory procedure that suits him. Finally, it should be pointed out that the state of deep reflection, or whatever state an individual selects, is apparently effective only before a period of hard work.

DREAMS

An altered state of consciousness that each of us experiences is the dream. Man has always concerned himself with the significance of dream content. It has been used for prophetic purposes, as in the biblical story of Joseph and his brothers, and it has been used to understand better the psychological characteristics of the dreamer, as in psychoanalytic therapy. More recently, eye movements and electroencephalographic recordings have enabled researchers to investigate the nature of the dream process under more controlled conditions. All of which, while yielding important information about the dream, also indicates that we still have much more to learn about it.

Insofar as creativity is concerned, the dream process, involving relationships between day residues and both latent and manifest dream content and such mechanisms as condensation and symbolization, contains many similarities to what presumably goes on in the creative process itself. Hence, the more that is learned about the dream process, the more enlightened we will be about the creative process.

Among the characteristics of the dream state is a relaxation of controls, a lessening of censorship, and a consequent combining of various elements and factors that may have seemed very disparate. Because of these characteristics it is not uncommon to suggest to someone who has been working unsuccessfully on a problem for a long time that he "sleep on it." The suggestion is that getting away from the problem for a while, plus the ensuing relaxation, might have salutory effects. Suggesting that he "sleep on it" also indicates the awareness in our folkways of the dream's problem-solving characteristics. An individual who, in his waking state, is unable, for one reason or another, to satisfy his drives or motives occasionally comes upon a solution to his problem in a dream.

Needless to say there is no documentation of the frequency with which individuals have used their dreams to solve problems and achieve creative solutions. But, some individuals do keep pads of paper or dictating machines alongside their beds so that they can note ideas that occur to them just before they fall asleep or just as they wake up. How frequently these have resulted in creative solutions is not known, but some have found this procedure helpful.

A recent study that sought to investigate the problem-solving characteristics of dreams was conducted by Snyder and reported in a paper by Parloff (1972). In this study a sequence of letters followed by two blanks was presented to the subjects. The sequence was O, T, T, F, F, ___, ___.* The subjects were told that once they knew the relationship between the letters, they would be able to fill in the two missing letters.

This problem was administered to subjects in the dream research program at the National Institutes of Health. EEG (brain waves or electroencephalographic patterns), respiration, and eye movement patterns were studied. On the basis of

---

*The letters stand for the sequence, One, Two, Three, Four and Five, and the two missing blanks for Six and Seven.

these data, one could test whether or not the subject completed a dream. When he had done so, the subject was awakened and asked where he stood with the problem. The study was conducted for several months, and although there was evidence that the subjects were dreaming, there was little evidence that they were dreaming about the problem.

It may be that the results of this study will be consistent with future research efforts in which there will also be little or no research evidence for the problem-solving character of dreams. Nevertheless, some very important items need to be kept in mind in evaluating this study. The potential effectiveness of dreams in problem solving may well depend on a variety of factors not possible to control or not well controlled in the study just described. Creative solutions in dreams may well be a function of the amount of time and effort an individual has devoted to trying to solve his problem, his motivation to do so, and the fact that the individual has selected his own problem and tried to solve it in his own way. It is quite evident that none of these obtained in the study cited.

Another factor probably associated with the potential value of the dream in problem solving is the amount of experience and training an individual may have in the effective utilization of his dream content. Individuals in psychoanalytic therapy learn that they recall more of their dreams and interpret them more fully during and at the end of the psychoanalytic process than at the beginning. Some of this is no doubt a function of the therapy but some is probably also attributable to what goes on in learning how to do so.

Some of us are unable to make good use of our dreams, let alone whatever value they may have for creative purposes, because we would rather repress or suppress its content. Also, our society has not institutionalized the use of dreams other than in such instances as psychotherapy. Not all societies behave in this manner. The Senoi in Malaya teach their people very different attitudes toward dreams. The Senoi are also taught how to use their dreams in daily life. Stewart (1969) who reports on this matter believes that we lose a good deal by not recognizing the social importance of dream content and by not making the interpreting of dream content part of our educational process.

Is it possible therefore that as we become better educated in the dymanics of the dream process we could have both waking and sleeping hours available to us for problem solving that could result in creative solutions?

ALCOHOL AND CAFFEINE

Numerous studies have been conducted on the effects of alcohol and caffeine on psychological processes. To summarize them all here is beyond the scope of this endeavor, because they do not concern themselves with creativity. We have limited ourselves to one study comparing the effects of caffeine and alcohol because its approach is typical of the studies in this area and, more importantly, because the investigator, Nash (1962), has something to say about creativity. A study by Roe of the liquor-drinking habits of a group of eminent painters will also be presented.

Nash (1962) studied the effects on 56 normal adult volunteer subjects (including 13 women), whose average age was 24, of the equivalent of two cups of coffee (caffeine alkaloid) and the equivalent of two and four martinis (a small and a large dose of ethyl alcohol) on several of their cognitive functions and affective states.

In general, allowing for variations in the effects of the drugs on the different psychological functions, Nash (1962, p. 45) says, "it is plain that *over-all intellectual efficiency was enhanced by caffeine, impaired by the heavy alcohol dose, and affected little (if at all) by the mild alcohol dose*" (italics Nash's). Guilford (1967) points to another possible generalization of Nash's findings that the recall or retrieval of information from memory storage is facilitated by caffeine.

Caffeine had two rather marked effects on specific cognitive functions. Individuals were more spontaneous in their associations; thought more quickly; had more associations; and were less likely to be at a loss for words or ideas. Their work on mechanized logical tasks was facilitated with caffeine. Guilford (1967) says the fact that the subjects were rarely at a loss for words would reflect the importance of the convergent production of semantic units (terms used in his classification system).

The second major effect of caffeine was that subjects were better able to organize and assimilate information that they heard. While both these effects might well be regarded as positive, to counterbalance these, Nash points out that previous studies in the literature revealed a decrease in hand steadiness as an effect of caffeine.

With regard to alcohol Nash's work indicated that a small dose, equal to two martinis, did facilitate somewhat the individual's associative process, and no other important effects were obtained. But the heavy dose of alcohol apparently disturbed visual acuity, perceptual closure, and the ability to coordinate eye movements. Thus, the heavy dose of alcohol interfered with the subject's ability to take in visual details quickly, to discriminate rapidly among the details, and to make sense out of meaningful visual patterns that had been disrupted. The capacity to recall impressions that were just memorized was also impaired. Apparently, there was also impairment of the subject's cerebellum, and horizontal writing extent was increased.

In evaluating the effects of alcohol and caffeine as well as the drugs to be considered later, we have to keep in mind that some of the effects reported may be direct effects of the alcohol, or caffeine, etc., but that some effects may also be indirect in the sense that a subject's behavior may be affected secondarily and additionally after he has observed the effects that could be directly traced to the alcohol or caffeine. This feedback can either reinforce an individual in his behavior, so that he persists in it, or influence him to compensate for the effects. Thus, should he observe that he is doing very poorly, the individual may exert himself all the more to make up for the deteriorating effects. Or if he does poorly, he may give up and do even less well. On the other hand, if he does well, he may be reinforced in his behavior, become more confident, and do even better.

It is therefore conceivable that some of the positive effects reported for caffeine stem from the subjects' feeling good about their increased performance and so doing even better. On the other hand, subjects who had alcohol might have done less well than they did if they had not compensated for how poorly they saw themselves doing.

Turning to the matter of creativity specifically, if the small dose of alcohol produced a freer flow of ideas, the question can be raised whether small amounts of alcohol can be said to promote creativity. Nash (1962, p. 109) says,

> This is a controversial question. Many authorities state categorically that alcohol has *no* beneficial effects on the intellect. But the present findings suggest that alcohol can induce a freer flow of ideas ... While creative solutions to difficult problems are unlikely to be conceived and fully elaborated under the influence of large quantities of alcohol, more moderate quantities of alcohol may shake one's everyday, unquestioned views, or otherwise render permeable the boundaries of previously fixed belief. Such altered ideas, even if not acted on at the time of intoxication, may provide a basis for later constructive action.

Unfortunately for our purposes, Nash did not study the quality of the ideas produced by his subjects to determine whether under certain conditions they were not only increased in quantity but also improved in quality. In Nash's study an increase in quantity of ideas was found.

There are no studies, to our knowledge, in which caffeine and alcohol are related to manifest creativity status—that is, no studies testing whether there is a relationship between how creative a person is in terms of acknowledged creativity and how much alcohol or caffeine he drinks. What is available is a study by Roe (1946d) of the relationships between drinking habits and some aspects of painting in a group of "eminent" painters living in the vicinity of New York City. To be included in this group an individual had to be eminent in painting and live in New York City. Roe found that none of these people abstained from drinking.

On the basis of her interviews and psychological tests, Roe reports the following.

1. The painters grew up in homes where their parents had liberal attitudes toward drinking. And they continued to live in a social environment which also had more liberal attitudes toward drinking than was true of the general population.

2. Several of the painters said they began to drink because it was prohibited, and they regarded this prohibition as an infringement upon their personal liberties.

3. Most of the painters avoided too much alcohol because they believed it interfered with their work. Nevertheless, they did consider it a means of relaxation. Roe relates this to the painters' intense devotion to their work and the amount of effort they put into it. Also, although these painters generally have a great deal of freedom (e.g., in how they will use their time), to make effective use of such freedom involves a strain and much personal discipline. Consequently, to seek a means of relaxation through drinking is understandable.

4. With one exception the painters said they did not regard alcohol as an effective stimulant to creative work and they did not use it as such. Some said they could and have drawn or painted while drunk but (with one exception) these pictures were a little distorted. As one moderate* drinker said,

> I just don't believe that drinking is a creative helper. You have to have a carefully careless kind of thing. You can't paint with someone holding your hand. You must paint with freedom but also within a discipline. I believe in discipline within a certain range—ordering the thing so you get the most out of the things you have to deal with. When drinking you get the careless touch all right, but not the careful part, and you must have discipline [pp. 429-430].

And an excessive drinker said,

> I can't paint at all when drinking. I think it isn't true the heavy drinkers just don't paint during the day. You can paint from a model or landscape while you are fairly tight because you have something to follow but when you work out of your head you have to be sober and well. I can sketch in a barroom but I can't remember making a drawing. If you are doing a job you have to be sober. You become freer while drinking, very dashing and expressive, and up to a certain point you can keep your technique. I stop at the point where I get out of control. I think it's more fatigue than anything

---

*Since none of Roe's painters abstained from drinking, she divided them into moderate, social, and excessive drinkers.

else; drinking on top of being very tired gets to you faster. I do a lot of night work [p. 432].

5. Roe noted a possible relationship between a painter's general style of painting or the type of painting he was currently involved in and the degree of drinking he indulged in. Indeed, this may be a "chicken-and-egg" problem since it is possible that the same type of person may become involved in drinking as may become involved in specific painting styles. It need not necessarily follow that drinking results in selecting these painting styles. Regardless of what is cause and effect, it is worth taking note of Roe's observations: Among the moderate alcohol users all the men were realists, none of them tried abstractions, none of them tried any of the painting "isms," none were extremists, and none of them changed his style appreciably throughout his career. Roe also regarded this group as "well adjusted" on the basis of the psychological measures used in the study.

The steady social drinkers had a wide range of styles, from academic to abstract and surrealist. Several of them were portraitists and one was a noted cartoonist, although the group also contained painters who never painted people. Some of the men in this group experimented with different styles at different times, but most of them have not changed their styles much since they began painting.

Men in the excessive drinker category tended generally toward greater shifts in their paintings. Fantasy was noted in the paintings of a number of steady social and excessive drinkers (but was not present in the moderate drinkers). As an interesting distinction, Roe points out that interest in the social scene by the moderate drinker-painter may be manifest in the individual; when this appears in the work of excessive drinkers it comes out as satiric comment.

6. For all six of the painters in the excessive drinker category (four of whom she regarded as compulsive drinkers and two of whom she regarded simply as excessive drinkers), alcohol had an anxiety-reducing function and this is one of the reasons they drank. But the causes of their anxieties were different. One extremely interesting observation that Roe makes about the life histories of her excessive drinkers, and which she did not observe in any of the steady social drinkers, was that the fathers of five of the six men in the excessive drinker category were artists or wished to be artists. Four of these men clearly succeeded beyond their fathers in purely creative work. In each of these instances, there was some inner lack of drive in the father. In commenting on these data Roe says,

If he [the son] identifies with the father to the extent of following his actual or wished-for vocation, and succeeds better than the father did, it is not inconceivable that the son should suffer under a heavy load of guilt, and it may be that this is particularly the case in a "creative" profession where the dynamics of father rivalry may extend to the deepest layers of the personality. Under such circumstances the presence of severe anxiety in these men is not surprising, and the fact that they have become excessive or compulsive drinkers is also not surprising, particularly where heavy drinking is a socially approved custom [p. 460].

7. As to the short-range effects of alcohol on Roe's subjects' paintings, we learn that

One artist thinks he paints more easily and better when drinking; 11 never paint when drinking; 7 say they may sketch or try to paint but the results are usually "cockeyed." Three mention the sedative effect of alcohol as its most desirable characteristic. Four say they can paint adequately with a hang-over and 3 say they cannot. Only 2 have noticed changes in color perception with drinking, and 1 thinks that even a single drink may affect his eye focus. It is clear that, with the one exception specified, all think that the short-term effects of drinking to any extent are deleterious to their work. None of them deliberately has recourse to it as a help in overcoming technical difficulties [Roe, 1946d, pp. 433-434].

8. As to the long-range effects, Roe reports: A few said that heavy drinking reduces their physical energy. A few said it had value for promoting new ideas, but even these said they could not use the ideas or that after the inception of the idea alcohol was disadvantageous. (One excessive drinker disagreed since he did find alcohol helpful in this regard.) Most of the artists felt that drinking did not stimulate them to new ideas for painting.

9. In terms of indirect aid there were reports of relaxation from intense periods of sustained concentration and tension. Some of the latter may stem from the work or from neurotic conflicts in other areas of living.

Nash's laboratory results and Roe's data from painters are remarkably consistent insofar as the negative effects of large doses of alcohol on the creative process are concerned. If anything, alcohol may serve the indirect purpose of providing some measure of relaxation from the stress of work, from the conflicts experienced in living, and from the strain of the self-discipline that is necessary to structure freedom effectively. Although some individuals may generate ideas under the influence of alcohol, and may try to work while intoxicated, the work they produce under these conditions differs from that which they normally produce. If alcohol were effective in producing the ideas, and this was not true in most instances, then it had a deleterious effect on the discipline and control necessary to bring it to fruition.

MIND-EXPANDING DRUGS

Another means of altering one's conscious state, of expanding one's mind and making it receptive to novel perceptions, that can be used alone or in combination with memories is mind-expanding drugs, to which access is now easier. As with other means of altering states of consciousness, one of the goals of using mind-expanding drugs is to achieve "deautomatization" to develop a new way of looking at the world. Since one is freed "from a stereotyped organization built up over the years . . . deautomatization is not a regression but rather an undoing of a pattern in order to permit a new and perhaps more advanced experience [Deikman, 1969, p. 217] ."

Several factors contributed to the use of drugs for the purposes of creativity. One was the similarity between the phenomena of the drug experience and the characteristics of the creative process. But there are other factors of a broader character on the larger social scene that also had influences in this regard. Among them we find in the field of contemporary American psychology the growth and development of what has been called a third force (Mogar, 1969). This third force is a relative newcomer to a field that has previously been occupied by two existing forces, psychoanalysis and behaviorism. This third force concerns itself with personal growth and the realization of human potential. It objects to the subordination of the individual to technological developments and the non- (or anti-) humanistic views of the world in which we live. It emphasizes realizing one's potential, and the individual's goal in this regard is to alter his current state of consciousness, to overcome functional fixedness, and to use flexibly previous experiences and thoughts and ideas stored in his memory in combination with immediate stimuli so that novel perceptions and affective experiences can be attained. Theories and findings of the third force could then be utilized as rationalization or reason for the taking of drugs to produce desired effects. Within this context, if the drugs could lead to extraordinary imaginings, then it is only a short jump to assume that rich imaginations and creativity are not exclusively limited to madmen or artists. Everyone can partake of them. Mogar (1969) in speaking of LSD points out that when conditions are right people can increase their experiences and still not diminish their capacity to deal with realistic situations.

The drugs to be considered in this section have been used to study thought processes, as well as psychoticlike behavior, because they induce the same effects as these processes and behavior and they have also been used for psychotherapy. To consider all of these would be beyond our scope, and the reader who is interested in these areas and wants one source for a good overview should consult the work edited by Tart (1969a) entitled *Altered States of Consciousness*.

There are several specific drugs that we shall consider in what follows, but before doing so it is perhaps wise to turn to some general comments about them as a group.

The drugs to be considered* have, as a group, been called "hallucinogens," psychotomimetic, and psychedelic. The term hallucinogen is a misnomer if it is accepted that hallucinations in their technically accurate sense occur. Technically hallucination is a perception in which the perceiver believes but for which there is no source in objective reality. In this sense hallucinations rarely occur with mind-expanding drugs (Barron *et al.*, 1964). The drugs are hallucinogenic to the extent that definite changes in the user's perceptions occur, but he can distinguish his visions from reality or he attributes them to the drugs.

The drugs have also been called "psychotomimetic" because the effects they produce are similar to what is observed in the psychoses. Finally, the drugs are also called psychedelic referring to the fact that in the perceptual changes that occur there are manifest characteristics of the imagination that were previously unsuspected (Barron *et al.*, 1964); if the emphasis is on mystical experience, religious conversion, or therapeutic change, then psychedelic, meaning "mind manifesting," is also used (Giarman & Freedman, 1965).

As indicated earlier, one reason that drugs have been considered as a means of stimulating creativity is that the phenomena they produce are similar to phenomena reported by creative individuals or in studies of the creative process.

Listing some of the similarities between hypnosis, psychedelic drugs, dream states, certain phases of the creative process, and sensory and dream deprivation experiences, Mogar (1969) says, "Reported communalities include significant alterations in perception, dominance of sensation and imagery over verbal-associative thinking, relaxed ego boundaries, changes in bodily feelings, and the suspension of conventional reality-orientation to space, time, and self [p. 385]."

Harman *et al.* (1969) present a table of characteristics of psychedelic experiences and divide them into two lists of ten each—those that support and those that hinder creativity. Among the former are increased access to unconscious data; increase in fluency of associations; more visual imagery and fantasy; relaxation and openness; more acute perception of sensory inputs; greater

---

*Mind-stimulating plants fall into two categories, those called "hallucinogens," psychotomimetic, and psychedelic, discussed above; and a second group that yield psychotropic drugs that usually calm or stimulate the nervous system (Grinspoon, 1971). Two plant narcotics that cause addiction and are physically dangerous are opium and cocaine (Grinspoon, 1971). The term "psychedelic" is attributed to Humphrey Osmond and was selected because it means "mind-manifesting." "Osmond felt that terms like 'hallucinogenic' or 'psychotomimetic,' commonly used to describe the effects of LSD-25, were misleading: they described drug effects obtained under special psychological circumstances which were *not* the most characteristic effects of the drug [Tart, 1969b, p. 321]."

empathy with external processes, objects, and people; greater aesthetic sensibility; greater "sense of truth" and capacity to "see through" false solutions; lessened tendency to censor oneself by premature negative judgment; and heightening of motivation.

Among the characteristics of the psychedelic experience that may hinder creativity Harman *et al.* (1969) list diminution in capacity for logical thought; reduction in capacity for direct concentration; lack of control over imaginary and conceptual sequences; anxiety and agitated states; constricted verbal and visual communication abilities; and greater attentiveness to internal problems of a personal nature. Since beauty is experienced, there is less motivation to achieve an aesthetic experience associated with the creative act. If a hallucination or illusion does occur, the individual may become absorbed in it. The psychedelic experience may be such that it becomes unimportant to find the best solution to a problem; motivation for "this-wordly" tasks may be lowered.

Before considering the specific drugs and their effects as related to creativity, it is well to point out some of the difficulties involved in doing research on drugs generally. (1) Researchers, as well as those using drugs, are aware that effects obtained with drugs are influenced by individual differences—the individuals' physiological and psychological states, their reasons for taking the drugs, and their fantasies about the drugs. (2) Another problem comprises the setting (including physical aspects of the setting) in which the drug is taken; the subject's relationship with the experimenter; and the experimenter's attitudes toward the subject, the drug, and the experiment. (3) Measuring devices adequate to study effects of the drugs are lacking. (4) A series of medical, legal, and social problems surround drugs and drug taking, making research in this area difficult. Grinspoon (1971), for example, reports that the Federal Bureau of Narcotics started a campaign to educate the American public about the dangers of marijuana and included in this campaign a statement that the taking of marijuana released hostility and incited people who were normal to become involved in crimes and in violence (Grinspoon, 1971). Reports on drug taking appear almost daily in the newspapers. Thus the May 18, 1971, issue of the *New York Times* (1971a) carried an item with a Washington, May 17, dateline reporting that two psychiatrists, going beyond a paper they published in the *Journal of the American Medical Association,* told the National Commission on Marijuana and Drug Abuse "that regular use of marijuana or hashish produced a toxic reaction in the central nervous system of adolescents, a reaction marked by distorted perception, listlessness and impaired judgment [*New York Times,* 1971a, p. 10] ." The same news item reported that these statements were challenged by other psychiatrists and drug abuse authorities, one of whom described the published paper as "full of inaccurate and inflammatory statements." In the same news item it was reported that John E. Ingersoll, head of the Bureau of Narcotics and Dangerous Drugs, "told the commission that he opposed legalizing marijuana."

But then, somewhat less than 3 months later, on August 8, 1971, a piece in the *New York Times* (1971b) headlined "More States Ease Marijuana Curbs" pointed out that there was a trend among many states to ease the penalty for possessing marijuana and "to shift the emphasis from punishing the occasional smoker to curbing the pusher [p. 39]." The harshest penalty in the United States (from 2 years to life imprisonment) was still to be found in Texas, but its legislature approved a methadone program and a law that allowed experimentation to determine the effects of marijuana. Nebraska, which had the most liberal law (a mandatory 7-day jail sentence for possession of less than a pound of marijuana), softened it still further by allowing the presiding judge to set a fine of $1 for the same violation. (5) Finally, another difficulty besetting research in this area is the lack of a theoretical model from which hypotheses can be drawn for further research.

In addition to the problems surrounding drug research, the quality of research available in this area leaves much to be desired. Grinspoon (1971), author of a very thorough scholarly work on marijuana, says that very careful investigations in this area became possible in the early 1940's as a result of the isolation and identification of tetrahydrocannabinol by R. Adams. Nevertheless, Grinspoon very critically points out that it is impossible to check the results of one study with the data from another since no two studies use the same amount of the same drug; they do not use comparable groups of subjects or representative subjects; and finally they do not measure the same behavior of the subjects with the same instruments or comparable ones.

Studies are not comparable, Grinspoon says, in terms of potency and substances used. In some studies an alcoholic fluid concentrate was used and in others finely chopped flowering tops and leaves of Indian hemp plants from around the world were used. Although the active ingredients of marijuana when smoked are not known, quantitatively speaking, they are not the same as when the drug is taken orally. Grinspoon points out that it is a principle of pharmacology that the effects of any substance vary with the route of administration (and with marijuana, inhalation, absorption through the digestive tract, or both have been used). Another principle is that the drug's effects are a function of the dosage used, but in the studies on marijuana the dosage is usually not defined.

Persons used as subjects in the different research programs are not comparable. They might be inmates of mental hospitals and prisons as well as bright, healthy, young students. Subjects are not randomly selected, and laboratory personnel administering the drug (and even the subjects themselves) may know whether the subjects are receiving a drug or a placebo.

Although any one or a combination of the difficulties or problems just mentioned would be quite damaging criticism of the research in this field, Grinspoon himself points out that although complete comparability between two studies does not exist, the specific findings of any one study can be evaluated in their own right provided all necessary data for such evaluation are noted. Furthermore, while there are individual differences in reactions to marijuana, Grinspoon (1971) says that certain responses or effects recur consistently and are so reported in the literature.

Several specific drugs will be considered in what follows, and it may be difficult to differentiate between them. Hence the following suggestions by Chein (1968) may be of help. Consider the case of the young man who is out on a date with his girl, says Chein. In this instance the young man may suffer from certain inhibitions, or the situation is such that it does not live up to his romantic expectations. What do heroin, alcohol, and marijuana have to offer him? If he takes heroin he will experience a "detachment from his troubles, a separation of the observing and active self from the self that is immersed in the activities of the world [p. 5]." He becomes like an observer immune from the stimuli and pressures around him, yet at the same time he has the illusion of being involved with the girl. If he imbibes in alcohol, he will become less inhibited, his impulses (e.g., homesexual or hostile) may come to the fore, he will be exposed to feelings of intimacy, and he may not be too clearly aware of the terror he is experiencing in the situation in which he finds himself. If he takes marijuana he then has "the promise of dressing a drab affair with an exotic aura that stems mainly from distortion of the sense of subjective time [p. 5]." The three drugs have one thing in common, according to Chein, they help "mask or mitigate" the "ineptitude" of the young man.

Before turning to the drugs themselves it is important to remember that there are three kinds of effects that might be investigated in a complete study of drugs: (1) effects directly due to the psychopharmacological properties of the drugs; (2) effects associated with drug behavior, such as effects following activities of procuring the drugs and administering them, all of which satisfy certain functions; and (3) effects associated with the meaning of drugs and drug misbehavior, such as masculinity, a hostility-expressing function, or a status-conferring function.

One of the concerns frequently raised about the mind-expanding drugs is whether they are addictive. To understand this matter properly it is necessary to start with a definition. Here again we draw on Grinspoon's work (1971) in which he discusses opium addiction as a paradigm for addiction and points out the following. (1) The addicted individual has undergone some sort of change such that if he gives up the drug for years he will become readdicted with a rather small number of doses. (2) When deprived of his drug, the addicted individual experiences withdrawal symptoms. (3) There is a strong craving for the drug which may be wholly or partly psychological or stimulated by the fear of withdrawal symptoms. Grinspoon points out that tolerance is regarded by some as an attribute of addiction. He himself does not regard tolerance this way because it also appears with nonaddictive drugs, such as LSD. Tolerance refers to the decreasing effects of a drug when the same dosage of the drug is repeated. To have the same effect or the same initial effect, the dosage of the drug must be increased.

According to Grinspoon (1971), the three criteria listed above exist or are likely to exist if the condition can be called one of true addiction. They are not in the case of marijuana; hence by this definition it is not addictive.

While marijuana is not addictive, in the terms just considered, some individuals point out that its use will result in psychological dependence and that this dependence will have a debilitating effect on the individual. Grinspoon (1971) argues that this kind of dependence may not be at all different from the kind of dependence an individual has on various of his possessions and that the critical question is whether this dependence results in any kind of individual and social harm. Insofar as creativity is concerned, then, if true addiction occurred, it is apparent that it would be quite debilitating. If psychological dependence occurred, its effects would be the same as those of any other dependence (which can, however, divert a good deal of energy from the creative process).

Marijuana

Marijuana is a crude preparation from the flowering tops, leaves, seeds, and stems of female plants of Indian hemp, which was named *Cannabis sativa* by Linnaeus in 1753. The intoxicating factors are found in the sticky resin produced by the tops of the plants, particularly the female plants. The male plants produce some resin but they are grown primarily for hemp. When the resin itself is used for smoking or eating, it is known as *hashish*. The potency of marijuana varies with the amount of resin; by the same token, the types of effects produced, physical symptoms, and distortions of perceptions and thought processes vary as a function of the quality of marijuana.

Marijuana is a mild drug and lacks the powerful consciousness-altering properties of mescaline, peyote, psilocybin, or LSD (Grinspoon, 1971). It shares the following characteristics with LSD: the wavelike aspect of the experience, distorted body perception, distorted spatial and temporal perception, depersonalization, increased sensitivity to sound, synesthesia, heightened suggestibility, a conviction that one is thinking more clearly and has a deeper awereness of many things. Both drugs can also result in anxiety and paranoid reactions (Grinspoon, 1971).

Grinspoon (1971) also reports the following *differences* between marijuana and LSD, peyote, mescaline, psilocybin, etc. The latter produce longer-lasting effects. Marijuana may produce sedation, whereas LSD and LSD-type drugs produce restlessness and wakefulness. Marijuana, unlike LSD, does not dilate pupils, nor significantly elevate blood pressure, reflexes, or body temperature. Marijuana is more likely to increase pulse rate. Tolerance develops for LSD but not for marijuana. The effects of marijuana can be controlled by how much the individual smokes (control is not as effective when the drug is taken orally). By limiting how much he will smoke the individual can control how "high" he will become.

Marijuana is classified by Tart (1969b) as a minor psychedelic drug. Tart regards the difference between minor and major psychedelic drugs as somewhat artificial because there is overlap in the effects produced by the various drugs. Nevertheless, despite the artificiality, he feels that the distinction is useful; hence we present it here. The minor psychedelic drugs have one or more of the following characteristics:

(1) the effects are felt to be under a fair amount of volitional control by most individuals who use the drugs; (2) the duration of action is typically short; (3) aftereffects are generally mild or nonexistent; (4) the effect of the drug experience is rarely strong enough to cause the user to actively proselytize and try to convince others that they *must* have this experience themselves; and (5) these characteristics make them highly suitable for research—because the Ss' welfare is not appreciably threatened in most cases, elaborate and costly schemes for protecting Ss are not as necessary as with the major psychedelics [Tart, 1969b, p. 321-322].

There are a variety of other characteristics of marijuana worth reporting from Grinspoon (1971). When marijuana is smoked, the effects are noticed within 10–30 minutes, and they last for from 1 to 3 or 4 hours. The physical effects have been reported as lasting up to 12 hours. The user falls asleep after about 6 hours. If the drug is taken orally, the effects occur more slowly, usually in about an hour or as long as 3 or 4 hours, and the effects are longer than when smoked. The last effect of the drug is sleep and, unlike the experience with alcohol, it is not followed by a hangover.

A person's initial reactions to marijuana are anxiety and agitation. These reactions are most likely if the individual is inexperienced with the drug or takes it in a nonsupportive environment, indicating the relation of the environment to the nature of the user's experiences. People sense a fear of death or vague distress. Experienced users, on the other hand, regard their anxiety as "happy anxiety." Thus, they learn to label their feelings and reactions differently than do the inexperienced users. Experienced users are also important in teaching inexperienced ones what to expect and how to regard their reactions.

After the initial anxiety state, the individual feels calm and relaxed and senses a state of euphoria or "high" which then alternates with a state of "dreamlike repose." There are feelings of slight dizziness and light-headedness; the body feels weightless; and walking is effortless. Sometimes the head and limbs feel heavy and there is an unpleasant pressure in the head. Users say their thoughts and associations are freer. Thought feels clearer and becomes more important to the individual. But attempts to speak about this or to get this across in writing frequently meet with failure (Grinspoon, 1971).

There is also a heightened sensitivity to external stimuli; attention shifts rapidly from one topic to another, and details that are usually overlooked now attract a good deal of attention (Grinspoon, 1971). Colors seem brighter and works of art that previously had no meaning now appear meaningful. Individuals also claim a better appreciation of music.

Under the effects of marijuana individuals report a distorted time sense with time being drawn out: 10 minutes, for example, feels like an hour. Paranoid thoughts do occur and some laugh at their thoughts whereas others find them confusing.

Physically the signs are few and it is difficult to make the diagnosis of being on the drug. There is no dilation of pupils and there may be slight tremors and ataxia. The conjunctivae are injected (Grinspoon, 1971). Dryness of mouth and throat and consequent thirst can occur. Occasionally the reaction is nausea, vomiting, and diarrhea, which generally occur when marijuana is taken orally rather than when it is smoked. There is generally a significant increase in pulse rate, and a striking symptom is hunger. This feeling of hunger is special. Under the effects of marijuana an individual can approach an ordinary meal as if it were a culinary delight and he were a gourmet (Grinspoon, 1971).

Marijuana has been used as an adjunct to psychotherapy, and Grinspoon (1971) in his review says that he is not impressed with the data available on marijuana used in psychotherapy nor is he impressed with its effects in his own experience working with patients high on pot. The patient may think he is communicating and gaining insight into himself and his problems but Grinspoon says he cannot empathize or go along with these reactions. What does happen is that the patient's associations are more fluid. For this reason Grinspoon suggests that it would be worthwhile to study further the value of marijuana as an adjunct to psychotherapy.

Marijuana does not tend to release aggressive behavior and may indeed inhibit it. Some reports indicate that marijuana does not "lead to" the use of addicting drugs. A study by the Issues Study Committee of the Bruin Humanist Forum (cited in Tart, 1969a) is quoted as saying, "Ninety-eight percent of heroin users started by smoking tobacco and drinking alcohol *first* [Mayor's Committee on Marihuana, 1944, p. 326]." In another report (Grossman *et al.,* 1971), we find that "as marijuana use increased, use of hashish, opium, speed, LSD, heroin, and barbiturates also increased significantly [p. 336]," but we do not know whether in this study the investigators had inquired with what (tobacco, alcohol, drugs) the subjects had first started.

There has been some research on the effects of marijuana on kinds of mental performance. Grinspoon (1971), who has reviewed this literature, says the results of these studies fall into two groups. One position is that marijuana has a detrimental effect on all aspects of mental functioning and the negative effects vary as a function of dosage. At the other extreme are those studies which indicate that marijuana has no, little, or even a positive effect on mental functioning or intellectual work.

An important factor in the discrepancy among the results is whether the subjects in the experiments were regular users of marijuana. In one study cited, users actually improved in their performance in one cognitive test and a test that measures coordination and attention. On a third test measuring sustained attention there was no improvement. In the same study nonusers also did not improve on this last test, but in the other, where the habitual users actually showed improvement, the performance of the nonusers was impaired. Apparently, the habitual user has the capacity to adapt or to compensate for any negative effects the drug may have.

In another study it was reported that only slight disturbances were found in attention, concentration, and comprehension. On the other hand, those whom Grinspoon (1971) calls the "authorities" (he includes the American Medical Association and physicians or officials connected with federal agencies) report such effects as impaired judgment and impaired memory, irritability, and confusion. The feeling of self-confidence that marijuana induces is regarded by them as questionable, as are the claims of clarity of conclusions, rapid flow of ideas, and the impression of brilliance. These sensations are said not to be deep enough to form an engram, so that they cannot easily be recalled. The LaGuardia Report (Mayor's Committee on Marihuana, 1944) said that marijuana has a temporary adverse effect on mental functioning. The amount of intellectual impairment, when it starts, and how long it lasts vary as a function of how much marijuana is taken. More complex intellectual functions are more severely affected than simpler ones. Negative effects are reflected in the falling off of both speed and accuracy of functions. Nonusers manifest greater impairment of intellectual functions and for longer periods than do users. But this same committee reported that taking marijuana did not, apparently, result in mental deterioration.

In introducing this section on drugs we said the goal was deautomatization— the overcoming of an automatic response to an object together with all previous associations that a person may have had with it. That deautomatization does apparently occur is well described by an Anonymous (1969) author who says that under the effects of marijuana a person thinks less of objects in terms of their functions or in terms of the memories they evoke. For example, as the author points out, when an individual sees a flower under usual circumstances he has an image of the flower and his memories of flowers—how they look and smell—are reinforced by the immediate experience. When under the effects of marijuana, the person has time and is not under pressure. He is not concerned with the uses or consequences of his experience. He is much more aware of the textures, colors, forms, smells, etc. of the flowers. He is much more involved with experience rather than the use of this experience. Under the effects of marijuana the individual does not impose upon an object what it ought or should be; rather he knows what the object is but is not limited to this one function or characteristic, but experiences the object in terms of a multiplicity of character- istics, functions, metaphors, and associations.

What has been described as "the first attempt to investigate marihuana in a formal double-blind experiment with the appropriate controls" and "the first attempt to collect basic clinical and psychological information on the drug by observing its effects on marihuana-naive human subjects in a neutral laboratory setting" was carried out by Weil and his co-workers (1968, p. 1235) with nine male volunteers who smoked tobacco cigarettes regularly but who had never tried marijuana and eight men who smoked marijuana regularly—every day or every other day. The ages of the men in both groups ranged from 21 to 26. The marijuana was prepared in cigarette form and two doses were used: a low dose of 0.5 gram and a high dose of 2.0 grams. For placebos, the chopped outer covering of mature stalks of male hemp plants, which does not contain any marijuana, was used. The order of placebo and the two doses of marijuana were varied systematically for naive subjects, whereas chronic users had only the large dose.

The experiment was conducted in a neutral setting. This is particularly important for comparing the effects of marijuana in this experiment with what is reported anecdotally and in sociological studies. From these reports we learn that the kind of reaction an individual has depends not only on the quality of the drug, but also on the person's attitude while taking it and the environmental (social as well as physical) setting in which it is taken. Since this study was conducted in a neutral setting, with no critical social interaction between subjects and experimenters or between subjects themselves, we do not know what the effects of the drug might be when the possibility for interaction is maximized—a situation that would be more comparable to real-life conditions in which the drug might be taken. It would be an error to assume, however, that the drug's effects depend completely on the nature of the interactions. The chronic users in this study reported that if the large dose of marijuana they had in this study were larger, it would be larger than they generally used. Chronic users also reported that they got "high" in the neutral setting in which they were studied. When asked to rate themselves on a 1-to-10 scale with 10 representing the highest they have ever been, most of them rated themselves 8 or 9, and all rated themselves between 7 and 10. The chronic users of marijuana did not appear to be affected by the fact that there was no social interaction.

Both physiological and psychological measures were obtained in this study. The physiological measures included those of heart rate, respiratory rate, pupil size, blood glucose level, and conjunctival vascular rate. The psychological battery consisted of (1) a Continuous Performance Test that lasted 5 minutes and was designed to measure a subject's capacity for sustained attention; (2) a Digit Symbol Substitution Test that took 90 seconds and measured cognitive functioning; (3) readministration of the Continuous Performance Test for 5 minutes with strobe light distraction. Previous research with certain drugs indicated that the drugs had an adverse effect on performance under these conditions. (4) Subjects were required to fill out a Self-Rating Mood Scale, which took 3 minutes. The results of this scale are not reported in the published paper but are to be reported at some later date. (5) Finally, subjects underwent a Pursuit Rotor Test that lasted 10 minutes and measured muscular coordination and attention.

Results of this study were as follows. Physiological effects were not very pronounced. Heart rate increased moderately, but respiratory rate and blood sugar levels did not change. Contrary to anecdotal reports, no change in pupil size was found in the short-term exposure to marijuana, but dilation of conjunctival blood vessels was found, which is consistent with reports that marijuana users develop red eyes.

In terms of subjective experiences, as was said previously, the chronic users reported they did get "high." Characteristics of this "high" were not reported. Naive subjects did not report having strong subjective experiences after smoking low or high doses of marijuana, and few of the effects they do report are like those usually reported by chronic users. They reported little euphoria, no distortion of visual or auditory perceptions, and no confusion; several did say that "things seemed to take longer [p. 1240]."

On the psychological tests, no effects were found on the subject's capacity for sustained attention as measured by the Continuous Performance Test, with or without strobe light distraction. On the Digit Symbol Substitution Test, which was used as a measure of cognitive functioning, there was a significant (at the .05 level) *decrement* in the performance of naive subjects following low and high doses at 15 and 90 minutes after smoking marijuana. The decrement was greater after a high dose than after a low dose 15 minutes after taking the drug, suggesting the possibility of a dose-response relationship. Although the behavior of the naive subjects on this test was impaired, the chronic users, who started with good initial performances, improved slightly after smoking the large dose. The investigators do not believe that the difference in performance can be accounted for by practice effects and regard the result as a trend.

Naive subjects also showed a decrement in muscular coordination and attention (on the Pursuit Rotor Test) that was significant at both 15 and 90 minutes, and there was a dose-level relationship. Chronic users started from good initial scores and improved slightly, but this slight improvement is regarded as due to practice effects.

In summary, then, naive subjects do show negative effects after smoking marijuana. Their performance is impaired on simple intellectual and psycho-motor tests and, in some cases, the decrement is related to the dose of marijuana they had. Chronic users did not show the same effects and, in some instances, their performance improved after smoking marijuana. Finally, the investigators report that in the neutral setting in which the study took place the effects reach their maximum within 30 minutes after inhalation; they start to diminish after 1 hour; and are completely gone after 3 hours.

A good summary of some of the effects of marijuana on consciousness is presented by an Anonymous (1969) author. He reports that the user's sensations are clearer and sharper. There is a change in his perception of time—time appears to go more slowly. There is a greater relaxation of controls, inhibitions, and suppressions so that he has a freer flow of associations, feelings, emotions, and thoughts and is not limited by his experiences with an object or the socially acceptable functions that have been associated with it. The kinds of effects that marijuana will have are, according to the Anonymous (1969) author, in accord with the conditions suggested by other writers—the kind of person who has taken the drug, the number of times he has taken it, how he has taken it, and the conditions under which it has been taken.

Several studies have concerned themselves with the relationship between marijuana and personality factors. A sampling of this work indicates the following. According to Grinspoon (1971), the 1944 New York City Mayor's Committee report on marijuana presents personality test data collected with the Downey Will and Temperament Scale. Grinspoon's summary of these data indicates that there are only minor personality changes. Those that do appear involve a lessening of drive, a decrease in aggressiveness, and a more positive attitude toward oneself. These variations apparently result from a lessening of control, greater relaxation, and more confidence in oneself. Most important, however, was the finding that only when large amounts of marijuana were taken was there evidence for changes in the individual's attitude to the world, his basic personality structure, or his general attitudes. And when such changes did occur they occurred in very few instances. If anything, marijuana tended to reinforce and accentuate a person's existing personality patterns—an introspective person became more introspective; a demonstrative person showed more emotion to others, etc.

Among the studies cited by Grinspoon (1971) are two that concerned themselves with the Rorschach ink-blot test. One study reported that subjects who were on marijuana attributed unusual importance to the details that made up the ink-blots. The number of interpretations of details was reduced and changed in character.

Another study using the Rorschach found a slight increase in number of responses, talking, and amount of extraneous comment. Subjects in this study allowed themselves much freedom in their interpretations of the blots, going off on tirades, playing with answers, repeating themselves, and at the same time trying to get their ideas across clearly. The effects on both user and nonuser were essentially the same, but although the number of individuals studied was quite small, the trend was for a greater disorganizing effect on the neophyte.

Grinspoon (1971) says that although marijuana does not provide motivation, an individual who has a "social marijuana high" and who has a specific task to perform will do it as well as if he were drug-free and in some instances will do it even more efficiently and accurately. Due to the social effects on marijuana, an individual's lack of motivation can be dispelled if he receives praise or encouragement for his work. When a nonuser takes marijuana, however, he may well be prevented from completing a task, and with increasing dosage of marijuana, impairment of function is also increasingly likely.

Brill *et al.* (1971) studied the relationship between personality factors and the extent of marijuana use in young college students. They studied four groups of students who differed from each other in frequency of use. At one extreme were those students who used marijuana less than once a month; at the other were those who used it almost every day. These students were compared with two control groups on four Minnesota Multiphasic Personality Inventory (MMPI) scales, a risk-taking propensity scale, a stimulus-seeking scale, nine specially constructed items, and a number of demographic variables. The results indicated that the more frequent use of marijuana was significantly related to higher scores on the stimulus-seeking scale and the MMPI psychopathic-deviate scale and to "true" responses to these items: A person should not be punished for breaking a law he thinks is unreasonable; and, As long as I can remember, I have had more emotional problems than other people.

In this study the regular use of marijuana was very significantly related to having tried other drugs. But there was no support for hypotheses about impaired relationships between parental identification, goal orientation, or the role of religion and frequency of drug use. The results did lend support to the notion that frequent marijuana users tend to be somewhat more hostile or rebellious and tend to seek stimulation. They more often report having long-standing emotional problems and less respect for the law than infrequent users. No significant differences were found between users and nonusers in measures of anxiety, defenses, and ego strength. As might be suspected, it is not known whether marijuana produces or is a consequence of these variations in personality factors.

McAree *et al.* (1969) found no differences in the MMPI profiles of students who used only marijuana and a population of normals. And Zinberg and Weil (1970) through clinical interviews found no clinical differences between users and nonusers. The latter study did find users to be more unconventional than nonusers. Norton (1968) found users preferred "aesthetic experiential values." Hogan *et al.* (1970), using the California Personality Inventory, found, according to Grossman *et al.* (1971, p. 335), "that users, as compared to nonusers, were more socially poised, open to experience, adventuresome, impulsive, rebellious, and pleasure seeking. Nonusers as compared to users were more rule abiding, responsible, inflexible, conventional, and narrow in interests. Nonusers were said to do slightly poorer academically." The general personality profiles, as Grossman *et al.* (1971, p. 335) point out, "are all indicative of the creative personality," but the same description could be used for the nonauthoritarian personality.

The study reported by Grossman *et al.* (1971) used these tests: the Personal Opinion Survey, a creativity measure; and the California F Scale, a measure of authoritarianism. They were administered to three groups varying in terms of frequency of marijuana use and a group of nonusers. Also used were a short form of the Taylor Manifest Anxiety Scale, the Marlowe-Crowne Social Desirability Scale, and a test for acquiescent response set. All of these were administered in group test administration to 316 college students at all levels of undergraduate work. Also obtained from the students were such data as age, sex, birth order, grade-point average, religion, and previous drug experience. The subjects rated themselves as nonusers; experimental users (tried marijuana a couple of times but do not expect to do so again); occasional users (three times a month or less); regular users (at least once a week).

The results indicated that with increased usage there was evidence of increased creativity and adventuresomeness and a decrease in the tendency to be authoritarian toward others or to be submissive to authority. There were no differences between users and nonusers in anxiety, and no difference in acquiescent response set. Nonusers did tend to score higher on social desirability but this trend was not significant. The biological data indicated that males were heavier users than females and that Jews were heavier users than Protestants or Catholics. Nonusers and regular users tended to be older than experimental or occasional users. Birth order and grade-point average did not yield significant differences between users and nonusers. Finally, as reported earlier, as marijuana use increased, so did the use of other drugs. These authors are aware that the students they studied at the two small eastern universities involved may not be representative of the general college population. Nevertheless, they point out that limiting our knowledge of the effects of marijuana to the uses made of it by persons with character defects or other psychological problems is quite inadequate. To understand well the effects of marijuana we need to study them with different groups of persons. This study with college students associated marijuana use with what some would regard as valued characteristics, such as creativity. The authors of this study also believe that "openness to experience" may be at the root of their findings. A person who is open to experience becomes creative, tries marijuana, and then experiences more than others who are less open to experiences (Grossman *et al.*, 1971).

Turning more specifically to the relationship between the use of marijuana and creativity, we again start with Grinspoon's work (1971), in which he cites a series of reports on the effects of drugs on writers who have written about their experiences—e.g., Gautier, Taylor, Baudelaire, and Ludlow. These reports he believes are invalid for an assessment of the moderate use of marijuana. Usually these writers took large doses of hashish mixed with other drugs. Furthermore, Grinspoon indicates that many literary accounts were written by people who read De Quincey's account of his unusual experience with opium as he described it in 1822 in his *Confessions of An English Opium Eater.*

About De Quincey's experience Grinspoon has an interesting comment. He says that De Quincey took his opium in the form of laudanum, a mixture of opium and alcohol. Some said it was not the opium but the alcohol that affected De Quincey, but according to Grinspoon, De Quincey's experiences did not result from the laudanum alone but from the interaction of laudanum and the characteristics of De Quincey's mind. It is probably well to heed Grinspoon's cautionary suggestion in reading literary reports of the effects of drugs: their effects are unpredictable when taken by individuals whose imaginative and creative minds are unpredictable.

On the contemporary scene, Allen Ginsberg, the poet, has written poetry while under the effects of marijuana and, as Grinspoon (1971) says, his ability does not appear to have been markedly affected in any negative way.

Grinspoon also cites other anecdotal material, this time from a biography of a "Mr. X," that he describes as "approximately accurate." Mr. X is a professor at a top-ranking American university and head of an organization producing important new research results. In the early 1940s he was recognized as a leader in his specialty.

In talking about his personal insights when on a marijuana high, Mr. X says there is a "myth" that the insights the user thinks he has under the effects of marijuana do not stand up under critical appraisal. He does not agree with this, believing that they are real insights, but the problem is how to present them to "another self" which is "down." Considering the effects of marijuana when he has used it to gain insights into problems in his own scientific field, this Mr. X reports that it works to some extent. He believes that he can make use of apparently inconsistent data, for he can make use of "bizarrre" possibilities that he might not have come up with without the drug.

From the field of poetry, Grinspoon (1971) cites another instance wherein marijuana had a positive effect on the creative work. This is a report of marijuana's effect on time perception as found in Michaux's *Conveyor Belt in Motion.* First, Michaux presents the poem as he wrote it under the effects of marijuana; then he presents his analysis of the poem. And in this analysis Michaux reports how each instant of time is separate, unique, and isolated from all other time instants.

Another area in which the relationship between marijuana and creativity has been studied is that of jazz music. Grinspoon cites Bloomquist (1968), who says that it is a myth that jazz musicians play much better when they are on marijuana. He says that they may be less inhibited and that they tire less easily but there it ends. In support of his conclusions Bloomquist cites a work by Aldrich (1944) in which he used the Seashore test of musical aptitude to study the effects of marijuana on musical ability and found that musical ability was not enhanced. This study was criticized by Winick (1960) because nonmusicians were used and their musical ability was tested with a test in which the pitch of two sounds was compared. Winick points out that this combination of person sample (nonmusicians) and this test of musical ability are not comparable to the creativity and expertise involved in a jazz musician playing in a group in which each member of the group reinforces the other and in which improvisation plays a very important role.

In his own work Winick (1960) did establish a relationship between jazz playing and the use of marijuana. But he did not find a positive relationship between the use of marijuana and the degree of professional success that the individual enjoys according to his peers. Winick (1960) reports that on the basis of data collected from a sample of 409 jazz musicians only a few, about 2% felt that altered time perception occurred as a result of marijuana use and could yield new space-time relationships for the musician which might enable him to play better or worse on certain occasions. When the musician's sense of space and time was expanded as a result of marijuana it seemed to retard the music's beat. Thus, the musician could feel that he had more time, more leisure, and less pressure to express his musical ideas. This might or might not be an advantage, depending on the music and the musician. Winick (1960) did find that a significant number of jazz musicians did use marijuana *after* playing emotionally demanding music after several hours. It helped them relax and thus served the same function as did alcohol in the study reported by Roe (1946d) for painters.

In concluding this section on the relationship between marijuana and creativity the best that can be said is that there are bipolar attitudes and evidence is variable. On the one hand, as Grinspoon (1971) reported, there is evidence that marijuana is valuable for the artist. In addition to some such evidence cited previously, he quotes Burroughs (1964) who wrote that, while he was working on *Naked Lunch*, marijuana helped him gain access to ideas that might not have otherwise been available to him.

On the other hand, there is the contrary report of the American Medical Association (1967), also cited by Grinspoon (1971), in which it was said that although artists may claim positive effects from taking marijuana, there is no evidence for such effects. Thus, although creative individuals, writers, artists, etc. claim they have been helped by marijuana, according to Grinspoon, medical experts, psychological experts, and would-be experts insist that whatever claims are made for creative effects from marijuana are only "illusory."

Morphine and the Amphetamines

Compared to a placebo, Evans and Smith (1964) found that subjects taking morphine showed significant improvement in the Perceptual Speed Test, the Logical Reasoning Test, and the Apparatus Test, which in Guilford's terms are tests of evaluation and implications. According to these researchers, these results were obtained because morphine decreased distractions. In the same study amphetamines facilitated performance on the Apparatus Test, Spatial Orientation Test, and Consequences Test. Neither drug helped with tests of Alternate Uses or of Anagrams, or with tests of ideational fluency, expressional fluency, associational fluency, or general reasoning. Most of these tests fall into what Guilford has called the divergent-production area and have to do with fluency and flexibility. Tests of divergent thinking, it will be recalled, are those which are expected to be related to creativity; thus, on the basis of this experiment amphetamines do not have a positive effect on factors presumably related to creativity.

LSD

To introduce this discussion, we present some general comments about hallucinogenic drugs (which include mescaline and psilocybin as well as LSD), and here we draw heavily on an article by Barron and his associates written for *Scientific American* (Barron *et al.*, 1964).

The objective and subjective effects produced by taking LSD, mescaline, or psilocybin orally are extensive, and the subjective effects of these drugs, as stated in the introduction to this section, depend on the potency of the drug itself, the subject's personality structure and current mood, and the social and psychological context in which the individual takes the drugs. This context involves what taking the drug means to the individual and how he feels about the motives of the persons who gave it to him.

Changes in visual perception are frequently reported after taking the drugs. With the eyes open, colors appear quite vivid and they glow; there is a reality to the space between objects; and the world looks beautiful. When the eyes are closed, among other things the subject can "see" all kinds of imaginary people and animals, and they appear in all kinds of fanciful places. The kinds of perceptual experiences the individual has are not always pleasant. The blackness that he can see is associated with "gloom and isolation [p. 9]." He may also sense his own body as if it were decaying and becoming distorted. People may appear as if dead, and if they are moving, as puppets. The disturbing effects of these perceptions can last even after the drug effects have worn off.

In addition to visual alterations, there are also alterations in the auditory sphere. The subject may hear voices talking in languages he does not know, or he may hear make-believe people talking to each other. Odors and tastes may be hallucinated. Synesthesia may also be experienced; thus, a sound or combination of sounds may stimulate the perception of a variety of colors. There are also changes in the experience of time—it may be slow, pleasant, or very boring. He may feel as if he exists beyond time.

The sense of oneself and one's body image is also affected. The subject may lose the sense of his own physical boundaries, of where he begins and ends, or of his inside and outside.

Insofar as sexual behavior is concerned, the hallucinogens are "neither anaphrodisiacs nor aphrodisiacs [p. 9]." Among the physiological effects associated with the drugs are dilation of the pupils, constriction of the peripheral blood vessels, raising of systolic blood pressure, and increasing excitability of spinal reflexes. Turning to psychological functions, it has been found that, when the individual is under the effect of a hallucinogenic drug, he does not do well in reasoning ability, memory, arithmetic, spelling, and drawing. Apparently, the decrease in performance level is not so much a function of lowered ability as a refusal to co-operate. Psychological dependence on the drugs can occur, as well as physiological tolerance, so that to get the same effects on two different occasions the user may have to increase the dosage the second time. However, if he does not take the drugs for a few days, then the physiological tolerance does wear off. Furthermore, the drugs are not addicting in the sense that no physiological dependence is established and increasing amounts of the drug are not required to maintain adequate physiological functioning.

The drugs vary in their potency. Thus, for an average adult male to show the clinical effects of a drug, he would have to take 500 milligrams of mescaline, 20 milligrams of psilocybin, or .1 milligram of LSD. There are also differences among the hallucinogens in the time of onset of effects and the duration of intoxication. The effects of mescaline when taken orally appear in two or three hours and last for 12 hours or more. The effects of LSD appear in less than an hour, last for 8 or 9 hours, and insomnia associated with it can last up to 16 hours. The effects of psilocybin start within 20 to 30 minutes, and its full effects appear in 5 hours. All of the effects are for the drugs when taken orally; if taken intravenously the effects appear within minutes.

In 1964 when Barron and his associates wrote their report they commented that there was relatively little incidence of serious negative reactions to such drugs as LSD, but such reactions were on the increase, possibly because more people were taking the drugs in environments that "emphasize sensation-seeking or even deliberate social delinquency [p. 11]." The character of the setting in which the drug is taken is important. However, the authors admit that it is difficult to characterize the environment in which adverse reactions will not occur. Hallucinogens have been used for therapeutic purposes but the studies in which they have been used did not use control groups, and hence it is impossible to evaluate their effectiveness.

While we shall be considering the relationships between the hallucinogenic drugs and creativity later on, we present here a study that includes data on several of these drugs, although the majority of the respondents may have been involved primarily with LSD. In 1967 Krippner (1969) surveyed 91 artists who said they had had one or more "psychedelic experiences." In this group of 91 "were an award-winning film-maker, a Guggenheim Fellow in poetry, and a recipient of Ford, Fulbright, and Rockefeller study grants in painting [Krippner, 1969, p. 287]." Of these respondents, 81% felt that the term "psychedelic artist" could be applied to them—in that their works showed the effects of a psychedelic experience that might or might not have been chemically induced. Ninety-six percent said that they had taken psychedelic drugs and 4% said no. LSD was mentioned by more of the respondents than any other drug; it was followed by marijuana, DMT, peyote, mescaline, morning glory seed, psilocybin, hashish, DET, and yage. Other kinds of drugs were also used. When asked if their psychedelic experiences, whether chemically induced or not, were generally pleasant, 91% gave an unqualified yes and 5% a qualified yes. When asked, "How have your psychedelic experiences influenced your art?" none of the respondents replied that their work suffered from the experience; some said that their friends might disagree with this evaluation; and 3% said their psychedelic experiences had not influenced their work. The others cited effects on content, technique, and approach (Krippner, 1969).

With regard to the content of their work, 70% of the respondents felt that the psychedelic experience had affected it, the most frequently cited effect being the use of eidetic imagery. Noticeable improvements in technique, specifically a greater ability to use color, was claimed by 54%. A change in their creative approach was attributed to the psychedelics by 52% of the respondents. Some felt they were less superficial and capable of deep experience. Some said that they experienced a turning point in their lives when they had their first psychedelic experience.

Krippner said that he rarely found artists among the casualties of illegal drug usage, probably because an artist, to create, must in some real sense be separate from his culture. Krippner also suggests that conceivably the person who will be least disturbed by his psychedelic experiences achieves most benefits from them.

With these general statements in mind, we consider more specifically LSD's effects on and relationships to several psychological functions, and creativity in particular. LSD (d-lysergic acid diethylamide) is derived from ergot, a fungus that grows on rye and wheat and was discovered in 1943. As regards psychological functions, it is said to result in greater plasticity of perception. Impaired concentration and negative effects on arithmetic performance have been reported (Levine *et al.*, 1955; Jarvik *et al.*, 1955a, 1955c), as have alterations in brain waves (Rodin and Luby, 1966; Werre, 1964; Horovitz *et al.*, 1965; Pfeiffer *et al.*, 1965). Whether these effects are simply transient or longer lasting (Milman, 1967) and the conditions under which they appear still are not clear. Levine *et al.* (1955) report a decrease of 11 points in IQ (from a mean of 122.9 to 111.8) after taking the drug. With the exception of the Digit Span and Object Assembly tests, significant losses were reported for all subtests on the Wechsler–Bellevue test of intelligence. Poorer concentration, greater distractibility, disturbances of conceptual abilities, and difficulty with shifting set presumably accounted for the results, and not anxiety (Guilford, 1967).

Significant losses in visual memory and one auditory memory test were reported by Jarvik *et al.* (1955b). In another study significant losses were obtained in tests of addition and subtraction with the material presented visually. Significant losses were also found in spatial orientation (Jarvik *et al.*, 1955c). Since these negative effects represent interferences with vision, it is conceivable that they resulted from hallucinations.

Goldberger (1966) compared the effects on cognitive behavior of a 100-microgram dose of LSD, 8 hours of isolation, and placebo on groups of normal males. The cognitive test battery was made up of (1) the Digit Span subtest from the Wechsler-Bellevue Intelligence Scale; (2) an adaptation of long and short passages from the Iowa Silent Reading Test (as a measure of comprehension); (3) two tests in which the subject had to keep several things in mind while he dealt with overlearned material—one test involved numbers, the other rhymes; (4) a word-naming test in which the subject was asked to name as many words as he could think of that contain a specified number of letters; (5) a counting task (subjects were directed to count backward by sevens from a certain number); (6) a simple rhyming test in which the subject was asked to give as many rhymes as possible for a given word. (7) To tap the subjects' abilities to deal with relatively unstructured material, they were asked to make up stories to two Thematic Apperception Test cards that were described orally. (8) Another test designed to test subjects' capacities to deal with unstructured cognitive material was one in which they were asked for a 10-minute monologue on a given topic—capitalism, racial segregation, etc.

The results of this study indicated that the 8-hour isolation and placebo conditions did not differ significantly from each other on any of the effects they produced on any of the cognitive measures. The data obtained from those subjects who took LSD were significantly different from the data obtained from subjects in both the isolation and placebo conditions, with the exception of the short-passage conprehension measure and Digit Span. On Digit Span the LSD results differed significantly only from those obtained with the isolation group, but those obtained under placebo conditions did approach significance.

In all instances where significant differences were obtained they indicated that impairment of cognitive functions occurred in the LSD condition.

Only the TAT stories and not the monologue were analyzed by the time the paper was published. These data also indicated that the LSD condition differed significantly from the isolation and placebo conditions, whereas the latter two did not differ from each other. Those who took LSD adhered less to the instructions and gave "shorter stories and greater amount of non-contributory verbiage as compared to both placebo and isolation [Goldberger, 1966, p. 7]." Although the monologue data were not completely analyzed, Goldberger reports that the trends in these data reveal "a similar pattern of findings" to that found with the TAT.

Turning to some of the specific effects of LSD on creativity, we find a report in Krippner (1969) after Rosenfeld and Farrell (1966) that LSD enabled Navy Captain John Busby in 1966 to work out a solution for a problem in pattern recognition. Trent (1966) reports that the psychiatrist Osmond and the architect Kyo Izumi used LSD when designing a mental hospital. Izumi took LSD while visiting traditionally designed mental hospitals in an effort to learn what effects such institutions have on persons in altered states of consciousness. The long corridors and the pale colors usually found in mental hospitals were experienced as frightening and bizarre. As a result, Osmond and Izumi developed a decentralized series of unimposing buildings with pleasant colors and no corridors.

Krippner (1969) reports receiving a personal communication from R. E. L. Masters in which mention was made of an attempt to study time distortion. A psychologist was given LSD and told that unexpectedly he would be given 1 minute of clock time to create a story. He was told that this minute would be all that he would need for his story. At the end of the minute, the subject did indeed produce a short story with a character description and description of other material.

Turning to the use of LSD for therapeutic purposes, it is reported that LSD helped actor Cary Grant (Gaines, 1963) and blues singer Ronnie Gilbert (Krippner, 1969).

Berlin *et al.* (1955), according to Krippner (1969), studied the effects of mescaline and LSD on four graphic artists of national prominence and among the results reported were: lowered efficiency in four of the artists in their finger-tapping ability and in their muscular steadiness. Nevertheless, all were able to complete their paintings. Art critics who evaluated the works they completed under the effects of the drug said they were better, of " 'greater aesthetic value,' " than their usual work, "lines were bolder . . . [and] use of color was more vivid [Krippner, 1969, p. 284]." Technically, however, some impairment was noticeable.

In 1964 McGlothlin, Cohen, and McGlothlin (1967) first conducted a pilot study with 15 subjects and then a larger study with 72 subjects. In the pilot study a variety of tests, including creativity, anxiety, and attitude tests, were administered before 200 micrograms of LSD were taken and one week after. No significant changes were observed in the creativity tests but changes were noted on the anxiety and attitude tests.

For the larger group of 72 subjects the experimenters conducted a more intensive study. A large battery of psychological tests was administered to these subjects and the tests were followed by three doses 200 micrograms of LSD. After the third dose of LSD, the tests were readministered at 2-week and 6-month intervals. The test battery included three art scales, a measure of artistic performance, a test of imaginativeness, a test of originality, four tests of divergent thinking, and a test of remote associations.

The investigators started with one experimental group and two control groups. The experimental group received 200 micrograms of LSD per test session, and then one control group received 25 micrograms of LSD per test session; the second control group received 20 milligrams of an amphetamine per test session. At the end of the study no differences were found between the two control groups; hence their data were combined for purposes of comparing them with the experimental group.

The results of this study indicated that after 6 months 62% of the subjects said that they had a greater appreciation of music. There was an increase in the number of records bought, time spent in museums, and number of musical events attended in the postdrug period. Scores on the art test, however, did not show an increase. These results suggest that greater aesthetic appreciation and increased participation in aesthetic activities were not associated with increased aesthetic sensitivity or performance.

On the 6-month questionnaire 25% of experimental subjects felt that LSD had resulted in enhanced creativity. The creativity tests, however, showed no evidence to support this report. One of the tests (called the Draw-A-Person test) is generally used for clinical purposes, in which context it is regarded as a measure of body image, but it may also be used with youngsters as a measure of intelligence. After 6 months, the subjects showed a significant decrease in their scores on this test. The authors regarded the test as a measure of artistic ability and thus would regard this datum as indicating a decrease in artistic ability (Krippner, 1969). However, if the test were regarded as measuring body image with this group of subjects, then it would indicate that more serious effects had taken place, effects that would indicate some greater possible psychological disorganization.

Other results of this study on the relationships between personality variables and the taking of LSD were rather interesting. Krippner (1969) tells us that the results indicated that individuals with personalities that emphasized structure and control did not like the experience of taking LSD and if they did they had minimal responses. The kinds of persons who had strong reactions were individuals who were spontaneous and who preferred an unstructured life. These persons were also individuals who were turned inward but not socially introverted. They had high scores on measures of aesthetic sensitivity and imaginativeness. They were not very conforming, competitive, or aggressive.

Thirty male subjects volunteered for a study by Zegans, Pollard, and Brown (1967) in an investigation devoted to understanding the effects of LSD upon creativity test scores. Before the LSD was administered, the subjects took the first battery of tests, after which certain physiological measures (blood pressure and pulse rate) were taken. For 19 subjects there was a dose of LSD equal to 0.5 microgram per kilogram of body weight added to their water; the remaining 11 subjects did not receive LSD. Subjects then relaxed in a lounge for 2 hours, and immediately prior to the second half of the test battery, consisting of alternate forms of the tests, the physiological measures were repeated. The test battery included a measure of remote associations, a test of originality of word associations, a test of ability to create an original design from tiles, a free association test, and a measure involving the ability to perceive hidden figures in a complicated line drawing. To determine speed of visual perception a tachistoscopic stimulation task was used (Krippner, 1969).

When the data were analyzed, the subjects who had taken LSD did significantly better than the control subjects on originality of word associations. While the other results also favored the LSD group, none of the other results were statistically significant. Therefore, the investigators in this study believe that giving LSD to a group of unselected individuals is not likely to increase their creativity. Further analysis of the data indicated that while LSD subjects did better on the word association test than the control subjects did, they did most poorly on tests of attention. Therefore, it appears that the drug may be effective in facilitating the appearance and development of unique ideas in those persons who were seriously involved in a specific problem (Krippner, 1969).

To conclude this section we present Krippner's (1969) report of Cohen's (1964) summary of the research data available on the relationships between creativity and the psychedelics. It is an open question, says Cohen, whether LSD does or does not increase creativity. People who take LSD do report, however, a subjective feeling of being creative. The critical word is, of course, *subjective*. For although subjective feelings may be precursors of significant behavioral changes and contributions, they may also be, and remain, feelings that have no realistic or objective base.

Another important point, and it may also be said for each of the drugs, is that there are a series of studies, as we have seen, where the drugs' effects are studied in terms of the changes that take place on psychological tests which measure variables that have been found to be associated with creativity. For example, ego strength has been found to be related to creativity; should an increase in ego strength or an increase in the number of associations be observed after use of LSD, some researchers would claim that the drug results in an increase in creativity. Obviously, more caution is needed here. That a single variable is related to creativity does not necessarily mean that it is related *only* to creativity (it may also be related to mental health, psychological well-being, etc.). Moreover, that a variable is related to creativity does not mean that creativity depends solely on it. The variable may be a contributing factor when it operates in concert with other variables. To demonstrate drug effects on only one variable tells us nothing about the other necessary and sufficient conditions operating in some pattern or gestalt which also have to be affected before it can be said that creativity is affected.

Mescaline

Mescaline, the active ingredient of peyote, comes from cactus. Indian groups take it during their religious ceremonies (Slotkin, 1952). Aldous Huxley described his experiences after taking 0.4 grams of mescaline dissolved in half a glass of water. His *Doors of Perception* (Huxley, 1963) contains an excellent description of several visual and psychological effects that could make taking of this drug seem attractive to some readers.

Spatial relationships, as we generally understand them, did not have the same significance after Huxley had taken mescaline as before the experience. Not that he could not find his way around objects in space, but he was not concerned with the positions that objects occupied in space, and dimensions were inconsequential. His "mind was primarily concerned . . . with being and meaning [Huxley, 1963, p. 20]." He would regard the furniture in his room not from a utilitarian point of view "but as the pure aesthete whose concern is only with forms and their relationships within the field of vision or the picture space [Huxley, 1963, pp. 21,22]." The books on his shelves had "brighter colors, a profounder significance. Red books, like rubies; emerald books; books bound in white jade; books of agate; of aquamarine, of yellow topaz; lapis lazuli books whose color was so intense, so intrinsically meaningful, that they seemed to be on the point of leaving the shelves to thrust themselves more insistently on my attention [Huxley, 1963, p. 19]." What he had seen gave him a greater appreciation of how creative painters may have seen the world around them. A table, chair, and desk composed themselves in a manner reminiscent of a painting by Braque or Juan Gris. A chair "was obviously the same in essence as the chair" Van Gogh had seen when he painted "The Chair." In looking at the folds in his own trousers, he was struck by "a labyrinth of endlessly significant complexity" reminiscent of Judith's pleated bodice and wind-blown skirts in Botticelli's painting, "Judith."

> But in Judith's skirt [Huxley says] I could clearly see what, if I had been a painter of genius, I might have made of my old gray flannels. Not much, heaven knows, in comparison with the reality; but enough to delight generation after generation of beholders, enough to make them understand at least a little of the true significance of what, in our pathetic imbecility, we call "mere things" and disregard in favor of television [Huxley, 1963, p. 34].

Just as there were changes in spatial relationships and in the intensity of color perception, so there was change in the time dimension. Things seemed to take longer, and time was taken up "without knowing, even without wishing to know, what it was that confronted me [Huxley, 1963, p. 53]." Time was also taken up with contemplation. He did not take up his time with unimportant or uninteresting things; he had better things to think about. There was no desire to do anything or to take an active role in anything.

This change in the "will," this change in ego function occurs in the context of another change in ego function which, although not frightening to Huxley, might be to other people. He experienced a dissociation between mental and bodily ego functions. He did not experience integration between body and mind. When he walked (and he could get around well), it was as if his legs were taking off by themselves. "It was odd, of course, to feel that 'I' was not the same as these arms and legs 'out there,' as this wholly objective trunk and neck and even head. It was odd; but one soon got used to it [Huxley, 1963, p. 52]."

Another potential source of anxiety was associated with the awesome quality of the experience itself. In describing his experiences as he walked about his garden, Huxley (1963) says, "It was inexpressibly wonderful, wonderful to the point, almost, of being terrifying. And suddenly I had an inkling of what it must feel like to be mad [p. 54]." At another point he says, "The fear, as I analyze it in retrospect, was of being overwhelmed, of disintegrating under a pressure of reality greater than a mind, accustomed to living most of the time in a cozy world of symbols, could possibly bear [p. 55]." Huxley discounts the frequency or intensity of these anxiety-producing experiences and points to the interaction between the drug and the physical and psychological condition of the individual taking it. "Most takers of mescalin experience only the heavenly part of schizophrenia. The drug brings hell and purgatory only to those who have had a recent case of jaundice, or who suffer from periodical depressions or a chronic anxiety [Huxley, 1963, p. 54]."

If, like the other drugs of remotely comparable power, mescaline were notoriously toxic, the taking of it would be enough, in itself, to cause anxiety. But the reasonably healthy person knows in advance that, as far as he is concerned, mescaline is completely innocuous, that its effects will pass off after 8 or 10 hours, leaving no hangover and consequently no craving for a renewal of the dose. Furthermore, mescaline does not result in fights, crimes, or accidents. The individual enjoys being by himself.

Summarizing Huxley's experience, then, we learn that mescaline does not have a negative effect on memory or thought; visual impressions are intensified; concern with spatial relationships is decreased, as is interest in time; volition suffers a change in which the individual does not see any reason for doing anything; and there are experiences which some individuals, depending on their physical and psychological condition, could find anxiety-producing. But, all told, Huxley's experience was a positive one. "For myself," he says, "on this memorable May morning, I could only be grateful for an experience which had shown me, more clearly than I have ever seen it before, the true nature of the challenge and the completely liberating response [Huxley, 1963, p. 42] ."

Turning to some laboratory research on the relationship between mescaline and creativity, we find a rather interesting study by Harman *et al.* (1969). This study is unique in that it utilizes to advantage what others find confounding or use to qualify the nature of their results. Specifically, studies of the effects of psychedelic drugs on creativity, or, for that matter, any other psychological functions, have suggested or indicated that the results are affected by the subject's psychological state at the time of the experiment, his belief in the drug's effectiveness, his trust in the experimenter, and his comfort in the experimental situation. While others state these effects in some way to qualify their results, Harman *et al.* (1969) start with this knowledge and use it by building up their subjects' expectations about a positive effect; they then test whether these positive effects do in fact occur. They tried to develop a way to make conditions as functional as possible to help produce whatever positive effects might occur.

Three major questions were asked in this research: Is creativity enhanced by the psychedelic experience and, if so, what is the evidence for it? Second, are the effects of the drug on creativity such that they are manifest, palpable, feasible as judged by the criteria utilized by industry and science? Third, are there long-term personality changes that involve or appear to be like self-actualization and increased creativity?

The subjects in this experiment were 27 men representing a variety of professional fields, including engineering, physics, mathematics, architecture, furniture designing, and commercial art. Most had had no prior experience with psychedelic drugs. They worked in academic institutions or industry and were selected for participation because it was felt that they satisfied these criteria: their jobs required creative problem-solving ability; the subject was determined by psychiatric examination to be psychologically normal and existed with stable life circumstances; and the subject was motivated "to discover, verify, and apply problem-solutions within his industrial or academic work capacity [Harman *et al.*, 1969, p. 449] ."

Prior to any experimental work each subject was asked to select one or more problems in his field that required a creative solution. Several subjects selected problems that they had worked on unsuccessfully for weeks or months. Then they had a psychiatric interview to assess their stability, and through this they also met and became acquainted with the psychiatrist who was going to supervise the psychedelic session. In addition to the psychiatric interview, each subject had at least one other interview with the investigating staff and at least one meeting was held of those subjects who were going to work together as a group so that they could get acquainted with each other before the experimental work began.

The interviews and meetings just described had the purpose of allaying the subjects' anxieties and of facilitating the establishment of trust and rapport among the participants. The meetings also provided an opportunity to tell the subjects about the structure of the sessions. Consequently, the subjects built up positive expectations about what they were about to experience; they understood what was going to take place; and they were prepared for any problems that might come up.

In the experimental session the subjects were given 200 milligrams of mescaline. This was followed by about 3 hours spent listening to music through stereo headphones. During this time the subjects were asked to relax, not to do any analytic thinking, to accept their experience, and to try not to control their environment.

Then the subjects were encouraged to talk with each other, they had some snacks, and about an hour was also spent on psychological testing. At the presession alternate forms of these tests had been administered. When the testing was completed the subjects spent 3 or 4 hours working by themselves on the solution to the problem selected. In the afternoon the subjects shared their experiences and sometimes worked together on a problem one of the participants brought in. By 6 P.M. they were driven home and supplied with a sedative to be taken if they had difficulty sleeping. The authors report that in many instances the subjects stayed up till the early hours of the morning working out insights they had discovered during the day.

To assess the effects of the drug the investigators used the following procedures. Psychological tests were administered before and during the experimental session; several days after the experimental session, each subject was asked to submit a report (subjective) of his experience. A questionnaire relating to various aspects of the experience was also administered to the subjects. Some 3-6 weeks after the experimental session, the subjects were interviewed by the psychiatrist and given another questionnaire about the effects of the drug on postsession creative ability and whether or not the solutions obtained met the criteria used in industry and science—that is, on the men's jobs.

These data were then utilized in three ways: change scores on the psychological tests (involving tests of creativity) were studied; the subjective reports were analyzed to discern the components of the creative process and the special features of creative solutions; and third, a determination was made as to whether the theories or solutions arrived at did or did not meet the pragmatic criteria of science and industry.

Considering the effects in terms of change scores on the psychological tests, we find that fluency of ideas under pressure did increase significantly but flexibility or range of solutions did not. These results were obtained with the

Purdue Creativity Test (Lawshe & Harris, 1960). On the Miller Object Visualization Test (Miller, 1955) the improvement in performance was significantly increased. For this test the subjects were asked to envision a two-dimensional outline figure folded into a solid. Behaviorally, the authors report that about half the subjects said the form of the test taken during the drug session was easier to do and they took about half the time they used in the nondrug session. About one-third of the subjects became more visual in the way they worked on the problem, and each of them improved his score on the second test.

The third test used was the Witkin Embedded Figures Test (Witkin *et al.,* 1971) in which, when presented with a complex figure, the subject has to pick out a simpler geometrical figure in it. Changes in performance here were quite significant indicating that the subjects improved in their capacity to recognize patterns, they were not affected so much by visual distractions, and, although an attempt was made to confuse them with colors and forms, they were able to do quite well with visual memory. As defined by Witkin *et al.* (1962) it could be said that the subjects shifted from "field dependence" to "field independence." In other words, instead of being dependent on the external environment for the stimuli for their responses, the locus for the stimuli was within the individual himself.

Following the experimental session the subjects were presented with a questionnaire containing nine characteristics relevant to creative problem solving and they were asked to rate each of these on a 5-point scale ranging from marked impairment to marked enhancement. The results here indicated that visual, verbal, and intuitive skills were at least temporarily improved.

The subjects' subjective reports were also studied to determine the extent to which they contained features of the creative process and creative solutions. Among the positive evidence Harman and his co-workers (1969) found were the following: lessened inhibition and anxiety; increased visual imagery and fantasy; improved concentration; more evidence for empathy with objects and people; a greater desire to achieve elegant solutions; unconscious material becoming more readily available.

Another interesting factor involved in the assessment procedures in this study, it will be recalled, was the investigation of the extent to which the theories and solutions arrived at were indeed pragmatically valued as judged by the academic institutions and industrial organizations in which the subjects worked. The variety of solutions arrived at do appear to have pragmatic value; some indeed were accepted by clients. Included among the solutions were: a new way of designing a vibratory microtome; a design for a building to be used for commercial purposes; experiments devised to measure solar properties; a design for a linear electron accelerator beam-steering device; improvement of a magnetic tape recorder; a model for a chair design; a design for a letterhead; a mathematical theorem for circuitry; a furniture line design; a useful new conceptual model of a photon; and a design for a private home (Harman *et al.,* 1969).

A total of 44 problems were worked on. On one of these there was no more work 1 month or more after the problem-solving session; on 20, new avenues for further investigation were opened; for one, a go-ahead was given for a developmental model to be tested; working models of two solutions had been completed; six solutions were accepted for construction or production; for 10 problems, there were partial solutions that were undergoing further development or were being applied in practice; and for four problems, no solutions were obtained.

Two weeks after the psychedelic session there was a short follow-up session, and the subjects reported a continuation of the positive changes they experienced during the drug state. The positive effects presumably lasted over the two-week follow-up period.

The results of the Harman *et al.* (1969) study are quite intriguing. Future research might well be oriented to replicating this study, as well as to extending it to include larger numbers of persons who represent different fields of endeavor. Care must be taken, however, to make certain that their unique methodology is replicated; and if this methodology is really found to have been the critical factor in attaining the results, then it would be a matter of great significance. It would set the groundwork and structure for proper utilization of mescaline or the other mind-expanding drugs for purposes of achieving the benefits to creativity that their use might facilitate.

Psilocybin

Huxley's experiences with mescaline, which were discussed earlier, are very similar to those described by Barron's (1961) subjects who took psilocybin, the synthesized form of the ingredients of the "divine mushroom." In pellet form, psilocybin, Barron reports, was taken by 30 persons—writers, painters, and scientists—individuals of "high degree of originality." A few days later, Barron asked them to report their experiences, and excerpts from the three anecdotal reports in the paper follow. There is no report as yet of the systematic evaluations of the data.

One of the subjects, a painter, reported several effects similar to those reported by Huxley. " 'I was most strongly aware of the effects of the drug upon my vision, not in the sense of optics,' he says, 'but in the disarrangement of the total process of seeing, including clarity, emphasis, perceptual focus, and spatial disarrangement. I do not believe that I underwent any hallucinatory visions . . .' [Barron, 1961, p. 14] ." More important for our purposes is not that these experiences support Huxley's but what this artist has to say about his work.

I attempted some drawings but found that my attention span was unusually brief. . . . Interruptions, such as the model moving, did not really bother me and on at least one occasion a considerable period passed between the beginning of the drawing and its completion . . . I simply picked it up and finished it when the occasion presented itself. I seemed to become unusually aware of detail and also unusually unconscious of the relationship of the various parts of the drawing. My concern was with the immediate and what had preceded a particular mark on the page or what was to follow seemed quite irrelevant. When I finished a drawing I tossed it aside with a feeling of totally abandoning it and not really caring very much. In spite of the uniqueness of the experience of drawing while influenced by the drug and my general "what the hell" attitude toward my work I cannot help but feel that the drawings were, in some ways, good ones. I was far better able to isolate the significant and ignore that which, for the moment, seemed insignificant and I was able to become much more intensely involved with the drawing and with the object drawn. I felt as though I were grimacing as I drew. I have seldom known such absolute identification with what I was doing—nor such a lack of concern with it afterward [Barron, 1961, p. 14].

A second painter confirmed what Huxley had said about the effects of the drug on the will and on action. "Several times," this painter says, "I was bothered by H. to do some drawings which seemed to be an invasion of privacy to even think of doing such a thing at that time. What was happening was more important to me than trying to record it. Being was the important thing and I didn't want anything to interfere with being [Barron, 1961, p. 16]."

But this negative effect on action is apparently short-lived. In the experience of this painter,

the most important part of what has happened to me since the experiment is that I seem to be able to get a good deal more work done. Sunday afternoon I did about six hours work in two hours time. I did not worry about what I was doing—I just did it. Three or four times I wanted a particular color pencil or a triangle and would go directly to it, lift up three or four pieces of paper and pull it out. Never thought of where it was—just knew I wanted it and picked it up. This of course amazed me but I just relied on it—found things immediately. My wife was a little annoyed at me on Sunday afternoon because I was so happy, but I would not be dissuaded. . . . When painting it generally takes me an hour and a half to two hours to really get into the painting and three or four hours to really hit a peak. Tuesday I hit a peak in less than a half hour. The esthetic experience was more intense than I have experienced before—so much so that several times I had to leave the studio and finally decided that I was unable to cope with it and left for good! I now have this under control to some extent but I am delighted that I can just jump into it without the long build-up and I certainly hope it continues [Barron, 1961, p. 16].

Barron (1961) summarizes the effects of psilocybin that stem from these positive experiences as resulting in the plasticity of visual perceptions; light and color appear as "though they were alive"; the world appears more beautiful and less composed of harsh outlines; the momentary event increases in importance and there is a consequent identification with objects perceived and an unconcern with them once they have passed out of sight. On the negative side, Barron points out that 10-15% of the experiences are either unpleasant or "hellish." A hellish experience is one that is

marked by a sense of impossible distance between people, of intrinsic solitariness of the self, of vast blackness and desolation throughout the universe, of the puniness of the shelters we have made for ourselves, the feebleness of fire against the outer coldness and blackness, and an anticipation of death or a feeling that one is already dead. The light and glow with which persons are suffused, or which come visibly from them, in the heavenly experience, seems to go out when the experience is one of hell. Or the person may seem to move in dark ugly red shadows, or to be a sickly green. Smiles become meaningless grimaces, and all human actions seem mere puppetry. In the hellish experience, time may seem impossibly slow and painful, and determinism is experienced as being a prison [Barron, 1961, p. 18].

A composer, whose anecdotal report is the third statement in Barron's (1961) paper, had one of these hellish experiences. His report contains the following statements:

A world of silent cathedrals
Thousands of magnificent cities
Measureless galleries . . . .
I am dead. That which men see in me is not me. They too are dead.
Inconceivably, the dead themselves are alive. What has happened is this: a world of the dead, dead men and dead things, but they think, eat, reproduce and die. The dead themselves die. . . .
The painters . . . above all, the sculptors and architects . . . are right. We musicians are involved in a childish game, which neither transcends nor even dies, so insignificant is it. The world is deaf and our struggles useless . . . deaf ashes, old, impenetrable and thick. . . .

Tomorrow I return to my old cellophane jacket, but first I must plunge into the dark waters of sleep, the waters from which rise, still wet, millions of dead men yawning [Barron, 1961, pp. 17-18].

Thus, the effect of psilocybin, like that of all other drugs and even of the nondrug techniques to be discussed later, depends on the physical and psychological state of the individual as well as on the drug. Whom the drugs affect in a positive way and whom they will affect adversely is still not clear. Furthermore, the anecdotal reports just cited were obtained from creative persons, some of whom were able to utilize their experiences and perceptions in constructive ways when the experience was not "hellish." They had the training and experience and talent to utilize their experiences. Would taking the drug stimulate creativity in individuals who had not yet manifested it? Will drugs by themselves make potential creativity manifest?

SUMMARY

It is apparent that there is no "little pill" available which when ingested will increase one's creativity. The studies presented indicate that caffeine has a stimulating effect on certain psychological functions, some of which may be related to creativity. Alcohol, when too much of it is taken, can have a debilitating effect on various psychological functions as well as on creativity. Indirectly it may have positive effects for creativity in that it may provide the creative individual with relief from tensions and an opportunity for relaxation after time and effort has been spent in the creative process.

The evidence relating to the psychedelic or mind-expanding drugs is quite varied. Limiting ourselves to the subjective reports of individuals who have taken these drugs, we find data indicating that these people believe their creativity has improved, and that they attribute this improvement to the drugs. Then, too, there are studies which indicate that certain psychological variables or functions which are related to creativity are sometimes positively affected by the drugs, and in some cases negatively. From such results, some investigators assume, without providing any direct test, that because the drugs affect a specific variable or function they also affect the total process. This would still have to be demonstrated. Obviously, the most potentially persuasive evidence comes from studies which were concerned with specific effects of the drugs on concrete, manifest, and demonstrable aspects of creativity. Here the evidence is wanting, with one important exception. A study by Harman *et al.* (1969) utilizes a methodology that might be very critical in providing data from which better arguments could be developed for or against the use of the drugs for purposes of creativity. Research on drugs indicated that the subject's attitude, his psychological state, the dosage, the subject's relationship with the experimenter, and the atmosphere in which the experiment is conducted all, in one way or another, affect the results obtained. Rather than becoming distressed at this phenomenon, Harman and his colleagues utilized all of this information. They established good relations with their subjects, created a friendly atmosphere, achieved rapport, and made a definite effort to diminish and allay the subjects' anxieties and to facilitate their effort to control obtrusive psychological thoughts and visions that might have negative effects. Having established these conditions with their subjects, who were men working in academic and industrial situations where they were counted on to provide creative solutions to the problems assigned them, Harman and his colleagues came up with positive effects in their study, where mescaline was the drug. This study was exploratory and requires further replication with larger groups representing more working areas in an effort to determine whether the first positive results obtained can indeed be obtained with other persons, and if so, whether the results can be even further extended. Indeed, this study is cited specifically for replication since the results were so promising. Replication is obviously desirable for the other studies as well.

The introductory remarks to this chapter pointed out that there are many problems in conducting psychological research on the effectiveness of the mind-expanding drugs. Not least is the problem that drugs and their effects are part of our cultural environment. Consequently, if good research is to continue in this area, it must be done by responsible and ethical investigators who can enlist the support of society and the government in obtaining the necessary opportunities and conditions, as well as good-quality drugs, to carry out their work.

Moreover, should the drugs be found to be effective for facilitating and stimulating the creative process, some form of control would be needed for their use. Obviously, this would be essential so that possible ill effects would be limited and corrected as early as possible. With such efforts and controls available, it would then become possible to conduct research in a very significant area without fear of interference or reprisals. In concluding this chapter we join Barron *et al.* (1964) in raising the question of whether it will be possible to discover means to make effective use of the drugs and to control their negative effects. It appears that "The hallucinogens, like so many other discoveries of man, are analogous to fire, which can burn down the house or spread through the house life-sustaining warmth. Purpose, planning and constructive control make the difference [p. 11]."

PART IV

PROCEDURES FOR AFFECTING THE INDIVIDUAL STAGES OF THE CREATIVE PROCESS

The stages of the creative process overlap. They do not follow each other in an orderly manner. By the same token, the characteristics that may facilitate the process at one stage may be equally helpful at another. It is only for heuristic purposes that we have separated the stages in a systematic manner, and in this section have tried to separate the techniques that will be most helpful at specific points. But, again, the reader should make his selections in terms of his needs.

According to our conception of the creative process, we have considered it as consisting of three stages—hypothesis formation, hypothesis testing, and the communication of results. We do believe that the creative process does start with the formation of ideas or orientations about the work that is to follow. The question is, how far back do we go? How many of the antecedent conditions and circumstances should we consider? Should we consider all of the developmental factors in the life history of an individual that preceded the beginning of his creative work? Indeed, they probably were significant influences on the creative work. But we have to stop somewhere and, while we still believe that the process itself starts with hypothesis formation, it is necessary to consider what some might like to call an earlier phase—the individual's education, or what we have called the *preparatory stage*. Our primary reason for discussing this stage is that a great deal of work has been carried out in the educational area that concerns itself specifically with trying to stimulate creativity in the individual while he is in the school system. The fact that these techniques may prove of value to educators, students, parents, and all concerned with the educational process, and that these techniques might be viewed as examples of procedures that can be used for stimulating creativity and are relevant to the different areas in life that set the stage for the creative process that is to follow, are other reasons for presenting them here. Therefore, after considering the preparatory phase with its characteristics and some of the procedures for setting a fertile groundwork that may help future creativity, we shall turn to the techniques that can help hypothesis formation, hypothesis testing, and the communication of results.

Chapter **VIII**

Affecting the Preparatory (Educational) Stage

In one sense, the creative process begins with hypothesis formation—going through the process of arriving at or having ideas from which the creative person selects what should later be tested, pursued, altered, and developed into that one idea which solves the problem, or results in the completed canvas, novel, or invention. But in another sense, the creative process starts earlier. It starts with all the prior "inputs"—the knowledge and experiences that the individual has had that could affect his attitude toward creativity and innovation as well as his receptivity to ideas that involve the creative solution. As Pasteur suggested, the creative idea occurs to the prepared mind.

Individuals vary in their life histories and experiences. Some are predisposed positively to data and information they can use creatively, whereas others when presented with the same information are blind to its potential creative use. From the variety of such experiences we have selected the early educational experience for further discussion. Youngsters at this level are still sufficiently malleable so that much can be done to facilitate the manifestation of their creativity or to stimulate it if necessary.

Although the educational system even at the elementary level can affect the child in a multiplicity of ways insofar as creativity is concerned, we shall limit ourselves to two areas—the pupil's social relationships with his teachers and classmates, and some aspects of the teaching situation.

SOCIAL RELATIONSHIPS IN THE SCHOOL ENVIRONMENT

A youngster's relationships with teachers and classmates constitute a core of experiences that can affect his attitude toward himself, creativity, and future social relationships involved in the creative process. Interactions with teachers affect not only *what* is learned and *how well* it is learned but later attitudes to superiors or authority figures who play significant roles in the creative process. Interactions with classmates may reinforce an individual's creative behavior or be inhibitory and constricting. Classmates are frequently a child's playmates in and out of school, so that acceptance by them can loom large in his life, but probably no larger than do relationships with colleagues at the adult level. Experiences with his classmates are significant precursors of a person's future relationships with colleagues, peers, and co-workers. The social context in which creativity occurs at the adult level is affected by much that occurs earlier in life.

Teachers

For pupils, teachers are potential models to be emulated or rejected. What teachers do, their values, the rewards and punishments they mete out, the classroom atmosphere they create, may affect the child's attitudes, values, and behavior and foster or inhibit the development of his potential. These statements characterize not only the general effects teachers may have but also the very direct effect they may have on a pupil's creativity. Consequently, it is important to know how teachers regard, reward, or punish behaviors related to the current or future creativity of their pupils.*

Torrance (1962a) studied how teachers regard creative students by looking at the characteristics that differentiated highly creative students from less creative ones. The definition of creativity he used in this study was how well the students scored on Guilford-like tests. The highest-scoring (most creative) boy and girl in each of 23 classes in grades one through six in three elementary schools were so selected. They were matched with other pupils (lower-scoring and less creative ones) on sex, IQ, race, school grade (and therefore teacher), as well as age.

Studying his groups, Torrance (1962a) learned that the highly creative pupil's work was "characterized by humor, playfulness, relative lack of rigidity and relaxation [p. 78]." Their ideas were " 'off the beaten track, outside the mold' [p. 78]." What kinds of reputations did these highly creative pupils have? That

---

*A good deal of the research on creativity at the elementary and high school levels has been conducted by Torrance. Much of what is presented in this chapter is based on his work, and additional material can be found in his books that are listed in the bibliography.

they (and this was especially true of the boys) had "silly, wild, or naughty [p. 8]" ideas. Thus, although the pupils scored high on tests of creativity, and therefore we might assume they had good ideas, those ideas they verbalized in class were denigrated. While it may well be that the test scores and verbalized ideas are not correlated, it is implicit in Torrance's presentation that they are and that the good ideas are denigrated.

To learn the kinds of behaviors actually rewarded or punished by teachers, Torrance *et al.* (1964) undertook a cross-national study involving Germany, India, Greece, the Phillipines, and the United States and found that there was undue punishment "of the child who is courageous in his convictions, the intuitive thinker, the good guesser, the emotionally sensitive person, the individual who regresses occasionally, the visionary person, and the one who is unwilling to accept something on mere say so without examination of evidence [p. 24]." This is the kind of behavior that would be associated with creativity.

If this is the kind of behavior that is punished, what kind of behavior is rewarded? In the study just reported Torrance *et al.* (1964) found that "being courteous, doing work on time, being obedient, being popular and well-liked, and being willing to accept the judgments of authorities [p. 24]," are rewarded. All of this sounds very much like the picture of the highly socialized, conforming, and noncreative child.

These results obtained at the elementary school level are consistent with those obtained by Torrance in 1959-1960 in a survey of high school science teachers in Minnesota. These teachers were asked about their teaching objectives, which were then classified as belonging to one of the five mental operations that are so central to Guilford's work: *cognitive,* in which the individual becomes aware of and familiar with material; *memory,* in which the emphasis is on memorizing and thorough learning; *convergent,* in which the emphasis is on the correct attitude and correct solution; *divergent,* independent, creative thinking; *evaluative,* critical thinking, judging, and assessing.

The data in Torrance's survey indicated that, by far, the teachers' objectives fell into the cognitive area (70.7%), the next largest percentage fell into the convergent thinking area (18.7%), and the smallest percentage (1.7%) in the divergent thinking area. The divergent thinking area is regarded as most related to creativity, yet the smallest percentage of objectives for these high school social science teachers fell into this area.

That which teachers reward is reflected in day-to-day teaching activities, but it is most concretely and most importantly, and with some degree of finality, manifest in the grades teachers give their students. Drews (1961) gathered data in this area by studying the grades teachers gave three types of gifted high school students: the studious achievers, the social leaders, and the creative intellectuals. Teachers, it was found, gave poorest grades to the creative intellectuals. However, when the groups were tested with a test of a wide range of information, the creative intellectuals performed better than either of the other two groups. Apparently the studious group reviewed and prepared for the examinations, as usual. The social leaders, who read very little, studied what they knew would yield a "pay-off." The creative intellectuals read college texts and books on philosophy or some other book which, on the face of it, had no immediate relevance to the examination.

At the college level, with engineering students, it was found that teachers' judgments of their students' creativity correlated with the students' achievements in these courses (MacKinnon, 1961b). In other words, these teachers were saying that they rewarded creativity. It would have been interesting if there had been an opportunity to relate the predictive value of the grades in this study to future creativity. Since the data in this study indicate that teachers believe they are grading creativity, it is reasonable to ask whether their concept of creativity is the same as that held by others outside of school. A follow-up of this group could provide an answer to this question. Other studies of the predictive value of grades lack data on earlier teachers' judgments of creativity.

At the moment available research indicates that grades are not good predictors of students' future creativity. MacKinnon (1960, 1961b), for example, found college grades do not predict well the future creativity of the architects and research scientists he studied. Indirect corroboration for this finding comes from a study by Holland (1960) in which it was found that the personality characteristics of students who get high grades are different from those that characterize creative adults.

We see then that the cumulative research evidence indicates that teachers, in general, and no doubt there are exceptions, do not foster the development of creativity. They denigrate the ideas of students who are otherwise regarded as creative; they reward conformity. While some of them may believe they are rewarding creativity, the grades others give their pupils do not predict or correlate with creativity in the "real" world of adult life. (College and graduate school admissions officers, as well as personal officers in companies, and those who give scholarships and grants on the basis of grades might well take note of this last point if they wish to pick creative people, for all too often they make their judgments of students on the basis of grades in the school transcript.)

With the foregoing summary in mind, three questions arise: First, are pupils aware of other reactions to their behavior? Second, are rewards actually effective in reinforcing creativity? And third, are teachers' attitudes and motivations as important as we suggest?

Torrance and his co-workers conducted studies that provide indirect evidence in answer to each of the questions. They (Torrance *et al.*, 1964) asked children they studied to make up stories about animals and people who do not do the usual thing, who do not conform to the group but rather differ and diverge from it. Analysis of these stories indicated that in half of them the children perceived "some kind of pressure against divergent characteristics [p. 35]." Assuming that they identified with the heroes of the stories, it is apparent that the pupils are aware of reactions against characteristics related to creativity. And if so, it is conceivable they might be reluctant to reveal their uniqueness, individuality, originality, and creativity. It might take a good deal of courage to fight perceived pressures against differences. Not many pupils have such courage. Do we lose a number of potentially creative adults as a result?

That rewards in the school system can direct children's behavior into more creative channels is indicated in another study reported by Torrance *et al.* (1964). In it, pupils were asked to write an imaginative story. In one set of conditions the primary reward was for originality, and the secondary reward was for correctness. In the second set of conditions the primary reward was for correctness and the secondary reward was for originality. What were the effects of this differential reward system? When the primary reward was for originality, pupils "wrote more original and more interesting stories than their peers in the other condition and tended to write longer stories but made more errors [Torrance *et al.*, 1964, p. 15]." When originality and fluency were selected for primary and secondary rewards, it was again found in a creative writing experiment that when the primary reward was for originality pupils "produced almost twice as many original ideas as their peers in the other condition and their fluency was not significantly reduced [Torrance *et al.*, 1964, p. 15]."

With regard to the effects of teachers' motivations and attitudes there is still another study by Torrance *et al.* (1964) in which pupils of teachers with positive attitudes to and motivation for creativity were compared with pupils of teachers who felt less strongly about creativity. These pupils were studied with tests of creative thinking administered 4 months apart and in a creative writing experiment carried out over a 3-month period. During the time periods that elapsed the pupils were in the classes of the teachers of different attitudes as indicated above.

Few significant differences in pre- and posttest measures of creative thinking were found. But there were significant gains in creative writing. A study by Brandwein (1955) also found that some teachers played important roles in the lives of creative persons. These teachers did remarkably well in producing students who were creative in their later years. Unfortunately, Brandwein does not present a full discussion of these teachers' characteristics.

Possibly teachers who emphasize creativity or who serve as models for creativity for their pupils are in the minority. This seems to be the conclusion one is drawn to as a result of the observations of researchers and workers in this field. Torrance (1962a) tells us, "From my observations of many elementary and secondary teachers, it is clear that many of them endeavor to reduce the variability among the students whom they teach [p. 144]." One teacher is quoted by DeHaan and Havighurst (1957) as saying, "When I am finished with my class in June, the slow children are a little faster, and the fast have slowed down a little [p. 208] ." With this kind of homogenization, the autonomy and individuality that breeds creativity is unlikely to survive.

A study that Torrance (1965) conducted in this area involved an attempt to learn how teachers and student teachers talk with children about creative writing and creative work. The teachers were presented with stories written by two elementary school children and asked to tell what they would say to them. "Many of the plans offered," says Torrance, "reflect again man's strong needs to punish and to pity. Criticism and praise are among the favorite weapons and defenses of the respondents [p. 186] ." The teachers did not try to involve the pupils' problem-solving skills or their self-evaluative approaches. Few of the teachers and student teachers other than those who were mental health students were aware that the mental health of the pupils who wrote the stories might have interfered with what they did. According to Torrance these teachers "apparently lack the concepts and/or vocabulary with which to communicate with children about their creative writing [p. 186] ."

The Teacher in the Social Context

The material presented thus far paints a rather dismal picture of the teacher's negative relationship to pupils' creativity. Is this a deserving description, or does a teacher merely become a target for criticism when creativity is blocked? There is good evidence that teachers do not necessarily reinforce their pupils' creativity and they are directly responsible for failing to do so. At times, however, it appears as if the teacher becomes a target for criticism because he or she is an available target but not necessarily the correct one.

That they are sometimes needlessly blamed in this area occurs even among researchers. Getzels and Jackson (1962) expressed surprise that teachers preferred high IQ students over the average students but the high creativity students they studied were not so preferred. Unfortunately a reevaluation of their data by other investigators (Wallach & Kogan, 1965) did not support this statement. The reevaluation indicated that while teacher preference scores for the high IQ students were higher than those obtained by the high creativity students, the difference between the two groups was not statistically significant. In other words, statistically speaking, the teachers did not actually prefer the high IQ to the high creative students. There were no real differences in how the groups were preferred.

Teachers are part of a social system and subject to all the pressures in it that may militate against creativity. Their social system is composed of their pupils' parents, a board of education, a principal, etc. If these others do not want creativity, the teacher is unlikely to foster it. Torrance *et al.* (1964) report that "teachers may volunteer to carry out creative thinking activities, [but] they tend to be inhibited in doing so, if the principal is not involved in the experiment and does not give his direct approval [p. 33] ." This is consistent with results of another study (by Jex, reported in C. W. Taylor, 1963). Jex gave a written test of creativity to high school science teachers who came to the University of Utah to obtain their master's degree in science. Their scores on this test correlated negatively with the ratings they received from their supervisors or principals for their previous year's work. Those with the higher creativity test scores received the lower ratings from their principals. Torrance *et al.'s* and Jex's material would support the idea that, if teachers are not rewarded for their own creativity, why should they be expected to reward the creativity of their students? The material also points to the possibility that the problems do not always lie with the teachers, and that to have the school system become more oriented to stimulating creativity and rewarding it, it is necessary to start at the top.

Starting within the society and at the top of the educational system would certainly have important effects for stimulating more creativity in the school system. Some specific suggestions in this area will be made later. At this point, though, one potentially potent group that can be of much influence in this regard is the pupils' parents. It is likely that if parents demanded an educational system that emphasized more creativity, they would get it. Parents should influence not only the school system, but their own children in this regard. Consider the effect if mothers were to ask their children not how good they were but how creative they were in school that day. Is it not plausible that parents' lack of concern with creativity is the reason that schools do not do more in the direction of focusing on and rewarding creativity?

Classmates

The other critical social ingredient in the classroom is a pupil's classmates, who constitute the peer culture. Small children in groups can be as constructive or destructive as any adult peer culture. They serve not only as an audience for a child's behavior but also as a social group within which the child can find satisfaction for his social needs. The peer group plays very critical roles. Its receptiveness or criticism of a child and his ideas, the subtle social pressure it exerts that leads to acceptance of the child as a member of a group or to isolation may serve to reinforce certain behavior patterns and inhibit others.

As with teachers and adults, so a child's social and emotional experiences with his classmates may affect his feelings of self-worth and confidence—feelings that are critical for effective fulfillment of the creative process. On the cognitive side, the child's attitude toward knowledge, his capacity and willingness to learn on his own, his capacity to evaluate the validity of data, his reasoning and problem-solving ability may also be critically affected by the total educational experience.

Classmates as well as teachers in the study (Torrance *et al.*, 1964) reported earlier regarded pupils with high scores on creativity tests as "naughty," "silly" and as having "far out" ideas. One might well wonder if classmates arrived at such evaluations by themselves or whether they were merely imitating their teachers. No data are reported on this matter in this study but in another. The other study is one by Torrance *et al.* (1964) that focused on the creative child as a minority of one in a group. (This is a particularly interesting study because adults often complain of what happens to them when they are a minority of one in their scientific, artistic, or work groups.)

If one child is definitely superior to others in his group on creative thinking ability, he usually finds himself under pressure to be less productive and less original. And when he makes good contributions to the group's successful achievement of its goal, he is usually not given credit for his contribution (Torrance *et al.*, 1964).

In this study, Torrance (1962a; Torrance *et al.*, 1964) worked with groups of five children. One of the five scored high on divergent-thinking tests; the other four did not. All groups had the task of planning a demonstration of how a toy works. Of the 25 children who were high on the divergent-thinking tests, 70% initiated more ideas than other members of their groups. What were the reactions of the other children? They resented the most creative member. Only 25% of these other children were willing to recognize that his contributions were the most valuable. The typical group also developed sanctions and methods for controlling the behavior of the most creative child. These took the form of openly expressed hostility, criticism, ridicule, rejection, and ignoring the creative child. In the higher grades (five and six) "organizational machinery" was used to control the creative child. He was elected to an administrative position (shades of adult life) or he was made to record the minutes of the group or appointed secretary with paper work to do—no doubt to keep him occupied and to make certain that he would be kept quiet and not offer suggestions.

In another study Torrance *et al.* (1964) asked, what would be the effect on a child's abilities if he were put in a group of children with the same ability (homogeneous grouping) as against a group in which the children had different abilities (heterogeneous grouping)? In this study two groups of students were established—one on the basis of IQ and the other on the basis of divergent-thinking scores. The students in all groups were asked to explain how a scientific toy worked. Among the results found were that when creative problem solving was required, homogeneous grouping reduced stress, the less creative participants could become more productive, and all participants enjoyed more what they were doing. Members of the homogeneous groups were more satisfied with their work. Less capable children in homogeneous groups felt more self-confident and had more self-esteem. The more able student was more modest and self-effacing in homogeneous groups, and the child with the highest IQ in the heterogeneous groups was expected to produce more ideas, and when he failed, he felt that he had let the group down. Heterogeneous and homogeneous groupings thus can have a variety of effects. Comparing the data from the study of the minority of one with the grouping data, it is apparent that homogeneous grouping has a more positive effect on the creative students and that less creative ones also do better under these conditions.

Competition can be characteristic of the classroom situation. How does it affect creativity? Torrance (1962a; Torrance *et al.*, 1964) studying children in grades one through six found that competition produced greater fluency, flexibility, and originality in creative thinking tasks. When the effects of competition were compared with those obtained when pupils were given practice in thinking up ideas, the effects of competition were reduced but not eliminated.

These findings were obtained in a study by Torrance (1962a; Torrance *et al.*, 1964) where he asked elementary school children to recommend improvements for a stuffed toy dog. An award was promised to one group for the best solutions. The performance of this group was then compared with another group that had had previous practice with a similar task in which the toy was a fire truck. The competitive group did better than the practice group in scores on different divergent-thinking measures. The competitive group was better in fluency scores only in grades four to six and in flexibility scores in grades two and four.

The effects of competition are no doubt numerous and require further study. If nothing else, it is conceivable that their effects may vary as a function of age. There is some indirect evidence at the college level that competition may work to the detriment of creativity. Buhl (1961) administered the AC Test of Creative Ability to 167 freshman engineering students. One finding of this study was that the highly creative student as measured by this test wants to be an average student. Apparently, one of the reasons for this is that if he excels, he will be alienated from the social relationships he desires. The highly creative student admits to being faster than most but believes that, with the exception of sports, he must conform to the average.

Data have been presented on some of the negative effects that peer groups can produce. Can they also produce positive and constructive effects? The results are not highly conclusive, although they lean in a positive direction. Torrance (1965) found that when classmates evaluate a work creatively (by suggesting additional possibilities) rather than critically (in terms of its flaws and deficiencies) "the weight of the evidence definitely leans on the side of the creative rather than of the critical peer evaluated condition [p. 170]."

Creative Pupils' Reactions to Classmates' Behavior

How do creative pupils respond to their classmates' reactions to them? To illustrate these we limit ourselves to the study presented earlier in which the creative pupil was a minority of one. In this study (Torrance *et al.*, 1964) a variety of reactions was found. Some of the creative children reacted to the behavior of their peers with compliance and going along with the wishes of the group. Others became aggressive against the group or showed a great deal of persistence in spite of everything; they ignored the criticism or acted the clown (which appeared to be their means of directing attention away from their ideas and gaining group approval for their exhibitionism). Others went off and worked by themselves, particularly those in the lower grades. Some became apathetic and were silent and preoccupied. Some fluctuated from one strategy to another, in a trial-and-error attempt to make an adjustment to the situation. Still others foreswore their intellectual leadership and offered minor aids to others.

It would appear from all that has been said about teachers' and classmates' reactions to the creative pupil that he or she is the "poor" and "helpless target" of others' jibes—the undeserving target of their criticism. Before accepting this idea uncritically, though, we have to reflect that creative school children sometimes provoke others' reactions and bring on their own problems, difficulties, and social rejections. At the second-grade level Torrance (1962a) found that the highly creative pupils were unpleasant, inconsiderate of their groups, possessed little or no goal orientation and little or no identification with the group, and did not pay attention to the leaders, who might have been their less creative peers.

At the third grade, creative students tended to work independently and were ignored. The same held true for the fourth grade. In this grade they also assumed little responsibility for leadership and, in turn, received little credit for their contributions. In the fifth grade the highly creative children showed more leadership "than in the fourth grade but brought upon themselves open criticism and attack for 'being too scientific,' 'being too greedy,' and such [p. 124] ." In the sixth grade these patterns became more pronounced.

One of the problems inherent in the study just presented is the proverbial chicken-egg problem: are the creative children provocative because that is their motivation and personality, or are their negative personality characteristics reactions to the frustrations they experienced and defenses they have erected against the barbs and taunts of others? Since the criterion of creativity in many studies presented is a Guilford-like test or one developed by Torrance, we must bear in mind that these are primarily verbal tests rather than tests of mechanical or scientific creativity. It is therefore conceivable that pupils who score high on these tests may be so verbal in the presence of others as to irritate them. On the other hand, several studies were presented in which teachers and classmates were quite negative to creative pupils—witness especially the study where the creative pupils were a minority of one and how "organizational" procedures, like making them secretaries, were utilized to constrict and confine them. Also, they were not even given credit for their good ideas. Similar experiences by creative adults stir them to antagonism; consequently, can we not expect similar behavior on the part of youngsters?

Whatever the case, it is apparent that to gain better understanding of the behavior of the creative pupil and reactions to him, longitudinal studies starting with the early school years and going on for some period of time would be desirable. In such longitudinal research attention might well be paid to the areas in which pupils manifest their creativity, for it is conceivable that the negative reactions reported are consistent with the verbal rather than the nonverbal creativity areas.

The Atmosphere of Schools "in General"

To know how the teachers, classmates, and school "atmosphere" affects a pupil's creativity requires the study of each situation separately. To characterize schools "in general" is hazardous. Nevertheless, investigators who have studied the problem of stimulating creativity in the school system have found that pupils do encounter numerous obstacles and stumbling blocks to their creativity.

Previously (page 156) Torrance's (1965) work was reported on how teachers and student teachers lacked "the concepts and/or vocabulary with which to communicate with children about their creative writing [p. 186]." There are other reports also.

Suchman (1961), involved with the development of "discovery through inquiry," observed that pupils lacked in autonomy and productivity probably because they relied on "the authorities"—teachers, parents, books—to shape their ideas. When these children were given new data, they did not organize what they had; they did not go about seeking more data; and they rarely tried to test hypotheses or draw inferences. They would, instead, offer conclusions they could not support or produce "a string of stereotyped probes that led nowhere [p. 155]." They did not try to discover any new concept even when everything necessary for doing so was available to them, presumably because they were accustomed to having things explained and presented to them.

Covington (1968), another worker in the area of stimulating creativity, had experiences quite similar to Suchman's. He felt that most school children are not well prepared for creativity. At the fifth and sixth grades, for which he had data, he felt that the students were sorely lacking in ability to think of any kind of ideas, let alone clever or novel ones. The students did not understand originality and were not capable of planning their work so that they could get involved in a creative project for any prolonged period.

Before turning to what can be done about the problems raised in the research presented and what can be done to stimulate creativity, let us turn to another important area of inquiry—the teaching techniques used.

TEACHING TECHNIQUES AND PRACTICES

Needless to say, there are many teaching techniques, and to deal with them all here is beyond our scope. Those selected for discussion are ones that result in problems and obstacles for creative work, and at the same time there are procedures discussed elsewhere in this book that can counteract these effects. The first problem area involves the effects of a teaching practice on a student's set or attitude to prior information. The second practice involves the use of evaluation as part of a teaching technique.

Set or Attitude to Prior Information

One of the age-old findings in psychology relates to the effects of *set* or *attitude* on human behavior. When a person is given and accepts instructions in a psychological experiment, he is set to respond in a certain way. He will behave in terms of his set or attitude and disregard or omit from his response that which is not consonant with the set. If the experimenter instructs a cooperative person to say what he sees on a chart that has both red and black figures, the person will be free to select what he wishes; but if he is told to see what the red object looks like, he will most likely respond only to it and not to anything else. This is obviously a simplified version of the effects of a set. Nevertheless, it makes the point that we carry within us sets or attitudes that determine what it is we select and respond to from all that is available in our environment. This is most apparent in the layman's use of the term attitude. We ask someone for his *attitude* to something with the knowledge and expectation that he carries within him tendencies or sets to respond in certain ways to stimuli, events, people, etc. in his environment.

Sets and attitudes are inculcated in us through a variety of life's experiences. Limiting ourselves strictly to the school situation, it is apparent that they get their start in how teachers ask or teach us to look for, respond to, or evaluate what they present or what they ask us to seek out. Investigators of teacher-student interactions (Torrance, 1965) point out that teachers emphasize critical and evaluative rather than creative attitudes on the part of their students. They are most likely to ask their students to look at a piece of work and to criticize or evaluate its deficiencies rather than to respond and add to its positive characteristics.

These sets are inculcated and reinforced throughout the pupil's experience. Consequently, if he is set to look for deficiencies, or if he has a negative attitude or approach to what is, for him, new knowledge or what the experimenters in studies described in the following paragraphs call *prior information*, then we can expect that the pupil will respond negatively and will not respond to, or will have difficulty responding to, stimuli creatively. This behavior may generalize to other situations. The student becomes quick to see deficiencies in his own as well as other's work.

While the psychological research literature contains many studies of the effects of set and attitude, we limit ourselves here to a sampling of those focusing on creativity. In one, undertaken by Torrance *et al.* (1964), each of three groups of students was given different types of instruction to apply to their readings: (1) to retain ideas that they read about; (2) to evaluate them; and (3) to improve upon them (the creative set). These groups was later given four types of tests: cognitive, memory, evaluative, and creative. The results were that the creative set group had the highest mean on the creative items; the evaluative set group had the highest mean on the evaluative items; and the memory set group had the highest mean on the cognitive and memory items. Thus, the kind of set an individual takes to new information affects how he deals with it.

If, then, teachers are more involved in giving their students sets to be creative rather than critical, the former should produce more creative ideas than the latter. These are the results obtained by Torrance (1959) with students in an educational psychology course. They were asked to examine reports in the literature that they selected themselves. The 100 graduate students who participated in this research were divided into two groups. They did not differ from each other in a pretest of "Creative Thinking in Mental Hygiene." One group was to examine research reports critically, and the other was to examine them creatively.* When the new ideas were evaluated during the second half of the course, those who had taken the creative attitude had produced more good ideas.

Since Torrance's students were permitted to select their studies from the literature, the results might have been affected by *either* the students' attitudes *or* the type of information to which they were exposed. To answer the questions involved, Hyman undertook two studies. In the first (Hyman, 1961) engineers participated in the study and in the second (Hyman, 1964) students participated. The combination of both studies provides rather interesting information.

For the first study Hyman worked with 36 recently hired engineers at the General Electric Company, to whom he presented a practical problem—one that had been worked on by other engineers already employed in the company. The problem was entitled the Automatic Warehousing Problem which involved the development of a system for the automatic recognition of boxes to fulfill certain requirements. The 36 engineers were divided into four groups of nine each on the basis of type of information they received and the kind of evaluation they were to carry out. There were two categories of information—homogeneous and heterogeneous. The former consisted of four solutions which had previously been developed by already employed engineers, and the solutions were so selected that they were essentially variations of each other. For example, boxes

*Reports on the research were completed by the first half of the course, and the new idea project was completed during the second half of the course. New ideas were evaluated on five criteria of "inventive level" and five criteria of completeness and adequacy of presentation.

could be marked by colors, magnetic materials, radioactive paints, etc. The heterogeneous condition also consisted of four solutions which had also been developed by already employed engineers. These were "four different and non-overlapping answers [p. 153]"—e.g., separating the boxes by size and shape, position of the boxes on the conveyor belts.

Each of the informational conditions was associated with two evaluation conditions: Constructive Evaluation, in which positive aspects or advantages of the solutions were to be noted; and Critical Evaluation, in which as many faults that could be found in the solutions were to be listed.

When the engineers completed their evaluation tasks, they were asked to develop their own solutions to the problem; to select what they regarded as their best solution and to develop it in some detail; and then to rate how well they were satisfied with their solutions. Finally, to determine whether there was any carryover, or transfer, of their experience, they were asked to think up new and useful applications for a process that involved changing the temperature of certain crystals and the consequent changes that then appear at the ends of the crystals. Relatively little is known about this process. In working on this problem the subjects again had to develop as many applications of the process as they could think of, to select their best idea and develop it in detail and, as before, to indicate how satisfied they were with their solutions through the use of 21 different bipolar adjectives: "ordinary-unusual,' 'unsound-sound,' 'original-unoriginal,' etc. [Hyman, 1960, p. 74]."

Before turning to the results of this study, it is important to point out several aspects of its design that make it relevant to our purposes. The problem that the 36 newly hired engineers worked on had already been worked on by others and solutions had been suggested. This is analogous to the student's situation in which he is presented with problems in his field and the kinds of solutions that others have already thought of. Consequently, this study concerns itself with whether knowing what others have done on a problem affects what one does. This is an extremely interesting question, for sometimes we wonder if learning what others have done with a problem might not stultify our own efforts. A person might have solved a problem differently if he had started off without any previous knowledge of what others had done. And as with educational materials the student can be presented with answers that are essentially variations on a theme (homogeneous information) or answers that are quite different from each other (heterogeneous information), suggesting that variety in solution is expected and reasonable.

Students can take certain attitudes to their information, so the experiment concerned itself with constructive and critical evaluation conditions. A student can read and learn information in a "friendly" manner, with the attitude that he can build elaborately upon it, or he can orient himself to looking for and concentrating his effort and attention on its deficiencies.

Of significance to educating for creativity is not only the students' attitudes to creativity but whether or not these attitudes will actually affect students' behavior when they have to develop their own solutions. So Hyman asked his engineers to come up with their own answers; pick their best one; and tell how satisfied they were with their solutions. Is it possible that just as they are instructed to think of others' work constructively or critically, they will think of themselves and their own work in the same way?

Turning to the results of Hyman's study, we shall consider first the results of the Automatic Warehousing Problem and then the transfer problem. It will be recalled that after the subjects evaluated the information they were given, they were asked to come up with their own solutions to the Automatic Warehousing Problem. These solutions were rated for creativity by engineers already acquainted with the problem. The results confirmed Torrance's findings. The subjects who were in the Constructive Evaluation condition produced ideas that were rated significantly higher in creativity, and they tended also to produce more ideas than those in the Critical Evaluation condition.

The specific evaluation condition also affected the content of the final solution to the Warehousing Problem. The most common solution to the Warehousing Problem was marking the boxes in some way. And all of the solutions that were high in creativity fell into this common category. Significantly more of the individuals who were in the Constructive Evaluation condition came up with such answers than did those in the Critical Evaluation condition.

No significant effects were found as a result of type of information condition or due to interaction of the evaluation and type of information condition.

Regarding the other question raised by Hyman—whether the effects of the evaluational and informational conditions carry over to another problem—the data indicated that as before and as in Torrance's study, the Constructive Condition again resulted in solutions that were rated higher on creativity than those in the Critical Condition. The Constructive Condition also resulted in a significantly larger number of suggested solutions.

The effects of type of information involved approached but did not achieve significance. In this instance heterogeneous information tended to facilitate creativity. There was no significant interaction between evaluation condition and type of information.

It will be recalled that in the Warehousing Problem the evaluation condition was related to the content of the final solution. For the transfer problem it was found that the type of information rather than the evaluation condition was related to content of solution. Thus, significantly more subjects in the homogeneous condition developed a solution involving temperature; heterogeneous groups tended to develop more uncommon and unique solutions and more different solutions (Hyman, 1960).

There were no significant differences on the transfer problem in the subjects' ratings of their own satisfaction with their solutions. Looking at the adjectives the subjects checked, "the Homogeneous Groups tended to describe their solutions as more 'sound,' 'satisfactory,' 'clear,' 'valuable,' 'inspired,' 'practical,' and 'sensible' [Hyman, 1960, p. 82] ."

In conclusion, Hyman's study shows the effect of an individual's attitude toward prior information on how he handles later problems. A person's attitude operates independently of the type of information involved. It is conceivable, however, as Hyman points out in the next study, that in certain circumstances type of information may be more important.

This second study (Hyman, 1964) is very similar to the one just described except that students rather than engineers were involved. They were 74 male and 92 female undergraduates who were exposed to different types of information under varying sets. The problem the students were asked to solve was how to get more European visitors to the United States. The two types of information consisted of four common ideas and four rather uncommon ideas. Again, the studies had two sets: a constructive evaluation set in which the students were given 20 minutes to list as good characteristics as they could think of about the ideas they were presented with; and, a critical evaluation condition in which the subject had 20 minutes to list all the weaknesses of the ideas. Thus there were four groups. (1) A group that worked constructively on common ideas. (2) A group that worked constructively on uncommon ideas. (3) A group that worked critically on common ideas. (4) A group that worked critically on uncommon ideas. A fifth group was added as a control group. It worked for 20 minutes on syllogisms.

After the students worked as just described, they were given 20 minutes to come up with their own solutions to the tourist problem and then they worked on two other problems to study transfer effects. Finally, the students rated ideas related to the Tourist Problem.

The students' solutions were rated on a "global scale of overall effectiveness [p. 72] " and while both male and female constructive groups produced more effective solutions, the results were not statistically significant. But there was a difference in the *content* of the solutions as a function of the experimental conditions. The constructive groups *used* the ideas they were given. In a sense they grafted something of their own onto these ideas. The Constructive-Common group produced ideas that were a little different from those produced by the control group. The Constructive-Uncommon group produced ideas that were quite different from the control group.

The critical evaluation groups essentially did not employ the ideas to which they were exposed. The Critical-Uncommon group produced ideas only slightly different from those produced by the control group, and the Critical-Common group produced ideas that were greatly different from the control group. Since the Critical-Common group was forced to come up with responses that were different from the common or "dominant" ones, this was the one group that Hyman says could be said to have engaged in problem solving.

All groups were equivalent in quality of ideas produced, as previously pointed out. Therefore, Hyman says, if one should want to say that the group that achieves its quality through more unusual methods can be said to be more creative, then under these conditions the Constructive-Uncommon and the Critical-Common groups "produced the most 'creative solutions' [p. 73]." The Critical-Common group was the only one apparently involved in "thinking" since they were the only ones that seemed to be doing any work to arrive at their solutions.

Hyman also had the students in this experiment rate 13 different ideas produced by other students to the Tourist Problem. Among the ideas rated were both the four common and four uncommon ideas that the students worked with previously. Constructive groups rated these previously evaluated ideas only a little more positively than did the control groups, while the critical groups rated their ideas much more negatively (and significantly so) than did the control groups.

Hyman points out that it should be noted that the effect of the students' attitude was quite specific and that it did not spread to the other items. Those individuals who were made more negative about a set of items limited their negative attitudes to these items only. Their negative attitudes did not spread to the other items.

Important differences between this study and that reported previously for the engineers on the Warehousing Problem need to be underlined. In the study with the engineers, constructive groups produced significantly more creative solutions than did the critical groups. The effects of the constructive and critical conditions spread to another problem. In the student study the effects were limited to the particular information evaluated. They did not spread.

To account for the differences in the results Hyman suggests two reasons. The two groups were differentially prepared for their tasks. The engineers dealt with a problem central to their professional interests, and they had had experience with different aspects involved in the solution to the problem. The students dealt with a problem that was peripheral to their main interests, and they had little knowledge about it. These differences might account for the differences in results. Since the ideas the engineers were to evaluate were central to their interests, the effects of the evaluation would therefore be more central and widespread. For the students the problem and its issues were not central to their interests, hence little spread of effect would be expected.

The second reason Hyman pointed to was the task's characteristics. The Automatic Warehousing Problem "demanded a tightly organized system to meet certain requirements. The possible answers were mutually exclusive in the sense that the proposal of one system necessarily ruled out the proposal of other systems [Hyman, 1964, p. 75] ." The students' problem, the Tourist Problem, "could be handled by a loosely organized package of ideas for dealing with various subproblems [p. 75] ." Thus we have here the importance of the task and the demands it makes on critical variables in such research. Hyman (1964) says,

> Our subjects were quite consistent in stating that the task demands practical and effective ideas, but no original or creative ones. They seem to be saying that, until the more obvious ideas for solving the Tourist Problem are tried out, we cannot tell whether there is a need for "a more creative approach." I think in retrospect that they are right. It is only when the common ideas are shown to be ineffectual, or if competing goals have to be satisfied, or if some other hurdles have to be overcome, that creativity may be called for. In line with this thinking, we have already started to build hurdles and conflicting goals into the experimental tasks that we give our subjects. The slight evidence that we have accumulated so far suggests that we may be right in surmising that our induced attitudes and informational conditions produce more general effects under conditions where subjects are solving problems with built-in conflict [p. 76] ."

In summary, then, research on the effects of sets on prior information indicate that teachers need to be quite cognizant of how they predispose or orient their students to available information. The orientation or set that students are given (or that we as adults take) affect that which we select from what is available and how we will use it. In general if we are oriented creatively we are more likely to build on available information and probably even elaborate upon it creatively. On the other hand, a critical orientation will also affect what we select and retain. Moreover, it will have a limiting effect on the use of information for creative purposes. In general this statement is no doubt valid, but future research will probably indicate that it varies as a function of types of persons and types of problems involved. As more of this evidence becomes available we shall be in a better position to tailor orientations to the characteristics of both students and problems in the hope that more of available creative potential will be manifest.

EVALUATION AND PRACTICE

One of the most ubiquitous characteristics of classroom situations frequently commented on is *evaluation*. Students are constantly reminded by their teachers of how well they are doing. And when teachers themselves do not evaluate a student's performance, they will frequently have other students evaluate his behavior with the rationalization that it makes all students "sharpen their wits" and helps them develop their powers of critical thinking and judgment. All of this evaluation probably serves one major purpose—to keep the child in line. With evaluation of everything he does the child is unlikely to have any opportunity to play, explore, indulge his curiosity, etc. As Torrance (1965) puts it, "My hypothesis is that children need periods during which they can experiment, make mistakes, and test various approaches without fear of evaluation and the failure that making a mistake implies [p. 148]." Consequently Torrance undertook a series of studies of evaluation and a sampling of this research is presented here.

One of these studies (Torrance *et al.*, 1964) concerned itself with "Three Kinds of Evaluated Practice." In it Torrance studies all the pupils in the fourth, fifth, and sixth grades in one elementary school. To them he presented his Science Toy Task. This task was used both during a practice session and a test session. During the practice session the experimenters engaged in three kinds of evaluation—(1) criticism and correction; (2) suggestion of constructive possibilities; and (3) combination of criticism and constructive possibilities. Among the variables involved in this study were the number of toys demonstrated, the number of uses demonstrated, number of science principles explained, number of times experimental manipulation was invoked, etc.

Analysis of the data indicated that there were no significant differences in the behavior of the three groups. However, when the data were analyzed in terms of "frequency of application" of the experimental treatment, then the difference was in favor of that group which had least exposure to any of the forms of evaluation. In other words, the evaluations or the experimental treatments, whichever they were, apparently interfered with the pupils' behavior and actually served to inhibit them in their activities.

A second experiment by Torrance (1965) concerned itself with a comparison of the effects of unevaluated practice but encouragement to experiment and a second experimental condition in which the pupils received constructive positive evaluation. The pupils in this study were those who attended grades one to six in a Minneapolis public school. They were told that they were being studied to learn how people develop unusual, interesting, and original ideas. A prize would be awarded to each of three pupils who did in fact come up with the most interesting and unusual ideas.

There were experimental and test tasks. The former consisted of an Incomplete Figures Task in which pupils were shown six incomplete figures on a sheet of paper and asked to say what they could make from them. One form of this task was used for practice purposes and another for test purposes.

The second task was the Picture Construction or Shape Task, in which the pupils were given a sheet of paper, a small triangle, and glue and told to make a picture by pasting the colored shape wherever they wanted and to add whatever lines they wanted. They were asked to think of a picture that no one else would come up with. They could use pencils, crayons, or whatever else they wanted for their pictures. For the test experiment the pupils were given a curved shape instead of the triangle shape.

In the experimental condition that consisted of *unevaluated practice plus encouragement of experimentation*, the students "were told to experiment freely with different ideas and not be afraid to spoil or 'mess up' their drawings because the practice session did not count toward winning the prize [Torrance, 1965, p. 151]." The pupils' questions were answered as their questions arose. After 5 minutes on the practice piece they could show what they had done to the other pupils.

For the other experimental condition, that which involved constructive positive evaluation, the pupils were told during practice to think up more uncommon ideas, to put in more ideas, to elaborate and make their picture more exciting. They were not told that their work did not count for a prize. Too-frequent evaluation was avoided, as was the need to develop original and elaborated ideas.

Productions on both previously described tasks were scored for a number of dimensions regarded as related to creativity. The results are rather complicated, varying as a function of grade level, etc., but rather than involve ourselves with these specifics, it is best to point out that Torrance in summarizing his results says that apparently children in grades one through four, that is, the younger ones, were more strongly affected by adult evaluation than were the older ones (grades five and six). The younger ones produced more creative work after a period free from fear of making errors and lack of evaluation than was true of the older children. Moreover, Torrance suggested that under unevaluated conditions the younger children behaved more creatively "than under the best constructive evaluation conditions [Torrance, 1965, p. 161]."

Not only adults practice or are encouraged to practice evaluation in the school situation, but teachers also frequently encourage pupils, peers, to evaluate each other. Consequently, Torrance (1965) also undertook a study of peer-evaluated practice.

The design of this experiment was essentially the same as that in the one just reported. Again, the Picture Construction and Incomplete Figures tasks were used; students were told that experimenters wanted to learn how pupils thought up original ideas; that prizes would be offered; and that the practice session did not, but test session did, count for a prize.

In one condition, critical peer evaluation, the pupils were encouraged to evaluate each other's production at the end of each practice session. They evaluated each other's productions critically, pointing out what they thought was wrong with each other's ideas.

For the creative evaluation condition pupils were asked to suggest possibilities that would make stories more unusual and interesting. This creative condition emphasized possibilities, whereas the critical condition emphasized deficiencies.

After the practice sessions the two tests were readministered and the effects of the critical and creative conditions were studied in terms of gain scores. In other words, how well a student did in the test session over the practice session was considered a gain score. In addition to this total gain score, specific gain scores for specific variables, e.g., originality, elaboration, etc., were also calculated.

The results for this experiment were "not highly conclusive." Nevertheless "the weight of the evidence definitely leans on the side of the creative rather than of the critical peer evaluated condition [Torrance, 1965, p. 170] ."

Finally, we report one more of Torrance's studies. We have seen that evaluated practice of all sorts has a negative effect on a pupil's activities and that unevaluated practice seems most desirable. But only one study has been reported on this matter. Further support is necessary, and it comes from another study by Torrance *et al.* (1964). This study involved the investigation of teacher effectiveness in an experimental mathematics course. Effectiveness was defined by students' test scores before and after the course. It was found that effective teachers reported more "trouble-shooting or hypothesis-making [p. 23] " and less criticism and praise than their less effective colleagues.

In another study, beginning teachers, while developing plans for discussing creative writing with their pupils, were very concerned with the "critical and remedial." Experienced teachers, when encouraged to do so, did "show a slight predominance of creative strategies over the critical and remedial [Torrance *et al.*, 1964, p. 32] ."

In summary, observations of schoolroom situations reveal all too frequently that both teachers and classmates are quite prone to evaluation. In general, the studies discussed in this section reveal that when classmates are constructive in their comments, creativity is more likely to be manifest than when their comments are critical. As for teachers, any kind of evaluation during practice sessions is likely to have a negative effect on a student's behavior on a later similar task. No evaluation is better than constructive comments, for such comments call the student's attention to evaluation, and this can have negative effects, for the student is likely to evaluate too early in the creative process and to evaluate all he does. If the student is allowed to practice without evaluation but with encouragement to explore and be curious about his materials, then he is likely to be more creative than if he is evaluated.

Once again, however, it is necessary to express a word of caution. There is some variability in the comments just made as a function of the student's grade level, and no doubt future research may show that they will also vary as a function of the type of problem and type of student involved.

TOWARD A SCHOOL SYSTEM THAT IS MORE
CONGENIAL TO CREATIVITY

It is evident that problems do exist in school systems that frequently militate against creativity. The evidence presented earlier indicates the kinds of procedures and interactions that are not fertile grounds for future creativity. At the same time, the situation is not uniformly bleak. Indeed, creative adults have gone through our school systems. Some must have had their creativity nurtured and fostered in their schools, by their teachers, and even by their peers. Whatever the case, our intent here is not to focus on limitations but to help maximize the probability that creativity will be fostered in the future. Consequently, we turn to several considerations which, depending on specific needs in specific situations, may be of help.

Diagnostic Surveys

Schools at all levels in the school system vary in their attitudes toward creativity and in the values they place on it. All too often the community does not know where its school system stands on this matter; principals and teachers may not even know. Ignorance about general issues is accompanied by ignorance on specifics—the kinds of blocks and problems that exist within certain classes or within certain areas of the school or within the total school system in a community.

To foster creativity these problems need to be diagnosed and rectified. To help in diagnosis, survey questionnaires can be constructed which focus directly on the matter of creativity.* Techniques already exist for gathering data on critical variables involved in the educational environment at the high school and college levels (Stern, 1958; Stern & Pace, 1958; Stern *et al.*, 1961). These might be extended in some appropriate form to the elementary school level and, in each of these, specific questions about creativity could be included.

Such a survey would be a step toward providing a community and a school system with an assessment and an inventory of where it stands with respect to creativity. Once the basic data are available, plans can be developed for creative and constructive solutions.

Selection of School Administrators

School administrators and school principals play vital roles in promoting and facilitating the creativity of their staffs, and especially of the pupils and students within their schools. They have power, status, and prestige, and play critical roles in deciding whether creativity will or will not be a value in the school system.

---

*For techniques for the study of another kind of environment, Research and Development laboratories in industry, the reader is referred to Stein (1959a-e).

If change in a direction that might hopefully produce more creativity is desired, one must start at the top. The school administrator must be influenced to introduce certain changes. If changes are not forthcoming from him, if he is not motivated to see them put into action, then little, if anything, is likely to happen. He must set the value system and framework within which specific methods might be developed and utilized to achieve desired goals.

A critical consideration for the principal in achieving his goals is how he gets along with his teachers. Consequently, it is important to have some framework or some guidelines in mind when selecting him. In this regard the following statements by Torrance (1961a, 1962a) might serve well. Principals and school administration might also be guided by Torrance's suggestions. He says that the good principal

1. Lets teachers know that he respects creativity and creative teaching.
2. Uses some regular system for obtaining teachers' ideas.
3. Tolerates disagreement with his own ideas.
4. Encourages experimentation.
5. Avoids loading teachers with too many extra duties.
6. Makes it possible to try out new ideas without failure being "fatal."
7. Makes school atmosphere an exciting, adventurous one.
8. Avoids *overemphasis* on teamwork.
9. Holds meetings in which ideas are evaluated honestly.
10. Helps develop sound but exciting ideas from failure experiences.
11. Exposes teachers to the creative work of other teachers.
12. Makes it easy for new teachers to generate new ideas and stimulate the staff.
13. Facilitates communication between teachers in his school and teachers elsewhere working on related problems.
14. Occasionally questions established concepts and practices.
15. Carries on a continuous program of long-range planning.
16. Recognizes and tries to relieve tension when frustration becomes too severe.
17. Maintains frequent communication with individual teachers but lets them make most decisions alone [Torrance (1962a), p. 206].

What kind of a person is a school administrator who can do these things? On this Torrance (1961b, 1962a) also has some very valuable suggestions. First, as to the kind of person he is, Torrance (1962a) says

1. He is a man of curiosity and discontent. He is always asking, "Why did this happen?" or "What would happen if we did it this way?"
2. He is a man of unlimited enthusiasm for his job. He is restless, intense, strongly motivated—completely wrapped up in what he is doing.

3. He is a man with the talent of transmitting his enthusiasm to his associates. He creates an atmosphere of excitement and urgency.

4. He is flexible. He keeps an open mind and is willing to accept and use new information. He listens to new ideas and does not flatly dismiss ideas with "don't be ridiculous" or "we tried that before."

5. He is unorthodox and boldly questions conventional ideas. He is goal-oriented, *not* method-oriented. He is willing to pay the price in physical and mental labor to achieve goals and is impatient with anything that gets in the way [p. 207].

And finally, Torrance (1962a) suggests that the administrator might check himself out on the following characteristics.

1. Makes certain that principals and teachers know that he respects creative thinking.

2. Uses some regular system for obtaining the ideas of teachers, principals, and board members.

3. Develops pride in the school system.

4. Makes it possible to try out ideas without failure being "fatal."

5. Offers opportunities and resources for exploration.

6. Does not settle school problems by fiat.

7. Does not coerce conformity to his own ideas.

8. Gives others credit for ideas.

9. Finds a place for divergent talents in the system.

10. Helps teachers and principals obtain financial resources to implement or demonstrate new ideas.

11. Facilitates communication among teachers in different schools within the system working on similar problems.

12. Leads a continuous program for long-range planning.

13. Avoids screening out the truly creative in selecting teachers.

14. Sees that divergent or minority ideas receive a hearing.

15. Maintains frequent communication with individual principals but gives them freedom to make certain decisions alone.

16. Gives principals and teachers time to work out and test new ideas.

17. Finds fascination in every facet of education.

18. Browses extensively in many fields of interest, other than education [pp. 208-209].

All of these are obviously goals and desiderata which, if achieved, would provide a top-echelon group that could develop a proper atmosphere for creativity and select and stimulate teachers in their efforts to foster their pupils' creativity. We now turn to the teachers.

Selection of Teachers

It is difficult to conduct systematic large-scale research to establish the characteristics of teachers who produce pupils who become creative adults. The problem involves collecting data at a point in time when we do not know whether the teacher will indeed produce creative adults. These data have to be filed away for several years after which criterion and evaluation data become available. If it were possible to collect such data, it would not only tell us what characteristics to look for in new teachers but it would likely answer another set of important questions. Is it necessary for a person to be creative himself to produce creative people in the same or different fields? Many individuals would answer "yes" to this question, probably because they believe in an apprenticeship system. Other people would say "no," implying that the person who is himself creative has all his energies tied up in that work and has little left "to give" others. No matter how the question will be answered, such research would, if undertaken, provide important information about the nurturing of creativity.

As was said previously, there is little information on teachers who produce creative adults, but there is some that can serve as a base for selecting such teachers in the future. For example, McCardle (1959) administered the Minnesota Teacher Attitude Inventory to 29 teachers to obtain a measure of their ability to establish good relationships with pupils. Participants taught first-year algebra. After controlling for certain factors, McCardle related teachers' scores on the test to the pupils' achievements. He found significant relationships between the teachers' scores and the pupils' scores in arithmetic reasoning and functional competence in mathematics including skill in what had been learned. In discussing this study Torrance (1962a) points out that while pupils of both kinds of teachers may learn the proper skills, those who were the pupils of teachers skilled in good relationships were more likely to be better off in using what they learned.

Some individuals have written about teachers who encouraged the creativity of their pupils (Hobelman, 1957; Barkan, 1960; Wessel, 1961). Summarizing these works, Torrance (1962a) says,

> All of them are highly sensitive, resourceful, flexible, and willing to "get off the beaten track." Perhaps much of their secret lies in their very uniqueness or diversity. However, perhaps most important, is their capacity to form good relationships with their creative students. We find in their behavior characteristics which would ordinarily alienate many students from them. These characteristics apparently become unimportant, since they have such great capacities for creative relationships with students [p. 195].

These teachers also "tackle difficult tasks, sometimes too difficult [p. 195]." They are hard workers and have occasional failures.

They may have some oddities, be nonconforming, and at times be childish. They may even defy conventions of courtesy, seem uncultured and primitive, and be unsophisticated and naive about many things. They are too absorbed in helping children develop to be concerned with being sociable or socially skilled [Torrance, 1962a, pp. 195-196].

Others may be put off by some of the characteristics of creative teachers.

Outwardly they are frequently rather bashful, and somewhat withdrawn and quiet. Their ideas have perhaps been laughed at so often, that others may have to demonstrate the genuineness of their friendliness and interest. At times creative teachers may seem haughty and self-satisfied, but this just exemplifies their independence in thinking. They may also appear discontented and fault-finding. And at times, they may feel that "the whole parade is out of step." This may be a part of their ability to sense problems and defects. If they are creative, however, they will have some constructive ideas about how the deficiencies may be alleviated or remedied [p. 196].

These characteristics certainly make sense. They require additional research support and could serve as a basis for the selection of teachers who can foster pupils' creativity.

Testing of Students

Within a framework oriented to facilitating and nurturing the creativity of pupils at the early grades, one may need, in addition to diagnostic surveys and proper selection of school principals, administrators, and teachers, further understanding of the pupils' intellectual potentials, capacities, and abilities. Typically, on the current educational scene pupils are likely to be tested with intelligence and achievement tests. It is apparent from what is currently available that adding tests like those used by Guilford (1967) and Torrance (1962a) and personality tests would go a long way to giving us the data we require. These data would not only provide us with what we need to possess for a better understanding of the pupils but also for the development of an atmosphere and a curriculum that would be congruent with the further development of their potentialities.

We are aware that some persons have grave objections to tests for fear that they are not culture-free or that they invade others' privacy. Needless to say, adequate discussion of both issues are beyond the scope of this book. We can say, however, that the first is a test development problem and no doubt can be appropriately resolved, given adequate time and resources. The matter of privacy is a red herring from our point of view. The history of medicine is replete with such red herrings that blocked important medical developments. Every physical examination can be regarded as an invasion of privacy, yet every examination conducted by professionals under professional conditions can be used to help the person involved. Our attitudes toward these matters and the standard we set up for them are the critical factors. Most crucial, of course, is to have appropriate knowledge of the pupils' abilities, so that their potentials can be fulfilled.

Guidance Counselors

The creative pupil, because of his individuality, autonomy, tendency to divergent thinking, etc., deviates from other pupils. His personality, thought processes, and behavior may all be different from those manifested by others. Until parents, principals, teachers, and the pupils themselves know how to take these differences in stride, so that the creativity of the pupil is not adversely affected, there is going to be the need for persons, like guidance counselors, who can explain what is going on to all concerned, and so either remedy or prevent problems from occurring that may have adverse effects on the pupil's creativity.

Guidance counselors are certainly not to serve creative students alone. Many different kinds of students can use their help. Our point here is to indicate the kind of role they can play with creative children. In this regard we follow Torrance (1962a), who says that in working with creative children there are six roles to be played by guidance workers: "(1) providing the highly creative individual a 'refuge' [p. 8]." Because creative children are likely to be estranged from their parents, teachers and peers, counselors might provide them with a safe environment. "(2) being his 'sponsor' or 'patron' [p. 8]." In playing this role the counselor as sponsor "encourages and supports [the child] in expressing and testing his ideas and in thinking through things for himself. He protects the individual from the reactions of his peers long enough for him to try out some of his ideas and modify them. He can keep the structure of the situation open enough so that originality *can* occur [p. 9]." "(3) helping him understand his divergence [p. 8]." Creative children are frequently disturbed by their sensitivity and divergent thinking and other characteristics. Being understood by a sympathetic and important adult such as the counselor is very important to maintaining their creativity. "(4) letting him communicate his ideas [p. 8]." Torrance says that teachers and classmates frequently said creative children did not speak out their ideas and they usually did not because their ideas were so far ahead of others'. But they need to communicate these ideas and to find they are accepted by others. The counselor can perform this role demonstrating that he respects the child for his thoughts and ideas. "(5) seeing that his creative talent is recognized [p. 8]." This is the same as a point we made previously regarding the testing of children to learn what abilities they have and to see that these are properly nurtured. And the last role that Torrance sees for the guidance counselor is "(6) helping parents and others understand him [p. 8]." Because others do not understand creative children, they frequently become angry with and hostile toward them. The counselor can help the creative student by explaining to these people how their behavior and reactions to the creative student can hurt his creativity. He might also explain to the young person how his behavior affects others so that he can, as one method, select individuals who are better able to communicate with him.

Continued Research on the Characteristics of Creativity within the Developmental Process

In addition to what has already been said, there is also the need for continued efforts in other areas. There is the need for continuous research to help us better understand characteristics of creativity throughout the school years so that if problems do occur they can be rectified. Other areas would be work on teacher training and teaching techniques.

To illustrate the kind of work that may help further our understanding of creativity within the developing child, consider the work of Legon (1957). Some of the characteristics he finds at different age levels are: Until the age of two the child questions the names of things and tries to reproduce sounds and rhythms. From two to four the child learns through direct experience and repeats his experiences in investigative play. He starts to develop a sense of autonomy. From four to six there is experimentation with a variety of roles in play. From six to eight the child turns to realism and rejects pretense. From eight to ten the child begins to use skills creatively, identifies with heroes, can undertake long projects, ask critical questions, etc. From ten to twelve, children enjoy exploration. Aptitudes for art and music develop during this period. The child can derive principles or generalizations. With this kind of knowledge about the pupil's developing characteristics, appropriate teaching methods that can foster his creative abilities can be developed.

Torrance (1962b) studied the variations in creative thinking abilities at different class levels and found that creativity increased steadily from the first through the third grades; that with one exception, it decreased markedly from the third to the fourth grades and then recovered a bit in the fifth and sixth grades. Between the sixth and seventh grades it dropped and subsequently was followed by a period of growth that lasted almost until the end of the high school years. One of the creative abilities that was an exception was the ability to formulate causal hypotheses. Children were slow in developing these skills but their development continued through the fourth grade and did not show the slump found in other types of creative thinking.

Torrance (1962b) suggests that future research might be able to show to what extent either personality or physiological factors, or both, may be involved in the slumps he finds at different periods for the creative thinking abilities. On the psychological side he draws on the theorizing of Sullivan (1953), who for example pointed out that the transition between the third and fourth grades is a time when most children experience subordination and accommodation, ostracism, segregation into groups, disparagement, stereotyping, competition, and compromise. During this period there are pressures toward socialization; unusual ideas are laughed at, ridiculed, and condemned. People are seen as potentially humiliating, anxiety-provoking, and punishing. (Therefore, why communicate new ideas to them?) At the seventh grade there are other pressures to conformity that can produce feelings of inadequacy and insecurity, and the anxiety experienced can result in further constriction of thought processes in general and creative thinking abilities in particular.

On the physiological side, Torrance suggests that the slump at nine years of age may be accounted for by the fact that children of this age have the "worst possible visual organization" and the decline at about the seventh-grade level might be accounted for by the changes and conflicts that accompany the beginning of puberty.

It is conceivable that with such data available for the whole developmental scale, planning for pupils could be more adequate throughout the school system. By the same token, continued research on proper teaching techniques to foster creativity would also be quite valuable in this regard.

Teacher Training

Teaching teachers to improve their methods so that their students' creativity can be improved is possible and requires continued attention. Torrance *et al.* (1961) taught teachers the following five principles of how to teach creatively: (1) treat pupils' questions with respect; (2) treat imaginative ideas with respect; (3) show pupils that their ideas have value; (4) permit pupils to do some things "for practice" without threat of evaluation; and (5) tie evaluation in with causes and consequences. The teachers taught this way for four weeks. A control group of teachers taught according to their usual procedures for the same period of time. Pre- and posttests of the pupils in these classes showed superior gains for the pupils in the experimental group. They had higher scores for originality and elaboration in four of the six grades studied, superiority in fluency in three, and superiority in flexibility in two.

It is worth noting that in this study a third of the teachers were unsuccessful in understanding the principles the experimenters tried to teach them. These teachers, it turned out, tended to be authoritarian, defensive, dominated by time schedules, insensitive to their pupils' intellectual and emotional needs, preoccupied with disciplinary problems, and unwilling to give much of themselves.

Another study by Torrance *et al.* (1964) also indicated that while an inservice training program for developing creativity may not produce very dramatic effects, it is a step in the right direction. Although teachers in this kind of program did not initiate any more creative activities than their colleagues under control conditions, their pupils showed greater growth in creative thinking.

Similarly, Rusch, Denny, and Ives (1965) compared an experimental group that was taught creatively for the school year and a control group that was taught in the regular manner. Two teachers and two classes of sixth-grade students were in each group. Seven divergent-thinking tests were given at the beginning and at the end of the school year. The experimental group gained significantly more on five of the seven tests, and in none of them was the control group's gain superior. It appears, then, that teachers can be trained rather successfully to teach for creativity.

Developing New Teaching Techniques

New ideas for teaching methods and teaching content have to be developed. They would sustain the curiosity, interest, and motivation of manifestly creative students and stimulate the creativity of those other students who have not yet fulfilled their potential.

One of the newer developments in this field is computer-assisted education and teaching machines. Before turning to these, we shall discuss another approach that is not as expensive as a computer and that may be adapted to a variety of educational situations. This technique is really a project named *Arcturus IV*. It implicitly involves role playing, a technique discussed in Chapter V (page 63). In role playing an individual assumes the role of another person and behaves in accord with the assumed person's characteristics. By going out of himself and behaving like his image of a creative person, for example, an individual may well fulfill his creative potential. For the project to be described, the goal of stimulating students' creativity is achieved by getting them to go "out of this world."

Arcturus IV

Arcturus IV is the name the late Professor Arnold gave a project he used first with his students at the Massachusetts Institute of Technology. Arcturus IV is a mythological planet for which Arnold specified certain characteristics: its specific gravity was 11 times that of the earth; it had peculiar atmospheric conditions; its inhabitants had six fingers, they were birdlike in appearance; etc. Arnold presented these data to his students and asked them among other things to develop a numbering or counting system for the inhabitants of Arcturus, and appliances and machinery compatible with their environmental conditions.

The goal of the Arcturus exercise is to disrupt whatever rigidity exists in a student's perceptual orientation and thought patterns. It seeks to undercut automatic reliance and dependence on that which exists. Indirectly, it stimulates thinking about experiences, systems, and procedures that are usually taken for granted—e.g., numbering and counting systems.

Arnold's project may help a student by removing him from a situation in which he feels blocked. It might well be combined with other techniques discussed in this book in a format where the student's project is to develop things for other people, and when he becomes blocked he might use brainstorming, attribute testing, morphological analysis, etc.

Projects like Arcturus IV can be adapted for all educational levels to enable students, by going "out of this world," to break the fetters that control and inhibit their creativity.

The Metaphor in Education

Gordon, the originator of Synectics, gave a rather central role to the use of the metaphor in this group procedure for stimulating creativity. Then, on the basis of his experience with the creativity of individuals and groups, he developed the use of the metaphor as well as associated teaching aids which he utilized in actual teaching situations. We shall present some of this work in Chapter XV, after we have had an opportunity to present the broader framework of Synectics so that we will be better prepared to understand these rather unusual and promising educational procedures and materials.

Teaching Machines

Schools of education, teacher training programs, etc. are constantly exploring different ways of improving teaching techniques. One of the more recent developments is the use of teaching machines, programed instruction, or computer-assisted instruction. These have also found their way into the area of creativity. A good number of years ago, B. F. Skinner, the psychologist who has made many significant contributions to learning theory and whose research and efforts have been quite instrumental in the development of teaching machines, pointed out in an article for a popular scientific magazine (Skinner, 1961), that a technology existed for the development of teaching machines that would "equip students with large repertories of verbal and nonverbal behavior [p. 91]." Furthermore, the students' experiences would be such that they would continue to be rather excited about additional education.

Skinner noted the fears and concerns that different groups of people might have regarding teaching machines. Some might fear that teaching machines would be a threat to the teacher; some might think it would make the educational process a cold and mechanical one; some might be concerned that they would "turn students into regimented and mindless robots [p. 92]." Skinner brushed all these aside, saying they had no foundation in fact. For Skinner the function of a teaching machine is "to teach rapidly, thoroughly and expeditiously a large part of what we now teach slowly, incompletely and with waste effort [p. 92]" by pupil and teacher. Skinner also believes that teaching machines could also teach subtle behavior that was beyond the reach of other teaching methods.

Whether the fears are groundless, as Skinner says, is a question that will be answered by future experience and research. Some of the research evidence is being collected in studies such as that conducted by Hess and Tenezakis (1970), who concern themselves with "the socializing role of computer-assisted instruction [p. xiii] ." Their first study is currently available. It focuses on attitudinal data obtained from junior high school students who were assigned to a computer-assisted instruction program in arithmetic that was of a remedial nature. The students in the research group were predominantly Mexican Americans who came from lower socioeconomic groups. The attitudes of the students who worked with the computer were compared with those who did not.

Both groups were found to have very positive feelings about the computer— "they liked it, thought that it gives right answers, and saw it as having a vast array of information available to it. They also saw it as fair, trusted its evaluations as well as its handling of task assignments, and sometimes attributed to it an almost human role [p. xiii] ."

Both groups of students evaluated the computer more positively than other sources of information and instruction. They felt that the computer had "greater expertise in processing and transmitting information [p. xiii] ." They had more trust in the computer than in the teacher. The computer had more charisma for them than did the teacher. Those who worked with the computer believed more than those who did not that the computer was not responsive to their desires for change in courses or content of the lessons.

The greater feeling of trust in the computer than the teacher Hess and Tenezakis suggest is probably due to the fact that the computer is seen as "task-oriented," whereas teachers are seen as evaluative. Specifically, teachers are seen as evaluating students' performance in mathematics on behavior not related to these tasks. The computer, on the other hand, is seen as "task-related." Interactions with teachers have affective and evaluative components that the students do not like. These results are consistent with those found by Torrance (1965) and reported previously. It will be recalled that he too found unevaluated practice was better than evaluated practice. The effectiveness of the former may lie in the fact that it does not provoke from the students affective responses, which they may find disruptive to learning and creativity.

From the foregoing it is quite apparent that computer-assisted instruction has "affective and social overtones in addition to its instructional function [Hess & Tenezakis, 1970, p. 102] ." Essentially the question is whether attitudes developed toward the computer in learning situations will be transferred to other situations outside of school. The school experience "may tend to establish patterns of interaction between the individual and a technological society [p. 101] ." It is necessary to keep this in mind in evaluating computerized educational practices and in considering their use in stimulating creativity. With this as a general caution in mind, let us return to the teaching machines as they are used for educational purposes.

A teaching machine is "no better than the material fed into it [Skinner, 1961, p. 92]." And composing such material is still an art. Nevertheless, a useful teaching machine, according to Skinner, allows the student to compose his response rather than to select it from available choices so that a student may go through an arranged sequence that can be quite long.

The machine itself does not teach. It simply brings the student into contact with material developed by another and then programed. Although it may be used with large numbers of students, it tries by virtue of the characteristics of the program to maintain the student's interest at a high level. The machine tries to sustain activity. The student has always to be alert and busy. Before the student moves from one thing to the next, the machine "insists" that the first point be thoroughly understood. This is not true of lectures, textbooks, etc. These other means of teaching do not check whether the student actually understands what is going on. The teaching machine "like a tutor" presents the student with what he is ready for, and he is helped to come up with correct answers. Toward this end, a well constructed program is one that gives the student hints and suggestions, and rewards the student when he is correct. In this way, the student's behavior is shaped and his interest maintained (Skinner, 1961).

Several novel approaches for programed learning have been initiated and others are still in the process of development, at the very early levels of education and also for adults. At the prenursery, nursery, kindergarten, and first-grade levels, Moore (1963) utilized automated and nonautomated equipment in a permissive atmosphere to help both ultraslow and ultrarapid learners gain intrinsic and extrinsic satisfaction from the learning process.

At the fourth-grade level experiments with programed instruction have been developed by Torrance and Gupta (1964) and by Crutchfield and his co-workers at the fifth- and sixth-grade levels (Crutchfield & Covington, 1965). Parnes (1958) has programed brainstorming procedures (to be considered in Chapter XIII) as a means of stimulating students' creativity at higher educational levels.

At first we are struck with a seeming paradox between programed instruction and creative work: The paradox, according to Crutchfield and Covington (1965), involves the fact that since the programed instruction material is prestructured, and since the student is led through the material step by step, there is danger of training individuals all of whom will think about the same problems in the same way. Prestructured material, it could be argued, does not allow the student to think in ways that are natural to himself, nor does it allow him to follow his unique approach to material. This militates against the possibility that a student will make the most of his own distinctive style. Programed instruction also runs the danger of requiring little effort on the part of the individual and might diminish the amount of energy put forth for mental searching and striving. Consequently, the individual may not be stimulated to seek creative pursuits. While creativity involves rejection of authority, programed instruction provides the student with no opportunity to reject the material presented to him. This experience might result in developing too much deference to authority. A good program involves clarity and precision. Such an experience might develop in the student ways of behaving and thinking that could interfere with his capacity to tolerate ambiguity and complexity—which some researchers have come to regard as necessary for creativity.

These are some very real problems in the use of programed instruction as a means of fostering creativity. To develop good programs for these purposes, as for teaching purposes generally, involves a great deal of ingenuity on the part of program writers to avoid "overly strong commitment to rigid forms of programing and by inventing new programing techniques that are positively adapted to the requirements of creativity training [Crutchfield & Covington, 1965, p. 8] ." We can put to good use "the self-pacing, self-directing, and self-administering features of programed instruction [which] lend themselves directly to the requirements of creativity training, for these characteristics do place the focus of cognitive initiative in the individual, and they open the way for an optimal accommodation of the program to the distinctive cognitive style of the individual [Crutchfield & Covington, 1965, p. 8] ."

To illustrate the kind of material involved in these programed procedures, consider that utilized by Crutchfield and his co-workers, which focuses directly on creativity. After thorough analysis of both the cognitive and personality factors involved in the creative process, and with certain carefully thought-out assumptions of how an auto-instructional program should be constructed, Crutchfield and his co-workers developed a 13-lesson program for fifth- and sixth-grade children (Covington & Crutchfield, 1965; Covington, 1968). The program is made up of simple detective and mystery stories selected so that they will be of interest to children. They are illustrated by cartoons and presented in booklet form with 30 pages per lesson. Each lesson is self-administered and the student paces himself. The stories combine the basic elements of problem solving and situations that involve various areas of curriculum content.

In each lesson a mystery problem is presented, followed by clues and information. The child is to discover the solution by himself. Continuity is maintained throughout the lessons by two school children, Jim and Lila, who are brother and sister. Jim and Lila learn to be detectives by taking lessons from their uncle who is both a science teacher and a spare-time detective. Jim and Lila serve at least two important functions. First, for feedback purposes, novel and uncommon responses are presented as Jim's and Lila's ideas. Thus, first the student generates his own responses, then Jim and Lila tell theirs. Second, Jim and Lila serve as potential models for the students to emulate. The student, therefore, participates with two very positive models that he can identify with and imitate. The models are not perfect but they learn from their mistakes. They start off poor in problem solving and then become progressively better. It was hoped as the student went through the program that as a result of his experience with the models in the stories, he would develop a sense of his own improvement and progressive development in the various thinking skills.

How effective are these programed instructional techniques? In one study two pairs of fifth-grade and one pair of sixth-grade classes (making a combined total of 195 pupils) were involved. Prior to their use of the programed instruction materials a 6-hour pretest battery was administered to the students. This pretest battery consisted of creative thinking tests and an attitude inventory for problem solving (Covington, 1966). The pairs of classes were closely matched on intelligence, attitudes, and initial creative-thinking and problem-solving skills. One class of each pair served as the control, while the other participated in the programed instruction program as part of their regular classroom work for 1 hour a day for a 3-week period. Children worked individually. At the end of the training period, an 8-hour posttest battery was administered, and then 5 months later as many of the fifth-grade children who could be located were given a 1-hour battery to determine whether the effects of training lasted until that time.

The results of the first part of the study are rather exciting. The 98 students who were instructed did very much better on almost all of the problem-solving tests than did the 97 control subjects. Not only were the differences between the two groups statistically significant, but they were also large on an absolute basis.

Of particular interest to us is the fact that among the tests for which differences were found were tests of divergent thinking, which Guilford tells us are related to creativity. On the pretest form of one of these tests children were given squares and asked to draw as many different objects as they could "that no one else will think of [Covington and Crutchfield, 1965, p. 4]." As an integral part of their drawings the children had to use the square. In the posttest the children used circles instead of squares. Each idea was scored for "originality" using Torrance's method based on statistical infrequency of occurrence. The authors report that the trained children did markedly better than uninstructed children, and of course the difference between the two groups on the originality measure was statistically significant. This result suggests that the effects of the training program are generalizable since the students had nothing like this test in the training program. And, the same result was found with the other tests of divergent thinking that were part of the criterion battery (Covington & Crutchfield, 1965). Instructed children also showed significant positive changes in their attitudes toward problems. They valued problems more highly and the activities (question-asking and persistence of attack) associated with them.

To determine how permanent the effects were, a follow-up study was carried out 5 months after the study just described, and on both the problem-solving tests and the tests of divergent thinking the students who had been instructed maintained their superiority over the uninstructed students (Covington and Crutchfield, 1965). Furthermore, the training proved effective despite differences in intelligence, sex, and initial levels of test performance. Approximately the same size gains were obtained over a range of intelligence levels; boys and girls show the same effects.

While the report by Covington and Crutchfield (1965) is very sanguine about the long-term effects of the training program, a later report by Covington (1968) tempers these results somewhat. He reports that for measures of problem-solving ability, the experimental group did do better (and significantly so from a statistical point of view) than the control group, but the absolute differences were smaller than those obtained after the first posttest. The results for tests of creativity were inconsistent. In one study of 108 children, the experimental group performed better than the control group, and in another study where a somewhat larger number of students was studied, the differences between the experimental and control groups washed out. Thus, after five months the effects of training as manifest in creative thinking tests were "at best marginal." Covington says one should not be surprised at these results, for the problems in these tests were not focused on or trained for in the General Problem Solving Program. Therefore, they should "be more likely to reflect a greater diminution in training effect [p. 28]" than problem-solving tests for which the students could use the strategies that they had been trained in.

The study just referred to was carried out in 1963 and another study was begun in 1964. In the 1964 study the auto-instructional program was extended to 16 lessons (Covington *et al.*, 1966). New criterion items were developed to study the degree of transfer, and two criterion tests were included in the training program (after lesson 4 and after lesson 10) for information on how rapidly the instructed children increase their effectiveness over the control children. Finally, other experimental conditions were also included: (1) a Passive Exposure condition, in which the child read the materials as a story and was not instructed to try to solve the problems himself; (2) a Rules Only condition, in which the child was provided with a set of didactic rules to aid him in thinking. The sample for this study was 286 children and included both high and low achievers.

All aspects of this study were not completed in time for the published report (Covington & Crutchfield, 1965), but among results reported were that (1) instructed children showed marked superiority over the control children on the posttest battery on practically every one of the tasks in the criterion test battery and on each of the criterion variables. These results raise the question whether the children were trained in new problem-solving skills or whether there was an activation of the use of skills the child already possessed. The authors believe, because of the brevity of the training program, that there was an activation of the use of skills already possessed. (2) There is rapid acceleration in problem-solving efficiency with very modest training. After four lessons, which were followed by the first criterion test, the instructed children were found to be superior to the uninstructed children and to the Passive Exposure and Rules Only children. After 16 lessons the data for three problems in the posttest measure indicated that the instructed children widened their superiority over the controls; the Passive Exposure condition also came to "facilitate proficiency in thinking to a marked degree [p. 10]"; the Rules Only group also exceeded the control group, but it was not as effective as the Passive Exposure or instructed groups. The results in both the 1963 and 1964 studies were stronger for the fifth-grade than for the sixth-grade children and presumably, the authors suggest, indicate the need for a more advanced and possibly differently oriented program for the older children.

In view of the fact that results presented previously cast some doubt on the longer-term effects of the training program, Covington (1968) asks whether a creative thinking program is actually needed for children when one considers such a program against the background of the children's total educational program. Those children who were not exposed to the training program caught up with the experimental group either as a result of maturation or as a result of experience. It is conceivable, though, that more significant changes, and changes that would last much longer, could have been obtained if the training program lasted for the whole school year or longer. A well devised *long-range* program would be of so much greater benefit to the tutored child participant, that the untutored child would not catch up in the long run.

Furthermore, although the results indicated that the untrained students caught up with trained ones "in terms of sheer proficiency, they may be markedly deficient in the very attitudinal dispositions necessary to put such skills to meaningful use [p. 28]." Therefore, one should not lose sight of some of the values a creativity program may provide that a child cannot find elsewhere, such as the excitement of working on a complex problem and the satisfaction of finding an answer to it. Such experiences may be exceedingly crucial in a child's development so that he looks forward to fulfilling his creative potential. Indeed, Covington suggests it is conceivable that the development of positive attitudes to creativity and to the manifestation of one's creative potential may be more important than the development of specific skills.

Because of the encouraging results with programed instruction, further work is continuing at Berkeley with this orientation. The work involves further development in lessons that can be used for remedial purposes and lessons that can be used for providing a more direct link between the skills trained for and the skills demanded in the curricular subjects the students are studying. Other programs are being developed for areas of creative thinking, other than problem solving (such as creative understanding) and of innovation (currently, "for instance, to develop a play), and other techniques are being used where the aim is to help develop in the student positive attitudes as a creative thinker.

Covington's and Crutchfield's work is very much in process. New information about it is constantly being generated. Thus, while the studies already presented indicated that there was some variability in the method's long-term effects, more recent work again provided evidence of the existence of these effects. In response to a communication from us about the nature of these effects, Covington (1969, personal communication) wrote, "In our earlier work . . . we did indeed find wide variations in the effectiveness of the training materials from study to study; sometimes there were large follow-up effects and at other times little, if any, indication of them. However, in our most recent work in which we exercised a great deal more statistical and experimental control, we find a reasonably high degree of consistency in this matter—indicating a fairly powerful residual effect even after many months." Hopefully as experience accumulates in this area we will know more about what kinds of pupils will profit most from this type of instruction as well as the nature of the conditions that will make this possible.

There are other studies of programed instruction and creativity. Noteworthy among them is one by Torrance and Gupta (1964), who developed a series of audio tapes and programed materials to help stimulate creativity in the fourth grade because they observed a decline in creative thinking abilities at this grade level. Experimental and control groups in the fourth grade in three different states were compared. Teachers in the experimental classes used provided materials every 2 weeks. Teachers in the control group, among whom were some who had already worked out their own plans for encouraging creativity, were instructed to go ahead with whatever they had planned. To study the effects of the programed materials, Torrance and Gupta compared students' scores on tests of creative thinking abilities developed by Torrance, which were administered at the beginning and at the end of the school term. The authors report that "the evidence is in favor of the experimental procedures [Torrance & Gupta, 1964, p. 103]."

An interesting by-product of the experimental procedures was that students' attitudes toward school were also affected. There was a tendency for fewer of the experimental students to say they "hated" school than was true of the control students. The evidence on the degree to which both experimentals and controls participated in independent creative activities during vacation periods was inconclusive, but there was some evidence to suggest that, while the controls tended to participate in structured and academic activities, they were more adventurous, nonacademic, and playful.

There is some concern that concentrated effort devoted to creativity may interfere with a student's acquisition of traditional educational skills. Torrance and Gupta (1964) studied this problem but obtained inconclusive results. The experimental materials may have interfered with the acquisition of skills in one school, "facilitated their acquisition in another, and made no difference in the third. It would appear," they suggest, "that whether the experimental materials interfere with, facilitate, or fail to affect the development of traditional educational skills depends upon the way in which the teacher uses the materials and how well he pursues his usual goals [pp. 104-105] ."

Two other findings are reported by Torrance and Gupta (1964). There was no difference between teachers in the experimental and control groups in their ability to identify creative talent as measured by the creativity tests used. And finally, differences were found in the students' career aspirations. Those in the experimental groups chose a wider variety of occupations, and a larger proportion of their peers in the control groups chose occupations that were among the most popular for the fourth grade.

A third investigator in this area is Sidney Parnes, who is president of the Creative Education Foundation. He directs many brainstorming and creative problem-solving training programs as well as research in this area. We shall have opportunity to discuss his work at length later. At this point we focus our attention on his work on programed brainstorming procedures. To evaluate its effectiveness he studied 186 students equated for intelligence and education (high school seniors who were expected to continue further with their education), and divided them into three groups of 62 each. One served as a control group and received no training. The second studied the programed materials by themselves. The third group studied the programed materials under the guidance and supervision of instructors. All three groups just mentioned were further subdivided in terms of the type of school from which they came and were differentiated in terms of their rated emphases on academic matters and interest in both cultural and enrichment opportunities.

The two groups of students that had training with the programed materials had such training for 13 weeks. Two class sessions per week were held. Prior to training, students were tested for a variety of cognitive abilities and one personality factor—dominance. After training, the groups were retested for these same characteristics.

With one exception—associational fluency—there were no demonstrable effects of the training program on any of the cognitive characteristics in one type of school. The training also did not have any significant effect on dominance, the one personality factor studied. In a previous study devoted to the effectiveness of unprogramed creative problem solving (Meadow & Parnes, 1959) with older students in day and evening college classes, it was found that training did in fact produce positive effects on dominance which increased after training.

The real effects of the training program were manifest in the cognitive tests. Both groups of students who worked with the programed material made greater gains on the cognitive tests than did the control students (those who had no experience with creative problem solving). Further, those who worked under the guidance and supervision of instructors did better than those who did not. The latter group did better than those who had no experience, but they were not as different from this group as were those who worked with instructors.

Thus, programed instruction in creative problem solving, according to Parnes' (1958) data, has positive effects on cognitive factors, and these effects are stronger if the training is under the supervision of an instructor. If no instructor is available, then studying the materials alone is better than not having any experience at all. But no matter how an individual is exposed to the programed material, dominance, as a personality characteristic, is not affected.

After the course of the training experience was over, the students were asked for their reactions. Instructor-taught students found the course more interesting and felt they gained more from the course than did the others, but both instructor-taught students and those who worked with the programed materials by themselves reported they had used what they had learned and felt that they would continue to apply what they learned in the future.

The effectiveness of the combination of instructor plus programed instruction may be a lead to a means for overcoming some of the concerns expressed previously by Hess and Tenezakis (1970). As more experience accumulates in this area it is conceivable that the role of the teacher may become more critical in a conjoint effort with the teacher, and the student exposed to both teacher and machine will come away with a more humanlike experience than if he were exposed to the machine alone.

While teaching machines can be valuable to stimulating creativity, several cautions need to be kept in mind: First, the effectiveness of teaching machines for our purposes has been tested thus far only with *tests* of creativity. Indeed, at the grade level at which the machines are used this is about the only evaluation technique that can be used. Nevertheless, interest must still focus on whether or not the machines will facilitate the creativity of students later in life. Long-term follow-up studies are needed for this.

The second factor that needs to be kept in mind is the "Hawthorne effect." This effect is named after an experience in industrial situations where various attempts were made to increase workers' productivity. After the first technique was tried, workers' productivity did go up. But then it also came down. Another technique was tried and productivity went up. It also came down, and so on.

What seemed to be at the root of what was effective was not the specific technique that was tried but the fact that attention was being paid to the workers. It is still too early to say whether the positive results found with the machines are due to the Hawthorne effect.

In summary, potentially worthwhile activity is going on in the field of teaching machines, specifically, that hold promise for valuable findings and uses in the future. If nothing else, the teachers and school administrators are likely to become more aware of the roles they may play in inhibiting creativity and the roles they could play to stimulate it.

Affecting the Preparatory Stage Outside of the School Environment

This chapter has focused on the school environment and the critical role it plays for the preparatory phase in creativity. What can be done to stimulate the preparatory phase of the creative process at the adult level? The following are several suggestions.

One important problem to cope with is motivation. The individual must have a desire to innovate or be creative. Else, he will not deviate from the present and will not challenge that which exists. He needs to stir himself up, which can be done in a variety of ways—challenging himself to be creative or trying to emulate the lives and achievements of creative individuals, which can be found in biographies of creative individuals.

Having stirred himself, having become dissatisfied (and even irritated) with that which exists, one starts looking for questions, problems to be solved, things to do. This may entail getting additional training or some specific required information. If so, it should be sought out with a constructive and creative set. Choices need to be made but care needs to be exercised not to become involved in premature evaluation and criticism.

One may need to break through one's existing patterns of behavior and patterns of seeing and doing things. To achieve this goal demands new inputs and new experiences which can come from different sources. Travel to foreign countries implicitly requires changing some of one's behavior. It also exposes one to differences in people's attitudes, values, behavior, and technology. All of this can be compared with what one has himself experienced in the past. If travel is impossible then reading about different cultures is helpful. Visiting different ethnic communities is similarly helpful.

Museums, natural history, art, and technological-scientific exhibitions contain many idea-stirring materials. Lectures are another source and they need not necessarily be in one's own field. In all likelihood, lectures in different fields frequently result in "inputs" and ideas for which one can see uses in one's own field. And one need not seek for creativity in one's own field. For some individuals, one's own field can be so fraught with tension and anxiety that his creativity can be best manifest in a different field.

Gordon (1961), as we shall see in discussing his group technique, *synectics*, for stimulating creativity, suggests reading books on animal behavior for they are good sources for metaphors that can be of help in creative problem solving. Such books, as well as books on travel and science fiction, and catalogs of different subjects, may also be valuable sources of new inputs of information. Consideration might also be given to any of a number of university, privately held, or industrially sponsored seminars for stimulating creativity. And, the individual may wish to consider some of the self-help procedures for hypothesis formation considered in the next chapter, for they may be quite useful in starting the preparatory phase into action.

SUMMARY

The preparatory stage of the creative process begins long before the individual embarks upon the process. Theoretically the preparatory stage involves many experiences in the family and outside of it that predispose the individual to whether or not he will be motivated to embark upon the creative process, to the kinds of data he will be exposed to, and the kinds of solutions he will seek. This chapter was limited to the educational or school environment.

Within the school environment attention was focused on social relationships between the pupil and his teacher and pupil and his classmates. Research evidence indicated how the nature of these interactions could affect a young person's creativity. But left to their own devices both teachers and classmates are, in general, likely to engage in behavior that is oriented to keeping the individual from deviating from the group and from being creative.

Turning to a consideration of teaching techniques, attention focused on the effects of sets or attitudes a student was given or assumed as he was exposed to or as he learned about new information. In general a critical attitude resulted in less creative situations than if he assumed a constructive or creative attitude. Just as evaluation of prior information is critical, so evaluation of the pupil or student is likely to have critical effects. Here, if no evaluation but encouragement to explore occurs, it is best, and then positive evaluation is better than negative evaluation. Both these generalizations, that about prior information and that about evaluating the individual, require qualification, for a complete statement of the nature of the effects will depend on future research and when completed will no doubt be found to be related to the type of individual, the kind of prior information, the kind of evaluation, and the kind of solution sought.

To help facilitate a school system's efforts to the fostering and development of creative potential, it was suggested that schools consider the following possibilities: (1) Make use of diagnostic surveys to learn the assets and liabilities of the specific school as an organizational system including the qualifications of its personnel, physical plant, communication system, value system, etc. as they affect the pupils' or students' learning and creativity; (2) To orient a school to creativity one must start at the top and carefully select or evaluate the value system of administrators and school principals as well as how they interact with their teachers and pupils; (3) Similarly, teachers need to be selected so that their values and goals are also directed to creativity. For school administrators, principals, and teachers, specific characteristics that one might look for were suggested. (4) Psychological testing of students is very important to a better understanding of a pupil's abilities. To psychological test batteries currently in use it would be most desirable to add tests like those developed by Guilford and Torrance as well as personality tests so that one would have a better understanding of each pupil's potential for creativity. (5) Creative pupils may well find themselves in situations quite different from those other pupils are in. It would therefore be quite helpful if guidance counselors were trained to cover the range of pupils they are currently concerned with but also trained to help the creative child deal with his problems. (6) Continued research is necessary to facilitate further understanding of creativity as it develops throughout the school years. There is a developmental process here about which we should know more. (7) Teacher training programs might add to their curricula how teachers can teach for creativity. (8) New teaching techniques need to be developed, and along these lines the use of computers for assisted instruction is one of the procedures worthy of further considerations.

While this chapter focused primarily on the elementary and to some extent on the high school environment as critical to the preparatory stage in the creative process, some attention was also paid to what can be done in this stage outside of the school environment. This is especially important for the adult. For adults groundwork must be laid in motivation to be creative and a desire to change present or existing conditions. New inputs and new experiences would also be quite helpful. These might include foreign travel and/or reading about foreign cultures. Attendance at museums and exhibitions also add new inputs that can be used for later creative integrations. Reading books on animal behavior, science fiction, catalogs, etc. are sources of new inputs as well as of analogies that can be helpful for creative problem solving. Finally, attendance at university, privately held, or industrially sponsored programs for stimulating creativity might also be quite helpful.

Chapter **IX**

Stimulating Hypothesis Formation

Leonardo da Vinci, in his *Precepts of the Painter*, referred to "A Way to Stimulate and Arouse the Mind to Various Inventions"

> I will not refrain from setting among these precepts a new device for consideration which, although it may appear trivial and almost ludicrous, is nevertheless of great utility in arousing the mind to various inventions.
> And this is that if you look at any walls spotted with various stains or with a mixture of different kinds of stones, if you are about to invent some scene you will be able to see in it a resemblance to various different landscapes adorned with mountains, rivers, rocks, trees, plains, wide valleys and various groups of hills. You will also be able to see divers combats and figures in quick movement, and strange expressions of faces, and outlandish costumes, and an infinite number of things which you can then reduce into separate and well-conceived forms. With such walls and blends of different stones, it comes about as it does with the sound of bells, in whose clanging you may discover every name and word that you can imagine [MacCurdy, 1956, pp. 873-874].

In 1823 Ludwig Börne wrote an essay entitled, "The Art of Becoming an Original Writer in Three Days." [According to Ernest Jones (1953), Freud's biographer, this essay may have been one of the sources for Freud's discovery of the use and significance of free association as a procedure in psychoanalytic therapy.] Börne's work concludes with these suggestions:

> Here follows the practical prescription I promised. Take a few sheets of paper and for three days in succession write down, without any falsification or hypocrisy, everything that comes into your head. Write what you think of yourself, of your women, of the Turkish war, of Goethe, of the Fonk criminal case, of the Last Judgment, of those senior to you in authority—and when the three days are over you will be amazed at what novel and startling thoughts have welled up in you. That is the art of becoming an original writer in three days [quoted in Jones, 1953, p. 246].

These two suggestions, made between 150 and 200 years ago, are very similar psychologically to a number of the techniques discussed in this chapter. They are all self-help techniques that a person can use without formal training or guidance and they all have the same goal—to help increase the number of ideas or hypotheses available to a person for starting a process that will result in a creative end-product. They suggest a variety of ways of reaching this goal, such as: the "externalization" of the parameters, variables, and elements that make up the problem or which may play critical roles in its solution. The individual is encouraged to put these parameters, etc., "out there" instead of keeping them in his head. For example, the individual may be encouraged to make up two lists—one containing the variables and the other the conditions under which they might be used. Then by placing the lists parallel to each other and moving them up and down, the individual can look at each variable under all conditions. These permutations and combinations of variables and conditions may stimulate a variety of ideas. In so doing, the individual works in a concrete and observable manner to achieve results that the creative person achieves in his mind.

Also common to a number of the procedures is the encouragement given to the individual to remove, lower, or defer his standards of evaluation and censorship. He is asked to suggest freely any and all ideas that occur to him and then to wait and see how they turn out before trying to judge whether his work will justify his efforts and whether his ideas will meet with his or others' approval. Premature evaluations may lead to the discarding of some very promising possibilities. These may never be realized if the individual becomes too judgmental and evaluative.

Also implicit or explicit in a number of the procedures is the desirability of overcoming a number of past experiences with the objects or materials with which the individual works. All too often these objects and materials are perceived in terms of fixed and immutable functions based on accumulated experiences and habitual patterns of behavior. These then become fixed as limits placed on how these objects might be utilized in newer combinations with other objects and materials. The techniques to be considered try to help a person overcome such rigidities and blocks and to proceed with the creative process to a creative solution.

The procedures also include other suggestions. The problem the individual starts with or the manner in which he has phrased for himself the initial task, whether it be a painting, a theory, a technological problem, etc., is not necessarily the best statement of the problem if the creative process is to get off the ground. Sometimes it is necessary to break the first statement down into its component parts so that feasible ideas for each of them can be developed and as these are achieved the desired creative end-product can be attained. On other occasions a completely different approach is required. The way in which a problem is first seen has to be changed before effective work can begin. One of the best explications of this approach is to be found in Chapter XV where we consider a group procedure for encouraging creativity called *synectics* that was developed by Gordon (1961). There are two steps in this procedure that illustrate what we have in mind. One of these steps is *making the familiar strange* and the other is *making the strange familiar*. We shall discuss these later.

It is most important to the on-going development of the creative process to come up with a "good" question or "good" approach, etc. Some creative individuals do this by toying with ideas and images in their minds; others do it in some inspired manner; others intuitively; and still others use techniques such as those described here. No technique presented here can say what the criteria of a "good" question or a "good" approach are; they can only help in originating possibilities. How the "good" question is selected is, like "inspiration" and "intuition," one of the "intangibles" in the creative process. Some persons may select the good idea through a process of trial and error, looking at and testing every combination and permutation but, most usually, the creative individual has what we have called an "aesthetic feel" for the alternative with the most potential or for that suggestion or idea that will most likely lead to the creative end state.

In this chapter, various procedures will be considered for hypothesis formation, a first stage in the creative process. These procedures seem to be best suited to the development of ideas and alternatives to further action in the creative process. These procedures are not to be limited to this stage. On the contrary, the individual should choose and make use of whatever technique he thinks will help him in any stage of the creative process. Moreover, it is also important to keep in mind that the value of a technique depends not only on its specific content but also on the ability, motivation, and curiosity of the person using it. Effective use of these techniques requires in addition a desire to be creative, a high energy level, the ability to persevere and concentrate, and the desire to take chances; and throughout all this, probably in the midst of some confusion, anxiety, and self-doubt, the capacity to remain confident and optimistic that a creative goal will be attained.

By way of further introduction to the various techniques to be considered we shall now turn to a more thorough discussion of several matters that were only touched upon previously—perception, language, inspiration, and intuition, so that a more complete theoretical and research basis will be available for the techniques to be considered.

PERCEPTION

How an individual perceives objects in his environment will obviously affect what he can do with them. If objects were perceived strictly in terms of their formal and structured qualities, there would be difficulty in combining or integrating them or any part of them with other objects in the environment. So the possibility of developing novel end states, whether they be paintings or mechanical devices, would be limited. The perceptions of many people are perceived largely in terms of these structured qualities, and therefore they find their creativity hampered.

But people are capable of other kinds of perception, one of which is *physiognomic*. According to this perceptual style, how objects are perceived depends on the motor and affective attitude of the person. Werner (1957) has written about this kind of perception, but its investigation as a general principle of cognitive functioning remained unexplored (Gardner *et al.*, 1959) until Stein, with the aid of others (Stern *et al.*, 1956), developed a technique to explore it.

The quotation from da Vinci at the beginning of this chapter is an example of the kind of perception referred to. Previously (page 27) we presented another example of this kind of perception when we cited Werner's (1957, p. 71) reference to Kandinsky's biography in which the artist tells us how he sees rain drops on his palette "puckishly flirting with each other," which come together as "sly threads," mix in with the colors, "and roguishly skip about . . . ." According to Werner, physiognomic perception precedes concept formation. It has appeared in children's perceptions, primitive languages, poetry, and the language of schizophrenic subjects, as well as in the reports of subjects who have taken mescaline. Considered in these terms, it is apparent that physiognomic perception is a primitive (meaning it appears developmentally earlier and is superseded by other forms) form of perception, and individuals who are capable of using it constructively in their creative pursuits are presumably capable of what psychoanalysts call "regression in service of the ego" (Hartmann, 1964).

Because this concept of "regression in service of the ego" is a rather important one in the creative process, a digression to elaborate upon it is in order. Regression refers to a return to behavior patterns that are characteristic of earlier stages of psychological development. The phrase "in service of the ego" signifies that that which was returned to, that which was repressed, is now used for progressive adaptation, to further and enhance psychological development. This type of regression is to be differentiated from those instances where "regression" by itself is used to indicate that the person is involved in a retreat from anxiety and an environment with which he cannot cope to an earlier kind of defense and an earlier stage of development. The adult who regresses may become more immature in his behavior and the child who regresses may become even more childish (as the older child who has stopped sucking his thumb begins to do so, regresses, when a sibling is born). Also, when an individual regresses to earlier or more "primitive" adjustment patterns, it may suggest that a psychotic process is in operation. By contrast, when regression in the service of the ego occurs, that which is regressed to is used constructively. Creative adults who so regress may appear "child-like" but not "child-ish." The creative individual regresses knowingly, voluntarily, and without fear so that he can gain a new perspective of his surroundings and his work. He can become more playful and break up the rigid structures and functions that attend upon his adult psychological development and which interfere with his creative process. He then, as a result of his regression, can use his new found perceptions in conjunction with his adult knowledge, perceptions, and discipline to move to more creative results.

As was said previously, knowledge of physiognomic perception has been available, but techniques to study it and its associated psychological characteristics have not. However, with the development of a technique called the *Physiognomic Cue Test* by Stein (Stein, 1974) for studying physiognomic perception, systematic studies of the relationship between creativity and physiognomic perception were begun. The test, a rather simple one, consists of two sets of items. One concerns itself with what we call *feeling-physiognomic* and the other is *thing-physiognomic*. For both sets the person taking the test is presented with a visual stimulus and a continuum of alternatives along which he can indicate what the stimulus looks like to him. One end of the continuum is the physiognomic end and the other is the formal end. The continuum increases in score as the subject moves to the physiognomic side. The subject receives three scores—feeling-physiognomic, thing-physiognomic, and a total score that is a combination of the previous two.

An example of feeling-physiognomic is the visual stimulus ⊙, for which the formal alternative is "circle with dot in it," while the physiognomic alternative is "a feeling of smallness." For thing-physiognomic an example is ⌣, for which the formal alternative is "two arcs" and the physiognomic alternative is "open mouth."

A good deal of research still needs to be done with this test. Thus far it has been used in two studies where there were criteria of manifest creativity and in one rather large study devoted to determining the kinds of characteristics to which the physiognomic scores are related. One of the manifest creativity studies in which the test was used was conducted by Walker (1955), who studied mathematicians and found that the more creative ones did in fact score higher on this test—were more physiognomic—than their less creative peers. The other, a study of industrial research chemists by Stein *et al.* (unpublished), found that the more creative ones tended to be (but not significantly) more physiognomic than their less creative colleagues.

Rosett and his co-workers (1967) utilized the test in a study of 1,038 applicants to the Cooper Union for the Advancement of Science and Art in New York City. The total group consisted of 757 males and 281 females who applied for courses in engineering, physics, architecture, and art. The results were that females generally scored higher on physiognomic perceptions than males; artists generally scored higher than engineers or students who expressed an interest in physics; among students of art and architecture, a relationship between one of the physiognomic test factors and openness to affect-laden thoughts was found, but this was not true among the physics and engineering students; for art students the feeling factor in the Physiognomic Cue Test correlated with scores on a questionnaire developed by Rosett and his co-workers for feeling style and abstraction style but not with the score for shapes; the feeling factor also correlated low but significantly with a measure of art aptitude, and the thing factor was related to a measure of architectural aptitude; a low correlation was obtained between freshman art grades and the physiognomic feeling factor; the feeling factor correlated negatively with several of the scores involved in the admissions criterion for engineering and physics students.

Thus, there seems to be evidence that physiognomic perception is indeed related to various aspects of creativity. To our knowledge no training program actually trains a person to become physiognomic in his perceptions, but the concept is used in some training programs (e.g., in synectics, considered in Chapter XV). Individuals might find it helpful, therefore, to practice by themselves to attribute humanlike form or aspects to inanimate objects; to empathize with the different materials and objects in their environments, and through these procedures to break through the rigid categorization of objects that restricts the ways they are conventionally thought about and perceived.

LANGUAGE

Language affects much of what the creative person does, how he perceives the world around him, and how he thinks. People are likely to think of language simply as a means of communicating the end stage of the creative process. This is obviously insufficient. Language is more critical than that, as indicated by Korzybski's work (1941) and by what behavioral scientists call the Sapir-Whorf hypothesis.

Language serves as a tool for carving out of the environment that which "exists" and that which is to be worked with. A person may think he is dealing with or talking about objective reality when in fact he is in many respects at the mercy of the language he is using. The concepts of his language become his guides to reality. If his language is deficient in certain concepts, he will be limited in what he can do; if his language is rich in concepts, he is proportionately more powerful. We shall return to the Sapir-Whorf hypothesis in Chapter XI (page 300).

Language serves as a means of recording experience and as a means of defining, refining and reporting it. By increasing the range of available concepts (by expanding his vocabulary, technical as well as nontechnical), a person can become more creatively effective. But just as language can affect creativity positively, it can also affect it negatively. Naming objects gives us a sense of mastery and understanding. Many objects also involve implicit or explicit classification systems. These classification systems can assume rigid characteristics that are often difficult to overcome. DeBono makes the point: "The rigidity of words is associated with the rigidity of classifications. Again, the rigidity of classifications leads to rigidity in the way things are looked at [DeBono, 1967, p. 82]." If the creative process is to progress without too many hindrances, the rigidity of classification just alluded to must be overcome. This may not be as easy as it seems because the use of a naming and classification system can give a person a false sense of understanding and mastery.

Several of the procedures considered later are designed to help overcome the rigidity of classifications and break through the automatization of perceptions and responses. Brainstorming, attribute listing, and morphological analysis are all ways of overcoming rigidity of classification. Another way, though, is by simply becoming more aware of how we use words and language. Naming things, thinking about things in terms of names, and the use of nouns reinforce the classification approach. One way to circumvent this situation is to think of objects in terms of verbs, or in terms of their functions and uses. A chair is for holding things up, whether one sits or stands on it. In terms of material discussed in this book, we can talk about *perception* or we can talk about *perceiving*. The latter is the more appropriate here, for the verb form denotes that energy is involved in the process, whether a person actually seeks out material in his environment to attend to or whether stimuli from the environment impinge upon him. To speak of perception, in the nominative case, is almost to endow this *process* with a concrete existence outside the person, but when we speak of *perceiving*, we implicitly involve the individual in the process, be his role active or passive.

A third, more practical, illustration of our point here comes from *synectics*. Gordon, it is said, had the assignment from a client to develop a new can opener. Gordon did not tell members of his group what their goal was for fear of limiting their associations to existing objects. It is probable that saying "can opener" to himself would lead a person to think of a mechanical device, of something-on-top-of-something. Such specificity restricts the kinds of associations that can come to mind. On the other hand, Gordon suggested to the group that they think of *opening* in the hope that it might call to mind quite a wide range of possibilities from which they might make their final selection. At one point in the group's process one of the men suggested that nature had its own openers for its various containers, for example, the soft seam of the pea pod. Hence, instead of a can opener involving something-on-top-of-something, a novel approach became possible in which the "opener" (the soft seam which could be broken easily) was to be part of the container.

The technique just described in which a person uses the verb form of a word might also be combined with generalization to further increase the range of possible ideas available. For example, say a man works with duplicators. Shall we say he is involved only in duplicating and the making of additional copies of some typed or printed material? Or shall we say that duplicating material is a form of communication and he is involved in communicating information? If the latter is true, then in addition to duplicating by means of a machine, there are a large number of other ways of communicating information. One of these could be the use of the telephone for long distance transmission of information which can then be duplicated at a more distant point than would otherwise be possible. Or consider another example, the case of the individual who transports material by trucks. If we say he is involved in trucking then he will always be limited to the use of trucks but if we say he is involved in transporting materials, then use can be made of ships, airplanes, piggybacks, etc.

The concepts in this section are reminiscent of children's thought as expressed in *A Hole Is To Dig* (Krauss, 1952). Children think this way, but adults, because of the way in which they have been socialized, are more likely to think in terms of the formal aspects of the objects with which they have had experience, to assign names to the objects and to think in terms of nouns. It is suggested here that the individual can profit from thinking of things in less "adult" ways than usual (what we refer to elsewhere as regression in service of the ego). Several "regressive" forms are pointed out in Chapter XV, where we discuss a group form of creativity stimulation called *synectics*. All of these can be utilized to affect the individual's perceptions, language, and thought, thereby facilitating the creative process.

TWO OF THE MYSTIQUES—INSPIRATION AND INTUITION

Techniques for stimulating creativity are based essentially on the writings of creative individuals who have described their experiences and work habits and related them to the creative process. The validity and significance of these experiences and work habits can be substantiated in psychological investigations. Then the techniques which try to stimulate creativity either through duplicating a creative person's experiences or by providing some analogous way of achieving a similar result, also have a good foundation in available scientific knowledge.

There are, however, among the experiences described by creative individuals, some which have not been very thoroughly investigated, others which have not yet proven tractable to scientific investigation, and still others which possibly may not stand up well under further scrutiny. For the moment we regard these experiences as constituting the mystique of the creative process. Five experiences which make up part of this mystique have been selected for specific comment in this book. In this chapter we shall discuss three of them: inspiration, intuition, and at the end of the chapter, how a hypothesis is selected for further testing. In the next chapter we shall discuss what is involved in following through in the testing of a hypothesis and the decision as to when the final product is regarded as complete.

It is impossible at the moment to provide techniques to facilitate these mystique aspects of the creative process. What can be done is to describe them, to understand them better, to provide what laboratory evidence is available to substantiate their validity, to discuss tenable theoretical suggestions as to their plausibility, and, what might be most useful, to discuss the conditions that appear necessary for and conducive to their appearance and effectiveness. In these different indirect ways it is hoped that we can also provide some basis for future methods for stimulating creativity.

Inspiration

Many autobiographical and biographical accounts of the experiences of creative individuals describe how they became inspired by an idea that "took over" and eventually resulted in the novel product. Many of us are in awe of such experiences and envious of the creative person's accomplishments. Still others hope for and look forward to instant creativity and sit around waiting for an inspiration to occur.

There are no direct investigations of inspiration as it has been described in the creative process, for usually the experience occurs in the privacy of the creative person's laboratory or studio. The experience is therefore not available to another's observation and study. To some extent similar phenomena have been observed in experiments on productive thinking (Wertheimer, 1945) where a person who has insight behaves somehow like the person who is said to be inspired. The inspiration experience as it has been described by others, however, is more intense and more encompassing. On a theoretical level it may be that inspiration is associated with the individual's acceptance of ideas and feelings that were repressed in the unconscious (Lee, 1947).

On the basis of available experimental knowledge and theoretical hypotheses, it might be said that to achieve a state of inspiration an individual would have to prepare himself intensively in his field and devote himself sincerely to the work he has undertaken. He would need to discover the nature of the environmental conditions that he finds most conducive to creative work and to make use of them as he pursues a creative solution. Simultaneously he would need to relax and disinhibit those forces controlling access to and awareness of unconscious factors. Such "relaxing" behavior entails being unafraid of what is buried in his unconscious and being secure in his ability to deal with the repressed.

If nothing else, it should be apparent that it is foolhardy to sit and wait to be inspired, for inspirations occur to individuals who have spent much time in preparation, who have access to unconscious material that they can use effectively and then, when the inspiration does occur, have the discipline and perseverance to work it out effectively.

Intuition

Another experience contributing to the mystique of the creative process during the hypothesis-formation stage is intuition. And just as it is impossible to tell someone directly how to be inspired, so it is impossible to tell him how to have an intuition or a hunch, or how to intuit a potential answer to a problem. Some believe that it may be possible to teach this capacity, although it has not yet been done (Bruner, 1963). To be able to train people to be intuitive would be most desirable, for as Bruner (1963) points out, "The shrewd guess, the fertile hypothesis, the courageous leap to a tentative conclusion—these are the most valuable coin of the thinker at work, whatever his line of work [p. 14] ."

Intuition is a method of formulating or solving a problem in which the person has no conscious awareness or knowledge of how he arrived at the answer or what stimuli led him to it.

What are typically regarded as analytic modes of thought are not involved in the intuitive process, but these are necessary and must be used to check on the validity of the intuitive hunches. They will be considered in the next chapter.

There are relatively few experiments in the psychological literature devoted specifically to intuition.* Westcott (1964) attributes this lack to psychology's philosophical heritage. Citing Wild's (1938) review of the philosophical literature on this problem, Westcott says that this body of knowledge differs on several points. One is whether intuition is indeed based on sensory processes and hence can be studied, or whether it is based on abnormal, nonsensory processes that cannot be studied psychologically. At the moment, philosophy accepts the second point of view—that intuition cannot be studied psychologically.

Despite the stated philosophical view, there is, according to Westcott (1964), some general agreement between philosophical and psychological approaches. He says (and we agree)

---

*Westcott(1964, 1968) has reviewed the available work on intuition. He has also made several significant contributions of his own to this area (Westcott 1961, 1964, 1966, 1968; Westcott & Ranzoni, 1963; Westcott & Tolchin, 1968), some of which are cited in this chapter.

It is generally conceded that, when an individual intuits, he reaches a conclusion, a synthesis, a formulation, a solution to a problem or whatever it might be, without being aware of the basis on which this conclusion or synthesis is erected. ... As empirical scientists we are committed to our notions of intellectual and cognitive processes and to the sensory way of knowing things, and can operate successfully on the premise that the absence of support of conclusions in an intuition is only an apparent absence [p. 35].

There are only two experiments in psychology that have actually used the word "intuition" (Westcott, 1964). We introduce one of these by presenting a study that actually relates to what psychologists call "insight and/or unconscious concept formation" which is regarded as containing "the rudiments of exactly the same process" as that involved in intuitive breakthroughs in the sciences [Westcott, 1964, pp. 36, 38].

This study of insight and unconscious concept formation is an unpublished study by Snapper, cited by Westcott (1964). (The results of this study might also be interpreted as reflecting the effects of operant conditioning.) In this study the subject was given 400 cards that differed in their various characteristics and designs, so that no two were the same. On the cards were stars, crosses, circles, etc., in different numbers and colors. The cards also had cut or notched corners, etc. The subject was also given a sample card that was pasted over a box, and his task was to put each of the 400 cards either in this box if there was similarity between his card and the sample card, or in a "reject" box. As the subject went through this sorting procedure the experimenter told him whether he was correct or incorrect. A subject was regarded as having performed successfully in this experiment if he performed "correctly" on 25 successive trials.

Of the 52 subjects who participated in this experiment, 33 failed completely and 19 were successful. Among these 19 were 6 subjects with a performance curve that was "a simple learning curve"—it increased slowly to the criterion of success. For the remaining 13 an "insight curve" was obtained—after some sorts of the cards, there was a sharp jump in the number of the subject's correct sorts.

Looking at the 19 subjects who solved the problem successfully it was found that the 6 whose behavior looked like that of a learning curve required fewer trials to achieve the criterion of success than did the 13 who solved the problem by what seemed to be insight. Furthermore, the 13 presumably insightful solvers of the problem were able to verbalize the principle involved in the solution they achieved. On the other hand, those who achieved the success criterion slowly could not offer any principle or any "sensible reason" why they were successful. Some of those in the latter group were finally able to state some principle. Others did so only after very much encouragement, but the principles they offered were not accurate. Finally, in this experiment it was noted that those who were unable to verbalize the principle were more relaxed and casual in how they worked on the problem than were those who did verbalize the proper principle. It is this group of nonverbalizers that Westcott (1964) regards as intuitive.

We turn now to Westcott's own work which both supports the effectiveness of intuition and provides us with information as to the characteristics of intuiters. Westcott (1961) considers intuition manifest when a conclusion is arrived at on the basis of what might generally be regarded as insufficient evidence information. This he differentiates from "ordinary inference," in which the conclusion can be seen as stemming from the available evidence. Consequently, in his experimental work Westcott studied individuals in terms of how willing they were to make inferences on the basis of little information and how correct the conclusions were in these circumstances.

To study this problem with adult college students, Westcott developed a series of 20 problems. For each problem there were "clues" that the subject could obtain in a fixed order. If all of the clues were exposed simultaneously, a solution would be reached for which there could be a great deal of agreement. The problems consisted of both verbal and numerical series as well as both verbal and numerical analogies. The subject was directed to select one clue at a time by breaking a seal that revealed a clue. He could offer his conclusion at any time, or wait until he had broken all the seals. One subject, by definition, would be regarded as more intuitive than another if he used fewer clues and if he were correct in solving the series.

To illustrate the problems used, one five-clue verbal series problem consisted of the sequence of letters A, C, E, G, I; the subject had to indicate what the next letter (K) would be. For a numerical analogy the subject was presented with 4:2, 9:3, 25:5, 100:10, 64:8, and then told to complete 16:___ .

Using this approach Westcott (1961) found that people vary in (1) how much information they demand before solving a problem; and (2) their ability to arrive at correct solutions regardless of the amount of information they take. Moreover (3) the ratio of the number of correct solutions to the amount of information demanded varies between people; (4) whether much or little information is sought is not related to the correctness of the solution; and (5) the confidence that people have in their solutions is positively related to how efficient they are in solving the problems.

Westcott (1966) also found his measures of intuition to be consistent or statistically reliable at any one testing session, and that individuals were consistent in their intuitive behavior over a 3-year period—those who were more intuitive than others in one experiment maintained their relative standing three years later. Another study by Westcott and Tolchin (1968) in which incomplete line drawings were used found differences in intuitive behavior in subjects from nursery school through college. On the basis of this work, Westcott and Tolchin suggested the possiblitiy that the tendency to behave intuitively may be set early in life.

Finally, Westcott and Ranzoni (1963) studied the relationships between intuition and several psychological characteristics—measures of intellectual capacity and personality—in several groups of college females. Of particular interest to us are the characteristics of the four groups of subjects the experimenters established by using two variables—how much information the person demanded before offering a solution and how successful or accurate her solutions were. The subjects in these experiments were Vassar College students.

In one experiment Westcott and Ranzoni (1963) studied the relationships among three variables: information demanded, solution success, and a third derived measure, Efficiency, which is Success/Information Demand. These three scores were then correlated with the SAT verbal and mathematical scores (obtained from the College Entrance Examination Board Scholastic Aptitude Test), and cumulative grade point average. The results indicated a tendency for low Information Demand and high Success to be correlated with a high SAT math score. The data for the SAT verbal score were also in the same direction but not as strong. No significant relationships were found between any of the scores and cumulative grade point average.

Consequently, Westcott and Ranzoni (1963, p. 598) conclude that intuitive thinking as measured in this study was not related to college grades and that conventional measures of scholastic aptitude are "significantly but not profoundly related to intuitive thinking" as measured in their study.

A second study reported in the same paper (Westcott and Ranzoni, 1963) investigated the relationships between the same three variables and personality-attitude variables. There were three personality-attitude variables—one was of anxiety as measured by the Taylor Manifest Anxiety Scale (Taylor, 1953), and two were taken from the Vassar College attitude inventory. One was a measure of Impulse Expression (Sanford, Webster, & Freedman, 1957) and the other a measure of Flexibility. The results of this second study did not reveal any significant relationships between the problem-solving variables and the personality-attitude variables measured.

The two studies by Westcott and Ranzoni just reported were correlational studies with the results based on the total sample of subjects involved in the study. For the next three studies reported in the Westcott and Ranzoni (1963) paper, subjects were selected from the extremes. They were subjects who were at least one standard deviation (1 SD) high or low on both Information Demand and Success. On this basis four groups were established: (1) "Successful intuitive thinkers"—who were at least 1 SD *low* on Information Demand and at least 1 SD *high* on Success; (2) "unsuccessful wild guessers"—who were at least 1 SD *low* on Information Demand and at least 1 SD *low* on Success; (3) "careful successful problem solvers"—who were at least 1 SD *high* on Information Demand and 1 SD *high* on Success; (4) "careful but unsuccessful problem solvers"—who were at least 1 SD *high* on Information Demand and 1 SD *low* on Success. The number of persons in each of the groups varied as a function of available data.

The selection of extreme groups was one of the ways in which the last three studies differed from the first two. Another difference was in the kind of available information. In one study, rather than use the total scores obtained from the personality-attitude scale mentioned in the second study, the authors used an item analysis of the scale and studied the ways in which persons in the four groups just described responded differentially to these items.

The data for the fourth study were interview data which included the answers to such questions as the subjects' reactions to the testing sessions, whether the subject had a "consuming passion," whether she liked to take chances, etc. In the fifth and last study the subjects were given a checklist of 307 adjectives from which they were told to select those that applied to them.

Rather than present how each of the four groups differed on the various measures, we quote and paraphrase from Westcott and Ranzoni's summary description of each of the four groups.

(1) The "successful intuitive thinkers" did not differ very much from the other groups in mathematical or verbal aptitude scores or in college grades. Although they tended to be more impulsive and flexible than the other groups, these were not critical differences. What differentiates this group from others is that they saw themselves as unconventional and felt comfortable about it. They were very involved emotionally in what they were doing, although their affect fluctuated a great deal, but this did not worry them. They were not fearful individuals. They accepted challenge but could also live with doubt and uncertainty. Members of this group enjoyed risks and sought instabilities in the world. They made commitments to causes and were capable of creating. They were able to change their behavior and could be influenced by others, provided such influence affected their own development. They saw themselves as others did: "alert, independent, foresighted, confident, and spontaneous [Westcott & Ranzoni, 1963, p. 610]."

(2) The "unsuccessful wild guessers" were individuals who tried their hands at intuitive problem solving but failed. They were close to the average of the combined groups in this study on verbal and mathematical aptitude and their grades were not too different from those obtained by the other groups. They were somewhat impulsive and less flexible compared to the successful subjects. Like the successful intuitive thinkers, they were unconventional, but their defiance of convention had a desperate and anxious quality about it. They behaved as if they had to be different from others. They did not get emotionally involved in tasks but concentrated more on themselves. They tended to become

afraid in a crisis and were not confident with risks. They responded to risks with "grim determination." Compared to the other groups they were not very interested in other people, "not inclined to produce creatively" nor to get too deeply involved in causes. Although they admitted others had influenced them, they did not believe they had changed much. They regarded themselves as "alert, quick, headstrong, and cynical" and to these adjectives the investigators added "anxious and troubled [Westcott & Ranzoni, 1963, p. 611]."

(3) The "careful successful problem solvers" required a great deal of information and then offered successful solutions. They were not very flexible but "more characteristically . . . cautious, conservative, and compliant." They were quite socialized and it would have been very unusual for them to do anything out of the ordinary. They did not think others had influenced them or that they had changed much. They did not regard risk as very enjoyable. They felt quite confident about their stand on social issues and did not want to change the world. They regarded themselves as "cautious, kind, modest, confident, but also . . . as resourceful, foresighted . . . and spontaneous." They got along very well in their conventional, conservative world [Westcott & Ranzoni, 1963, p. 611].

(4) The "careful but unsuccessful problem solvers" demanded much information but still failed. They were very similar to the other groups in verbal aptitude but their mathematical aptitude scores were somewhat lower. Because they did poorly in problem solving in this study, they might be suspected of having low grades. In fact, their grades were not lower than those of the other groups. Members of this group were as cautious and conservative as members of Group 3 but they did not like it, and yet they "cannot entertain the incaution which the preceding group can [p. 612]." They saw themselves as living in a risky world and oriented themselves to minimizing the risks. Most of the people in this group were interested in sports and people. They did not get very involved with intellectual matters. They believed they had changed and that others had influenced them in making these changes but they could not provide very specific information on this score. They were not certain whether they took chances nor whether doing so was even desirable. In a sense, they did not know whether they had a choice in the matter of taking chances. They described themselves as lacking in self-confidence, cautious, kind, and modest.

These, then, are some of the psychological differences reported by Westcott and Ranzoni (1963) on a group they regard as intuitive thinkers and on others who follow different problem-solving strategies. These are valuable data in a pioneering effort that requires further work and replication to substantiate whether indeed intuitive thinkers are as different from others as described. Meanwhile, the evidence just cited lends credence to the efficacy of intuition, and those who believe they possess it might well try to utilize it effectively in their creative processes by substantiating it with further analytic procedures.

SELF-HELP PROCEDURES

On a more practical and applied level we now present a series of techniques that a person can use by himself as a means of fostering the development of hypotheses. Since these are self-help techniques, their effectiveness depends a great deal on the individual's motivation, drive, and perseverance. There is usually no one else around to provide stimulation, encouragement, or that extra prod to get down to work. Encouraging printed words, of which there are many associated with these techniques, are no substitutes for human beings. Consequently, many individuals prefer training sessions in groups. Nevertheless, for such persons as well as for those who work by themselves, these techniques contain ideas and suggestions that can prove of much help.

Many of the techniques to be described are most useful in applied, scientific, or technical areas, where the variables can be stated and manipulated to achieve various permutations and combinations. The artist, writer, poet, etc., will not be likely to find these self-help techniques very useful. At the least, however, the techniques will serve to demonstrate to persons in the arts the means that persons in other areas have found useful to encourage hypothesis and idea formation. Conceivably these examples can then serve as appropriate stimuli for artists who also find experimentation and flexibility critical to their creative developments.

Self-help techniques are usually presented in a rather simplistic, exhortative, and inspirational manner. The reader is told that his untapped creative potential can be unleashed by practicing the techniques described. Frequently, anecdotes, aphorisms, statements, or experiences of creative men are cited to serve as models for creative behavior. Such support is without doubt helpful to some individuals; others can find what they want by limiting themselves to the techniques to which we now turn.

Brainstorming

Brainstorming is the name Osborn (1963) gave to his technique for stimulating creativity, and the term* is so popular that it has been applied generally to all techniques for stimulating creativity. While Osborn's *Applied Imagination* sets forth the basic principles of brainstorming, others (Clark, 1958; Parnes, 1967)

---

*The most frequently used term for the procedure described is *brainstorming*. In some quarters, however, more likely among researchers in the field rather than among laymen, there is some disagreement about the term to be used. Parnes, one of the major researchers and trainers in this area, suggests that "brainstorming" be limited to a group of people applying certain principles that will be spelled out later (Chapter XIII). At the risk of contributing to further confusion, the term brainstorming is used here to apply also to individual use because there is a significant tradition of such use.

have also written and elaborated upon it. Brainstorming is best known for its use with groups of individuals, but it can also be used by individuals working alone. Indeed, as Osborn himself recommends, brainstorming, like so many of the other techniques to stimulate creativity, is probably best used in some combination of individual and group practice. Both because brainstorming is best known as a group technique and because most of the research on it has been with groups of individuals, a lengthy and thorough discussion is presented in Chapter XIII. Here we will simply discuss some of the highlights of the process as an individual procedure.

For Osborn creativity consists of these stages: *Orientation*, in which the problem is defined and an approach that may aid in solving it is selected; *preparation*, in which facts and all relevant material that may be useful are gathered; *analysis*, in which what has been gathered is studied and analyzed; *ideation*, in which tentative solutions are produced (many of the techniques for stimulating creativity have their value and function primarily at this stage of the process); *incubation*, in which conscious effort is suspended but unconscious effort continues; *synthesis*, which involves putting the parts together; and *verification*, in which the ideas and solutions developed are checked against the problem to determine whether they work.

With this as background, Osborn (1963) sets up four basic rules for brainstorming:

(1) *Criticism is ruled out* . . . . (2) *Free wheeling is welcomed* . . . .
(3) *Quantity is wanted* . . . . (4) *Combination and improvement are sought* [p. 156].

It is apparent from this that in brainstorming the individual is encouraged to remove any kind of conscious evaluation of ideas that may come to mind. He is not to be afraid of "wild" ideas; as a matter of fact, the wilder the better, for it is easier to "tame down than to think up [Osborn, 1963, p. 300]." Furthermore, the individual is to strive for quantity of ideas, on the assumption that the more original ideas will come later in the course of his thinking processes; hence, it is better to think up the largest number of ideas possible. Finally, the individual is encouraged to combine ideas that occur to him and to think up improvements on them.

In addition to these four basic rules, Osborn provides a variety of questions that one can ask oneself to help stimulate ideas, as well as other aids that can facilitate the creative process (Osborn, 1963, especially Chapters XX–XXIV).

Some of the thoughts and ideas that a person is likely to have as a result of the brainstorming process might be immediately available for use. Others, and this is more frequent, are likely to be leads for ideas that will eventually be of use. With technical problems it is more likely that the results of brainstorming will be leads that will have to be worked out in some way. Brainstorming works best for problems for which there are a number of alternative solutions and least well for problems with only one or a limited number of answers. If a problem is too broad, it is worthwhile breaking it down into narrower problems and then to proceed with the brainstorming procedure as it is described in Chapter XIII.

Morphological Analysis

This technique was developed by Dr. Fritz Zwicky, who published *Morphological Astronomy* in 1957 and *Discovery, Invention, Research: Through the Morphological Approach* in 1969. Another book solely devoted to this approach was written by Allen (1962a); others also discuss it (Guilford, 1967; Osborn, 1963; Parnes & Harding, 1962; Goldner, 1962).

This technique consists in dividing a problem into its parameters or independent variables, which are then divided into subvariables or the different forms that these variables would take in a variety of situations. Theoretically, combinations of these subvariables should result in a solution. Where two variables are involved, we may visualize them as constituting a square. The vertical axis represents one variable and the horizontal axis a second variable, but since each of these variables is divided into subvariables, each smaller square can be visualized as a potential solution. If there were three variables, solutions would be visualized in the form of a cube.

Whiting (1958) gives an example of the use of morphological analysis where the goal is to obtain various combinations in a two-color scheme where one major variable is blue and its subvariables are shades of blue. The other variable is red and its subvariables are shades of red. Sixteen possible combinations of these four variables exist. A three-variable problem, also presented by Whiting (1958), is a bit more interesting. This problem involves the construction of a large cube which is then subdivided into a series of smaller cubes. The problem is to develop a new type of packaging for selling milk. The three variables are size, shape, and material. The size variable would be divided into all sizes (pint, quart, etc.) to be considered; the shape variable would consist of the different possible shapes; and the material variable would consist of different materials, such as glass, metal, plastic, paper, and cellophane.

In this example [Whiting, 1958, pp. 65-66 says] we have set up 225 possible solutions: each small cube within the box can be thought of as a drawer containing a particular alternative which may or may not be worth considering. Each of these possible solutions should be considered in turn. Some of them can be interpreted as already existing types of milk packaging, such as a quart glass cylindrical container, and a quart paper rectangular container. Others, such as a round metal 2 oz. container, are obviously impractical. Theoretically, in examining each of the boxes, we will develop some potentially useful problem solutions that might have been overlooked had we used some other method. Solutions such as a conical paper quart or a rectangular plastic quart are among those which, on the surface, would seem to have some potential.

McPherson (1967, p. 9) selects "the problem of getting something from one place to another via a powered vehicle." He then develops three independent variables: "1. Type of vehicle. 2. Media in which the vehicle operates. 3. The power source [p. 9]." These three independent variables and their subdivisions form a cube or three-dimensional figure, and by studying the matrix of the subdivisions a total of 224 combinations were possible, although obviously not all of them would be practical or feasible for a variety of reasons.

Goldner (1962) presents morphological analysis as a play between two children, one of whom is the son of a management consultant, and the other a neighbor's child. The neighbor's child comes for a visit and sees a cabinet. He is told that the cabinet is set up for a conference that the father has to attend. On one side of the cabinet are a series of boxes representing the different places where the toy (the product in this case) may be sold. These include and are marked local, state, regional, national, and international. The other side of the cabinet (or major variable) is the method of distribution—general distributors, franchised distribution, manufacturers' representatives, company-owned retail stores, independent retailers, direct sales, and mail order. Then there are boxes that go in and out, and they are marked to cover the various ways of transacting a sale: cash on delivery; cash only, less the discount; outright purchase; trade-in plus cash; rental purchase; lease; and time sale.

By playing with different dimensions of the three independent variables, 280 combinations were available. Examples of the kinds of combinations that arise are (1) international, general distributors, on a time sale basis, which is really the installment plan; and (2) international, through independent retailers, on a rental basis plan, which might be, it is suggested, a good combination for a $50 toy.

Psychologists who are acquainted with Guilford's (1956) work on *Structure of the Intellect* will note its morphological aspects in the cube, each of whose sides represent, in turn, contents, operations, and products.

While the images used by Guilford, for example, are three-dimensional, Allen, who has also written about morphological analysis (Allen, 1962a), has published a technique called *The Allen Morphologizer* (1962b), which he regards as a "device" that "enables" the user "*to find multiple solutions to any problems you might have by magnifying your brain power by a factor of 2,401. It will help you to achieve your goals in life rapidly and easily—to get anything you want* [Allen, 1962b, p. 1]." This device can be bought from Allen's publisher, or can be made out of paper by oneself.

Combining what is said in his book (Allen, 1962a) and in *The Allen Morphologizer* (Allen, 1962b), Allen suggests the following steps.

1. All material should be gathered, no matter how unimportant, and without evaluation for the problem under consideration. This material could include ideas for solving the problem, achievements desired, names of people who are involved with the problem, books that might be consulted about the problem.

2. All ideas should be typed or written, with the 3-inch side horizontal, on 2½ by 3-inch cards.

3. Disregarding order, the cards should then be laid out in groups of 12 that are three cards wide and four cards high. "Leave about one quarter of an inch between individual cards, and one inch between blocks of cards. This arrangement has worked out to be the best of the many different plans that I have tried [Allen, 1962, p. 182]."

4. The cards are then read rapidly four or five times. "This transfers the ideas into your subconscious mind and starts the morphological process [Allen, 1962b, p. 1]."

5. For the next half hour it is recommended that the individual leave the cards and occupy his mind as completely as possible with other matters. Even though the individual occupies himself with another activity, he need not worry, for his unconscious mind is working away at the sorting process.

6. The individual then studies and categorizes the cards into what he calls "friendly" or "congenial" groups. "If you had started with 500 cards you might wind up with from 20 to 30 of these friendly groups [Allen, 1962a, p. 182]."

7. A title card, different in color from the others used or written on in different ink, is prepared for each group and placed on top of it.

8. Each group is then treated as was each of the cards in Steps 3-6; These groups are then reduced to a smaller number of groups, preferably four but no more than seven. These final groups are called *parameters*.

9. Each parameter is then analyzed into no more than seven subgroups, called *components*.

10. The four parameters are placed in columns across the top of a page, and the seven components of each parameter constitute the rows.

11. Four vertical strips of paper or paper pasted on cardboard (or along the dotted line, if the morphologizer is used) are then cut. Each strip then consists of a parameter and its seven components.

12. The four strips, laid down side by side, are then moved up and down so that different combinations of the components can be viewed by the person; from these combinations he can more readily move on to his solution.

13. The individual using four parameters and seven components is confronted with the possibility of 2,401 combinations. The number may be more or less, depending on the number of parameters and components. Whatever the case, some individuals may have no difficulty selecting the best ideas, whereas

others might. To help those experiencing difficulty, Allen (1962a) suggests using Dr. Zwicky's "King Value."

> By this Dr. Zwicky meant what one objective is the most pressing, the one that above all others will, if achieved, indicate a successful solution of the problem of concern. The identification of this "King" value, and a keen appreciation of its stature, makes possible the elimination of enough irrelevant or minor elements so that it is possible to evaluate those remaining [Allen, 1962a, p. 58].

It is apparent that the potential usefulness of morphological analysis depends on the number of available variables or parameters. When a problem with many variables is undertaken, a very heavy, if not impossible, burden is imposed on the individual because it becomes increasingly difficult to integrate all the possibilities and to profit from this procedure. When there are too many variables they can be restated so that they are broader in character. It is also possible in such cases to make subproblems from the larger problem and build up to the larger solution only after amassing more information from and about the independent variables. Whiting (1958) is quite skeptical about this approach:

> If we had ten possible forms for each of five major variables, we would have to contend with 10^5 or 100,000 different possibilities. Since most problems are composed of a significant number of major variables, each of which has innumerable minor variations, it would seem that while morphological analysis may be appealing in a theoretical sense, in practice it has few practical applications [p. 66].

In contrast to this opinion, we have seen that morphological analysis has provided very valuable results as used by Guilford in his studies of the structure of intellect. Unfortunately, as long as there is no systematic manner of, nor any one place for, gathering data about, and accounts of experiences with, the use of these techniques (which, on the face of things, appear practical), we cannot provide "hard" data on how helpful a given technique may be.

Attribute Listing

This method, described by Crawford (1950, 1954), consists first in the isolation and selection of the major attributes or characteristics of a product, object, or idea. Then each of these in turn is modified in every possible way without evaluation or judgment. Only after all the ideas or possibilities are out are the modified attributes evaluated.

The screwdriver with its traditional characteristics is selected by McPherson (1967) to illustrate this approach. During the course of time each of the attributes of the screwdriver has undergone some kind of modification. The formerly round shank now has a hexagonal cross section, which is easier to grip with a wrench to gain more torque. For longer use, the handle is now made of plastic rather than wood. The traditional flat wedge-shaped end has been modified for use with many more different types of screws. Electric motors now provide power and there are screwdrivers that develop torque by being pushed rather than twisted.

Whiting (1958) uses the telephone as a possible object for modification, selecting four attributes for this purpose. The traditional black color of the instrument could be made any solid color, two-tone, plaid, illustrated, etc. Its plastic construction could be metal, glass, wood, lucite, etc. Its dial could be replaced by a push-button, lever, or abacus system, among others. Its handset could be made more square or more oval, and its base lower.

One of the problems with attribute listing as a technique to stimulate creativity is that it is possible to get very involved with a variety of attributes, and to spend valuable time in areas that are not quite central or critical. To cope with this problem, Whiting (1958) suggests differentiating between characteristics that are common to many products and those which are unique to the product itself. Then,

In the majority of cases, simple variations of these basic attributes do not tend to be extraordinarily original. Quite often, the majority of the most practical of these variations have been tried at some time in the past. It is in the area of the more unique attributes that the greatest opportunity for original variation exists. In the case of our example [the telephone], a more unique attribute would be the dial [p. 47].

It is also possible for the user of this procedure to feel limited to minor variations of the product. To deal with this problem, he should consciously direct his attention to those attributes that are regarded as the object's chief function (Whiting, 1958). For the telephone this would be transmitting messages; for a pencil it would be writing; and for a lawn mower it would be cutting grass. Concern with the major attribute is more likely to result in basic changes. A rather interesting variant of this procedure is presented by Goldner (1962), who refers to this process as "attribute shifting." The technique is basically the same in that the individual examines an idea or object very carefully. Then he selects its dominant attributes. These are then applied or shifted to an area or object that is not now using this attribute. For example, Goldner presents a problem in which a client requires 50,000 square feet of space in a specific location where only 10,000 square feet are available. Zoning regulations permit only a one-story building. The solution he suggests is to construct a five-story building with four floors underground. The shifting in this case is from area to height and from up to down.

Another problem presented by Goldner (1962) involves a food company confronted by increasing packaging costs. The recommendation is to install storage bins in the client's facilities and to ship food by bulk. In another case, attribute shifting occurred between a variety store or supermarket and a diamond mind. Since the diamond mine owner found it unprofitable to operate the mine, it was suggested that he convert it into a form of entertainment, charge admission, and make it a self-service mine. In still another problem, attribute shifting involved renting a home as against buying a home and the advantages of professional laundering as against do-it-yourself laundering: The problem was that drip-dry clothes were cutting into the profits of a laundry. The recommendation was that the company buy clothes for its customers and rent the clothes to them so long as the customers had their clothes laundered at the laundry.

Checklists

There are two kinds of checklists; Whiting refers to them as "specialized" and "generalized." Among the specialized checklists are those which present the different ways of introducing a new product, making a sale, or closing a sale.

> They remind the user of essential steps in a particular process, and can also be helpful in the training of personnel. They are probably most useful in the adaptation of ideas from a former situation to the present one, whereby these ideas can then be considered new or original according to our limited definition [Whiting, 1958, p. 61].

The disadvantages of the checklist approach are that it may be restrictive (when the individual considers only the categories on the list), and that specialized checklists tend to be inflexible, since they can only be used with problems that occur frequently.

The generalized checklist, which, as its name suggests, can be applied to a variety of situations, can be more flexible and is potentially more valuable for generating ideas (Whiting, 1958). A good example of such a generalized checklist is Osborn's list of questions as presented by Whiting (1958, p. 62) which contains nine basic categories for altering an existing idea, object, or product:

> *Put to Other Uses?* New ways to use as is? Other uses if modified?
>
> *Adapt?* What else is like this? What other idea does this suggest? Does past offer parallel? What could I copy? Whom could I emulate?
>
> *Modify?* New twist? Change meaning, color, motion, odor, form, shape? Other changes?
>
> *Magnify?* What to add? More time? Greater frequency? Stronger? Larger? Thicker? Extra value? Plus ingredient? Duplicate? Multiply? Exaggerate?
>
> *Minify?* What to substitute? Smaller? Condensed? Miniature? Lower? Shorter? Lighter? Omit? Streamline? Split up? Understate?

Substitute? Who else instead? What else instead? Other ingredient? Other material? Other process? Other power? Other place? Other approach? Other tone of voice?

Rearrange? Interchange components? Other pattern? Other layout? Other sequence? Transpose cause and effect? Change pace? Change schedule?

Reverse? Transpose positive and negative? How about opposites? Turn it backward? Turn it upside down? Reverse roles? Change shoes? Turn tables? Turn other cheek?

Combine? How about a blend, an alloy, an assortment, an ensemble? Combine units? Combine purposes? Combine appeals? Combine ideas?"

Goldner (1962) has a variant on the checklisting technique which he calls "vice-versa." In this case the individual thinks of whether he can make something heavier or lighter, thicker or thinner, larger or smaller, etc. For example, railroads run on the ground with wheels. What is "vice-versa" to wheels on the ground? The individual begins by visualizing wheels in the air, proceeds to transpose the wheels from below the vehicle to above it, and so on, until he arrives at the monorail, with the wheels at the top, tracks overhead, and "roadbed" and right of way supported from and determined by towers.

Forced Relationships

There are a series of techniques that depend "upon the creation of a forced relationship between two or more normally unrelated products or ideas as the starting point for the idea-generation process. Because of their essential similarity, they have been designated collectively as forced relationship techniques" (Whiting, 1958, p. 52). They have been used, according to Whiting (1958), by people who require new and original ideas in a fairly broad area. Among such individuals would be cartoonists, advertising copywriters and art directors, sales promotion personnel, some professional writers, etc.

Three such techniques are discussed by Whiting (1958): *catalog technique, listing technique* and *focused object technique.* The *catalog technique* consists simply in the selection of a word, object, or picture at random and without judgment from a catalog, magazine, journal, etc. Another object, word, picture, is then also selected in the same manner. Both elements are considered together and any kind of relationship is forced between the two. "Since neither element is controlled, the area in which ideas are needed must be extremely broad; thus, for most of us, the catalog technique is probably of limited usefulness [Whiting, 1958, pp. 53-54]."

Another kind of forced relationship technique of limited usefulness is the *listing technique.* Here an individual thinks of a general subject area and lists a number of objects or ideas that are associated with the general subject. These ideas are numbered and then the first item is considered in relationship to all of the others. The same is done with the second item, which is considered in relation to all of the other items, and so on, until each item has been considered in combination with each of the other items.

Whiting (1958) presents the example of a manufacturer of office equipment who wishes to develop ideas for new products. The first step would be to list and number the products in his line: (1) desk, (2) chair, (3) desk lamp, (4) filing cabinet, (5) bookcase. Then the relationship between the desk and the chair would be considered: the manufacturer would start freely associating to this combination. Among the associations there might be a combined unit, or a unit that allows for storing or recessing a chair in the desk. No time is given to evaluation, which would come later.

The procedure then continues with other possible combinations, such as the desk and desk lamp. The lamp could be recessed in the desk or controlled by push buttons in the desk.

The third forced relationship technique is the *focused object technique* developed by Whiting (1958). It differs from the other techniques in this category in that there is a definite purpose in mind for one of the elements in the relationship, and this purpose is predetermined. "In short, the focused object technique can be applied to a specific existing problem. In any of the other forced relationship techniques, all the elements in the relationship have been selected more or less arbitrarily, making it almost impossible to apply these techniques to a particular problem. They are useful only when ideas are needed within a broad field [Whiting, 1958, p. 60]." The first step in this process is to select the fixed element and to focus your attention on some other element, which is usually in the individual's immediate vicinity. "The physical presence of a specific object seems to make it easier to develop ideas from the forced relationship, though it is of course possible to visualize an object in one's imagination [p. 56]."

> Once both the fixed element and the randomly selected element have been chosen, the forced or unnatural relationship has been established. This is now used as the basis for a free-flowing chain of free associations from which we are hoping new and original ideas will develop. Usually, the first ideas will come from a simple transfer of the attributes of the random to the fixed element; in other words, the color, shape, and other characteristics of the random object will serve as the basis for ideas for modifying the pre-selected member of the forced relationship [p. 56].

For example, Whiting considers the manufacturer who is concerned with a new design for chairs. A chair is then the fixed element and the random element he lights upon is the common light bulb. He starts a series of forced relationships and comes upon what Whiting calls, "first level ideas," such as glass chair, thinner chair, bulb-shaped chair, screw-plug construction, electric chair, electrically operated chair. Then, too, "Even similar-sounding words may suggest possibilities; glass might be interpreted as class, and might lead to a suggestion that a chair be designed specifically for a particular class market, or that the line of chairs be classified in any number of ways [Whiting, 1958, p. 57]."

Probably more useful ideas occur from "second level ideas . . . which develop from the chain of free associations that the first level ideas initiate [Whiting, 1958, pp. 57-58]." Thus, from "bulb-shaped chair," one of the first level ideas, two paths are available, one starting with "bulb" and the other with "shape." From *bulb* Whiting lists the possibilities: "Flower bulb, Flowers, Floral designs for chairs, Flower scent," etc.; and from *shape* "Shaped to fit the human body, Glamour girl . . . Movie star signature chairs . . . Crucible steel, Steel band, Trinidad steel bands," etc. [Whiting, 1958, p. 58].

At the second level there is usually little, if any, relationship between the suggested ideas and the original random object. "This is as it should be, because the focused object technique is merely a device designed to *initiate* creative thought. The forced relationship provides a starting point, and since it is almost always an unusual starting point, the chance that new, original ideas will develop is excellent [Whiting, 1958, p. 59]."

Free associations should be followed as long as they are fruitful. When they are no longer fruitful the individual can go back to the original random element, select a new first level idea, and start a new series of free associations. Finally, Whiting (1958) suggests that using a series of forced relationships with a variety of random objects is generally more productive than limiting oneself to a single forced relationship.

PakSA

This technique was developed by J. W. Taylor (1961) and refers to the PackCorp Scientific Approach in honor of the Packaging Corporation of America. Taylor himself regards this technique as a modification and extension of other techniques. He believes he has eliminated their shortcomings and extended their advantages. The technique consists of nine steps (Taylor, 1961).

1. PICK A PROBLEM—Define your problem—in writing. State what's *wrong*—what needs fixing. State your *objective*—what end-result you seek.

2. GET KNOWLEDGE—Get known facts. Get new knowledge. Study written references. Experiment. Explore. Research deeply and broadly. Talk with informed people. Check your findings. Put them in writing.

3. ORGANIZE KNOWLEDGE—Put your information into understandable form. Sort it. Organize it. Write it.

4. REFINE KNOWLEDGE—Screen knowledge for *relationships* and *principles*. Match fact against fact. Look for similarities, differences, analogies,

cause-and-effect, combinations, *patterns*. Apply "stimulator" questions. If new ideas still are slow in coming to mind. . .

5. DIGEST—Let the conscious mind get its "second wind." Put the subconscious to work. Relax, take up another problem, work at a hobby or enjoy some mild diversion—until refreshed. Then. . .

6. PRODUCE IDEAS—*ad lib*, or—Concentrate anew on your problem until ideas begin to emerge. As they occur, don't stop to judge them— produce them and write them. *Build up as many alternatives as you can.*

7. RE-WORK IDEAS—Check your new ideas for flaws. Examine each idea objectively—question it; challenge it; test it; re-work it; improve it; follow it through.

8. PUT IDEAS TO WORK—If the approval and acceptance of others are required, *sell* your ideas:

Plan each sale. Allow enough time. Get participation. Use "samples." Stress *customer*-interest. If new methods and skills are involved, *teach* them.

9. REPEAT THE PROCESS—Until it becomes a natural habit [pp. 185-186].

Input-Output Technique

Developed at General Electric, this technique usually involves the use of energy in one form or another. The first step in this process would be to establish the output, or the goal or the solution that is desired. The input involves the form of energy that gets the system going. Say, for example, that the problem is to develop a system for warning about a fire, an example given by Whiting (1958). In this case the input is "fire." In this problem there can be certain limitations or standards that the solution is supposed to meet (but these should not be too restricting, for they might then prove to be too inhibiting). Having established these three basic ingredients, we must then

determine how best various forms of the energy produced by it can be used to ultimately achieve the desired output (a warning of the presence of fire). This is done by asking a series of questions similar to those that follow:

(1) What outputs are produced directly by the input? Fire is characterized by the presence of a certain amount of heat and light, and the presence of the gaseous products of combustion and smoke.

(2) Can any of these phenomena be used to produce the desired output directly?

Without reference to the specifications, we might say that once the fire became large enough, a combination of its light and smoke, and perhaps heat, would supply its own warning signal. Unfortunately, however, by this time the fire has probably devoured a good part of the building, making a solution of this type most unsatisfactory.

(3) What reactions are caused by heat? light? smoke? This next question is a very important one. Here a serious attempt should be made to list all the possible physical and chemical reactions. Those caused by heat are expansion of various metals, liquids and gases; melting of metals; changes in the composition of certain chemicals. Light and smoke both can cause various physical and chemical reactions also.

(4) Can any of these reactions be used to achieve the desired output?

The melting of an alloy like Wood's metal, which melts at a temperature below the boiling point of water, could be used to break a circuit or to open a valve. Actually, Wood's metal is used in sprinkler systems designed to extinguish undetected fires. The expansion of liquids is the principle used in the thermometer. The unequal expansion of a bimetal strip when exposed to heat is the basis for the thermostat (actually, a heat-actuated electric circuit breaker). Light can be sensed by a selenium cell or an electric eye, while smoke can be detected by various chemicals [Whiting, 1958, pp. 49-50].

Up to this point, then, the individual has a number of alternatives for detecting the presence of fire, which is the first step in the process. This is followed by a consideration of all possible outputs that follow from a given input in a previous stage. In practice, several input-output steps may be combined. "However, if a strong effort can be made to consider each input-output step separately, the possibilities of arriving at a new, original, and better solution are much greater, because the different outputs stemming from each input are explored fully. This greatly reduces the likelihood that a stereotyped solution will be produced [Whiting, 1958, p. 51]."

As noted earlier, the input-output technique involves the use of one kind or another of energy and as such would be best applied by individuals with technical knowledge. Hence, its usefulness may be limited. Furthermore, several outputs can stem from each input, which can be confusing or time consuming. "The best advice to follow in regard to this point is to limit your use of the technique according to the importance of the problem under consideration. Thus, only those problems that deserve extensive treatment would get it [Whiting, 1958, p. 51]."

Use of the Ridiculous

Von Fange (1959) found that selecting what seems the most ridiculous idea in a list of ideas proved to be of such value that he recommends it as a specific technique. He reports, for example, that after one session dealing with the problem of "How to Fasten or Join Two Wires Together," the suggestion to "Hold it with your teeth" was selected as the most ridiculous. It was apparent that this idea would not work, but "Almost immediately the entire group [with which it was tried] realized that 'Alligator' clips and numerous other fasteners patterned after this very concept were already commercially available [Von Fange, 1959, p. 53] ."

To "Use chewing gum" was then selected as another ridiculous idea. And again Von Fange (1959) reports, "Almost as fast as they had settled on this, a chemist who happened to be in the group said that the base of most chewing gums is a common plastic which, by the addition of suitable chemicals, could be made to set very firm. And then another man suggested that most present-day power cords on clocks and radios have a molded plastic plug where the wire is held to the prong by this very expedient [p. 53] ."

Modification

When a person already has a good idea, a conscious attempt to modify it, as suggested by Whiting (1958), may make it into a great idea. He also suggests that such areas as advertising, and art, where slight modifications in wording or visualization can make important differences, can profit from the use of this technique. To use it, an individual might set a goal of the number of modifications he wants to achieve, which he then strives for in a very conscious fashion.

The "Fresh Eye"

This technique, described by Whiting (1958), involves selecting a commonplace object and examining it with a great deal of concentration. The goal is to find beauty in the object. Looking at the object closely brings to the fore new and previously overlooked characteristics. Seen in a fresh light, the object can then be used in a variety of ways.

ANOTHER OF THE MYSTIQUES—SELECTING THE "GOOD" POSSIBILITY

All of the techniques described have as their goal the generation of many hypotheses and ideas that may be used for later testing. What the techniques do not prescribe is how to select from the available ideas and hypotheses that one which will eventually lead to the creative end state. Indeed, just how creative individuals go about making such selections is another of the mystiques of the creative process. Some experience inspiration when they do so, others make their selections intuitively, still others probably do so in some as yet unknown ways.

Persons who use the techniques described here will no doubt find themselves confronted with the problem of making a choice from the numerous available possibilities. There are no guidelines available for making the "right" choice in one try without error. Either a person can decide to test systematically each of the available ideas or he can utilize his aesthetic sensitivity to select that idea about which he has a "gut feel" that it will lead in the desired creative direction. Some persons work under such pressure that they think they cannot afford the luxury of sitting back and just seeing how they "feel" about different ideas and possibilities. To that extent, they may fall short of creative goals. Creativity sometimes demands just such moments of leisure. Other persons may feel strange and uncomfortable with this approach because it does not seem very "rational" or "objective" to them. We can only suggest that they give it a try for after some experience, and hopefully some successes, the process becomes easier.

SUMMARY

Successful hypothesis formation depends in great measure on an individual's not being fixated on existing stimuli and structures in his past experience or immediate environment. Ways to achieve a freer orientation are discussed in this chapter. These ways include breaking up the perceptual field to make it more amenable to new combinations, and examining the way language (i.e., a person's vocabulary and linguistic norms) affects thought processes, so that static words fix ideas, preventing them from flowing into each other.

The results of studies investigating and supporting the effectiveness of intuition are presented. Instances where intuition has proved of much value are cited, and the hope that we shall be able to teach it to others in the future is voiced.

Finally, a series of self-help procedures intended to stimulate hypothesis formation in a variety of ways are discussed. One of the most common is to express, or externalize, the parameters and variables that creative persons usually manipulate in their minds. Such externalization procedures generally make it easier for many persons to develop new combinations and fruitful creative hypotheses.

The value of the outcomes of the techniques discussed depends not only on the specific techniques, but on the proper statement of the question, a person's motivation to be creative, his drive, and his perseverance. It also depends on having confidence in one's "aesthetic feel" in the selection of ideas for further development. The pitfall of developing ideas for the sake of developing ideas should be avoided. Selections must be made, and the chosen ideas submitted to further tests as described in the next chapter.

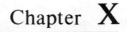

Chapter **X**

Making Hypothesis Testing More Effective

Garnering the available knowledge and coming up with an idea are only early stages in the creative process. Yet many individuals falter after one of these two stages. Some never get beyond acquiring knowledge. Others go on to the next stage, sometimes even describing themselves as inspired at this point. They can "almost see" the painting they "intend to" or "would like to" paint, or can "almost hear" the orchestra play their symphony. Similar imaginings are true of writers, scientists, and engineers.

Yet they are all only at the outset of the creative process, and their aspirations and fantasies have to be held in check as they move from hypothesis formation to hypothesis testing.

There are a number of reasons why so many would-be creative people falter early in the process. Some simply lack the requisite training in the methodology or technology of their field. Still others, who are well trained, fail to get through the hypothesis-testing stage for other reasons, which we shall discuss in this chapter. All these persons may at times derogate the significance of their craft or the methodology and technology of their field, suggesting that only the idea-formation phase of the creative process is truly creative—the rest is the province of technicians or craftsmen, who are expected to supply the (mere?) details. Then if the creative idea does not bear the envisioned fruit, these people have a

224

convenient whipping boy to blame for the lack of results. Those who limit themselves to ideas in this way seldom realize that they may lack the discipline, control, and capacity to move from a partially passive phase of the creative process (hypothesis formation) to a more active phase (hypothesis testing). They also often do not realize that novel ideas frequently require novel procedures, methods, and technology to make them work. Creative effort may be necessary to adapt existing forms and technology to a new idea.

Some people also object to the testing phase because it involves evaluation, which they downgrade as unnecessary in the creative process (and in all of life). These individuals like to talk about being creative because as part of the creative process they are encouraged to be nonevaluative. They forget that this is done only to facilitate letting down internal barriers to the free flow of ideas; evaluation or testing cannot be put off forever.

The individual who goes on to the idea-testing stage must be motivated to actualize his idea and to ascertain whether it will work out. Like the other parts of the creative process, this stage requires a willingness to take risks, a sense of optimism, and a feeling of confidence in one's ability to fulfill the creative process with a high degree of effectiveness. Some people are inhibited by anxiety: they fear that a test will prove that the time already spent on their idea was wasted. Others feel inadequate to produce in reality what the mind conjured up in fantasy. Some fear that testing the idea will make it prosaic; its "grandeur" will be diminished. Such individuals do not appreciate that in the process of testing an idea they may come upon possibilities not thought of before. The painting becomes better as the artist sees new possibilities in what is being worked out on canvas. The novel improves as the author perceives the depth of his characters develop; and the new apparatus becomes capable of unthought of functions as its inventor considers different kinds of material for its construction. A test or evaluation may even show an idea or product to be more worthy, valuable, or significant than was originally imagined. If, however, an earlier stage has been characterized by exaggerated feelings and attitudes, then any subsequent stage in the creative process is likely to be regarded with some trepidation, hostility, and derogation.

The hypothesis-testing stage consists of a continuous dialog between the individual with the idea or hypothesis and his "environment." The word "environment" is placed in quotes to call attention to the fact that its physical aspects are various. On the one hand, there is the environment of the researcher, engineer, or scientist: a laboratory with equipment that may or may not take up all available physical space. On the other hand, there is the environment of, for example, the writer—that blank sheet of paper in the typewriter—or the painter—that untouched canvas. The scientist's laboratory environment is sometimes envied by the writer because it seems to afford so much to work with. And the blank piece of paper is occasionally envied by the scientist, because the writer's environment appears so uncluttered and the writer himself so unfettered by existing conditions. Needless to say, these interfield jealousies are groundless; they are mentioned only to illustrate that fields of creative endeavor do differ, and that when we speak of a dialog with the environment we know that the writer and painter "start from scratch" and continually make and remake their environments. On the other hand, in some fields individuals have more available to work with, in the sense that *something* is there, but this something may also have to be changed and adapted to different needs as the problem is resolved.

Even within fields, there may be differences between problems that are of a very similar character. Moreover, in some instances an individual may have a reasonably clear idea of what the end state should be (e.g., a better mousetrap); hence, to arrive at it he can, in a sense, work backward from this goal. With other problems it is necessary to work from the overall conception or even a tentative goal toward the end state. There is, for example, an obvious difference between painting a portrait or landscape and painting an abstract work. The figure for the portrait (or scene for the landscape) is *there*, for reference, whereas the abstract conception exists only in the mind of the artist.

The great variety of problems confronting the creative individual indicates that different specific approaches and different attitudes are needed to solve them. These differences are reflected in the personalities of the individuals who work in different fields and in the approaches and work methods of different people. The point of this discussion is that we cannot deal here with every possible kind of problem, nor with the many kinds of personalities best suited to handle various kinds of problems. We will, therefore, present those general and specific statements about the hypothesis-testing phase of the creative process we believe will enable the reader to weigh the alternatives and select the appropriate course of action.

THE DIALOG

We have said that during the hypothesis-testing stage the individual is involved in a continous dialog with his environment, which may be (among others) the equipment-filled scientist's laboratory or the blank-paper or empty-canvas milieu of the writer or painter. The characteristics of this dialog may be quite varied. At one point there may be a clear and direct statement, followed by ambiguity, fuzziness, a retreat (sometimes far back) to a previous statement, a leap forward, etc. The dialog is also characteristically very dynamic, in that during it the individual alternates in attitude, shifting from creator to critic. What was inside him is now externalized, so that he can stand back from his work and assume the role of his own audience. His work is now an object for evaluation.

Individuals vary in their capacity to shift roles. Some are able to maintain only the subject role; unable to become their own audiences, they frequently lack self-criticism and produce idiosyncratic works that are rejected. Over their protest that others do not appreciate their art, the audience perceives the lack of discipline inherent in the creation of such a work.

Whereas the lack of discipline and self-criticism can be a hindrance, too much discipline can also be a drawback. The individual may get only partway through a statement before rejecting it as not good enough. Or, as the statement is elaborated, excessive discipline can generate undue concern with the minutiae of method and form at the expense of the idea, so that the product appears formal, rigid, lifeless, or lacking in utility.

Another pitfall in this process is that the opportunity to develop and explore alternatives may lead to an obsessive inability to make up one's mind. So much seems possible that the individual succumbs to vacillation and self-doubt, shifting from one alternative to another but never following through on any one.

These self-doubts may have their sources in or may stir up feelings of guilt and hostility, and this emotional disruption may generate depression, self-recrimination, and a sense of inadequacy. If these feelings become severe and serious impediments to the creative process, help from an individual trained in dealing with psychological problems may be needed. Less serious problems may be alleviated by spouses, friends, superiors, colleagues, and others, who serve as either sources of encouragement or good sounding boards. They can, verbally or nonverbally, indicate their acceptance of, confidence in, and support of the individual. By reassuring him that they regard him as "good" no matter what he produces, they can create an emotional atmosphere in which anxieties are reduced and attitudes conducive to creativity can flourish.

However, when the creative process is not hindered or obstructed by the problems just discussed, the individual can often, when the work is completed, trace its development, perceiving how one thing led to another. When the hypothesis-testing stage proceeds with reasonable effectiveness, the blending of the uniqueness of the idea and the autonomy of the creative individual as regards his self-discipline and the exigencies of his craft or field is such that what is produced has a creative novelty, which is useful, tenable, or satisfying.

THE MYSTIQUE IN THIS PART OF THE PROCESS

Just as there is a mystique associated with the hypothesis-formation stage of the creative process, so there is a mystique associated with the stage of hypothesis testing. During hypothesis formation, the mystique involves inspiration, intuition, and selection of the potentially correct solution in terms of some aesthetic or "gut" feeling. During hypothesis testing, the mystique is associated with the capacity to "feel with" the strains and stresses of the problem or work and the capacity to "know" when the work is complete.

"Feeling with" the Stresses of the Problem or Work

During the course of the dialog between the creative individual and his work, the work may be conceptualized as containing various stresses and strains or as being made up of a variety of forces. Therefore, to arrive at the creative solution, it is important to move with these forces in whatever direction they lead. It is almost as if the problem contains the solution, and to arrive at it, the individual has only to sense and "feel" how the problem is directing him. This kind of behavior is to be distinguished from that in which a solution is imposed upon a work and all of the component parts are forced into a preconceived conceptualization or that in which the conceptualization is simply inadequate for all of the component parts. The solution in these last two instances is inappropriate.

To be able to follow a problem's direction, an individual must possess that which, for want of a better word, we call an "aesthetic feeling." Sometimes this feeling cannot be described very well. The individual does not have the words for it and sometimes may not be aware of the basis of his reactions and behavior. Furthermore, those who listen to him may become irritated and may deny or discredit his experience for they insist on rational, practical, and concrete terms. For those who have the experience of utilizing their capacity for aesthetic awareness, the experience is very clear. We shall later present a laboratory study of problem-solving behavior in which we shall present evidence that comes close to supporting what we have just said. This evidence does not come directly from a study of creative activities but from a study of how creative individuals perform in a problem-solving situation. The study also includes data on the relationship between a measure of aesthetic value and problem-solving behavior.

"Knowing" When the Work Is Complete

The second mysterious aspect of the hypothesis-testing stage of the creative process is being able to recognize when a problem is solved and when a work is complete. The point here is not only that there is a solution to a problem, but that there is a creative solution. For example, two mathematicians may devote themselves to the derivation of mathematical formulas. Both may come up with the same or with different formulas for the same problem but among their colleagues, the mathematician who produced the elegant solution will be regarded as the more creative. The field of painting also yields examples to illustrate this point. Some artists have difficulty in recognizing when a painting is complete: they overwork it or "mess it up." They have to be told when to stop working on a canvas, while other artists recognize this point without too much difficulty. The latter "know" in a not necessarily rational way when their work is complete.

The examples just presented share the characteristics of what the Gestalt psychologists call a "good gestalt": a wholeness, completeness, and satisfying quality that prompts the creative individual to say, "This is it!"

Once again it is impossible to describe how to acquire and control the vital elements of this stage of the creative process. It is very important, however, to relax sufficiently to be available and accessible to "aesthetic feeling" and awareness of completion. Later we may be able to offer more precise helpful suggestions. Gordon (1961), originator of synectics, a group technique for stimulating creativity which is discussed in Chapter XV, suggests that tape recordings of creative sessions should be frequently reviewed by the group members to see if they can recognize from the sessions the conditions and experiences antecedent to the creative solution. If there were characteristic communalities in these conditions, the group members might utilize these cues in future situations as recognition points indicating that a solution or a good gestalt may be at hand.

Related to this matter is an experiment conducted by Blatt (1960, 1961) involving a problem-solving experiment in which he studied the relationship between the rhythm of his subjects' heartbeats and the solution of the problem. He found characteristic changes in heartbeat that paralleled the problem-solving process. Specifically, there was a change in heartbeat before the subject solved the problem. Subjects were not consciously aware of these changes. Is it possible that these physiological autonomic responses were directly related to the approaching solution and that they were manifestations of awareness at some nonrational, nonconscious level? If so, it may in the future be possible to train and teach people to be more sensitive to these levels of autonomic reaction and to use this "information" effectively for creative work.

For our further consideration of the characteristics of the hypothesis-testing stage of the creative process and the easiest ways for an individual to cope with them, we shall examine briefly two psychological theories—associationism and Gestalt psychology—and what they have to say about problem solving. After relating these theories and some of the research they stimulated to hypothesis testing, we shall then discuss the distinctive styles of work and behavior that various types of people utilize in creative work, emphasizing that different kinds of people can achieve the same end result through diverse pathways. These pathways are congruent with their own personalities. Thus there is no single pathway to creativity. Hopefully the reader will find the style that is best for himself and develop it. We shall then conclude with a number of specific suggestions and aids intended to help the individual when he encounters obstacles and blocks during the hypothesis-testing stage of the creative process.

THEORIES

The problems, difficulties, issues, and frustrations that occur during hypothesis testing may be resolved through serendipity, discovery, trial and error, and problem solving. In serendipity an individual comes upon the answer to his problem, or a clue to the answer, while he is looking for something else. But he recognizes the answer because his mind is *prepared*. As we use the term, it applies to the individual who, although carrying out his daily functions, is nevertheless alert to possibilities that may be helpful in the successful fulfillment of the creative process.

Discovery involves characteristics similar to those involved in serendipity—the alertness and readiness of the prepared mind to recognize and accept the appropriate finding or stimulus. The individual's search, however, is more directed and overt in this case. Discovery and serendipity differ in that in the former the individual consciously and purposefully engages in seeking behavior directed at a predetermined goal.

Trial and error is a procedure well known to most people. As the terms convey, it consists of trial followed by error followed by another trial and still another error, and so on, until a trial is followed by a success. This, to some extent, is the procedure Edison used to determine the best filament to use in the incandescent light. Occasionally referred to as *"simply* trial and error," this process of studying the effects or results of all permutations and combinations of all the elements involved is actually quite demanding. It requires knowing what kinds of elements or basic factors to look for, which to combine, and what criteria to use to determine when the desired result has been obtained. The tendency to belittle successes achieved through trial and error is shortsighted, since such results in fact stem from astute selection of the elements to be combined, commendable perseverance, and an appreciation, understanding, and acceptance of the result when it appears.

Trial and error differs from the last way we shall consider to obtain results in the hypothesis-testing stage of creativity—problem solving—in that problem solving characteristically entails more thinking: Either before or during a period of working with, studying, and manipulating objects in the environment or thoughts in his head, the individual is engaged in thought.

The fact that these four methods differ should not deter anyone from using the method with which he feels comfortable.

To further elaborate and clarify several of the points just made it might be well to put them into a theoretical context. Once again, the two major psychological theories drawn upon for the hypothesis-testing stage of the creative process are associationism and Gestalt psychology. The reader interested in problems related to the creative process need not be concerned with taking sides on these two theoretical orientations; even in the psychological literature, both theories have been utilized in understanding creative persons' thought processes. Thus, for example, Mednick and Mednick (1964), in a paper entitled "An Associative Interpretation of the Creative Process," apply associationism to an understanding of Einstein's processes, while Wertheimer (1945) in his book, *Productive Thinking*, also has a rather lengthy discussion of Einstein's thought processes, only this time they are examined from the point of view of Gestalt psychology.

Associationism

This theory says that the individual's capacity to solve problems is affected by his capacity to generate associations. These associations may be stimulated by concrete objective stimuli in the environment, or by already formed associations to stimuli or to the relationships between associations.

To have a variety of associations the individual requires a reasonable amount of "input." In other words, associations are more easily developed and have a wider range if prior responses to a variety of stimuli are already stored somewhere in the brain. To make effective use of this storage system involves in part not evaluating one's thoughts or ideas too strictly nor having too many barriers between them. The associationists believe that to test ideas adequately an individual needs to associate. Some of the techniques for facilitating this process were discussed for their value for hypothesis formation in Chapter IX. The techniques presented there are relevant to the testing phase as well. Applying them simply involves stating the problem or difficulty as if the individual were in the idea-formation stage. In other words, each time there is a problem, it is a stimulus for hypothesis formation.

For the Mednicks (Mednick & Mednick, 1964), who developed the Remote Associates Test (RAT), "*Creative thinking consists of forming new combinations of associative elements, which combinations either meet specified requirements, or are in some way useful. The more mutually remote the elements of the new combination, the more creative is the process or solution* [p. 55, italics Mednicks']." This definition specifically emphasizes remoteness of associations as a manifestation of creativity, just as in brainstorming the quantity of associations is said to be positively related to the quality of associations.

In support of their orientation, Mednick and Mednick (1964) cite authorities in the arts.

André Breton [cited in Ghiselin, 1952] describes a collage by Ernst as being distinguished by a "marvelous capacity to grasp two mutually distant realities without going beyond the field of our experience and to draw a spark from their juxtaposition." Robert Frost (1962) said in an article in the *Atlantic Monthly*, "Let's put this straight. The coupling (and here he is talking about the coupling of poetic ideas) that moves you, that stirs you, is

the association of two things that you did not expect to see associated"
[p. 55].

According to Mednick and Mednick (1964), three mechanisms facilitate "the
ideational contiguity of otherwise disparate ideas [p. 55]." If the contiguity of
remote ideas can be maximized, then the probability of a creative solution is
increased. The mechanisms are (1) serendipity—the appropriate stimuli may
appear in the individual's environment by accident. Furthermore, two ideas
quite unrelated to each other may occur to an individual, only then to be
integrated into a creative solution because each idea was evoked by two stimuli
in the environment that simply happened to occur together. (2) Similarity—
associations may occur because of "the similarity of the associative elements,"
and associations "may occur in certain kinds of poetry, music, and painting
where similarities in form, in sound, and in colors are very important. This mode
of creative solution may be encountered in creative writing which exploits
homonymity and rhyme [p. 56]." (3) Mediation—Mednick and Mednick regard
mediation as the most important associative mechanism. Two or more ideas that
never belonged together are brought together by the mediation of an idea that
belongs to all three. The Mednicks (Mednick, 1962) based their RAT for the
study and selection of creative individuals on this mechanism. An example from
this test illustrates this mechanism. The subject is presented with three words,
"white," "out," and "cat," and is asked to give one word that relates to the
three. The correct answer is "house" because there is a White House, an
outhouse, and a house cat.

Like others who believe in associationism, the Mednicks believe that associations may be stimulated by environmental factors or previous associations, or
may be mediated by ideas related to other associations. Many permutations and
combinations are therefore possible. Other people in this field, like those
involved in brainstorming, suggest (in a sense agreeing with the importance
Mednick assigns to remote associations) that quantity will breed quality. The
individual therefore needs prior experience or exposure to stimuli; knowledge
and experience; the personal flexibility to develop various permutations and
combinations; and finally, the capacity to make the correct selection.

Gestalt Psychology

There are several points of disagreement between the associationists and
Gestalt psychologists. We cannot go into all of them, and for our purposes a brief
discussion of two of them will suffice. Gestalt psychologists object to the
associationists' emphasis and dependence on the individual's past experiences.
Associations, as we have seen, stem from prior "inputs" and unless an individual
has access to this storage (or memory) system of inputs, no new ideas can be
formed. Gestalt psychologists argue that ideas based on the past can result only

in *reproductive* thinking, whereas *productive* thinking stems from responding to structural forces in the field [with the "field" consisting of (1) the stimulus regarded as figure; (2) the background in which it occurs; and (3) the person involved].

Among the different kinds of evidence cited by Wertheimer (1945) in support of his position are case studies of Galileo's, Gauss's, and Einstein's thought processes during the course of their work.

Another objection of the Gestalt psychologists is that the associationists concern themselves with parts and pieces. An object for the associationists is built up out of its parts, so that a square for them is made of its four constituent parts. For the Gestalt psychologists, on the other hand, squareness is *given* in the figure, and each part has its role, so to speak, by the organization of the whole or, in this instance, the square. The whole determines the parts.

Regarding problem solving specifically, we find that for the Gestalt psychologists a problem begins when an individual experiences a gap or lack of closure in a situation. The individual may be the passive receiver of the gap or he may actively go out, seek, discover, or create a gap in his environment. For example, a situation may be thought of as complete, fully structured, without gaps or without problems—when along comes an individual, who, in the sense we are talking about, makes a problem. In Barron's (1958) framework, he makes disorder out of order only to create still another better order.

According to Gestalt psychology a problem (consisting of the gap or the lack of closure and the field it is in) contains structural forces. If the individual allows himself to "feel with" and follow them he will be able to resolve the problem. There is a situation (call it S_1) in which the actual thought starts and then another situation (S_2) in which the process ends and the problem is solved. Gestaltists posit that there are structural features in S_1 called forces or vectors, with direction, quality, and intensity, that set up requirements to be followed and fulfilled if effective solutions are to be attained. For the Gestaltists this development is a manifestation of the so-called Prägnanz principle—that the field situation is organized as simply and as clearly as is possible under the existing conditions. The forces in the vectors lead to the formation of a good gestalt.

The vectors in S_1 gradually lead to change and improvement which at S_2 (the end state) result in a condition or state in which the inner forces are held together harmoniously. The parts are determined by the whole and the whole by the parts. The good gestalt has been achieved.

It would appear from this description that the problem-solving process should run off very smoothly and solutions be found rather easily. There are several reasons why this does not happen:

(1) An individual may have an inadequate view of the situation and be unable to grasp the structure of the gap in the situation that confronts him. The individual may be too narrow or too overextended in his point of view. When he

does have the sense of the structure of the problem at the beginning, he may lose it afterward if he becomes too involved in details or by leaping ahead too quickly on the basis of a general overview.

(2) Individuals are seduced by possible shortcuts to goals. They may be so concerned with getting a result that they concentrate on what is close by, overlooking the possibility that by a "detour," by "going out of the field" momentarily and then coming back into it, they might find the more effective solution.

(3) S_1 and S_2 are each part of the same field and both are embedded in a larger field, consisting among other things of the current state of the art and knowledge available, the social situation at the present time, and the individual's own life history. All of these can break into this separate part-field of S_1 and adversely affect the possibility of solution.

(4) For some problems, the structural nature of the problem determines the vectors and the individual and his personal interests play no role. Indeed, if these personal motives or interests do begin to play a role, then it may be disturbing to the problem solution. There are other problems in which the individual's personal needs are the source of the problem, but here too "the problem may remain insoluble so long as one focuses on one's own wish or need; it may become soluble only if, viewing one's desire as part in the situation, one realizes the objective structural requirements [Wertheimer, 1945, p. 196]."

(5) Wertheimer (1945) interestingly points out that in some situations the real, important, and critical achievement is to realize that a problem exists, that change and improvement are required. "To envisage, to put the right problem," Wertheimer says, "is often a far more important achievement than to solve a set task [p. 197]." Some individuals do not take the time to formulate the right problem before they start their work.

(6) Some individuals do not allow themselves to sense differences in the character of the problems they work on. They always try to proceed in the same direction. But in some areas, as in music and art, Wertheimer points out that the beginning is with the end state (S_2) and "the artist is driven towards its crystallization, concretization, or full realization. Characteristically, the more or less clearly conceived structural whole-qualities of the thing to be created are determining in the process. A composer does not usually put notes together in order to get some melody; he envisages the character of a melody *in statu nascendi* and proceeds from above as he tries to concretize it in all its parts [p. 197]." When conditions are ambiguous, the forces in the problem may seek clarification of the central issue for a period and then move to the parts, and so alternate following the "structural requirements" until the goal is achieved. Some individuals cannot follow such an alternating pattern. It is too irregular and "too messy" for them. Consequently they impose a framework on the problem rather than following its leads.

(7) In the foregoing, so much emphasis has been placed on the structural characteristics of the problem that we might assume that the role played by the individual is unimportant. It is therefore wise to quote Wertheimer at this point:

> When a picture is given here of the inner structural dynamics in the determination of processes, it does not mean in this development man is merely passive. An attitude is implied on his part, a willingness to face problems straight, a readiness to follow them up courageously and sincerely, a desire for improvement, in contrast with arbitrary, wilful, or slavish attitudes. This, I think, is one of the great attributes that constitute the dignity of man [Wertheimer, 1954, p. 198].

A Study of Feeling with a Problem's Forces—Part of the Mystique

The Gestalt psychologists have tested their hypotheses about the problem-solving process in a variety of laboratory experimental studies. As pointed out previously, insofar as creativity is concerned, their work has also involved case studies and analyses of the work of such people as Galileo, Gauss, and Einstein (Wertheimer, 1945). Investigation in the same Gestalt tradition in which currently creative individuals were studied was undertaken by Blatt and Stein (1957, 1959). In this work, first, hypotheses were developed regarding efficiency in problem-solving behavior; then efficiency in problem-solving behavior was related to creativity.

The work first focused on efficiency and problem-solving behavior, involving 35 industrial research chemists, all of whom had their PhD's. Later in the same study the authors were concerned with the relationship between efficiency and creativity. This involved two small groups (and therefore the need for caution in evaluating the results) who were part of the larger sample. One was a group of eight men who were rated as "more" creative, and the other was a group of nine who were rated as "less" creative by their peers and superiors.

A "rational" problem, one that consisted of logical relationships, was selected for the study. It involved the use of a device developed by John and Rimoldi (John, 1957) which made it possible to determine not only whether a problem was solved but also the process through which it was solved.

Using Gestalt psychology, it was reasoned that the problem-solving process could be regarded as consisting of two phases, an analysis phase and a synthesis phase, both of which are separated by a "lag" phase. As the term implies, during the analysis phase the individual spends his time analyzing the problem and being exposed to the information (both necessary and sufficient) that it contains or, stated differently, he becomes better acquainted with its structure. For most problems it is most difficult, if not impossible, to have a well-defined measure of the information they contain, and it is also difficult knowing whether the person has been exposed to the information, let alone whether he has been aware of its significance. For the problem used in this study, the information that made up the problem, or the information needed to solve it, as well as whether the subject had been exposed to it, was available to the experimenters. As we shall see later, the person's behavior while working on the problem was monitored on tape.

Theoretically, after having garnered the necessary information during the analysis phase, the individual should be able to synthesize his data, thereby solving the problem. But this is an oversimplification of the relationship between problem and individual. Some people, as we have seen, have difficulty following the structural forces of a problem. Consequently, a lag phase usually occurs between the analysis and synthesis phases during which the individual's problem-solving behavior begins to shift from analysis to synthesis. Blatt and Stein actually divided the analysis phase into two parts, an initial phase and a lag phase. The initial phase extends from the beginning of the problem-solving process to that point at which the subject has been exposed to the necessary and sufficient information making up the problem. It is followed by the lag phase, which is concluded when the subject's predominant mode of activity shifts from analysis to synthesis. In the synthesis phase, the subject's behavior reflects primary concern with coordinating the information he has obtained.

In the Blatt and Stein (1959) study of efficiency in problem solving, efficiency was defined as the absence of unnecessary questions. If an individual were sensitive to the stresses and strains or the demand characteristics of the problem he was working on; if there were no interferences from personal or other field forces, then he should solve the problem with a minimum of unnecessary questions. Basically it was expected that the subject would spend his time during the analytic phase sensing and learning the field forces. Once he knew these, there should have been little or no time wasted in shifting from the analysis to the synthesis phase. Ideally, there should have been only one coordinating move that integrated or synthesized all of the material and brought about the solution.

This was the theoretical orientation. The research procedure involved using the apparatus, mentioned earlier, developed by John and Rimoldi (John, 1957). This electromechanical device has a face panel that consists of a center light and a circle of several lights and buttons. A disk can be placed over the center light and between the circular set of lights. On this disk are several arrows that run between some of the lights. In some cases a single arrow extends between two lights, and in some cases two arrows, each from a different source, converge on one light. The arrows indicate something of the nature of the relationship between the lights. A single arrow between two lights means that if the button at the tail end of the arrow is pressed it will send an impulse along the path of the arrow and light the light at the arrowhead. Where two arrows converge upon a single light, it may mean either that the buttons at both sources need to be pressed to light the light on which the arrows converge, or that if both these buttons are pressed simultaneously, one will inhibit the other. The information contained in the single arrow is "given" and the others need to be learned. When they are all learned, the subject has to demonstrate that he knows them by pressing the correct sequence of three red buttons that are below the disk. This is not an easy problem to solve. In the study described, 37 minutes, on the average, were required to solve it.

This problem has two rather interesting characteristics. First, as mentioned previously, the experimenters know the characteristics of the problem and the information that the subject has to know and learn in order to solve it. Second, each button that the subject presses, which may be regarded functionally as a question, marks a moving tape. Markings on the tape can be analyzed to determine the number of questions that a subject has asked. Moreover, because the experimenters know the requirements of the problem, they also know which of these questions are necessary, and whether they are analytic or synthetic.

Using the apparatus just described and the lack of unnecessary questions as a measure of efficiency, Blatt and Stein (1959) found that (1) more efficient subjects did have a clearer delineation in the analysis and synthesis phases of the problem-solving process. (2) Efficient subjects asked a larger proportion of their questions during, and devoted proportionately more of their total time (and more absolute time as well) to, the initial phase. Relatively speaking, the more efficient subjects were less involved in the lag phase of the problem-solving process. They asked a smaller proportion of their questions in this phase. They also spent proportionately less time, as well as less absolute time, in this phase. (3) An efficient subject asked his questions at a slower rate, "suggesting that he may be doing more thinking, planning, and integrating of the data than the less efficient individual [p. 206]."

Turning to the relationships between efficiency and creativity manifest in the different behaviors of eight "more" and nine "less" creative PhD industrial research chemists, Blatt and Stein found that

> The more creative men tend to be more efficient (i.e., they tend to ask fewer unnecessary questions) and they tend to ask their questions at a slower rate. They also have a clearer *A-S* [analysis-synthesis] shift point, and tend to have a larger proportion of unique questions to redundant questions. Finally, they also ask a larger proportion of their questions in the initial phase, but they do not differ significantly from their less creative colleagues in the lag and synthesis phases [Blatt & Stein, 1959, pp. 204-205].

In other words, the more creative individuals in this exploratory study spent more time analyzing the problem on which they had to work than did the less creative persons.

In line with Wertheimer's suggestion that the person is part of the field, Blatt and Stein (1959) studied the relationships between person-related variables and the problem-solving process. They used one intelligence test [the Miller Analogies Test (1970)], an abbreviated form of the *F* (authoritarian) Scale (Levinson & Huffman, 1955), the Allport-Vernon-Lindzey Scale of Values (1951), the Taylor Manifest Anxiety Scale (Taylor, 1953), and the Freeman Manifest Anxiety Scale (Freeman, 1953). [Since the two anxiety scales did correlate significantly with each other (.36, $p < .05$), the scores on both tests were combined into a single anxiety score.]

The results of this part of the study were as follows. Previously, the analysis-synthesis shift point was shown to be related to efficiency, and in this part of the study it was shown to be positively and significantly related to the Aesthetic value but negatively and significantly related to the Social value of the Allport-Vernon-Lindzey Scale of Values (1951). There were some trends for the A-S shift point to be negatively related to the Political value and the Taylor Manifest Anxiety Scale (Taylor, 1953).

The total rate at which questions were asked "was negatively related to the Aesthetic Value and positively related to the Political Value. The relationships between rate and the Theoretical Value, the *F* Scale, Taylor, and Combined Anxiety Measures were all positive and close to significance [Blatt & Stein 1959, p. 208]." Considering the various phases of the problem-solving process, Blatt and Stein (1959) found that

> Personality variables were related only to the per cent of questions that were asked in the initial phase. The Aesthetic Value correlated positively and significantly with this dimension; the Social Value, the *F* Scale, and the Taylor Manifest Anxiety Scale were all negatively related and approached statistical significance. The relationship between the MAT and per cent of questions asked in the initial phase also approaches statistical significance but in a positive direction [pp. 208, 210].

There was one more variable to which Blatt and Stein (1959) related the personality variables—the proportion of unique to redundant question.

> This aspect of problem solving was seen as possibly indicating the ability to break one's set or as the capacity to develop restructurations of the problem. This factor was negatively and significantly related to only one personality scale, the Freeman Anxiety Scale. The relationships between the Aesthetic Value and Combined Anxiety Measure and this variable approached statistical significance. The former was positive and the latter negative [p. 210].

Thus we see that, consistent with Wertheimer's statement, there are personality factors that may obstruct and others that may facilitate the problem-solving process. The Blatt and Stein study suggests that individuals for whom aesthetic factors are important (i.e., who place high value on good form in the arts and in life in general), appear to have more capacity than others, who are not so inclined, for following the forces in the structure of the problems on which they work, and so are more efficient in their problem-solving efforts. When individuals try to dominate a problem and/or when their anxiety levels are too high, they become insensitive to the stimuli in their environment and become unable to utilize them effectively.

A Study of the Relationship between Heart Rate and Problem-Solving Behavior—A Potential Contribution to the Mystique

Blatt (1960, 1961) used the theory and technique of the Blatt and Stein (1959) study to investigate the relationship between one aspect of the autonomic nervous system, heart rate, and problem-solving behavior and so provided data that may well help alert an individual as to when he is approaching a solution to his problem. If people could be so trained, then a critical part of the creative process would no longer be so mysterious and more individuals would probably make creative contributions in the future.

In the study by Blatt and Stein (1959) described earlier, the problem-solving process was said to comprise an analytic phase, followed by a lag phase (which involved a shift in the individual's behavior from analysis to synthesis), and finally a synthetic phase, which culminated in the solution to the problem. The individual's behavior while solving the problem was ascertained from the study of a tape on which was recorded every button press that an individual made as he sought the solution.

Blatt (1960, 1961) followed up their earlier research by studying a group of subjects whose heart rate was recorded while they were working on the problem. Variations in heart rate were then correlated with problem-solving behavior. Analysis of these data indicated that the efficient problem solvers—those who asked the fewest unnecessary questions—had major changes in their heart rate at three points: (1) when all the questions necessary to solve the problem had been answered; (2) when their behavior shifted from analysis to synthesis; and (3) as they approached the final solution.

It would be interesting to investigate whether it is possible to train persons to become more aware of their autonomic reactions and to use this awareness more constructively in the solution of problems. Along with such studies we would need to keep in mind the kinds of problems to which information about heart rate or intuition can be applied. It should be noted that the problem used by Blatt and Stein involved one solution. We still need to know whether similar intuitive and autonomic behavior can be observed in problems with several solutions.

TYPES AND THE TESTING OF HYPOTHESES

Not all of the individuals who participated in the experiments cited earlier (nor all individuals who engage in hypothesis testing) behave in the same way. Such differences are "lost" for all intents and purposes since researchers are generally more interested in relationships between variables than in the persons involved in the experiments. At best, in these studies, individual differences figure only in the standard deviations calculated for statistical purposes. Consequently, individuals who seek information in the psychological literature on how to improve their creativity often come away with the feeling that there is only one approach to creativity, which is certainly not true. Different types of individuals can be equally effective in the same situation. For any one problem there are different pathways to the solution or goal, what general system theorists (Bertalanffy, 1968) call *equifinality*. Different types of individuals follow these different pathways or have different styles of work. What is important is to know oneself and to capitalize on one's style.

Just as there are types of individuals who can be effective in different ways on the same problem, so there are different problems or different problem areas in which types of persons can be differentially creative. We still need more research on this matter. Pending such research, we consider the available research data on types, so that at least the personality side of the problem can be illustrated.

One organization in our society constantly involved in the creative process is the research and development (R&D) arm of a company which employs scientists and engineers. Gough and Woodworth (1960) studied the research "styles" of men so employed by presenting 45 research scientists with 56 statements* dealing with scientific activity, values, and modes of research procedures, which they were to sort into five categories varying from most to least descriptive of themselves. By appropriate statistical analysis of these data plus psychological test scores and observer ratings, Gough and Woodworth (1960, pp. 95-96) came up with pictures of eight types of researchers. They were (a) the *zealot*: this type of researcher is dedicated to research and "sees himself as a driving, indefatigable researcher." (b) The *initiator* is the man who "reacts quickly to research problems," generates ideas, stimulates others, is a good team man. (c) The *diagnostician* sees himself "as a good evaluator, able to diagnose strong and weak points in a program quickly and accurately" and as a person who improvises "quick solutions" to problems. (d) The *scholar* has an exceptional memory and "an eye for detail and order," but he is not a perfectionist nor an "endless seeker for ultimates." (e) The *artificer* "sees himself as having a special facility for taking

---

*Gough reports (personal communication) that these statements have "been extensively applied in France with excellent results." And he also supplied these references: Bonnardel and Lavoegie (1965, 1966) and Giscard (1966).

inchoate or poorly formed ideas of others and fashioning them into workable and significant problems." (f) The *esthetician* is analytical in his thinking, "prefers research problems which lend themselves to elegant and formal solutions," and has a wide range of interests. (g) The *methodologist* "is vitally interested in methodological issues, and in problems of mathematical analysis and conceptualization." (h) The *independent* avoids administrative work and team activities; he thinks in "reference to physical and structural models, rather than in analytical and mathematical ways."

These types of researchers make a good deal of sense. It would therefore be of much value if future efforts were oriented to spelling out more fully how these types differ and how a person could ascertain whether he were a member of any of the eight types. Knowing this information and the conditions under which his type performs best would be most helpful to a person's creativity.

Another typology has been developed by Stein (1966; Stein & Neulinger, 1968); it has been used in the study of the effectiveness of a group of Peace Corps volunteers assigned to a community development project in Colombia, South America, and is discussed in the next chapter (in the section on the intermediaries in the creative process). At this juncture we alert the reader to Stein's typology because it differs from Gough and Woodworth's (1960). Their typology is based on the activities that the individual performs; Stein's is based on the individual's motivational needs and then related to how he goes about solving a problem involved in his assignment. Specifically, Peace Corps volunteers who Stein studied were involved in community development activities which required helping people to organize themselves to fulfill their mutual needs. Different types of volunteers achieved this goal through processes and styles that were quite congruent with their own personalities (cf. pages 283-287). Various styles, related to personality factors, successfully achieved the same goal.

SPECIFIC SUGGESTIONS

We now present some specific suggestions, drawn freely and flexibly from all the theories and approaches mentioned earlier, for facilitating the hypothesis-testing stage of the creative process. Although some of the suggestions reflect the operation of the same psychological principle and might have been presented under the same rubric rather than separately, the latter procedure was followed in an effort to broaden the reader's perspective by emphasizing the various specific ways in which he can make effective changes in his hypothesis-testing behavior.

Knowing Yourself

As we pointed out earlier, not everyone follows the same pattern for attaining effective solutions to problems. It is therefore important for an individual to become aware of the processes that are most productive for him. Concomitantly, he should become aware of and proficient in securing the conditions under which he has been creative. The individual must work actively on the elements of his problem, but he must also be sufficiently passive so that patterns can be sensed and directions can be followed. Passivity alone or activity alone is insufficient to creative hypothesis testing.

Optimal Level of Motivation

There is an "optimal" level of motivation at which individuals can do their best. Creative individuals who feel "inspired" may be *so* inspired that the inspiration interferes with hypothesis testing. An individual may also be *so* motivated for a creative solution that his motivation interferes with the solution to the problem. It should be kept in mind, by creative individuals as well as by those responsible for the administration or supervision of creative people, that there is an *optimal* level of motivation for any activity. Many of us are likely to think that if something is good, a great deal of it is better and very little of it is no good. Hence, we orient ourselves to thinking of minima and maxima when we should be thinking of optimal relationships.

Experimental demonstration of optimal motivation was provided by Birch (1945) in an animal experiment in which he studied motivational factors and problem-solving behavior in chimpanzees. A chimpanzee in a cage was presented with the problem of getting at food that was outside the cage, beyond his reach. Also, outside the cage were two sticks, one longer than the other. Birch varied the complexity of the problem by how he placed the sticks and by their proximity to or distance from the food, hypothesizing that it would be more difficult for the chimpanzee to solve the problem if one stick were near the food and the other stick were further away from it than if both sticks were near the food.

In addition to varying the complexity and difficulty of the problem, Birch also varied the motivational state of the animal (in this instance, hunger) by depriving it of food for 2, 6, 12, 24, 36, and 48 hours before testing.

The results of the experiment indicated that when the chimpanzee was not very motivated (i.e., not very hungry), he was distracted from the problem by all sorts of extraneous stimuli. When very highly motivated (very hungry), the chimpanzee excluded everything else and concentrated solely on the problem. When habitual patterns of solving problems were frustrated, there were temper tantrums and screaming by the animal. The animals whose behavior was most flexible and directed toward a solution of the problem were those whose motivations were at intermediate levels.

Learn Different or New Ways of Solving Problems

A problem generally persists when our usual ways of coping with or solving it are ineffective. We tend to become habituated to certain specific ways of solving problems which we use automatically as needed because they proved successful for us in the past. We never feel the need for change until we are unsuccessful. We therefore need to increase our repertoire of ways of solving problems and this can be done through such activities as reading "how-to-do-it" books, which may put our techniques in perspective and give us new ideas for other potentially useful techniques. It can also be profitable to study principles of problem solving. Maier (1933) demonstrated this when a group of students he lectured to on reasoning and problem solving did better in solving a problem than a control group who had no such lectures.

Metaphors, Analogies, Auxiliary Problems

It helps, when trying to sense the stresses and strains in a problem, to recast the problem in terms of some kind of metaphor, analogy, or auxiliary or related problem. We shall see how this method, which is also suggested by Polya (1946), is used in group problem-solving situations when synectics is discussed (in Chapter XV).

Feel Free to Go Out of the Field

A fair amount of the theory of Gestalt psychology is based on these psychologists' analysis and understanding of the laws of perception. They emphasize the interaction between perception and thought processes. Perception has an organizing effect and characteristic, and the way in which we perceive a problem to be organized may block any effective solution.

A good illustration of this difficulty is the well-known nine-dots problem. The individual is shown three columns of three dots each. The columns are about one-half inch apart. The person is then asked to draw four straight lines that go through each of the dots without lifting his pencil off the paper.

The problem is solved by extending one of the lines beyond the square. Some people perceive the dots as forming one or more squares. The organizing effects of this perception is so strong that they cannot break it, even though solving the problem requires going "out of the field" of the square.

Avoid "Excess Stimuli" and "Mental Dazzle"

In trying to solve a problem we are occasionally hampered because the material we are confronted with is inadequate for solving the problem. The reverse may also be true, though: the stimulus field may contain too much information.

This is well illustrated in a study by David Katz (reported in Krech *et al.*, 1969). School children were presented with simple arithmetic calculations of addition and subtraction. Some groups of children performed their calculations with undenominated numbers, such as 10.50 plus 13.25 plus 6.89. Others worked with the same numbers except that they were preceded by a dollar sign. Still other numbers had the abbreviated symbol for foreign currency preceding them (e.g., Kr for kroner). Katz found that the difficulty of the calculation was increased by adding the monetary sign and that the problem became still more difficult when the symbol for foreign currency was added. Even with adults it was found that the time involved in doing addition increased by 12% when the dollar sign was added.

Overcome "Functional Fixity"

One of the difficulties in solving some problems is that the functions of the stimuli presented are *fixed* in terms of our past experience with them. The functions they served on some previous occasion stay in our minds, and the more important the function they served at that time, the more fixed the function is.

"Functional fixity" as a concept in problem solving was suggested by Karl Duncker (1945), a German psychologist. The manner in which it operates to impede problem solving is well illustrated in an experiment by Adamson (1952), in which each subject is asked to mount three candles vertically on a soft wooden screen using with these objects other objects that were also available and which included cardboard boxes, matches, and thumbtacks.

In presenting one group of 29 college students with the problem, the candles, matches, and tacks were put into three boxes. These were very likely seen as containers and not as supports or shelves, in which manner they had to be seen if the problem was to be solved. This "blind spot" may explain why only 41% of this group solved the problem. In another group of 28 college students 86% solved the problem; the boxes were empty and placed among the other objects. The "container" function of the boxes was thus not as fixed for the second group as it was for the first.

To overcome functional fixity it therefore may be helpful to move the stimuli around. Different perceptual combinations may suggest different functions. Learning the different functions of an object early in one's experience with it may also prevent functional fixity from occurring.

Break Down "Embeddedness"

One of the difficulties in problem solving is that of finding the right kind of material for the solution. To be sure, at times this material is simply not available in the immediate area. At other times it is, but it is embedded in other material so that its possible functions go unrecognized.

For example, in a ring-and-peg problem the subject is asked to put two rings on a peg that is at one end of the room. The two rings are near the peg at the far end of the room. The subject stands behind a chalk line near which are two sticks.

The solution involves getting the two sticks together and making a longer stick out of them. On the wall is a calendar that hangs from a nail by means of a piece of string. The problem is to "disembed" this piece of string from its situation (or field). Unless the subject perceives the possibility of removing the piece of string from the calendar and using it to tie the two sticks together, he will not be able to reach the rings.

For effective problem-solving behavior, an individual needs to feel free to shift from the stimuli in his environment. The capacity to break the embeddedness problem is so important that it is part of a test of cognitive functions called the Embedded Figures Test (Witkin *et al.*, 1971).

The effects of embeddedness are further highlighted by work done by Scheerer (1963). When 16 subjects were given the problem with a piece of string hanging alone from the wall, they used the string to tie the two sticks together. Knowing then that the string, if it is not embedded, functions to fulfill the purpose in the experiment, Scheerer then used it to suspend objects that had no real function—a piece of blank cardboard, an outdated calendar, and a cloudy mirror. Under these conditions subjects again used the string for the purpose for which it was intended. When the string fulfilled a *meaningful* function, however—when it was used with a current calendar, a clear mirror, and a "No Smoking" sign—56% of the subjects failed to use the calendar string, 69% failed to use the mirror string, and 53% failed to use the "No Smoking" sign string.

The subjects in the experiment were asked to verbalize their thoughts as they went along, and from this it was learned that those who thought they were forbidden to use the string simply did not do so. It was also learned from what the subjects said that everyone decided early that a string was needed. In this part of the experiment, then, more than half of the subjects looked for a string for the whole time of the test but did not think of using a string of which they had full view.

Feel Free to Play with the Spatial Arrangement of the Stimuli

When objects important to the solution of the problem are in the subject's visual field, it is more likely that the problem will be solved. This was demonstrated in the early research studies in Gestalt psychology. Köhler studied chimpanzees' behavior in the use of implements to solve problems. He was particularly interested in whether or not the animal could use sticks as rakes to pull in food and found that even if a stick had been used as a rake on a previous occasion, it was not used again by the chimpanzee for such purposes unless it was in the same visual field as the food.

From this it would appear that moving objects around might facilitate solving the problem. *The Allen Morphologizer,* as we saw in Chapter IX, has possibilities in this connection. Some individuals may find it more effective to shift variables around visually while others may prefer talking about them in various ways.

Shifting objects around may not only put them into closer proximity with the goal (hence expediting the solution), but may also shift an object away from other objects with which it is generally seen, and so facilitate the development of new and different uses. For example, a knife may be seen as a food utensil, but when juxtaposed with hammer and nails it may be seen as a potential screw-driver.

Break the Time Set

Just as things are spatially organized, so they can be temporally organized. And just as spatial organization of stimuli may affect problem-solving behavior, so may their temporal organization. In other words, over time an individual may become more and more accustomed to certain ways of solving problems. Having used these ways effectively, he is more likely to use them to solve a new problem than to adapt the solution to the requirements of the problem. Psychologically speaking, the individual has become set, and the set can interfere with problem solving.

This was very well illustrated in a study by Luchins (1942) in which he presented individuals with a series of problems. He so trained them that they had to solve problems in a complex manner and when they came to a problem that could be solved in a simple manner (which the subjects had also demonstrated they could do), they did not do so but used the more complex approach.

Luchins used a water jar problem with which many people have had experi-ence as youngsters or teenagers. For example, in one problem the individual has two empty jars, one that holds 29 quarts of water and another that holds 3 quarts of water. The subject's task is to end up with one jar containing 20 quarts. To do so he starts with an empty 3-quart jar and fills it 3 times from the 29-quart jar.

A more indirect solution is apparent in the second problem where the student has three jars, a 21-quart jar, a 127-quart jar, and a 3-quart jar. His task is to end up with 100 quarts of water. To achieve this he fills the 127-quart jar first, spills off 21 quarts, and then pours 3 quarts twice with the 3-quart jar.

In the Luchins study 57 subjects worked on the two problems just indicated and then went on to two critical problems. In one of these, each subject had three jars with respective capacities of 23 quarts, 49 quarts, and 3 quarts. His task is to come up with 20 quarts. Those subjects who had only the first two problems solved this critical problem and one other in a direct and rather simple manner. Indeed, this was true of all the 57 individuals. On the other hand, 79 subjects had had not only the first two problems but also a third one before they were exposed to the last two critical problems. On the intervening four problems the subjects had to use all three jars and their solutions had to be rather indirect. When these 79 subjects were confronted with the last two problems, 81% used indirect solutions; only 17% used direct solutions and 2% used other solutions or failed.

Knight (1963) also studied the effect of set and contributed some new information. He used five rather than three jars in an experiment with two groups of college students who were to solve 21 problems. One of the student groups was designated the High Effort group because they were presented with a problem that was difficult to solve. The second, or Low Effort, group was presented with an easier problem. The same principle was involved in solving either problem and, as might be expected, the High Effort group took a longer time to solve its problem. This group showed a much stronger effect of set and continued using a more complex principle when a simpler one was available. Then, when this group had a problem on which it could not use the initial principle, it continued to develop more complicated principles. The outcome of this was that on the last problem only 7 out of 22 students in the High Effort group were aware of the obvious solution, whereas in the Low Effort group 18 out of 24 were aware of it.

Krech *et al.* (1969), in commenting on this study, say, "The more we invest initially in deriving a certain problem-solving principle, the more likely we are to stick to it. Whether this 'investment' is cognitive, motivational, or emotional, we cannot say—it is probably a bit of each—but the practical implications of this finding . . . are not difficult to see [p. 426]."

It is well to keep these points in mind, for there are individuals who are likely to overlook the obvious because they had to struggle so hard in learning or testing problems initially. The point is also relevant to the evaluation of courses and programs designed to stimulate creativity. Individuals who go through such programs may come up with answers to problems. These answers can then be utilized to evaluate the program. One would do well, however, to evaluate how well the response compares with the simplest ones. Hyman (1960) found that individuals who went through a brainstorming course selected more complicated responses, whereas experienced engineers selected simpler ones.

Just-Completed Conventional Uses May Block Novel Uses

Among other fixations that may block problem solution is the inability to use an object for novel purposes if it has just been used in some traditional manner. Duncker (cited in Scheerer, 1963) gave subjects the problem of suspending string from a wooden ledge. The subject was given a gimlet but no hooks. The solution involved putting the gimlet in the wood and hanging the string on it. Duncker found that individuals who had used the gimlet to make holes were less likely to use it as a peg.

Another study that falls into this category is the ring-and-peg problem described earlier (see "Break Down Embeddedness"). Other experiments showed that if the string was embedded in a meaningful situation it was not used by the subject. By the same token if it were used for its conventional purpose, it was also not used for tying things together. For example, if a secretary came in and asked the subject to help hang up a mirror, the subject, who had been at work on some unrelated written material, helped do so and then went back to his work. Fifteen minutes later subjects were given the ring-and-peg problem and although they had had experience with the string, 50% of them failed (Scheerer, 1963).

However, when the string was handled as a string, results were different. In this study (Scheerer, 1963) subjects were told that they were participating in a study of "manual dexterity." They were to hang up on the wall an old calendar, a cardboard, or mirror using a tweezers to tie the string. After 15 minutes the subjects participated in the ring-and-peg problem and only 1 out of 36 failed. Apparently, "the mirror and the string were perceived as two things. . . . The string remained a string, not just a means of hanging things [p. 124]."

Increase Psychological Distance

In Gestalt psychology when stimuli in a problem are presented to an individual, both the stimuli and the individual become part of a field. The critical word here is *part*. At one extreme is the case where the individual merges with the stimuli. Colloquially speaking, he loses himself in the problem. Technically, he has lost his psychological distance. Loss of psychological distance can result from an individual's very high motivation to do well, or from overanxiety, among other factors. (Embeddedness may also occasion loss of psychological distance.)

It is therefore quite critical that the individual maintain an optimal relationship with the problem. To see whether an individual's involvement in a problem can be overcome by increasing his psychological distance from it, Scheerer (1963) had individual subjects serve as observers while another person went through the motions of trying to solve the problem. In working on the problem, this person got as far as talking about the need for something to tie the sticks together. He was then stopped, and the subject who had been observing was asked to work the problem out in his own mind. In this experiment it was found that one out of seven observers failed to solve the problem properly, but more than half of the subjects who actually tried to solve the problem and who were deeply involved in it failed. Hence, psychological distance was an aid in solving the problem.

Adapt Your Response to the Problem's Pattern

According to the Gestalt psychologist each problem has its own demand requirements. The individual must sense them, be aware of them, fulfill them, and so solve the problem. Inability to do so is an indication of functional fixity, set behavior, and the like, all of which may be termed *fixations* that can interfere with the problem-solving process.

It is obviously impossible to consider every kind of problem an individual may be confronted with, but the three suggested by Krech *et al.* (1969) highlight the major characteristics we need to know. The three kinds of problems are explanation, prediction, and invention.

In explanation, the goal is *to seek an understanding of why a specified event has occurred.* In prediction, certain conditions are given, and the goal is *to anticipate the event that has not yet happened.* In invention, the goal is *to create a novel set of conditions that will result in a specified event* [p. 412].

Many creative solutions have been developed as a result of solving problems in explanation—by Galileo, Copernicus, Newton, and Einstein. And while explanation problems are often the simplest to solve, we must beware of all too common errors. The perception of cause may be influenced by the grouping phenomenon in perception. Thus, two events that occur simultaneously, if they are similar to each other or close to each other, are likely to be regarded as causally related to one another. Too few objects or stimuli in the environment may be available to solve a problem, but environmental stimuli may be so strong that we focus on this one stimulus source. And as we said previously, "mental dazzle" may affect us when too many stimuli are available. The explanation problem frequently presents us with a specified stimulus pattern, and it thus becomes difficult to break away from the first solution. It may, however, be the wrong solution.

A prediction problem is not as well structured as an explanation problem because it involves an attempt to understand a *future* event. Because the situation is less structured and ambiguous, mental sets can have greater effects and it is more difficult to follow the patterns or field forces. The prediction problem involves fewer stimuli, so it imposes fewer stimulus demands on the individual; he can therefore break away from solutions that do not work well.

Still less structure is involved in invention, because the individual actively strives for novelty. Since inventions, like all other problems, rely on some aspect of or some relation with the past for their solution, we must be aware of the possible negative effects of past experiences, for they may affect problem-solving behavior. In invention, also, the desired event, the goal, may shape the subject's problem-solving behavior and affect him so that he works from the "top downward," in contrast to working from the "bottom upward" as in the explanation type of problem.

Regardless of what the starting stimulus for the problem-solving behavior is, it is critical that the individual feel free to start at whatever point he sees a problem and thinks of some way to solve it. By thus breaking up a problem into subunits, important wedges into the broader problem may be found. Furthermore, as any part of a problem is solved, it may so alter the individual's perception of the existing stimuli by changing field relationships that new ideas and new attempts at more effective problem solutions become available.

SUMMARY

After having an idea, the individual engaged in the creative process must test and evaluate it. This hypothesis-testing process is often a problem-solving experience. The individual thus has to keep in mind the characteristics of the problem he is working on and adapt himself to them. He must have the capacity to tolerate frustration and have optimal motivation (Maier, 1969). It is important that he maintain his flexibility.

Teaching, supervisory, and managerial personnel should also be aware of these factors involved in hypothesis-testing so that they will not only be supportive and encouraging to their personnel—even to the point of suggesting they set aside a problem for an extended period of time so that they can acquire a fresh view and return with more effective behavior—but will also assume more direct action in learning about the types of men they supervise, their capabilities, and the problems assigned to them. In so doing they should be able to assign the right man to the right job—the man who has demonstrated most motivation and aesthetic sensitivity in working with certain kinds of problems so that creative results may be attained.

Chapter **XI**

Affecting the Communication of Results

Creativity, like all other behavior, is a function of the transactional relationships between a person and his environment (Lewin, 1935). The creative individual affects and is affected by the social context in which he works. All too often in the study of the creative process attention is focused on and limited to what goes on within the creative person. In the previous chapters on hypothesis formation and hypothesis testing we too attended to such matters and concerned ourselves with what are essentially *intra*personal communications. These were manifest in our description of the dialog that the creative person has with himself about his work, in his consideration of the implications and applications of a hypothesis, when he stands back from his work to assess it, etc.

But all that goes on within the person should not cause us to overlook the very important *inter*personal communications that occur during the creative process. They occur when the creative individual invites a friend or colleague to look at, listen to, or read his work, and the friend or colleague provides comments or evaluations that either implicitly or explicitly give the creative person emotional support and/or acceptance. Obtaining financial support also requires interpersonal communication as involved in filing applications for fellowships, grants, or an itemized budget to support the conduct of an individual's work. Options might be given for the later publication of the person's writing, and gallery owners and museum administrators might be contacted for the later showing of his work. These are some of the kinds of interpersonal transactions and communications that take place throughout the creative process. They vary in terms of the persons involved as well as in terms of the roles they play. At times, they serve as a fertile groundwork that nourishes, encourages, and facilitates the work of the creative individual. And at other times, following the concepts of evolutionary theory, they affect, if not determine, those works which will be allowed to come to fruition and those which will survive.

Critical interpersonal communications are manifest during hypothesis formation and hypothesis testing, but at no time do they stand out in such bold relief as when the creative work is completed and presented to others for their acceptance and evaluation. This, then, is the starting point for this chapter—a completed creative work. This work, in terms of our framework, now exists in a social context and has then to be communicated or transmitted to others in the society. The final target of the communication is an audience or the public. Before the communication arrives at its final target it may have to go through many persons whom we call *intermediaries,* and it may be affected by a variety of social forces. To be sure, not all creative works are communicated to the public at large. The target audience for a communication varies as a function of field of work as well as the goal and intention of the creative individual. Nevertheless, there are instances where the public is the final target. Consequently, it is germane to discuss the factors that affect its receptivity to creative works and the processes through which the public goes in accepting novelty.

It is unfortunate that the communication stage of the creative process has not been studied thoroughly in all areas of creative endeavor. Consequently, we are confronted with a state of affairs in which we cannot provide the reader with sufficient valid generalizations from which he can make appropriate inferences in all fields. Some readers may therefore become frustrated. It is conceivable that a creative painter who might have wanted to know more about the characteristics of gallery owners and museum administrators and how to communicate with them will not only be frustrated at the lack of such information but he may become more frustrated when he finds a section on county extension agents. Such a fictitious reader's reactions are quite understandable and indeed we sympathize with them. To be sure, data on the county extension agent will be of interest to those concerned with communication in rural areas and these persons have a good deal to gain from knowledge in this field that has been so intensively worked on these many years by the rural sociologists. Hopefully, though, the fictitious painter and others who read the material on the county extension agent will be motivated to determine whether there are persons in functionally analogous positions in their own fields and then to observe whether the behavior of these persons can be better understood in terms of the knowledge gained from reading about county extension agents. Hopefully, as a result of this book more effort will be devoted to collecting information on the communication stage in different areas of creative endeavor.

At this juncture it should also be pointed out that this chapter differs from preceding ones in a rather important way. In preceding chapters specific individual techniques were presented to stimulate the creative process. In this chapter the goal of stimulating creativity is approached indirectly. Rather than focusing on techniques, the orientation in this chapter is that an individual's creative efforts will be facilitated and less energy will be unnecessarily expended as the creative individual becomes aware of the persons and social forces involved in the communication stage of the creative process. Hopefully, too, the creative individual and others involved in the creative process will gain some knowledge of how to select individuals who can carry out the requirements of the communication stage effectively. And then, it is to be hoped that those who are described in this chapter will become more aware of the critical significance of the roles *they* play in the creative process. Much time and effort could be saved and devoted to new creative pursuits if these persons made more manifest their criteria of evaluation, if they were more rewarding, and if they were more willing to take risks.

RESISTANCE TO DISCUSSING THE COMMUNICATION STAGE

Creative individuals do not attribute much significance to the communication stage of the creative process or they are reluctant to discuss it. There are several reasons for this. Communication requires more contact with people than do the other stages of the creative process. Although the creative individual is not necessarily a loner, neither is he generally very outgoing or gregarious. He may prefer a small number of social relationships that are not too demanding, so that he can devote much of his energy to his work. The communication stage, however, brings him face to face with what he usually prefers to avoid.

There are also creative persons who, while they may be very skillful in their own fields of endeavor, are just not very skillful in verbal communication. They can be severely handicapped in discussing their works with others or in gaining others' support at the various stages of the creative process. Indeed, for these individuals it is most appropriate to say that their work must speak for itself. Such creative persons, therefore, are also apt to play down the importance of the communication stage.

Because of the difficulties, time, and effort involved in adequately fulfilling the requirements of the communication stage, creative persons frequently have to call upon others, whom we call intermediaries and whom we shall discuss later, who are more expert and who are professionally trained in such matters. From the creative person's point of view these persons fulfill their roles best when they are unobtrusive—when they do not seek much publicity or credit for themselves. At times the relationship between the creative individual and the intermediary works out quite smoothly and harmoniously. The creative person appreciates the fact that he has a relationship with someone who takes care of presenting his works to the public and selling them so that he can have more time for new creative efforts. The intermediary for his part may be respectful of his client's skills and appreciative of the fact that he has creative works available for sale. In other cases, a previously harmonious situation may deteriorate and resentment and conflict dominate the scene. The creative individual may feel that the intermediary is not really deserving of his fee because "the work could have sold itself," etc. And the intermediary might feel that the creative works would never have seen the light of day without his efforts and contacts. Therefore a potentially important and mutually reinforcing relationship becomes an impossible one. In this kind of relationship the pressure on the creative individual to share some of the honors accorded his creativity may lead not only to an exaggerated emphasis on the early stages and the intrapersonal aspects of the creative process, but also to a demeaning of the communication stage, the persons involved and the significance of their contributions.

During the communication stage the actual or potential commercial value of the creative product becomes a very important matter of interest. Some creative persons willingly and openly acknowledge their concern with such matters. They are not reluctant to talk of their interest in money. For example, after a Carnegie Hall concert, Walter Damrosch asked Rachmaninoff what "sublime thoughts" had gone through the latter's head as he looked at the audience while a concert of his was being played. " 'I was counting the house,' said Rachmaninoff [Oglivy, 1963, p. 21]." Other creative individuals feel that money has a debasing effect. They see it as related to commercialism rather than creativity.

Creative persons may also feel negatively about the communication stage because in this part of the creative process power plays and manipulations are most obvious. These they regard as external to the creative process, overlooking the fact that in their own motivational system there is probably also a drive for power that keeps the creative process moving along.

One aspect of power in the communication stage that evokes resentment in creative individuals is that others and not they have the power to decide whether they are creative, whether their works will be regarded as creative, and indirectly whether they might gain immortality by having their work become part of society's cultural heritage. Others do in fact pass judgment on what is to be regarded as creative. Others do in fact differentiate between and separate the creative from the "not-so-creative" and the noncreative. Among them are individuals who have the power to decide the manner in which the society and culture will grow. Because of their position in the creative process or in the society, they play very crucial roles in determining which novel products will become part of the culture. Creative individuals may believe that such determinations have more to do with the popularity of a work rather than its creativity. They will argue that a work should be judged on its own merits and that whether or not it is creative centers on the characteristics of the work. But the fact of the matter is that if the work is not brought before others who will make judgments before they accept it, then there is no one to acknowledge and recognize the quality of the work.

The communication stage when carried out effectively fulfills critical psychological functions for creative individuals. What is most obvious is that, when a creative work is communicated to and accepted by others, the recognition and rewards received are quite gratifying to the creative person. But according to some psychoanalysts (e.g., Lee, 1947) the creative process is initiated by an underlying and nonobvious motivational force—the creative individual's motivation to make restitution for destructive impulses that have made him feel very guilty.

It is beyond our purpose to discuss this matter fully here; nevertheless, it should be pointed out that if this theoretical orientation is valid, one of the consequences of the communication stage is that acceptance by others, which is part of this stage, helps ameliorate the guilt that the individual may have had to tolerate during the course of his work and at its completion. When the creative work is completed and accepted by others, the creative individual is absolved of his guilt and feels worthy once more. The sharing of this experience also forms a bond between the creative individual and his audience (Sachs, 1951). Hence, it is conceivable, from a psychological point of view, that having to wait for another's evaluation and acceptance and the consequent "absolution" is, by its very character, tension producing, irritating, and frustrating. In the face of such psychodynamic involvements, it is understandable why creative persons should feel reluctant to pay much attention to the communication stage of the creative process.

These are some of the reasons why creative persons do not necessarily wish to regard the communication stage as part of the creative process. Others, like the intermediaries, whose reasons will be discussed later, are also frequently reluctant to discuss the communication stage. And finally, investigators in this field also omit the communication stage as one of their research considerations because they concentrate solely on what goes on in the intrapersonal life of the creative person. Our point of view, as we have said, is different. We regard the intrapersonal aspects of the creative process as important but we do not stop there. We also regard the interpersonal aspects as important. All manner of reluctance and negativism could obscure the actual and potential significance of the communication stage in the creative process. Hopefully, by having made explicit some of the problems involved in discussing the communication stage, we have helped overcome or diminish some of the resistance to what follows. Then, by 1aking explicit some of the problems and obstacles to effective communication, readers may find it easier to arrive at constructive solutions.

We begin with a consideration of the creative individual, his personality and diverse roles, to indicate how they may affect communication. This will then be followed with a presentation of various kinds of intermediaries and the significance of their roles in the creative process. And then we shall discuss the audience or public and consider briefly some of the socio-cultural factors that may affect their acceptance of creative works, the characteristics of some creative works that facilitate their acceptance, the process through which the public goes in accepting novel works, the subgroups within the public and their differential receptivity to creativity and, finally, a consideration of some studies on the overcoming of resistance to change.

We reiterate that research on the communication stage in different areas of creative endeavor has been quite scarce. Consequently, it is impossible to generalize across fields, and we are limited to a consideration of singular instances. Hopefully, readers will not find the immediate lack of relevance to their own field too disconcerting but will try to infer from examples in other fields to relevant instances in their own creative areas. If so trained and disposed, they might regard what is presented as an example of the kind of research that should be conducted in their own areas to provide further understanding of the creative process.

THE CREATIVE INDIVIDUAL

His Personality

Personality characteristics of creative individuals such as those summarized on pages 58-60 are based on studies in which creative persons were compared with less creative persons. The different stages of the creative process were not considered in these studies and relationships between psychological characteristics and effectiveness in each of these stages were not investigated. Hence we cannot say which of a creative individual's personality characteristics facilitate his efforts to cope with the communication stage of the creative process. We do know that many, if not all, of the characteristics listed on pages 58-60 are probably more likely to be an advantage during the hypothesis formation and hypothesis testing stages than during the communication stage. Such psychological characteristics as autonomy, independence, dominance, aggressiveness, etc., are more likely to be of positive value during the earlier stages than in the final stage of the creative process in which, if nothing else, the individual has to consider and take the point of view of the person with whom he is communicating. If not, then the creative individual runs the risk that he will not be understood or accepted. Moreover, he may also run the risk that he may not have further opportunity for creativity or be sorely limited in this regard.

All of this is of course speculation; pertinent data are lacking. Unless we focus our studies on the communication stage specifically, we are unlikely to learn the psychological characteristics that may facilitate an individual's efforts in this stage of the creative process. At this point, therefore, all we can do is to point out that when difficulties in communication do arise, we should not overlook the possibility that the creative individual himself may be responsible for some of the problems.

A notable example of deficiency in communication is Pasteur, of whom it has been said that "Even his most sympathetic biographers seem to be agreed that he struck the majority of his contemporaries as an insufferable egoist with not a little of the paranoiac about his behavior. He was dogmatic, cocksure, conceited, contentious, and extremely sensitive to criticism [Barnett, 1953, p. 316, following B. J. Stern, 1927]." He was elected to the Free Association of the Academy of Medicine by only one vote. Although first on the list of eligibles, he was so personally unpopular that he was almost not elected to the seat. His manner was offensive and people responded violently to him.

Semmelweis, originator of the theory that puerperal fever is a contagious disease, is another whose personality affected the reaction to his discovery. According to Barnett [1953, p. 316], Semmelweis had been described by one biographer as "irascible, impatient, and tactless." And Jenner ran into difficulties when he insisted on exclusive credit for vaccination. In industrial research organizations it is not unusual to come across the "prima donna" whose personality and behavior can be quite irritating to most of those around him.

Fortunately, the creative contributions of the persons just cited and others like them were not completely blocked by the personalities of their originators. Society still reaped the benefits of these creative developments. But, is it not conceivable that potential creative contributions were either temporarily or permanently delayed because the persons who originated them so antagonized or irritated others that they did not get opportunities to develop the works further or to get a hearing or a showing of the creative work?

By calling attention to those instances of "negative personality characteristics" our intention is not to suggest that submissiveness or self-denigration is the answer either. First, we do not feel that the creative person could behave in this manner. And second, it is quite apparent that such ways are also no guarantee of effectiveness in communication. All we can do is call attention to an area of behavior that may be overlooked as we try to solve problems that arise during the course of the creative process.

His Diverse Roles

Creative persons work in rather complex situations. This is not immediately apparent to an observer whose attention might be focused on the creative person's autonomy and the control he exercises over his working house and working environment. In such a focus, sight is lost of the fact that the creative person is also expected to fulfill financial obligations, those that are involved in the cost of his materials, etc., and those involved in supporting himself and his family if he has one. In addition, the creative person may fulfill a role in his professional contacts with colleagues or he might, to supplement his income, be involved in a teaching role.

The roles of the creative person can be quite diverse and more critically, they may even conflict with each other. Just how roles vary and how they interact with each other have not been studied in relation to different fields of creative endeavor. One area that has come under rather intensive investigation and which illustrates what we mean by role diversity and potential role conflict is that of the researcher in the industrial research and development (R & D) organization (Stein, 1962, 1963).

Based on his observations, Stein suggests that the industrial researcher has five roles to fulfill: the scientific role, the professional role, the employee role, the social role, and the administrative role. These roles, or the expectations that others have of the research man, are described more fully elsewhere (Stein, 1962, 1963); hence, we limit ourselves to brief descriptions here.

In the scientific role the individual researcher communicates with other scientists or engineers, individuals who, like him, have been trained scientifically and technically. The researcher shares information with them and gets feedback from them on this information. The second major role of the researcher is that of professional. In this role he relates to a client, whereas the scientific role did not involve a client. In communicating with his client, the researcher provides him with what Hughes (1952) has called "esoteric service."

With only two of the five roles defined, we perceive complications and potential problems. The industrial researcher in his scientific and professional roles has two distinct audiences. Each requires different kinds of communication and different emphases within these kinds of communication. In his scientific role the researcher's language is generally technical, and he and his audience are interested in precision, thoroughness, completeness, feasibility, etc. In his professional role, however, the researcher has to communicate with a member of the company's executive and decision-making staff who may or may not be technically trained and capable of understanding what the researcher has presented. The executive staff's interest is not limited to such matters as feasibility; it includes (or centers on) whether what is being worked on will make money for the company. Furthermore, due to limitations and demands on the executive's time, the researcher's project has to be presented, explained, and even defended with the utmost conciseness.

To fulfill the professional role properly, a researcher has to be quite proficient in at least two areas. First, he must be able to communicate well in layman's terms. This is a skill that researchers are not taught in college, nor does the organization necessarily train researchers in this skill, although it demands it of them. Usually, the researcher tries to learn such skills as best he can on his own. In other situations, the organization might send a researcher to a seminar where he will learn how to write reports, or the company will employ a technical writer or rewrite man, whose job is to "translate" technical reports so that they can be easily understood by management and possibly the stockholders and the public.

The researcher must also be able to evaluate the financial worth of his work. In most industrial situations such assessment is left up to the new products committee, with the creative person whose work is being considered participating little, if at all, in their deliberations. Among inventors, a group that is probably not too different in many respects from industrial researchers, it was found that their lawyers regard them as "poor" in business sense— implying that they could be taken advantage of. Although it is unlikely that industrial researchers would be taken advantage of within their organizations, their lack of business sense and knowledge of and ability to analyze the potential market for their products is a shortcoming when it comes to communicating persuasively and effectively with those empowered to authorize production of the products, devices, or appliances they develop in their research.

In addition to scientific and professional roles, the researcher in industry has to fulfill an administrative role, which involves supervision of and taking responsibility for others. On the one hand, it includes activities that may be described as the administration *of* research—conducting work on, and supervising the work of other scientific, engineering, or technical personnel on technical problems or projects. On the other hand, it requires involvement in various administrative matters—budgetary, space, personnel, etc.—that help keep the conduct of research activities moving smoothly. As with his other roles, the industrial researcher usually lacks appropriate training for this administrative role. Nevertheless, it is quite important that he fulfill it, for the rewards in industrial research organizations are usually given for administrative ability. A person can go far if he has both administrative and creative talent, but will not do as well if he has only creativity. To compensate for this, some organizations have what they call two ladders on which men can rise in the organization—an administrative ladder and a creative or scientific one. A researcher who has difficulty administering or communicating with others can presumably still rise in such organizations, but the top of the creative ladder is not so high as the administrative ladder.

The remaining two roles of the industrial researcher are the employee role and the social role. If either role is not fulfilled, the results can be serious. In the employee role the researcher is expected to obey many of the rules and regulations governing other employees, though he frequently experiences conflict and frustration in doing so. For example, in organizations where clerical and secretarial employees are required to punch a time clock, researchers may also be asked to do so, or at least to account for and record their time in some way. Even if he objects to this requirement, the researcher has to conform or else encounter administrative reprimands that could affect raises, promotions, etc.

Similarly, in terms of the social role, some organizations expect their researchers to comport themselves in a manner that reflects the organization image. Both the employee and the social roles press the researcher into conforming behavior—behavior that is antithetical to his creative behavior.

The roles just discussed were used by Stein (1959d) in constructing a series of questionnaire items that were submitted to researchers as well as laboratory executives. The researchers were divided into two groups—one judged "more creative" and the other "less creative." Both groups of researchers and the executives were asked to use these items to tell what made for success and what made for creativity in their organizations. The data from the two groups of researchers were correlated with those obtained from the executives. Greater agreement was found between the data obtained from the more creative men and the executives on what made for creativity and success than was found between the data of the less creative men and the executives. These correlations were obtained at all administrative levels in the organization. Therefore it was argued that the correlations in all likelihood were not due to the more creative men currying favor with their superiors, but rather that they indicated that the more creative men really perceived the research organization very much as their superiors did. Consequently, the creative group no doubt communicated better with their superiors. These data were supported by interview data in which it was learned that the researchers, regardless of their creativity status, believed that in addition to the four years it may take for a man to get his PhD, "another four," during which he learns how to communicate and get along with others, are usually needed to earn the "industrial PhD."

To highlight the kinds of problems and role conflicts confronting the researcher in industry, Stein (1963) prepared a list of "commandments" that reflect the kinds of behavior the industrial researcher may have to engage in to fulfill his roles adequately and to obtain the opportunity to pursue his creative interests. (These precepts should not be taken too literally: poetic license was taken with the data for emphasis or to make a point.) Stein says

1. The industrial researcher is to be assertive without being hostile or aggressive.

2. He is to be aware of his superiors, colleagues, and subordinates as persons but is nevertheless not to become too personally involved with them.

3. He may be a lone wolf on the job, but he is not to be isolated, withdrawn, or uncommunicative. If he is any of these he had best be particularly creative so that his work speaks for itself.

4. On the job he is expected to be congenial but not sociable.

5. Off the job he is expected to be sociable but not intimate.

6. With superiors he is expected to "know his place" without being timid, obsequious, submissive, or acquiescent.

7. But he is also expected to "speak his mind" without being domineering.

8. As he tries to gain a point, more funds, or more personnel, he can be subtle but not cunning.

9. In all relationships he is expected to be sincere, honest, purposeful, and diplomatic, but never unwilling to accept "shortcuts," be flexible, or Machiavellian.

10. Finally, in the intellectual area he is expected to be broad without spreading himself thin, deep without becoming pedantic, and "sharp" without being overcritical [p. 124].

Role analyses like the one just presented are not yet available for creative persons working in a variety of fields. If they were, we could possibly understand better the role conflicts that all creative persons endure and possibly develop ways of coping with them. In this manner not only would creative persons have more time and energy available for creativity but there would also be less confusion in the communication between creative persons and others.

INTERMEDIARIES

Between the creative individual and the audience or public there are various intermediaries. They play important roles at all stages of the creative process and especially at its end. They serve both the creative individual and the public. For the creative individual they may be sources of emotional and financial support as well as sources of technical information and evaluation. They legitimatize certain works as creative and deny this status to others. As a result, they serve as selective filters for the society, as "gatekeepers" (Lewin, 1958) or as the governors, the controlling elements in the evolutionary development of the culture. What they regard as creative is presented as such to the public. On the other hand, negative evaluations by intermediaries may be a work's death knell unless rescued by an audience.

Some intermediaries like talking about their roles in the creative process, especially how they might be responsible for discovering an unknown artist or how they helped an already established creative person with his work. Others assume less obvious roles, working behind the scenes as they continue to help creative persons and make evaluative decisions about creative works.

There is a good deal of overlap in the functions intermediaries perform. Consequently, any classification, including the one to be used, is arbitrary. At best it selects some characteristic of a group of intermediaries and makes it more salient without denying that other categories could serve the same purpose.

We shall start with that group of intermediaries who provides the creative individual with emotional or financial support as well as with acceptance and recognition. This group we call *supporters* or *patrons*. The kinds of intermediaries we include in this group are: the "psyche" group, the entrepreneur, the executive, and the staffs of foundations.

The second group of intermediaries we call the *experts* and shall illustrate their importance by discussing two subgroups: "the authorities" and the critics. These intermediaries have achieved status as evaluators or judges of creative works. The authorities have status in the creative individual's own field because of their own creative contributions in the same area. On the other hand, critics need not necessarily have demonstrated expertise or creativity in the same field they evaluate but are accorded their status because they have demonstrated their capacity for understanding and appreciating a creative work and for clearly communicating their insights to the public.

The third group of intermediaries we call *transmission agents*. These persons have most direct contact with the public. Their job is to get the public to become aware of the creative work, to make it easily accessible to the public, and to have it accepted and used by the public. One subgroup of transmission agents are county extension agents. This subgroup has been studied quite intensively by rural sociologists. It is presented not only because as a group it facilitates the communication of creative works and products but also because the range of studies carried out on this group illustrates the kinds of variables that should be included in studies of other intermediaries as well.

A second subgroup among transmission agents are the Peace Corps volunteers. Attention is focused on this subgroup not because it is involved in the transmission of creative works, but because of the relevance of the fact that in one study of a group of Peace Corps volunteers a psychological technique was used that could be of value in the selection of future transmission agents.

After county extension agents and Peace Corps volunteers are discussed, we shall turn to a consideration of three additional subgroups of transmission agents: gallery owners, salesmen, and advertising agencies. All three groups are or can be involved in selling creative works. Not only are they involved in making creative works available but they are also involved in persuading the public to buy them and, most obviously, they are involved in making a profit from selling creative works. These groups carry out functions for the creative individual during the communication stage of the creative process that would not only take much of his time and effort but also a good deal of money which he probably would not have. These groups possess a kind of expertise that is completely separate from that which the creative individual has but which affects the communication of his work. To illustrate some of the factors involved in such expertise, attention is called specifically to the advertising agency. And finally, we shall discuss a group of persons, the opinion leaders, who also play critical roles in spreading the word about new ideas and creative works.

Supporters and Patrons

The first major category of intermediaries we shall consider includes those who give the creative individual emotional support throughout the creative process. When he encounters stress, when he wants relief from the doubt and concern about his work, when he wants someone with whom to share the excitement of a completed creative work or the happiness of receiving recognition for a completed work, then the creative individual can call upon persons in this group of intermediaries.

Throughout the creative process, intermediaries in this group are also among those usually called upon for financial aid and support. With the possible exception of one subgroup to be considered—the psyche group—intermediaries in this group expect something in return for their efforts. Financial support may be given in the form of a loan to be repaid, an honorarium or gift for a completed work, an option to buy the completed work, or a credit line indicating source of sponsorship for the work.

Even if the relationship is marked only by emotional and social support, there still may be various expectations. The creative individual may be expected to fulfill his patron's needs—to socialize with him when the patron wants his company and, should the creative individual become famous, popular, and sought after, to be at the patron's disposal and to introduce the patron to his new found contacts and relationships.

Creative persons need to maintain and sustain their financial and emotional contacts or else these valuable sources will not be available when they are needed most. It takes time and energy to do this. Although others may envy the creative individual who has a patron, this relationship is not always a happy one as witnessed in the relationship between Pope Julius and Michelangelo.

The Pope had commissioned Michelangelo to paint the Sistine Chapel. The artist was aging fast, the chapel was not yet completed, and the Pope became impatient. Papini (1952) quotes Ascanio Condivi, who describes the situation as follows.

"... The Pope gave the painter no peace so anxious was he to arrive at the hour of the uncovering of the ceiling. He reproved the artist during every visit, every word was a goad. Finally one day the explosion occurred.

"Michelangelo desiring to go to Florence for St. John's day asked the Pope for money; and the Pope demanded when the Chapel would be finished. Michelangelo, as was his custom, answered: 'When I am able!' The Pope, who had a short temper seized the stick which he had in his hand and struck Michelangelo with it, shouting: 'When I am able! When I am able!'

"Michelangelo infuriated by this new insult instantly went home and prepared to leave for Florence, perhaps with the intention of his earlier flight, never to return to Rome. But the Pope, who remembered the earlier flight also, and perhaps repenting of his hasty blow as though he were beating a groom, sent for his favorite, Accursio, and gave him five hundred ducats to take to Michelangelo and also his excuses for that unpontifical and un-Christian beating. Michelangelo accepted the money and the excuses, nevertheless he departed the same day for Florence [pp. 166-167].

Some creative persons on the contemporary scene, most usually in the arts and humanities, find themselves in positions analogous to that of Michelangelo. And among them are creative persons who are quite content with the relationship. On the other hand, there are those who feel that they must avoid relationships with supporters and patrons because patrons are not likely to be satisfied unless the individual sells his soul to them and then they might interfere with the work. Rather than spending their time communicating with such supporters and patrons, some creative persons circumvent the need for a patron by alternating between the pure and applied aspects of their work. The painter may turn commerical artist to earn money in order to be free of financial arrangements while he carries out his "pure" work. The writer may spend his days writing copy for an advertising agency but his free time on his novel.

The "Psyche" Group

The psyche group is a reference group for the creative individual. It is generally an informal group of supporters that gathers around or is sought out by the creative individual. They and the creative person are bound together by professional ties or long-term friendships. The creative person can go to the psyche group throughout the various stages of the creative process for emotional support, advice, criticism, clarification, or even to discuss the testing of some of his ideas. Discussions within this group may be one of the early manifestations that new ideas are developing or that still newer and different ones are yet to come. The size of the group may vary from one to several persons. A particularly good example of a psyche group is the group of artists who gathered around Diaghilev in the early nineteenth century. Dancers, painters, musicians, and writers, many of whom later became foremost in their fields, helped and stimulated each other in the face of a skeptical public.

Freud's relationship with Fliess, when it was still a positive one, is an example of a psyche dyad. One of the values of this relationship for Freud is reflected in the following excerpt from one of his letters to Fliess. The letter was written to tell Fliess that he (Freud) was unable to keep a meeting in Berlin (Freud, 1954).

I do so most unwillingly, because I expected a great deal from meeting you. Though otherwise quite satisfied, happy if you like, I feel very isolated, scientifically blunted, stagnant, and resigned. When I talked to you, and saw that you thought something of me, I actually started thinking something of myself, and the picture of confident energy which you offered was not without its effect. I should also have profited professionally from meeting you, and perhaps I should also have benefited from the Berlin atmosphere, because for years now I have been without anyone who could teach me anything and have settled down more or less exclusively to the treatment of neuroses [p. 60].

Relationships with older individuals, masters of the field in which an individual works, although qualitatively different from those established with his peers, may also constitute psyche groups. Such relationships may be on the decline on the contemporary scene.

Dahlberg (1971), speaking as a writer, says, "The most prodigious mishap of the young American writer is that he has no Master, or an elder of letters to guide him; and so he relies wholly upon himself, a very unreliable teacher. I was lucky; I knew Theodore Dreiser and Sherwood Anderson [p. 2]."

To have a psyche group with which to communicate openly and frankly can be extremely valuable to the creative person. He does not feel evaluated by this group and hence can freely alter ideas already expressed or receive encouragement to go off to new uncharted areas of creative endeavor.

The Entrepreneur

The financial characteristics of the patron's role become most salient when we study the entrepreneur who provides the risk capital necessary to invest in the origination, development, and marketing of the creative product. Entrepreneurs are most likely to have contacts and relationships with scientists and inventors rather than with creative persons in the humanities and the arts.

Entrepreneurs, because of the financial risks they might take, are among the most hard-headed of the intermediaries and they share with other intermediaries the job of critically evaluating creative works. Consequently, entrepreneurs are responsible for many creative technological developments. They have turned down many "crackpot" ideas and so have saved the public much time and money. But some of their decisions have either delayed or obstructed for significant periods of time, if not forever, a number of creative developments.

Hooke, for example, invented the spring balance that was the basis for a marine timekeeper. But he lost interest in it and did not himself employ the balance in a timepiece because he could not form a syndicate that would provide support to exploit the invention (Usher, 1954). Selden similarly encountered difficulty in obtaining support for the automobile engine he invented and built. He went from door to door presenting his drawings and patent application in an effort to raise funds. "He is a lawyer. He understands patents. But he is so far ahead of his time that they will not believe him. They even take their legal business out of his hands because 'Well,George is . . . you know . . . he's off on *that* thing again!' [Ellis, 1954, p. 112]." Another instance was that of Dr. Fritz Zernike, who did not get support for his phase-contrast microscope because some said it could not be done. Later, however, it won the Nobel prize for him (*Time*, 1953).

We should not be too quick to blame entrepreneurs for all such difficulties. Creative persons themselves share this responsibility too because they do not make the necessary effort to comprehend the entrepreneur's frame of reference, value system, and the mode of communication he understands best. Inventors, who are most common among those who require frequent financial aid and who should therefore know better, have been found to be lacking in business sense (Rossman, 1931) and without this we can well imagine the kinds of problems that could ensue.

The Executive

The organization of research activities in institutes, academies, Research and Development departments, etc., has placed executives who administer these various organizations in important roles as intermediaries. These executives may themselves have been creative persons but this need not necessarily be the case. The top level administrator may have risen to his post as a result of other business experience, for example, sales. Presumably, if the executive was a researcher he might be able to communicate more effectively with his subordinates but this too is not necessarily so for when the executive is an ex-researcher he may try to pit his own expertise against that of his subordinates and in that instance will serve very much like the subgroup of experts to be considered later.

Whatever the case, the executive as intermediary either by himself or in concert with his assistants and advisors passes on the plans, proposals, and projects that other potentially or manifestly creative persons will undertake. The executive decides how space will be used, how assisting technical personnel will be allocated, and most certainly how funds will be used and for how long financial support for a particular endeavor will be available.

One of the communication problems that frequently arises between the executives and those they supervise revolves about the fact that executives are not always clear as to what they really are interested in supporting and eventually even marketing. This lack of clarity sometimes stems from the difficulties of long-range planning. On other occasions, it stems from the fact that executives are quite content to let their subordinates proceed as they wish. When the subordinates' work is completed, then the executives can select what they want from the array of creative results that become available. Planning meetings in which personnel at all levels as well as executives participate would go far in overcoming some of the difficulties in this area. New product committees composed of both personnel and administrators would also be helpful in this regard.

More communicating and joint planning between executives and subordinates before work gets underway and while it is in process would also help foster the development of creative efforts.

Just as executives can help facilitate the communication process by the various means just indicated, so subordinates can also initiate steps to improve communication. Their academic training usually provides them with experience in writing research reports. But then, their audience is usually other researchers. When they become professionaly employed they need to learn to write reports that their superiors, especially those who are not technically or scientifically trained, will read and understand. They need to learn how to get all the necessary information about their creative work plus the money it will make and related financial matters onto "one page or less." The researcher who does not already know how to do this can learn by obtaining necessary training within his organization, management training programs, correspondence courses and college programs that do not conflict with his working hours.

On pages 258-260 we presented our conceptualization of the researcher's roles. It is interesting to compare that list with a list of executive characteristics compiled by Prince. Prince (1970), on the basis of his experiences with executives, has compiled a list of executives' characteristics, which he believes will facilitate subordinates' creative work. Such an executive is

> A risk taker who absorbs the risks taken by those who work for him— a man or woman who relieves his subordinates of the burden of failure for ideas that don't work.
>
> A man who can live with half-conceived, half-developed ideas and not insist on considering only finished products.
>
> A man who is willing to find ways to get around company procedures that impede achievement.
>
> A man who has a fast take-off time, who is willing to take action with an idea that looks good even when complete data are not available.
>
> A man who is a skillful and constructive listener.
>
> A man who doesn't dwell on mistakes—either his own or others'.
>
> A man who relishes what he is up to [p. 176].

Such an executive is an ideal partner for the creative individual throughout the course of the creative process.

Foundation and Government Staffs*

The business executive described above has his counterpart in the nonprofit foundation or the government money granting agency. The difference is that

---

*Since this was written, a book has been published by Nielsen (1972) that will provide the reader interested in foundations with much more information.

those in foundations and government probably do not oversee a person's work as frequently on a direct or indirect basis as do those in industrial organizations. Presumably because they are not as interested as business executives in making profits they should be interested in supporting long-term efforts needed to produce creative works. This is frequently the case. But sometimes the pressures on them from their trustees are such that they too concentrate on picking "winners." Then one cannot tell the difference between their behavior insofar as creativity is concerned and that of those desiring to make a profit.

Foundations, like business organizations, have delimited areas or activities they will support. The range for governmental agencies is obviously much broader, but their concerns also are focused. Artists and scientists are not always cognizant of these different interest areas. When such information is not available, much time and effort may be lost in writing applications and in being turned down because the application may not be appropriate to the funding agency. To cut down on some of the time and effort that might be lost, it would be of value to consult such directories as: *United States National Institutes of Health, Division of Research Grants, Research Grants Index; United States National Science Foundation, Grants and Awards; Annual Register of Grants and Support.* If these directories do not have the necessary information then librarians might be able to supply the proper source. Writing, calling, and even visiting (despite the extra time and money involved) a foundation or government agency might supply the applicant with the information he needs.

To obtain support from foundations or government sources usually requires written application in which the project is described and a budget supplied. It is critical that the work be described completely and clearly for it is very unlikely that the applicant will have an opportunity to present any kind of verbal defense. Obviously persons who are not accustomed to writing applications may lose out. There is a skill to writing them and persons who do so with some frequency are aware of a quality called "grantsmanship"—defined as demonstrated proficiency in obtaining grants. The term is not unqualifiedly positive for it may be used with the implication that the application's content is not as good as its persuasive power to obtain the funds.

In addition to the description of the project, the preparation of the budget also requires knowledge, time, and experience. The applicant needs to know figures on salary levels, fringe benefits, overhead charges, equipment costs, etc. Indeed supporting agencies, if they approve the content of a grant, are sometimes willing to hold off its approval until necessary changes are made in the budget. On other occasions, applications for supplemental funds are possible. If the applicant is part of an organization like a university, there is usually someone in his own department who can provide the necessary information or there is an administrative staff member who has this information.

Applying for a grant is not the only occasion on which demands are made on the individual's writing skills. There are usually requirements involving progress or follow-up reports and a final report. All of these may not only be requirements when the funds are accepted but eventually also serve as bases for future grants.

Foundations and government agencies could help stimulate creativity, if only indirectly, if they were more clear as to their interest areas, provided help in writing applications and preparing budgets, had reasonable demands for reports, and, if the application is turned down, provided the applicant with some information as to why. This is usually not done because foundations and governmental agencies fear they would constantly be harassed by questions from rejected applicants.

Finally, it is important that funding be granted for a period of time necessary to bring the work to fruition. No doubt in many instances this is the case, but on some occasions or in some areas, problems may arise. One area where hardship may occur is playwriting. Walter Kerr (1972), drama critic of the *New York Times,* discussed the difficulty of the playwright who obtains a grant sufficient to see a first production of his work. In the framework of the creative process discussed here, this production would constitute hypothesis testing. After its first presentation, the playwright is in a position to revise his play, taking the audience's and critics' responses into account in his revisions. Even after he has done so, the play may still not be quite ready for the commercial theater. At this point, foundations, according to Kerr, are unlikely to provide support, presumably because they are afraid of getting too close to having a commercial success. It is conceivable that some of their fear may be related to a concern about their nonprofit status. But whatever the reason, the playwright is deprived of "the years in which, after having got rid of his baby fat, he is slowly and painfully putting insight and technical expertise together, training his hand to truly convey his thought [Kerr, 1972, p. 9]." The young playwright may get help to get started on a production of his work, but may not get support sufficient to see the work through its variations and changes before the final product can be produced.

Although there are communication problems with foundation and governmental agency staffs, it is well worth the effort to surmount these, for, as in the problems of the playwright just cited, once the hurdle is overcome, contact established, and the first grant obtained, it is likely that if the individual continues to perform creatively that he will have a constant source of support.

There is no satisfying everybody, for if foundations and governmental agencies continue support of manifestly creative persons, then there may be less left for new applicants. Whether or not there is an expanding money supply, any irritation that could arise from this kind of situation could be diminished or eliminated if these agencies would make their criteria public.

We mentioned previously that relatively little systematic research information is available concerning the communication stage of the creative process. Studies of the deliberations of foundation and governmental staffs would go far in providing desired data. Provision could be made that no confidential material would be revealed and no one's privacy invaded in order to overcome the usual objections to such studies. Such studies would contribute not only to our understanding of the communication stage but also to the development of techniques that would help in overcoming problems at this stage. Data from these studies could be used to develop ways of making the deliberations of these groups more effective and for the development of criteria and procedures for the future selection of persons who would have the greatest probability of being creative.

Experts

A second category of intermediaries consists of a group we call experts. We have chosen this title for this group, although it is apparent that other groups of intermediaries are also experts. The distinguishing characteristic of this group is that it has recognized expertise and authority in a specific field or discipline. Its positive judgment about a work marks it as a significant contribution to a specific area of work. Deliberations and evaluations of other intermediaries may affect a work's support and whether or how it will be transmitted to others. The experts in the category considered here not only affect these same factors but their evaluation practically determines the status that a work will have among other creative works in the same area.

As examples of experts we consider two subgroups, the authorities and the critics and reviewers. No doubt there are others who also belong to this category, but the two we consider should suffice for our purposes.

Authorities

Every field of creative endeavor has its own group of authorities who have achieved their status by virtue of the fact that they made creative contributions to their fields or they made contributions which were otherwise significant. Whatever the case, the assumption is, although untested, that the individual who has been creative himself is equally capable of recognizing another's creativity or the creative value of his work. One might argue that this procedure has worked since there is a constant supply of creative works. But this argument is open to question and should be tested for it is equally conceivable that the supply exists in spite of the experts or because their decisions can be circumvented. Authorities may be able to recognize a creative work but there is also the possibility that they can frustrate it or put obstacles in its way.

There is the story of a now very creative and prominent physiologist who, when he was a young professor, found that before his department would allow him to send off a research proposal requesting funds for his work, its faculty had to approve it. He followed the prescribed procedure, presented his proposal and was turned down by his faculty, being told that the work he projected in his proposal just could not be done.

The young professor, so the story goes, left dejected and in about a year's time returned to the same group with another proposal. Again, he was told that his projected work could not be done. This time the young professor turned to the professors who were his seniors and said, essentially, "Gentlemen, I am not asking whether my projected plans can be carried out. I am only asking you to approve my proposal so I can get research funds. As a matter of fact, I have done the work. I learned from my previous experience with this group that I was completely dependent on your approval to obtain funds for my research. I then decided to do my research project, prepare a proposal for it and then use those funds for another idea or work that someone would feel could not be done."

Authorities may not approve potentially creative works because they simply do not evaluate correctly and also because they may be envious of and competitive with the people they judge. Whatever the case, the fact remains that, although authorities are frequently regarded as being very objective in their decisions and crucial keepers of the discipline's or culture's heritage, they can become bottlenecks in the communication stage of the creative process— witness the experiences of several notable researchers in medicine whose work was evaluated by the medical fraternity (Barnett, 1953, following B. J. Stern, 1927).

Vesalius was attacked by his contemporaries because he challenged the authority of Galen on human anatomy. He was called a madman, and his resort to dissection to acquire knowledge was labeled impious. Harvey met with opposition of the same sort, and on the same grounds, with the publication of his researches upon the circulation of the blood. At least twenty authorities upon anatomy challenged his views in print, and many others ignored his discoveries or abused him personally. Lister's insistence that antisepsis would prevent the suppuration of wounds provoked attacks from many quarters, and for several reasons; but the really damaging contentions were those of medical authorities, such as James Simpson and James Morton, who either denied his method any originality, belittled its effects, or advocated some other causes for the good results that he was able to demonstrate. When Semmelweis announced his theory that puerperal fever was a contagious disease and was not due to any supernatural influences, he was violently assailed by members of the medical profession and experts in related fields. Virchow ignored him with pontifical disdain. Others fell upon him with ridicule, misrepresentation, and personal vilification [p. 316].*

---

*While the negative responses of the experts in these instances may have had rational bases, it is equally possible that they may have been provoked by the researchers' personalities. We previously noted that Pasteur was regarded as an "insufferable egoist" and somewhat paranoid, and that his behavior almost cost him his seat in the Free Association of the Academy of Medicine. Similar negative personality characteristics were evidenced in the cases of Semmelweis and Jenner (cf. page 257).

Newton also had his problems with authorities. Although the Royal Society accepted his telescope, it was not as receptive to the paper spelling out the work on which its discovery was based. "The paper [on optics] touched off a storm—not because the experiments were not accurate and the conclusions drawn from them indisputable, but because his findings did not square with certain theories then held. So many voices were raised in complaint that Newton finally exclaimed in disgust, 'I see a man must either resolve to put out nothing new, or become a slave to defend it.' From that time forward he was more reluctant than ever to make his discoveries known [Strother, 1955, p. 25]." And for those who did want to know more about his discoveries he hardly made it easy for them. Strother reports that "Even mathematicians found the book [Newton's *Principia*] difficult to read, not only because the problems dealt with are difficult, but because Newton purposely made it tough so that he wouldn't be bothered by 'little smatterers in mathematics' [Strother, 1955, p. 26]."

Creative persons and experts can play all manner of such "games" but would not the creative person have more time and energy for creative pursuits if this part of the creative process—the communication stage—were fraught with fewer interpersonal conflicts and problems?

Critics and Reviewers

The second subgroup in this category whose primary role is that of evaluation are reviewers or critics who write opinions and evaluations of art shows, plays, books, journal articles, etc. These persons need not and usually do not demonstrate the ability to do what they are evaluating. They need not be novelists, dancers, painters, or whatever. But they are regarded as capable of passing on developments in these areas and of telling others what their evaluations are.

Reviewers' or critics' views and opinions, regardless of whether their criteria are explicit or implicit, frequently become the standards for others. And, when they have access to the public through important newspapers or other media, they frequently function as tastemakers. Because some of them practically monopolize channels of communication to the public (newspapers, for example, generally cannot afford to have more than one reviewer write a review of the same performance) they become rather powerful in their roles. They can "make or break" a play, an author, etc. Word of the likes or dislikes of these powerful critics spreads, with the result that performances may be tailored in accord with their preferences. For example, in New York young pianists had been told not to play Chopin on their program because some music critics in New York had the preconceived idea that only an older person has the sensitivity to do so.

Reviewers play critical roles in the evaluation of works and because critics and their points of view vary over time, the works that are regarded as creative also vary. In discussing this matter Jacques Barzun (1955) points out that we could be led to

. . . the strange conclusion that great creations are made such after the fact, by a retroactive decree of the human spirit. As the Lord looked back upon His creation and saw that it was good, so among mortals a providential critic, coming after a longer or shorter time, falls in love with a certain work and persuades the heedless throng to look back and stare. Until then the creation lacks the very qualities that later make it unique and wonderful. A hundred years ago, all the merits of "Moby Dick" were defects, and Melville was a bungler. And in this centennial year of homage to Whitman, we find it hard to acknowledge that "Leaves of Grass" was then an obscure and obscene oddity [p. 1].

Needless to say reviewers and critics defend their roles while those whom they criticize believe that they function on rather irrational bases.

Wilfred Sheed, both writer and critic, talking rather cynically about some of the satisfactions of reviewing books in an essay for the *New York Times Book Review* (February 7, 1971) tells us that he once wrote what he regarded as a dishonest review which nevertheless elicited a postcard from the writer whose work he had reviewed telling him that he was the only one who understood his work.

Authors, Sheed says, can hate a great deal, and for them to receive "a bad review is like being spat on by a complete stranger in Times Square . . .". While an author may forgive a reviewer, his wife will not. She will accuse the reviewer of asking for the book just to give it a bad review and "destroy the author's earning capacity . . . you can't get published yourself; you are a racist, a sexist, and either a fag or a fag-baiter . . . [p. 2] ."

John Simon, theater critic for the magazine *New York,* believes that critics whatever their orientation, earnestly try to differentiate between good work and bad work. Although it may appear at times that their criticism may destroy the very field they are reviewing, Simon reassuringly tells us about his own field, theater reviewing, where theater reviewers share "an earnest desire to keep show-biz alive . . . lest they lose their livelihoods. Before long, therefore, they'll discover a few unquestionable gems that will put the theater on its feet, their quotes on display, and your teeth on edge [Simon, 1971, p. 54] ."

But then of course there are those who have been reviewed who disagree and believe that reviewers' opinions do not always have rational bases. Thus, John Steinbeck (1955) said:

We are likely also to forget that critics are people with all the frailties and attitudes of people. One critic explained to me after the fact that he had given me a ferocious beating because he had a hangover. Another, with a reputation for blistering anything he touched, suddenly went enthusiastically appreciative of almost everything. The explanation was not hard to find. He had published three novels which failed and his fourth was well received and his whole approach changed. Another reviewer uses a neurosis stemming from his birth under unusual circumstances and from unusual parents as the gall in which he dips his pen. Still another critic of personal indecision, reviewing a novel with a homosexual theme, attacked it hysterically on points of grammar [p. 20].

It would be most enlightening to have systematic data available on reviewers' personalities, motivations, and interactions with the persons they review. Some psychoanalysts have written papers in this area from which potentially fruitful hypotheses can be gleaned. For example, Kris (1952) suggests that the critic's attitude, positive or negative, may result from the fact that the critic recreates the artist's experience. He may identify positively with the experience and the artist or he may become rivalrous with the artist. The critic's reactions therefore may be a function of unconscious factors in his own personality.

Weissman (1965), also a psychoanalyst, in discussing the critic in the arts and specifically the theater, says that since the critic does not have the urge to be creative in the area in which he is working, he is in a better position to receive the creative person's communication and pass judgment on it. Weissman believes that there is some relationship between critics' noncreativity and the fact that they are often childless, citing twelve of fourteen critics who were childless: Samuel Johnson, Pope, Saint-Beuve, Macaulay, Pater, Ruskin, Lamb, Berenson, Beerbohm, Shaw, Mencken, and George Jean Nathan. The remaining two of the fourteen were Emerson, who had two wives and four children, and Addison, who had one child who was apparently mentally defective (Weissman, 1965). Childless critics in this view give up their procreative wishes so that they can then allow themselves to be curious "and aggressively critical of their creative parents [p. 57]." These hypotheses obviously require much systematic research to confirm them.

According to Weissman (1965), from a psychoanalytic point of view, the critic identifies with both the artist and audience. On both preconscious and unconscious levels he identifies with and responds to the artist's work and considers it in terms of aesthetic factors. While the artist regresses to his unconscious and utilizes its products for his creativity, the critic and the audience proceed otherwise. They proceed, according to Weissman, from conscious perception to preconscious elaboration which reverberates with the unconscious. The critic moves from "a conscious perception to a preconscious infiltration and unconscious responses [p. 59]." The critic moves beyond what the audience is able to do. He takes the material from all levels of consciousness and considers it in terms of an aesthetic experience. "A critic approximates the state of optimal functioning when his aesthetic evaluation encompasses and communicates an integrated account of both the artist's and audience's conscious, preconscious, and unconscious participation in a creative experience [Weissman, 1965, p. 59]."

Possibly with the accumulation of data based on some of the speculations and hypotheses just presented, we would have greater understanding of the interaction between reviewers and those whom they review and be in a better position to present and understand the different factors involved in the communication stage of the creative process.

Transmission Agents

The third group of intermediaries we call transmission agents because their role is primarily to make accessible or to sell creative works to the public. These people have also been called *change agents* but we feel that all groups of intermediaries are involved in change and consequently a more neutral phrase like *transmission agents* would be more appropriate.

The transmission agents may be expert in the field in which the creative work was developed. But whether or not they have much of such expertise they at least have a good deal of knowledge about the creative work. What characterizes them best is expertise and effectiveness in making others aware of the creative work, in persuading them to buy and use it. These transmission agents may look for specialized subgroups within the public or the total public as its target, or they may focus some or all of their attention on persons who are opinion leaders or tastemakers in the community whose endorsements frequently convince others to follow their leads.

Four subgroups of transmission agents will be discussed and each for a different reason. The first subgroup will be that of county extension agents presented because it is probably the most thoroughly studied subgroup. From the studies done, we may get ideas of the kinds of questions to be asked and data to be obtained from future studies of other intermediaries. The second subgroup is Peace Corps volunteers. A study we did of one such group (Stein, 1966) will be presented to illustrate how the effectiveness of techniques for selecting intermediaries might be improved. Since transmission agents do play such critical roles in the creative process, the whole course of the process could be improved if we were able to select them with increased effectiveness.

The third subgroup is salespeople, including all kinds of salespeople as well as individual entrepreneurs such as gallery owners. The last subgroup is the advertising agency because it plays such a critical role on the contemporary social scene and because advertisers, being much more self-conscious and aware of the effectiveness of their techniques, have provided data on their methods' that give us more understanding of the complexity of the communication stage. Procedures used by other intermediaries are not so explicit. And finally, we shall consider opinion leaders. They are persons who, because of their status in the society, are regarded as also having the ability to evaluate the creativity of a work. The areas in which opinion leaders have status and the area of the work need not be the same. Nevertheless, because of the opinion leaders' status,

whatever the field or whatever the reason, their endorsements frequently facilitate the adoption and communication of a work.

County Extension Agents

Probably no other subgroup of intermediaries has been subjected to such
intensive study for as long a period of time as the county extension agent. This
stems from the interest of the United States Government, the Department of
Agriculture, the land grant colleges, the rural sociologists, etc., because of the
critical role the county extension agents play in transmitting information about
new agricultural procedures, materials, or products to farmers and in getting
farmers to use them. The following is a sample of the findings we culled from
Roger's (1962) work in which he presents various studies of the county extension agent.

Just as the industrial researcher is exposed to role conflict (cf. pages
258-260), so is the county extension agent. One source of potential conflict for
the county extension agents is his relationship to the extension service. He is
frequently confronted with the problem of whether to adhere to the demands
and pressures of the extension service or to work around them in some way.
Preiss (1954), according to Rogers, reports that the more successful county
extension agent concerns himself more with the extension *service* than with the
extension service *bureaucracy* (italics ours).

Another source of potential conflict exists between the extension agent and
his clients. In a study conducted in Wisconsin (Wilkening, 1958), extension
agents saw their roles as giving their clients basic education and as being involved
in the transmission of creative works, but their clients saw them as providing
speakers for their clients' organizations.

A number of studies have also been carried out on factors related to the
county extension agent's effectiveness and the areas in which he can be most
effective. It was previously pointed out that the successful agent concerned
himself more with the extension service than with the extension service bureaucracy. It was also found in a study of factors contributing to agents' success in
Missouri (Nye, 1952) that their personality characteristics were most important,
and these were followed by the kind of training the agents received and their
vocational interests and attitudes. A county extension agent's effectiveness may
also be a function of his social status relative to the people with whom he
communicates and the various ways in which he is perceived by different members of the community (Rogers, 1962). Finally, his effectiveness, defined as the
number of innovations adopted by farmers in the area he covers, appeared to be
a function of the intensity of his promotional efforts. A study of county extension agents' efforts in promoting artificial breeding of dairy cattle from 1943 to
1949 indicated that from 1943 to 1946 the rate at which this breeding technique was adopted was almost directly related to the number of days a year that

county extension agents spent on promoting the idea. After 1947 the agents' efforts decreased, but farmers continued to adopt the idea at a constant rate. Presumably this was due to one farmer telling another about artificial breeding. Those who adopted the technique earlier than others (called "early adopters") were opinion leaders who influenced their neighbor farmers to adopt the idea (Stone, 1952).

Rogers (1962) suggests that rate of adoption of an innovation may not stem directly from a county extension agent's efforts but rather that a county extension agent's efforts may be a function of the existing rate of adoption of an innovation. Thus, when a county extension agent observes that an innovation is adopted, he interprets its acceptance to mean that the people need it. He therefore increases his effort to get it accepted. Increase in rate of adoption may then lead him to increase his efforts rather than vice versa.

There are many other studies reported by Rogers (1962) but let this sample suffice to indicate how the role, personality, perseverance, etc. of an intermediary during the communication stage relate to his effectiveness in transmitting creative works, new products, new ideas, innovations, etc. to various specialized audiences and/or the public.

Peace Corps Volunteers

For the communication stage to be carried out effectively people are needed who can fulfill the requirements of their roles. In the hope that the selection of such individuals can continue to improve, we present the findings of a study we undertook of Peace Corps volunteers (Stein, 1966). This was the first group of volunteers to be assigned to Colombia, South America. They were in a community development program in which their task was to help village groups organize themselves so that they could work together in the building of community roads, schools, health centers, etc. At first blush, it would appear that this has little to do with the creative process because roads, schools, health centers, etc., are not in and of themselves creative works. Indeed, this is true, but the fact of the matter is that Peace Corps volunteers could just as well have been involved in the transmission of creative works. Under such circumstances we would still want a technique to help improve the selection process.

The technique used in this study is a Self-Description Questionnaire (Stein, 1965; Stein & Neulinger, 1968), which is based on Murray's (1938) need system. There are 20 paragraphs that a person is asked to arrange in a rank order from that paragraph that describes him best (assigned to a rank of 1) to that which describes him least well (assigned a rank of 20). The person's ranking is then processed by a computer which matches it against the rankings of existing profiles of different personality types that were established in previous research. The subject is then assigned to that type or profile to which he is closest. If he is not sufficiently close to any of them, in terms of certain criteria, then the subject is regarded as unclassified.

In the Peace Corps study the following types predominated.*

The *socially oriented* type† is dedicated to people. He assists helpless people and supports, comforts, and protects them. He is deferent to authority and conforming.

The *intellectually oriented* type also enjoys working with other people but is more achievement oriented. He is more likely to follow his own point of view and enjoys sensuous impressions and aesthetic feelings.

Action oriented individuals see themselves as controlling situations and getting things accomplished. They are doers and achievers rather than players or thinkers.

Unconventional type persons aid and comfort the helpless and receive the same in return. A member of this type is not discriminating in his social relationships. He regards himself as a free soul who likes to have others around so that he can be seen and heard, can entertain and amuse.

Resourceful individuals are also oriented to achievement. When their freedom or position of mastery is threatened, they feel under pressure and become anxious. Soon, however, they recover their resources and find new means of coping with their problems. Thus they are flexible and can make compromises to achieve their long-range goals.††

These types were not actually used to select the volunteers in this program but to study the selection process. The results yielded by this research (Stein, 1966) that are of interest to us are:

1. The selection committee, composed of psychiatrists and persons involved in community development activities, appeared to have a predilection in favor of action oriented volunteers. The selection committee obviously had no prior knowledge of the types. Their choices were such that all of the young men who were classified as action oriented volunteers were selected for service in Colombia, while only varying proportions of the other types were selected for this activity.

2. Among those individuals who were sent to Colombia, it was found that the action oriented volunteer, at the end of his two years of service in Colombia, was regarded has having done less well in his assignment than the socially oriented, intellectually oriented, unconventional, and resourceful types. This was particularly interesting because the selection committee, as indicated in the first point, chose all the applicants who were later classified as the action oriented type, but of the remaining applicants they chose only a little more than half the

---

*These are brief descriptions. Fuller descriptions may be found in Stein (1966).

†Currently this type is referred to as the *conformity oriented* type.

††These were the main types in the Peace Corps study. Currently there are additional types: forceful, S, T, and unclassified.

men from each of the other types. Implicitly, therefore, they were counting on members of this type to perform with greater effectiveness than the other types of volunteers.

3. In retrospect, it appears that the action oriented type was so involved in getting things done, and quickly, that he had difficulty making contact with the people in a culture that had a different time table. These action oriented volunteers might have done very well in another site but not in the one to which they were assigned. If transmission and change agents are to operate with maximum effectiveness there needs to be a match between the individual's personality and the requirements of his job situation.

4. There seemed to be a relationship between a man's personality type and the style of his behavior as he fulfilled his community development assignment. On the basis of observational and interview data, the following was learned:

An *action oriented* volunteer contacted influential people in the community and urged them to tell the people to come to community meetings. Consistent with his personality, this type of person was involved with power, status, and control.

An *unconventional* volunteer told two or three people in his community that he was there to work *with* them and that he was not going to work *for* them, after which he left.

A *socially oriented* volunteer spent weeks visiting the families in the community to establish contact with them and when he felt there was sufficient interest, he called a community meeting.

An *intellectually oriented* volunteer went around explaining, discussing, and putting up notices on the school bulletin board asking the people to come to a town meeting.

Finally, a *resourceful* type followed quite a different approach from all the others. He ran a village bazaar, and when the people came to it, he organized a meeting.

These observations and data are based on only a small sample of volunteers but they indicate how different personality types can actually fulfill the same role—in this instance, that of community developer. And, in fulfilling this role, their styles reflect their individual signatures. Effectiveness in a role as a transmission agent is not limited to a single personality type. Different personality types may be equally effective in the same role. They differ in their styles. Hence, those involved in selecting them can help maximize the probability of their effectiveness by matching their style with groups of persons with whom they have to communicate and who are responsive to these styles.

Salesmen

If a person has any hesitation in accepting the place of the communication stage in the creative process, he need only observe the efforts of a salesman of creative work to acquaint himself with the possibility that some creative works might not have left the creative person's studio, laboratory, etc., without the salesman's effort. The salesman may also spend his time developing a receptive audience for creative works.

The kind of salesman we have in mind is someone who knows at the expert level, or not far from it, what it is he is selling and he also has thorough knowledge of the people to whom he is selling. The importance of both areas of knowledge should not be underestimated, nor should we underestimate the time and energy involved in obtaining such knowledge and in developing beneficial social contacts.

An excellent example of a very effective and famous salesman in the art world who illustrates very well what we have in mind was Duveen. Behrman (1951), in his write-up of Duveen, provides a great deal of material to illustrate the different aspects of the role he played. The following is only a segment of that role.

Probably never before had a merchant brought to such exquisite perfection the large-minded art of casting bread upon the waters. There was almost nothing Duveen wouldn't do for his important clients. Immensely rich Americans, shy and suspicious of casual contacts because of their wealth, often didn't know where to go or what to do with themselves when they were abroad. Duveen provided entrée to the great country homes of the nobility; the coincidence that their noble owners often had ancestral portraits to sell did not deter Duveen. He also wangled hotel accommodations and passage on sold-out ships. He got his clients houses, or he provided architects to build them houses, and then saw to it that the architects planned the interiors with wall space that demanded plenty of pictures. He even selected brides or bridegrooms for some of his clients, and presided over the weddings with avuncular benevolence. These selections had to meet the same refined standard that governed his choice of houses for his clients—a potential receptivity to expensive art. . . . In negotiating with the heads of noble families, Duveen usually won hands down over other dealers; the brashness and impetuosity of his attack simply bowled the dukes and barons over. He didn't waste his time and theirs on art patter (he reserved that for his American clients); he talked prices, and big prices. He would say, 'Greatest thing *I* ever saw! Will pay the biggest price *you* ever saw!' To this technique the dukes and barons responded warmly. They were familiar with it from their extensive experience in buying and selling horses [pp. 33, 35].

Salesmen, to be effective in their roles as transmission agents, need to know what they are talking about. And, although they are involved in selling, their knowledge of their products is most critical. This is strongly reflected, because of the nature of their field, in the efforts of the pharmaceutical detail men. They are employed by drug companies to keep doctors current with information about old and new drugs and thereby induce doctors to buy from their employers. Doctors are quite busy and cannot always keep up with current literature as well as they would like. Hence, detail men are important sources of information to doctors (Hawkins, 1959). But, detail men, as no doubt other intermediaries, are not always given credit for their work. For example, Ferber and Wales (1958) asked 210 doctors to keep diaries of information about new ideas. A study of the diaries revealed that detail men were more important as sources of information than doctors said they were. Van den Ban, according to Rogers (1961a), found a similar phenomenon with farmers. In 1952 he asked 200 farmers in Wisconsin their source of new farm information. Approximately 3% reported commercial agents. When these same farmers were reinterviewed in 1957 and asked about the sources of information they used for specific farm ideas that they had adopted from 1952 to 1957, more than 30% mentioned commercial change agents.

Salesmen encounter other obstacles in the communication process. Thus, they are not trusted as much as some others who have information about new products. Farmers, for example, placed more trust in what they heard from their farmer neighbors about new products than in what they heard from salesmen. Rogers (1962) reports a study in which 97% of the farmers interviewed said they were more likely to be convinced about a new idea if they talked with a farmer neighbor than if they talked with a salesman. Salesmen's motives were suspect. They were strangers and they were always suspected of trying to sell more and more. When salesmen were perceived by their farmer clients as more like themselves, they were regarded as more trustworthy. This was found by Rogers and Leuthold (1962) in a study that involved farmers who had been hired as part-time salesmen by various companies. These farmer salesmen were seen as peers by the farmer clients and not primarily as salesmen.

People go through various stages* in adopting a new product. Salesmen apparently are more effective with people who are at the first stage (the trial stage) than at any of the other stages (Ryan & Gross, 1943; Beal & Rogers, 1957; Rogers, 1962). The salesman is relied on more heavily in the trial stage because at this stage the individual buys small amounts of what he needs to test the product before he decides to adopt it for more frequent use.

Gallery Owners

The role of a salesman-intermediary can be as complex as that of a creative individual. We have already considered the salesman's role in relation to clients, as reflected in Behrman's write-up of Duveen. Salesmen may also play important

*The adoption process is discussed on pages 290–297.

supporting roles vis-à-vis creative individuals. This is particularly manifest in the art world among gallery owners who, while not big enough to be entrepreneurs, are "bigger" than salesmen. They seem to us to be closer to salesmen and therefore they are presented here.

Stevens (1971) in an essay for the *Wall Street Journal* entitled "The Artist as an Affluent Man," discusses the various financial relationships between printmakers and gallery owners. She points out that when a gallery owner accepts a work for sale, the work is usually taken on consignment. According to a marketing study in 1964 referred to by Stevens, artists did not necessarily like this arrangement, for they were not protected against the loss or damage of their works. And, if a dealer sold their work they did not necessarily get paid for several months. In such instances, gallery owners use the artist's share of the money interest free. To be sure, not all galleries operate this way; there are very reputable galleries that pay their artists a specified number of days after they sell a work.

Artists, usually the better-established ones, have all sorts of arrangements with their galleries. One painter-printmaker, Krushenick, according to Stevens, receives a monthly check from the gallery that sells his work. This check is for less than he earned during the month. And, if he needs more money he writes the gallery. According to Krushenick, to take all his earnings from a gallery as they accumulate is to put a strain on the gallery.

Still other artists, because of their varied experiences, have worked out still other kinds of business arrangements. One artist, to avoid bookkeeping headaches, will give a gallery 50% off if it buys directly from him. But, if it buys on consignment, it gets only 40% off.

The economic conditions and status of printmakers are quite varied. At one extreme, the established ones can sell their works for high fees. But a younger and less well-established person may have to sell an entire edition of his work for a flat fee, in addition to teaching to support his family. While this may sound like a very difficult way to earn a livelihood, some young artists prefer it, for if they sold their works by themselves they might have to wait a long time for their money. This way they get their money right away. Indeed, when they are established and recognized and command high fees, they have some economic security and can afford to take the time necessary for the fees they desire.

The Advertising Agency

One of the more ubiquitous intermediaries on the contemporary scene is the advertising agency. Rarely, if ever, does an advertising agency represent a creative individual directly. (We should clearly note that we are not talking about creative persons in the advertising agency. We are focusing on the agency in its role in a continuous process from creative individual to audience or public.) Rather it will represent the company or organization in which the creative individual is employed. The advertising agency will usually not have any contact with the creative person. Some creative persons may not like to see what is done to their work and yet will be helpless to do anything about it; others disengage themselves from this experience.

Advertising agencies are among the best examples of intermediaries. They are very self-conscious about their roles, and their representatives as well as others have written a good deal about how they can fulfill their clients' needs and how they can communicate with the public. We have selected samples of comments from several persons that seem to illustrate best the reciprocal relationship between client and advertising agency as well as some comments about the effective use of channels of communication. Creative individuals might do well to attend closely to how advertising agencies go about their work. They are "pros" in communication and consequently the creative individual who may want to improve his skills in the communication stage of the creative process, might profit from trying to develop procedures of his own on smaller scales that are analogous to those used by the advertising agencies with a larger scope. We shall consider in this section the relationship between client and advertising agency, and later, some suggestions about the media and the message that is to be communicated.

The relationship between client and agency has been characterized by David Ogilvy, Chairman of the Board of the advertising agency, Ogilvy & Mather, Inc., as being as intimate as that between doctor and patient. In his book (Ogilvy, 1963) he presents several suggestions that both advertising agency and client need to consider if their relationship is to be mutually satisfying and is to result in successful advertising campaigns.

For the agency Ogilvy suggests that: (1) The agency staff should have a personal commitment to the product. If the staff privately despises the product, the campaign is likely to fail. (2) Products with a history of falling sales should be avoided because it may indicate that the product is no good or that the management is incompetent. These deficiencies cannot be overcome by advertising. (3) Agencies should accept new products only if they are included with other products that are distributed nationally. This is an economic consideration, for not all new products make it past test markets. To take a new product through a test market is a costly matter and an agency's profit margin does not allow for such a level of risk. (4) Will the client want the agency to make a profit? Is advertising only a marginal factor in their marketing program? The answer to the first question should be yes. If the answer to the second question is also yes the potential client should be avoided. Advertising agencies, according to Ogilvy, should avoid clients who want to hire persons they consider central to the advertising campaign and who do not wish to leave the hiring of such persons to the advertising agency staff.

Considering the relationship from the point of view of the client, Ogilvy suggests that: (1) Clients select their agencies on the basis of careful evaluation, including evaluations of the agencies by previous clients. (2) They should set high standards for their agencies and reward them when these standards are attained and criticize them when they are not. (3) Agencies should be thoroughly briefed on the client company's activities because the more they know, the better off they are. (4) The client should not make the agency feel it is always looking for a better one. This makes the agency insecure. (5) If the client has an in-house advertising group, it should not be made to compete with the outside agency.

It would be extremely valuable if creative persons working by themselves could select their intermediaries with the care and standards just prescribed. In all likelihood, only if the financial stakes are high enough, and only if the creative person's reputation is sufficiently well established, can the creative person be involved in such care and standards. Nevertheless, it is something to aim for and to emulate whenever possible.

Opinion Leaders

The last group of intermediaries we shall consider are the opinion leaders in the community. These are persons with high status for one reason or another in their field or community. The term "opinion leader" is older than most synonymous terms. It was used by Lazarsfeld *et al.* (1944) in a now classic study of the 1940 presidential election. Other names in the behavioral science literature for the same role are: key communicators (Lionberger, 1960), influentials (Stewart, 1947; Merton, 1957), tastemakers (Opinion Research Corporation, 1959), and gatekeepers (Lewin, 1958).

The opinion leaders serve as intermediaries in their own right when they come upon a creative work and then purposefully communicate its value and significance to others. Or, because others see that opinion leaders use or have a creative work, they then feel they should also have it. The "it" must be good because opinion leaders have it, or there is now status attached to possessing the creative work. The opinion leader may also be regarded as a subintermediary because intermediaries, such as those considered previously, make opinion leaders special targets of their communications. A salesman may try to sell an opinion leader on a work, or he may give the opinion leader the creative work for free just so he can say that an opinion leader has it and then others will want to pay for it.

Who are these opinion leaders and what are their characteristics? Rogers (1962) reviews a number of studies from which the following has been gleaned.

In general, opinion leaders are more likely to be innovators than are their followers (Rogers, 1962). Influential farmers are more innovative than their followers (Lionberger, 1953, 1955; Marsh & Coleman, 1954; Rogers, 1962). Doctors who convinced other doctors to use a new drug were themselves early adopters of the drug (Katz, 1957). At the same time that they manifest innovative behavior, opinion leaders generally reflect the values of their community. That is, they conform more to the norms of the particular social system in which they live than do others. In a study of 13 Kentucky neighborhoods, the opinion leaders in those communities that were regarded as modern were more innovative than the followers. In traditional neighborhoods opinion leaders were less innovative.

Moreover, an opinion leader in one area is not necessarily an opinion leader in another. A woman who leads in one area is not likely to be a leader in another (Katz & Lazarsfeld, 1955). The leaders in farm innovations were not found to be leaders in local politics or other community affairs (Emery & Oeser, 1958) or in church or school matters (Ryan, 1942). There might be a relationship between the developmental level of a culture and the presence of opinion leaders who are leaders in one or in several areas. Rogers (1962) suggests the possibility that in less developed countries or in traditional societies there is likely to be more polymorphic than monomorphic influence, to use terms originating with Merton (1957). (Monomorphic refers to influence in one area, and polymorphic to influence in several areas.)

There is a difference in the sources of information used by opinion leaders and their followers. The former use sources that are more impersonal, technical, accurate, and "cosmopolite" (a term used by sociologists to mean coming from sources other than or in addition to those existing where one lives; the opposite of "cosmopolite" is "local") than those of their followers. Opinion leaders read the mass media, while followers rely on ideas transmitted from person to person, and the latter are more likely to distort the information. Influential farmers subscribed to more magazines and newspapers (Lionberger, 1953); influential doctors received their drug information from professional journals (Menzel & Katz, 1958); farmer opinion leaders subscribed to more farm magazines and papers and watched more TV farm shows than did the followers (Rogers, 1962); farmer opinion leaders are more likely to seek out technically accurate information from county extension agents and agricultural scientists than are the followers.

Opinion leaders are more aware of and more oriented to what goes on outside their communities. In this sense they are more cosmopolite (Rogers, 1962). Doctors who are opinion leaders are more likely to participate in more out-of-town meetings (Katz, 1957); farmer opinion leaders belong to organizations outside their rural community (Lionberger, 1953).

Opinion leaders engage more in social activities than do followers. They participate more in their community's formal and informal organizations, but they do not necessarily hold power positions in their communities (Rogers, 1962).

Opinion leaders have higher social status than their followers. In one study by Lionberger (1953) it was found that, among farmers, opinion leaders are likely to own their own farms, have larger farms, and have higher incomes and greater community prestige. Another study by the same investigator (Lionberger, 1959) revealed that farm opinion leaders, although found in all social classes, were more often found in the upper social classes.

Personal Influence

Opinion leaders are effective because they exert personal influence, and indeed personal influence exerted by persons other than the opinion leaders is also very effective and very critical for the communication stage of the creative process. It has been said (Rogers, 1962) that after 10–20% of an audience adopts an innovation, it may be impossible to stop its spread because of the effects of personal influence. In a consumer study undertaken by Katz and Lazarsfeld (1955) it was found that personal influence was mentioned more frequently and was more significant in the decisions that people made about a product than were any of the mass media. Coleman *et al.* (1957) found that doctors who were regarded as opinion leaders were more influential in determining the time at which a new drug was adopted by other doctors than were any of the other factors studied. Neighbor-to-neighbor communication was more important than any other source of information in convincing Iowa homemakers to purchase synthetic fabrics (Rahudkar, 1958). And, as Menzel and Katz (1958) point out, in politics the newspaper editor or the ward heeler does not have as much effect on an individual politically as do his parents, spouse, or his ethnic or religious loyalties.

Personal influence serves to make people aware of a creative work. But since most people rely on impersonal communication in the mass media for this, it is likely that the influence on awareness is more important for those who adopt creative works or innovations later in time than for those who adopt them quite early. Once an opinion is formed, it is reinforced by talking about it with a person's peers. Personal influence networks generally communicate the norms on innovativeness, and these norms are probably most important when the individual evaluates a new product and is trying to make up his mind about it. The opinions of his peers may be a substitute for trying out an innovation. This would be particularly important where it is impossible to try out an innovation by himself.

According to Rogers (1962), personal influence is also helpful in other ways, such as in overcoming what he calls *selective exposure*—the tendency to expose himself to communications that agree with his own. Personal influence can break through this. Individuals tend to make their decisions on the basis of past experiences and ideas—what Rogers calls *selective perception*. Personal influence from others gives an individual another point of view to take into account. And lastly, Rogers points out that personal influence is valuable in overcoming *selective retention*—the remembering of ideas that agree with the individual's existing opinions.

Personal influence can overcome the barriers of selective exposure, selective perception, and selective retention because, as Rogers (1962) points out:

1. When a person discusses a matter with a friend, he does not know in advance the ideas that will be discussed; hence, exposure to personal influence is less selective than exposure to the mass media on a topic.

2. During the course of a dialog an individual has an opportunity to voice his opinion and to have it corrected, or contrasted with differing views. This, of course, is not possible with the mass media.

3. With mass media, an individual may have one exposure, but in personal communication an individual can be reminded about a new idea on several occasions, although he might at first not have been interested in it.

Dichter (1966) in his study of the effectiveness of word-of-mouth communication was interested in learning what prompts a person to talk about a product or service and what induces a person to listen. Dichter says that "The power and the significance of everyday Word-of-Mouth lie mainly in the *speaker's* lack of *material* interest [p. 148]." The speaker does expect to get something out of his communication. He expects the listener to do something about what has been said. Dichter sees speakers' motivations as falling into four categories:

1. *"Product involvement"*—the user's experience with a product stimulates tension within him that he must talk out.

2. *"Self-involvement"*—the speaker's emotional needs are satisfied through talking about a product. As a result of talking about a product, the speaker, according to Dichter, may gain attention, show connoisseurship, feel like a pioneer, suggest that he has inside information, suggest that he has high status, allow himself to feel as if he were involved in a good cause with a "gospel" to spread, confirm his own judgment, and assert superiority.

3. *"Other-involvement"*—the speaker is concerned with giving something to the listener (the recommendation is a gift).

4. *"Message-involvement"*—the speaker's talk is based on how the product has been presented in the mass media and not on his own experience.

Judging from 488 instances where purchases were made on the basis of word-of-mouth information, Dichter concluded that the listener made his decision to buy on two conditions: "(a) that the person who made the recommendation is interested in him and his well-being, and (b) that the speaker's experience with and knowledge about the product are convincing [p. 152]."

Breaking down the recommending groups, Dichter identified seven:

1. *Commercial authorities*—people who work close to a product and appear to or should know more about it than the average person; this group, which included *professional experts* like mechanics (who recommend cars) and beauti-

cians, accounted for 3% of the sales. The group also included salespeople, who accounted for 6½% of the sales.

2. *Celebrities*—radio, TV, and theater personalities who recommended products accounted for 7½% of the purchases.

3. *Connoisseurs*—people who have a close "but nonprofessional contact with the product"—know about and enjoy the product but do not make a living from it. A person in this category is the car enthusiast who reads all the automobile magazines, etc.; 10% of the purchases were made on this basis.

4. *Sharers of interests*—people having a similarity of interests or tastes (e.g., young mothers or junior executives) accounted for 18% of the buying decisions made.

5. *Intimates*—members of the buyer's family and his close friends. This group accounted for 14% of the purchases.

6. *People of goodwill*—people seen by the buyer as having his well-being at heart (included are very close friends, friendly neighbors, etc.). This category accounts for 24½% of the purchases.

7. *Bearers of tangible evidence*—speakers who have some tangible evidence that convinces the buyer. Of the total group 16½% fell into this category.

Personal influence therefore is a rather potent force in the communication stage of the creative process. It would be well if creative individuals could enlist the power of this force for their purposes. It is conceivable that then not only would the communication stage have been carried out with effectiveness but the time and energy that creative persons themsleves have to devote to this stage might be decreased and the creative individual would then have both more time and more energy for starting new creative works.

With the discussion of opinion leaders and personal influence we have concluded our survey of various types of intermediaries. Our intent was not to be all inclusive and no doubt the reader has thought of others who should have been discussed. Our intent was merely to discuss a selection of intermediaries to illustrate the variety of roles they fulfill both for the creative individual and their clients, the audience, or public. We also considered some intermediaries to illustrate other points—e.g., the county extension agent to illustrate the numerous variables studied regarding his characteristics and effectiveness that might also be studied to better understand other intermediaries. And in a discussion of one group of Peace Corps volunteers a technique was presented that might also be useful in the more effective selection of other groups of intermediaries.

With all that has been said of intermediaries it should be clearly understood that they do not supplant the creativity of the creative work. Their task in the communication stage of the creative process is to make certain that the creative work reaches the public and audience and thus satisfies or fulfills the needs of various subgroups in the society. In this manner intermediaries' efforts do serve to encourage, support, and maintain a value system in the society that makes it possible for creative individuals to carry on present and future efforts.

The Flow of Communication

The number and kinds of intermediaries involved in the flow of communication about a creative work no doubt varies as a function of what is being communicated and the complexity of the situation in which the communication occurs. Over time, behavioral scientists have shifted in their thinking about the flow of communication. At first it was thought of as involving one step, and then later as involving multistep channels of communication.

Prior to the study of the 1940 elections by Lazarsfeld *et al.* (1944), sociologists regarded the United States as a "mass society," in which the spread of information was assumed to be from the mass media to the public in one step. This was termed the one-step channel of communication. It was supplanted by the *two-step channel* of communication because Lazarsfeld *et al.* (1944) found that ideas flow from the mass media to opinion leaders and from them to the larger public. As elaborated by Rogers (1962), the first step involves primarily the "transfer of information," and the second involves the "spread of influence [pp. 211–214]."

The two-step flow of communication is, according to Rogers (1962), also too simple and probably does not do justice to the communication process in all instances. At any one point in the process there may be two steps, but a multistep approach is probably more generally applicable. For example, opinion leaders among doctors talk as much to their colleagues about drugs as do other doctors. It appears that their colleagues have even higher status than they themselves have and thus communication may take several steps and not just two (Menzel & Katz, 1958).

In terms of the multistep flow of communication, it is apparent that the type of communication channel used and its effectiveness vary as a function of type of problem involved and the type of information desired. Light is cast on these matters in a study by Menzel and Katz (1958), who divided medical problems in terms of the degree to which answers to them are generally well established and well structured. Two categories were established—acute and chronic. Acute problems require quick treatment and there are few variations in treating them. Success or failure in treatment is apparent in one or two days. Chronic conditions, on the other hand, have several possible treatments, and effectiveness of therapy is difficult to measure.

In the treatment of acute conditions it was found that 7% of the doctors called on colleagues for advice, whereas when conditions were chronic 22% called on colleagues. Thus, as the ambiguity of a problem increased, there was an increase in the use of colleagues for information. [This finding is consistent with a controlled laboratory experiment in which it was also found that influence of others was stronger in unstructured than structured situations (Sherif, 1936)].

Those doctors who received three or more choices as sources of information gathered their information at out-of-town meetings as well as from journals before deciding what drugs they would use. The doctor who was an isolate relied more heavily on commercial sources, such as detail men (drug companies' representatives), and on direct-mail advertisements. These sources, while they also come from "out of town," are less prestigeful, and are easier to keep up with. The detail men serve not only to disseminate information but also as a "near-professional companion" for the doctors who are isolates.

The number of channels involved in the communication process is obviously a function of a number of factors: the intermediaries involved, the media involved and the use made of them, the type of problem for which the communication is designed, the target group for which it is intended, etc.

THE ADOPTION PROCESS

Just as communication about a creative work does not flow directly from the creative individual to the audience or public but must go through one or more intermediaries and a process of communication flow, so there is an adoption process through which the audience goes in adopting the creative work. Complete and unconditional acceptance does not occur immediately.

What will be said about the adoption process is based primarily on information and data available from rural sociologists and their investigations of the acceptance of innovations in farming procedures and techniques. We think the general principles are applicable to creative works in other areas too and so present this work here. Hopefully, future systematic studies of adoption in other areas of creativity in the future would tell us the extent to which the processes are in fact similar or different.

In adopting an innovation the public (or its subgroups) goes through a five stage process, according to Rogers (1962): (1) awareness, (2) interest, (3) evaluation, (4) trial, and (5) adoption.

The *awareness* stage consists of exposure to the innovation. At this stage the individual lacks complete information about the innovation and is not yet motivated to seek out this information. Next, the individual, growing *interested* in the innovation, seeks information about it. He is, in a general way, favorably inclined to the innovation but does not know yet how he can use it. During the awareness stage the individual is passive, but in the interest stage he actively seeks information. His personality and values and the norms of the social system in which he lives affect where he seeks information and how he interprets it.

Evaluation is the third stage in the adoption process, and it is presumed to exist when the individual tries out the innovation mentally to determine how it would satisfy his needs. This stage, according to Rogers, is the least distinct of the stages of the adoption process, and it is most difficult to get information about it. The individual is uncertain at this point whether to adopt or not. He requires reinforcement, which he seeks by getting information from others. At this point, information from peers is more effective than that from the mass media because the latter is too general.

During the fourth stage, the *trial* stage, the individual actually uses the innovation on a small scale to determine how worthwhile it is. In this stage the individual can check out the innovation in his own immediate situation.

The fifth and last stage is *adoption,* during which the individual decides to continue full use of the innovation. If the results of the trial stage are positive, the decision is made for adoption.

An innovation may be rejected at any of the stages in the adoption process. If the process runs its course and the innovation is then rejected, this rejection is called a *discontinuance* (Rogers, 1962). Discontinuance may occur as a function of the characteristics of the innovation itself, as well as of the characteristics of the individuals involved. Rogers points out that those who adopt an innovation after most others have already done so are more likely to discontinue use of an innovation than those who adopt it earlier. This may be a function of the fact that those who adopt an innovation later have lower incomes, and their lack of financial resources may be one cause of their discontinuing use of the innovation.

The time involved in each of the stages of the adoption process has been studied and it has been found (Beal & Rogers, 1960) that the rate at which awareness occurs is faster than the rate of adoption. More time elapses between awareness-to-trial than between trial-to-adoption. Adoption generally follows directly after the trial stage. If an individual can be encouraged to and does try an innovation, it may well speed up the time to adoption. Giving away samples or a free trial of the new product can speed up adoption of the new product immeasurably (Klonglan *et al.*, 1960).

Sources of information are of differential effectiveness during the various stages of the adoption process. Information sources from outside the individual's social system are more important at the awareness stage of the adoption process and local sources are more important during the evaluation stage. From this it is apparent that generally speaking mass media are more important at the awareness stage, and that personal sources of information increase in importance from the awareness stage to the evaluation stage. Personal sources of information fall off in importance at the trial stage. Personal sources are likely to be most important at the evaluation stage. Also, at this stage the opportunity to engage in a dialog with another person enables the interested person to learn additional information about the innovation as well as to obtain clarification of his thoughts about and experiences with the innovation (Rogers, 1962).

Characteristics of the Media

Just how well the adoption process runs its course is, as we have seen, a function of a number of factors. We shall limit ourselves to further comments on two of them. The first is the characteristics of the media that were part of the communication process, and the second is the characteristics of the innovation itself.

Different media have different demand characteristics and requirements. It is important that these characteristics be understood, for the kind of copy that will be effective in transmitting the message with one kind of medium may not be as effective with another. McLuhan (1964) has made some general differentiations among the media, and Ogilvy (1963) has suggestions to make about specific aspects of the media, all of which we present not only because of their inherent value and interest, but also because they serve to demonstrate how much one may need to be aware of, if the communication stage of the creative process is to be carried out with effectiveness.

McLuhan (1964) differentiates between "hot" and "cool" media. Among the "hot" media are: radio, movies, phonograph, the phonetic alphabet, and paper used for writing. Among the cool media: telephone, television, cartoons, speech, hieroglyphic or ideogrammic written characters, and stone used for printing.

A hot medium is one that is "well filled with data." It does not require so much audience participation since it does not leave much to be filled in by the audience. In contrast, a cool medium gives little and the listener has to fill in a great deal.

Due to the characteristics of the media, they can affect messages in different ways. Thus, a hot medium may highlight or exaggerate a message, whereas a cool medium may tone down the same message. Where a cool medium may be appropriate for certain messages, a hot medium may not.

Just as media and messages interact, so there are likely to be interactions between media and the people with whom they are used. Some subgroups of people may respond differently to a medium with a specific message than do other subgroups. McLuhan does not present the kinds of reactions that different kinds of people have but he does have something to say about cultural differences, from which we can infer that differences between types of persons may also be involved. Russians' attitudes, according to McLuhan, toward material presented aurally and visually differ from the reactions of people in the United States to these means of presenting material. The telephone, for example, is very congenial to the Russians' oral tradition because of its "rich nonvisual involvement." The effects that the Russians associate with the telephone, people in the United States associate "with the eager conversation of the lapel-gripper whose face is twelve inches away [McLuhan, 1964, pp. 45–46]." These differences stand out in bold relief when the two countries' spying techniques are considered. "The Russian bugs rooms and spies by ear, finding this quite natural [McLuhan, 1964, p. 46]."

Ogilvy (1963) talks about the use of various media, and we have selected some of his comments about posters, illustrations, and television commercials to illustrate the critical differences in the effective use of the different media. With regard to the use of posters, Ogilvy suggests that they should contain "a remarkable idea" and be a "visual scandal." Strong colors with maximum contrast (or plain black and white) should be used. Subway and bus posters should not look like " 'baby billboards'—multicolored illustrations and short copy, set in large display type [Ogilvy, 1963, p. 127] ."

Regarding illustrations, Ogilvy suggests that their subject matter is more important than the technique involved in them. Photographs are better than drawings for illustrations and the photographs should arouse the reader's curiousity. Illustrations, he says, should not be judged when they are mounted on cardboard and covered with cellophane, for this process is misleading. They should be judged when they are pasted into publications. If the advertisement is designed to look more like the editorial page than like an advertisement, it "will attract about 50 per cent more readers [p. 122] ."

According to Ogilvy, what is shown on a television commercial is more important than what is said. Words only explain the pictures. If what is said is not illustrated, it may be immediately forgotten by the viewer. Television commercials should be built around one or two points. If the use of the product can be demonstrated, it should be. For such products "television is the most powerful advertising medium ever invented [p. 131] ."

However we differentiate between media, whether we call them hot and cool, or speak of them more concretely as posters, illustrations, or television commercials, or use some other terms, the point is that media do differ significantly from each other; information conveyed effectively by one medium may not be well conveyed by another. For effectiveness in the communication stage of the creative process we need to be aware of the possible interactions between medium, message, and audience.

Message. We have just made some suggestions about the medium and we shall talk later about the audience or public. Let us now consider the message. In doing so, it is necessary to differentiate between the creative product, which is a message in and of itself, and the message, or in advertising terminology, the *copy,* that accompanies the creative product and tries to communicate to the public the creative product's characteristics and worth and thus convinces or persuades the public to buy it. In this section, we are concerned only with the second type of communication.

Communication involves a dialog between the sender and receiver of a message. The receiver is not a passive receiver but responds in terms of messages that he understands. It is therefore necessary for the sender to consider the point of view of the receiver before he sends messages. It is quite sufficient for the abstract painter to communicate to his colleagues in technical jargon about his creative effort, but he will most certainly lose a nonprofessional audience if he tries to communicate in the same way. On the other hand, he may win a rather devoted and loyal audience if he does take the time to present the purpose and objective of his work in language that they can understand. Not only are all of these people potential purchasers of his creative work, but they do represent a rather large portion of society who should not be alienated if an atmosphere is to be created which will foster the development of a continuous flow of creative achievements.

Again, it is profitable to learn about characteristics of the message from the field of advertising, where communication is a most critical factor in its success. Dichter (1966), some of whose work was presented previously, places a great deal of emphasis on word-of-mouth communication. He believes that effective advertising might well be based on the principles that seem to be involved in the influence that word-of-mouth communication seems to have—and these same principles might well be adapted for various areas of creativity or at least they might serve as the basis for inferring how more effective communication might occur in different areas of creativity.

Dichter says that the message communicated should offer the consumer "a promise of emotional gain or some sort of mental gratification [pp. 161–162]." Consequently, he suggests that to stimulate word-of-mouth influences advertisers should [pp. 162–165]:

(1) *"Use the 'shock of difference'—but with an orientation":* Potential consumers should be told something very different about the product.

(2) *"Employ the effect of 'heightened reality' "(stagecraft):* Expressive use should be made of different art forms in staging reality.

(3) *"Invite 'listeners' to join you in poking fun at yourself":* This promotes friendship and has consumer feel he is in advertiser's confidence.

(4) *"Equip your message with 'wings' ":* People like to repeat what they can hear and quote. A message that is applicable to a variety of situations is best.

(5) *"Leave room for your reader's wit or ingenuity":* The reader should be allowed to fill in left-out words or to play with ambiguous meanings.

(6) *"Do not leave your customer alone with your product":* Tell the consumer some of the benefits he may reap from the use of a product, so that when he does use it he can recall what he heard.

(7) *"Link your product with needs and trends of the time":* If this is done, the product has a place among other topics that are talked about.

(8) *"Satisfy the urge for 'newness' ":* To prevent a product from being taken for granted, it should be presented from a new angle from time to time.

(9) *"Give your reader a chance to gain attention":* The potential consumer should be supplied with cultural, technical, or scientific information he can use.

(10) *"Provide him with 'inside information' ":* Show the potential consumer something of what goes on behind the scenes.

(11) *"Give him the feeling of secrecy or exclusivity":* The potential consumer needs to be made to feel he belongs to some kind of club.

(12) *"Make your reader feel that recommendation is a gift":* The potential consumer should be made aware of the things the product can do for those he cares for, and that therefore his recommendation is a gift to them.

(13) *"Offer a bridge of friendship":* The consumer might be able to send a free, gift-packed sample to friends.

It is obvious that Dichter's principles are of primary importance to the field of advertising to which he directed his comments. But the value of his comments should not be lost on others. It is sometimes too easy to fall into the trap of thinking that we can talk to all audiences just as one talks to one's professional, scientific, and artistic colleagues. Indeed, there are no doubt some creative persons who think it beneath them to talk in any other fashion. Furthermore, they might rationalize their behavior by saying that audiences or the public really do not want to be talked down to and therefore they talk the way they do. It is true that audiences do not want to be talked down to. They do want to understand what they hear and it is the creative person's responsibility to make sure he can take their point of view if he wants to communicate with them. If he does not want to communicate but feels that this is an important part of the process in which he is involved, then, as was said previously, he can hire any of a number of intermediaries to do this part of the work for him. What we intended to convey by citing Dichter's work is that one of the most effective selling techniques is not what might be referred to as the "fancy" techniques of advertising but what goes on in word-of-mouth communication every day. If the creative person can communicate in this manner, he will be most effective in this stage of the creative process.

Characteristics of Innovation

Another factor that affects the adoption process is the innovation's characteristics. This is rather crucial because the casualty rate of new products is rather high. It should come as no surprise that all new products introduced to the public do not survive—are not adopted. But what are the data? In 1962 Rogers reported that an industrial design firm said that 23 out of every 26 products introduced by industry fail.* A large advertising agency reported that only one out of 25 products that are test-marketed succeed, and a report of the United States Department of Commerce estimates that within four years of their release, 90% of all new products fail.

A study cited in the *Wall Street Journal* (1971) was reported to have surveyed 125 large companies that marketed new products and services during the preceding five years. The study found that the median percentage of major new

---

*One of the problems in evaluating the casualties for our purposes is that we don't know just how creative or how novel the new products really were. Conceivably, some might have been very novel, while others may have been variations on existing products.

products in the period that fell short of expectations in some important respect was slightly more than 20%, and about 5% were so disappointing they were taken off the market. The risks were the greatest for consumer product manufacturers, which had a median failure rate of 40%. Among the reasons for failures were product problems and defects, but "the leading reason was inadequate market research or simply overestimating the potential sales for a product [p. 1]."

With such a high casualty rate among new products, why do companies persist in coming forth with new products? Because, the *Wall Street Journal* report says, *"Six out of 10 companies in the survey anticipate new products will be more important in their sales over the next five years than in the last five-year period [p. 1]."* Because of the investment of the time and energy, and because of the risk capital involved, it is obviously of crucial value to learn as much as possible about the characteristics of innovations that affect their adoption. Rogers (1962) mentions five such characteristics, stressing that the objective evaluation of these characteristics is not as important to the adoption of an innovation as the individual's subjective evaluation. The five characteristics mentioned by Rogers are: "(1) relative advantage, (2) compatibility, (3) complexity, (4) divisibility, and (5) communicability [p. 146]."

Relative Advantage, according to Rogers (1962), refers to the extent to which an innovation has advantages over that which it would supersede. Its superiority may occur in any of a variety of areas: economic, labor, the job it performs, etc. Thus, an innovation may have an advantage because it is cheaper, it requires less labor to work it, it does the required job better than the one that exists. The advantages and significance of an innovation may be underscored by an existing crisis. Adler (1955) found, for example, that the adoption of educational innovations was delayed by depressions and wars, but that when these were over there was an acceleration in the adoption of the innovations.

The second characteristic, *compatibility*, refers to the extent to which an innovation is consistent with the values that exist in the society and the kinds of experiences that adopters may have had. The individual who adopts or is about to adopt an innovation gains a measure of security if the innovation is compatible with existing values and previous experience (Rogers, 1962). The adoption of birth control devices is slower in areas where religious attitudes exist that are against them. If an innovation is related to a previous one that had been evaluated negatively, then the adoption of the new innovation may also be delayed. The adoption of picture windows for private residences was delayed because people associated them with store windows and thus regarded them negatively for homes.

The third characteristic, *complexity*, refers to how difficult or easy it is to understand an innovation. This is a rather important variable in some areas. Kivlin (1960), in a study of the rate of adoption of farm innovations, found that the complexity of the innovation was more important than any of the other characteristics except relative advantage. It would be interesting to know whether this finding would be substantiated in studies of other kinds of innovations. We do know that what is perceived as complex by one group of individuals is not so perceived by others.

Divisibility, the fourth characteristic considered by Rogers (1962), refers to the extent to which an innovation may be tried on a limited basis. If the innovation cannot be divided for a small-scale trial, it might be tried over a period of time. It is as if the individual were involved in trying the innovation on the installment plan.

The last characteristic considered by Rogers is *communicability,* which refers to the extent to which an innovation, its characteristics and results, can be communicated to others. Some innovations are more easily described in these terms than others. (We shall have occasion later to present another approach, *benefit segmentation,* to understand the characteristics of the product that affects its adoption. This latter technique focuses on the attitudes of the public to the product rather than on the characteristics of the innovation itself.)

THE AUDIENCE OR PUBLIC

The communication stage of the creative process approaches its end when the creative work is presented to its target audience or public and ends when the audience or public accepts and uses it. The character and size of the audience or public varies as a function of the area to which the creative work belongs. In areas such as theoretical physics and mathematics, the sciences, the humanities, and some of the arts, the audience may be a group of experts and authorities— those whom we counted previously among the intermediaries—who become the final target audience with whom the creative individual communicates and who finally accept his work. In other areas—the theater, the dance, the novel, the more applied areas of the sciences and engineering fields (those that yield technological innovations)—the experts really serve as intermediaries and, while their acceptance is crucial, acceptance by the public marks the end of the communication stage and the creative process from our point of view.

Just as the creative work resonates with something important in the experts, so it must resonate with something crucial in the audience or public. A creative work cannot take hold for long without this kind of response no matter how much "selling" and persuasion has occurred. An audience or public responds positively to creative works that say or do for it what it has been unable to say or do for itself. The creative novel, play, and painting express something that the audience needs to say. The creative work, be it "happy," pleasant, rebellious, shocking, dismaying, full of doom, etc., resonates with a felt need in the audience. The creative individual's artistry or creativity may well lie in the fact that he knows how to give expression to this need and thereby how to satisfy it. In technological areas, creative works satisfy by extending man's capacities to master his environment, by making living easier, and by increasing man's capacity to earn his livelihood.

Just as we saw previously that there is potential conflict between the creative individual and the intermediaries during the communication stage of the creative process over such matters as sharing honors, so either the creative individual alone, or the intermediary alone, or both in concert may be in conflict with the audience or public. Sometimes this conflict is manifest in the criticism that the public "does not know anything" when it does not accept a creative work; sometimes in the idea that public acceptance has more to do with popularity or success than with creativity (and this is the attitude, usually, when someone else's work is involved). And sometimes creative persons and intermediaries form an élitist group that has little, if any contact with the public and becomes increasingly alienated and isolated from it. Under such circumstances creativity in the society can only diminish appreciably because valuable sources of support have been lost.

When creative individuals and intermediaries view themselves in transactional relationships with their audiences and public, when they see themselves as fulfilling the needs of the audience and public, of extending the audience's horizons and changing their audience's perceptions of the world around them, creative individuals will realize that the audience and public become for them important sources of emotional and financial support.

The creative individual and the intermediary can receive emotional gratification from the audience's and public's acceptance since it reinforces the creative behavior that is involved. Psychologically the public's acceptance of the creative work acknowledges and implicitly rewards the creative individual for being different, for having deviated from the group and its tradition to create something new. Less obviously, the audience's acceptance of the creative work also reinforces the behavior of the intermediaries involved. Such reinforcement provides them with valuable feedback that they made correct choices and decisions.

In addition to providing creative individuals and intermediaries with emotional support, the audience or public also provides financial support both directly and indirectly for creative works. Indirectly, its support comes through the taxes it pays that are converted into scholarships, grants, research programs, art councils, etc., which provide individuals with the opportunity to manifest their creativity. Direct support comes in the form of being active contributing supporters of creative persons or programs that support them and by being active purchasers of creative works.

Through their emotional and financial support, through their social and political attitudes, the audience and public create an environment with a positive atmosphere in which to receive creative works and from which future creative individuals and creative works can develop and be nourished.

The audience or public can play another important role in the creative process. It is generally assumed that the creative process starts with the creative individual and then moves to the audience or public. But the audience or public can help stimulate the creative process if the creative individual would only "listen" to its needs and desires. That more and more cognizance is being taken of this aspect of the public's role is attested to by the concern with forecasts of consumer spending (Bender, 1971), and the amount of time, effort, and money that is expended by the government, companies, economists, and market research groups to learn about consumers' attitudes and future plans (as manifest in the surveys undertaken by such organizations as the Survey Research Center at the University of Michigan).

In discussing the role and significance of the audience or public in the communication stage of the creative process we shall start by considering, only in a very brief fashion, several sociocultural factors that may affect the public's acceptance of creative works. Then because there is really no such thing as *the* public but subgroups within it, we shall turn to a consideration of both the methods used to segment the public into subgroups and the characteristics of these subgroups as they affect their receptivity to and acceptance of creative works. And finally, because subgroups within the public, as any individual, may have difficulty in accepting change and may become quite resistant to it, we shall present studies of attempts to overcome such resistances in the hope that they might stimulate additional ideas for overcoming resistance to change and creative works in areas of creative endeavor other than those considered.

Several Sociocultural Factors Affecting the Public's Acceptance of Creative Works

The audience and public are affected by a variety of sociocultural factors in its response to creativity. These very same factors also serve as part of the matrix of factors which affects the potential creativity of many individuals. It would take us too far afield to discuss all of these factors. Such a task would involve writing a social and cultural history of society. We have selected therefore only a few for comment to illustrate the various kinds of factors that are involved.

A public is responsive to and accepting of creative developments to the extent that it values change and is not afraid to depart from the status quo. Creative works deviate from that which exists. They challenge the status quo, the accepted, age-old belief systems and traditional ways of doing things. A people who are afraid of change because of the insecurities and anxieties it provokes in them, a people who are afraid of change because there are pressures to maintain traditional orientations are unlikely to accept creative works.

Economic and political conditions may so preoccupy a people that creative developments may go unnoticed. In an economic depression few, if any, funds may be available to support creative activity. In prosperous periods there may be more support for creative works. And, when there is economic inflation, there may be a distoriton of creative values so that works previously considered non-creative now become overestimated in significance. Wars may spur developments in war-related technology but inhibit or restrict creative developments in other areas. Religion may condone creativity in some areas and obstruct its development in others—witness the effects of Catholicism on church music and church art.

Whether a creative work is accepted or not by a people may be a function of the area in which the work was developed. People expect change in some areas of their lives and not in others. We may anticipate it "in our technology, in our art forms, in our women's fashions, and to some extent (slang) in our language. We do not anticipate it in our religion, in our political structure, or in our family organization [Barnett, 1953, p. 69]."

People vary in their capacity to appreciate and understand the purpose or function of many creative developments. And this lack of understanding might be attributed to the quality or breadth of the educational opportunities available to the people.

A people's time perspective—the emphasis and value they attach to the past, present, and future—will also affect how they respond to creativity. Some people are steeped in their past; they solve current problems as their forefathers did. For them tradition has the force of authority and any deviation from either tradition or authority is not permitted. Other people emphasize the present; the significant data for these people are those which occur in their own lifetimes. Finally, a third group studies history to understand it and uses the lessons it has learned from history to prepare itself for the future. Individuals in the first two types of cultures do not expect change and do not accept it even if it is forced upon them, whereas those in the third may not only anticipate change and accept it, but consider change and creativity as positive values in and of themselves.

These are some of the sociocultural factors that affect a public's acceptance of creativity. Some of them foster while others retard or prevent creative developments. Over time, they can result in an enviroment that stimulates and nourishes creative works, or they can operate actively to prohibit creative works or more silently to encourage resistances to change and creativity. Before this chapter is concluded, we shall focus on methods for overcoming such resistance to change, but before doing so let us consider the different subgroups that make up the public and discuss how these subgroups differ from each other in their attitudes towards creative developments.

Segmenting the Public

It is apparent when we speak of a public that there is no such single unit. There are subgroups within the public, each with its own characteristics and each with its own response to creative works. If the problems and difficulties in the communication stage of the creative process are to be kept to a minimum, it is important to know the characteristics of these subgroups. With such knowledge it would then be possible during the communication stage to focus attention initially on those who are expected to be most receptive to the creative work, so that the creative work "can take root." And when this happens, hopefully other subgroups, after observing the positive experiences and reactions of the first group, might then also accept and adopt the creative work.

Most of the work differentiating between subgroups in the public has been carried out by those interested in the adoption of new products or innovations that are of commercial rather than of scientific, literary, or artistic value. Some might question just how creative these works are, but even if we concur in such a questioning attitude, we should not be blinded to the possible existence of similar processes and variables with acknowledged creative works.

Four methods will be presented that have been used for segmenting the public—adopter categories, typologies, life-style, and benefit segmentation. [The first three are presented in this section, and benefit segmentation is presented in the next section (p. 312).] The first two methods involve two different statistical techniques, and the third and fourth share in a methodology that is different from the first two.

The method of adopter categories to be presented is that of Rogers (1962), some of whose other work has already been presented. Basic to Rogers' adopter categories is the normal distribution curve. In studying the rate of cultural diffusion, Rogers as well as others observed that there is at first a slow gradual rate of growth in the adoption of an innovation. This is then followed by a period of much more rapid growth, after which there is a period of decline that is more rapid at first than later on. In other words, the shape of the curve for the diffusion process is bell-shaped—the shape of the normal distribution curve.

Data for the diffusion curve, which was found to be bell-shaped, for most innovations were obtained by asking individuals to recall the date at which they purchased or adopted an innovation. The accuracy of this information is, however, sometimes open to question. Menzel (1957) in studying doctors' adoption of a new drug found that doctors' statements as to when they did adopt a new drug did not agree completely with druggists' records for when prescriptions were written. On the other hand, Havens (1962) found that farmers were accurate in reporting the dates on which they adopted bulk milk tanks. Such studies suggest the need for at least some caution in accepting the suggested shape of the curve for the diffusion process.

Nevertheless, having assumed the shape of the curve, Rogers (1962) utilized the mean and standard deviation of the normal distribution curve to differentiate between five categories of persons who made up varying proportions of the area under this curve. These subgroups of persons were named innovators, early adopters, early majority, late majority, and laggards. Since the normal curve is symmetrical, there should be an even number of categories to conform to this symmetry. Laggards could have been divided into "early laggards" and "late laggards," but Rogers points out that these two groups appear rather homogeneous, and hence there is no need for such distinction. The groups established by Rogers are not completely exhaustive since there is no category for nonadopters, and these do exist in the general population. The characteristics of these groups will be discussed shortly.

Another method for segmenting the public and for determining the different subgroups that make it up uses *Q*-factor analysis—a statistical technique for assembling persons into groups such that the members of any one group are more similar to each other than they are to members of other subgroups. Each group is then regarded as a "type" of person. This method was used by Stein (1965) in his study of personality types and by Demby and Cohen (1968) in a method they call psychographics which is oriented to elucidating the different types of consumers that exist.

The search for types of persons among consumers is a rather new development in the field of market research and consumer behavior. Prior to the inception of motivational research in the 1950's, market researchers concentrated on the percentage of the public who liked or used a product because of its taste, flavor, texture, etc. This approach was eventually supplanted by the study of demographic factors and their relationships to consumer behavior (Martineau, 1957; Warner & Lunt, 1941), and studies were conducted in which the public was segmented, for example, into lower, middle, or upper classes. The buying behavior of each of these socioeconomic subgroups or their attitudes toward different products were then studied. With such research data at hand, advertising copy directed at a specific group could then be written, and it was hoped that the copy would encourage a larger percentage of the target group to purchase the product.

In about the 1950's market researchers began to draw more heavily on psychoanalysis and dynamic psychology for theory and variables that would help explain better what was involved in consumer motivation. They also turned to the field of clinical psychology for techniques (e.g., projective techniques). This combination of theory, variables, and techniques provided market researchers with more personal information about consumers—more information about their life histories and personality characteristics—than was previously available and which could be related to their buying behavior. The next, and one of the most recent developments, is the search for subgroups of persons called types through the use of the statistical technique referred to called *Q*-factor analysis. *Q*-factor analysis in this area results in the development of a profile based on psychological variables. This profile is regarded as characterizing a group and differentiating it from other groups in the population. Because it involves a profile of interrelated psychological characteristics, this approach is regarded by its protagonists as yielding more meaningful data than previous approaches for the understanding of consumer behavior.

The third method to be described, *life-style* (Wells & Tigert, 1971), and the fourth, *benefit segmentation* (Haley, 1971), both share in a methodology that is different from the normal distribution curve used for adopter categories and the *Q*-factor technique used for types. It involves the selection of a criterion or a characteristic and then studies all of the other variables related to the selected characteristic. Thus, a relatively long questionnaire is administered to a population of respondents. Included in it are questions about the frequency with which different products are used, what the respondent likes about different products, or the benefits he has from using them, the opinions he might have on different matters, the magazines he reads, the sports he engages in, etc. The criterion or characteristic the investigator selects can be the frequency with which a product is used, or the benefits the consumer gets from using a product. In a life-style study, for example, the criterion selected may be "very frequent" use of a client's product—i.e., the investigators will select for further study those persons who say they use the client's product "very frequently" and then they may be compared with all other persons in the study—i.e., all those who use the client's product less frequently—on all the other questions in the questionnaire. After it is determined which items are answered significantly differently by one group as compared with the other, the group's responses can be integrated into a picture of its life-style. In this manner, the life-style of very frequent users can be compared with the life-style of less than very frequent users, and advertising copy can be written to reinforce the behavior of the first group or to encourage the second group to use the client's product.

In a benefit segmentation study the approach is very similar. Here, instead of frequency of usage, some benefit may be selected as a criterion and then the procedure is the same as with the life-style approach. Both life-style and benefit segmentation studies are very similar, in the structure of their methodologies, to early studies in the field of motivation research in which one would, for example, study the kinds of products used, magazines read, etc., by different socioeconomic groups.

With this information on the different methodologies and statistical techniques involved in segmentation studies in mind, let us now turn to the content of these studies with special attention to the various kinds of subgroups observed and the characteristics of these subgroups. Where research is available on subgroups involved in the creative process, it will be presented. In other instances research illustrative of the method will be presented which hopefully might stimulate use of that segmentation method for the further understanding of the creative process.

Adopter Categories

A statistical technique, the standard deviation, was used by Rogers (1962), in accord with usual practice, for dividing the area under the normal distribution curve and assigning the sections to the adopter categories. On this basis 2.5% of adopters are innovators; to the right of this group are 13.5% who are called early adopters; the next 34% are the early majority. This now brings us to the middle of the curve. The first 34% in the second half of the curve are the late majority, and the last 16% are the laggards.

On the basis of a number of studies, Rogers differentiated between various subgroups of adopters in terms of a variety of characteristics, and what follows is based on his discussion (Rogers, 1962).

(*a*) *Innovators.* The innovators are "venturesome," and in their social relationships cosmopolite. They travel in a circle of venturesomeness and spread new ideas, like circuit riders who spread the gospel. Being an innovator has several prerequisites, including control of substantial financial resources to absorb the loss resulting from an unprofitable innovation and the ability to understand and apply complex technical knowledge.

Innovators, both by definition and in terms of empirical research data, deviate from the norm. In statistical terms, they are two standard deviations away from the mean. Linton (1952), according to Rogers (1962), found them to be "misfits in their societies" and to possess "atypical personalities," and Barnett (1953) found them "truly marginal individuals." They are not necessarily perceived positively by their neighbors. A group of Ohio farmer innovators was asked how their neighbor farmers perceived them, and more than half of them said with lack of respect (Rogers, 1961b).

However, there are other data which indicate that how innovators are perceived by others is a function of the group's norm or the value it places on innovation. If the group or the system is traditional in its orientation, then innovators are not positively perceived. If the orientation is "modern," the innovator is likely to be perceived more positively.

Perceptions of innovators also vary by the respondents' own positions among the adopter categories. Earlier adopters tend to be more favorably inclined to innovators than later adopters. This may be because earlier adopters are more familiar with the innovators and more similar to them in social characteristics, and hence interact more frequently with them.

Innovators see themselves as deviant from the social system in which they live (Rogers, 1961b). With deviancy as a characteristic of the innovator, the question arises where and how the innovators obtain emotional and social support. Data cited by Rogers (1962) indicate that innovators are rather frequently cosmopolites—their reference groups are outside the community in which they live, and these groups probably supply them with much of the support they need.

(*b*) *Early adopters.* Following the innovators are the early adopters. They are more integrated into the community in which they live. While innovators are cosmopolites, early adopters are localites. They are oriented to their communities and not to outside groups. Early adopters are usually opinion leaders, since potential adopters look to them for advice and information about new products and ideas. This adopter category is generally sought by transmission change agents who want to speed up the diffusion process. Early adopters are models for others and are respected by them for their successful and discriminating use of new ideas. To maintain their positions in the community, early adopters know that they must continue to earn its respect.

(*c*) *Early majority.* The early majority, the third category of adopters, adopt new ideas before the average individual. Members of this group deliberate for a while before adopting a new idea. The time they take to deliberate is longer, obviously, than that for the two previous groups.

(*d*) *Late majority.* The late majority comes next, and its members are *skeptical*, according to Rogers. They adopt a new idea in response to social pressure and because such adoption has probably become an economic necessity.

(*e*) *Laggards.* The last group to adopt an innovation are the laggards; they are tradition bound. They are localites, oriented primarily to their local situation, and near-isolates. They are oriented to the past. By the time they get around to adopting an innovation, it probably has been superseded. They are suspicious of innovations, innovators, and transmission change agents.

The groups of adopters just considered also differ from each other in several other ways, according to Rogers (1962). For example, early adopters are younger, have higher social status, are better off financially, specialize more in their business operations, and have a different type of mental ability and flexibility than later adopters.

With regard to communication, early adopters consider impersonal sources of information more important than personal sources, and have a more favorable attitude toward cosmopolite than localite information. The opposite is true of the late adopters. Early adopters use sources of information that are closer to the origin of ideas than do late adopters, and the former also use a greater number of sources of information than do the latter (Rogers, 1962).

Personality Types

Stein used *Q*-factor analyses (Stein, 1965, 1966; Stein & Neulinger, 1968) to develop personality types where the basic data are a person's description of the hierarchy of his own psychological needs (Murray *et al.,* 1938). This method and the types it yielded were presented previously in the section on transmission agents (p. 277) where the effectiveness of Peace Corps volunteers was discussed. Both the same method and the same types (plus others) used in the Peace Corps study were used in a study of consumer behavior to investigate how types of individuals differed in their buying habits. Briefly, as a reminder, the types used were: (1) *socially oriented*—those persons who are dedicated to other people, deferent to authority, and conforming in their behavior; (2) *intellectually oriented*—members of this type are achievement oriented, likely to follow their own point of view, enjoy sensuous impressions and aesthetic feelings; (3) *action oriented*—these persons control situations, they are doers and workers; (4) *unconventional*—these people are not very discriminating in their social relationships, they do not seem to reject anyone, they accept their own impulses and see themselves as free souls who like to be seen and heard; (5) *resourceful*—members of this type are quite resilient. They are flexible and if one solution to a problem fails, they are quick to develop another.

In addition to these types, four others were included in the consumer study. They were developed after the Peace Corps study. Two types are identified only by letters, the S and T. Their psychological characteristics have not yet been completely determined. The third is the *forceful* type. Members of this type are oriented to mastery, domination, achievement, and high status. And finally, there is a ninth category, the *unclassified* persons—those who did not fit into any of the above-mentioned categories.

The self-description questionnaire used to collect the data for the personality types and a questionnaire for information on consumer behavior were both administered by interviewers on a door-to-door basis to a population of 40–49-year-old men (N=393) and women (N=397).

One question in the consumer questionnaire that is of particular interest to us was, "When a new product or a new appliance comes on the market, how soon are you, as compared to your friends and acquaintances, likely to buy it?" The respondents replied by selecting one of the following categories: (1) I am likely to be among the first 5% or 10% to buy it; (2) I am likely to buy it after about 25%; (3) or 50%; (4) or 75% of my friends have bought it; and finally, (5) I am likely to buy it after most, if not all, of my friends have bought it.

Among the 393 men it was found that the S and resourceful types said they purchased new products and appliances before 50% of their friends did, while the forceful, action oriented, and T types did not make such purchases till after at least 50% of their friends did so. The other types fell in between.

Among the women, 389 of the 397 studied responded to the same question, and among them it was found that the intellectually oriented, T, and resourceful types said they made their purchases before 50% of their friends did, whereas the forceful and unconventional types said they did so later.

The resourceful type, whether male or female, says he buys novel products *before* 50% of his friends do, and the forceful type, also whether male or female, says he buys novel products *after* 50% of his friends do. But other types show sex differences with males of one type behaving one way and females of the same type another way.

Stein's typological approach is a very new one in this area and its findings need to be replicated as well as extended to other problems—e.g., the relationship between personality types and attitudes toward various kinds of creative works; the media that different personality types read and the kinds of messages they attend to—so that the difficulties involved in getting creative works accepted by different subgroups would be diminished appreciably.

Psychographics

Another technique utilizing Q-factor analysis for the study of consumer subgroups is called psychographics, developed by Demby and Cohen (1968, 1969; Demby, 1970), president and vice-president, respectively, of Motivational Programmers, Inc., New York City. They developed this approach after questioning the use of demographic data (socioeconomic status, geographical location, etc.) in the study and prediction of consumer behavior after a period when significant changes had occurred on the socioeconomic scene in the United States. Considering income alone, Demby and Cohen (1969) point out that in 1950 only 3% of all households in the United States had incomes of $10,000 or more a year. In 1960 the figure was 14%, and in 1966 it rose to 30%. Because there are so many people with high income levels and because the purchasing behavior of people at these levels is so varied, they felt it was necessary to move "beyond demographics to find out how people live—what kind of a style of life they have adopted—because this affects the kind of products they buy and the way they respond to advertising [p. 2]."

In their study Demby and Cohen (1968) used a rather long questionnaire covering a wide array of attitudes and interests: political, economic, and social; books, newspapers, and magazines read; frequency of use and type of use made of TV and radio; drinking habits; purchases made of cosmetics and home furnishings; foods bought; etc. For additional data they also used a variety of psychological tests—including projective and self-concept tests.

The collected data were analyzed by Q-factor analytic procedures and two subgroups emerged—*creative* and *passive* consumers. They were so named on the basis of previous preliminary research in which it was found that the creative consumer not only was a heavy purchaser of new products, but also led a more outgoing and imaginative life than the passive consumer. The characteristics of each of the two groups that emerged in the larger study (Demby & Cohen, 1968) were as follows. Creative consumers buy new and interesting products and brands. They see themselves as imaginative, rather than self-controlled. They have strong interests in political and civic activities and go out a great deal to theaters and restaurants. They socialize frequently and do a lot of magazine reading but less TV viewing than the passive consumers.

Passive consumers buy fewer new products and see themselves as self-controlled rather than imaginative. They are less involved in political and civic activities and go out less often to movies and restaurants. They read fewer magazines and view more television.

The passive consumer is a less secure person than the creative one and is less likely to seek challenge. For example, when asked what they would do with an unexpected $25,000, the passive consumers said they would pay off debts, pay off mortgages, or put money in the bank. The creative consumer, on the other hand, said he would invest it.

With regard to purchasing behavior, Demby (1967) points out that the passive consumer is interested in purchasing the same kind of products the creative consumer buys. Specifically, it appears that the passive consumer has a long-time intention of purchasing new products but something always prevents him from doing so. Demby and Cohen, therefore, believe that one of the critical differences between passive and creative consumers may lie in the decision-making process of the two groups.

To check this out, Demby and Cohen asked both types of consumers whether they intended purchasing a new sports car at some time in the future, and if so, whether they intended doing so in the next three years. Among creative consumers, 87% said they expected to buy the new sports car within three years and among passive consumers, 40% said the same. But the future was more than three years away for 60% of the passives compared to less than 15% of the creatives.

The same was true for the purchase of another family car. A definite year in which they would purchase a new family car was mentioned by six out of ten creative consumers compared to four out of ten passive consumers.

Desire and purchase appear, therefore, to be correlated among creative consumers but not among passive ones. For the creative consumer there is "a time-limited future—the near future or close to the present." For the passive consumer "the future means a hazy, non-time-limited period [Demby, 1967, p. 17]."

There are therefore a number of characteristics of what Demby and Cohen have called creative and passive consumers. These characteristics are especially interesting when we recall that in the population studied by Demby and Cohen (1968), all of the individuals had incomes of $10,000 or more and that 64% were passive consumers and 36% were creative consumers. The cluster of characteristics that makes up both subgroups needs to be cross-validated and re-checked. Specifically, to answer the possible criticism of circularity in reasoning, the questionnaire should be administered to new populations and new groups of creative and passive consumers established. Then a follow-up of these groups should be made to learn if they do indeed purchase new products that were not on the market at the time they were assigned to their consumer subgroups. It would also be especially interesting to learn if subgroups already established by Demby and Cohen do, over a period of time, continue to purchase new products. If it is found that they do, segmentation in terms of psychographics may be of much value to anyone involved in the production and marketing of new products.

Life-Style

This approach was employed by Wells and Tigert (1971) with a questionnaire containing questions about a number of products plus questions about the frequency (on a seven-point scale) with which these products were used. Demographic questions as well as 300 questions having to do with respondents' interests, opinions, and activities, covering such areas as media used, art, clothes, cosmetics, homemaking, and other matters of general interest were also included. To develop life-style data they separated their respondents into two groups on the basis of the frequency with which they used a product. One group was on the very frequent user side, and the other hardly ever used the same product.

To illustrate what a life-style picture is, consider one of the products discussed by Wells and Tigert—eye makeup. Looking at how more frequent users of eye makeup differed from less frequent users, it was learned that: According to the demographic data, the more frequent eye makeup users were young, well educated, and lived in metropolitan areas. Working wives used eye makeup more frequently than did full-time homemakers, and use was higher in the West than in other parts of the country. More frequent eye makeup users were also heavy users of other cosmetics: hair spray, perfume, nail polish, etc. They were also above-average cigarette smokers and above-average users of gasoline and of the telephone for long distance use.

Answers to the activity, interest, and opinion questions disclosed a more complete picture. The more frequent eye makeup user was more interested in fashion, being attractive to men, and more meticulous about her person; she was not interested in housekeeping, rejected traditional ideas but accepted contemporary ones. In all these ways, the more frequent eye makeup user differed from the less frequent user.

The foregoing description stands out better as we consider another product and its life-style concomitants. The product is shortening. Compared with the heavy eye makeup user, the heavy shortening user was not as young, had a larger family, was less likely to have an outside job, and lived in the South. These women were not heavy users of eye makeup or other cosmetics but they were heavy users of flour, sugar, laundry detergent, canned vegetables, mustard, catsup, and the like. On the opinion, interest, and activity questionnaire, none of the items that correlated with eye makeup use correlated with the use of shortening.

After life-style data are collected they can be used as a basis for writing advertising copy. Life-style data, like other segmentation procedures, provide a basis for developing a picture of the group of people—the target group—that the client wants to reach. With this picture in mind, more effective copy can be written than is possible under usual circumstances because more concrete information is available about the target group.

Life-style data according to Wells and Tigert can prevent making mistakes in advertising copy. They tell of an instance where, because a product was new, it was planned to advertise it in the context of a theme representing the 21st century. When life-style data were collected, this plan had to be discarded. Potential customers, the life-style data indicated, were not interested in science, fantasy, or the future.

The purpose of all segmentation studies, then, is to provide better understanding of the subgroups of the audience involved so that communication can be more effective with them. The more one knows about a subgroup, the easier it should be to make contact with and to communicate with them. It is obvious that not all segmentation techniques have been used the study of novelty, but it is equally obvious that, by the addition of appropriate questions, data could be collected and then analyzed so that the attitudes of different subgroups toward creative works could be ascertained and more effective communications established with them. It is equally apparent that for subgroups not attracted to creative works, one might study specifically why this is so and why the subgroups are so resistant to change. With this knowledge steps might be taken to implement possible change. Some help in this regard may be obtained from the studies that follow.

OVERCOMING RESISTANCE TO CHANGE

In previous sections of this chapter attention was focused on the different kinds of individuals and processes involved in the communication stage of the creative process in the hope that, by making their roles and functions salient, and by providing some suggestions for dealing with them, creative persons might be better able to fulfill the requirements of this stage. By virtue of the fact that creative persons would then encounter fewer problems and obstacles in their work, and by virtue of the fact that intermediaries and the public would have been satisfied with the communications they received, a more positive atmosphere for creativity would exist which would provide continued opportunity for future creative developments.

The theme of previous sections in this chapter is that creativity may suffer from lack of stimulation because various people are ignorant of the different factors involved in the communication stage of the creative process. There is at least one other obstacle to creative works in the communication stage that needs to be mentioned—the resistance of intermediaries, the audience, or public to change. Some persons, when they are presented with creative works, novel ways of doing things, or novel ways of thinking about or perceiving their worlds or environments, refuse to adopt these novel products or approaches and persist in their old ways. Under such circumstances it would appear that the message—that is, the creative work—is simply not getting through to some larger segments of the public because of resistances. The reasons for the resistance may be varied. Resisting groups may well have been so saturated with all kinds of novelty that they refuse anything new; they may be anxious about change; they may be ignorant about a creative development; and, indeed, they may also have been so bombarded with advertising that tries to persuade them to buy a product that they develop "perceptual screens" (Haley, 1971) to make them impervious to such advertising. With regard to this last point, Haley reports the experience of an advertising agency that showed a film to a group of people who thought their only task was to evaluate the film. Embedded in the film, however, were three commercials that the investigator wanted the group members to evaluate. One day after the group viewed the film, its members were contacted and asked if there were any commercials in the film. Over a third, using perceptual screens, according to Haley, said, "No."

Perceptual screens against advertising may be on the increase. Haley (1971) reports that, using copy-testing data "based on an averaging of year-to-year rates of change for clients for whom the same brand had been tested on a number of occasions in each of two successive years [p. 5] ," and with data for 1960 serving as a base equal to 100, two measures of advertising effectiveness—recall and attitude change—both fell. The former fell to 52% and the latter to 0%.

Meyer (1970) in a study cited by Haley believes that such a drop might be accounted for by clutter in advertising, people getting bored with television, increased time spent on commercials, restrictions on the kind of copy used, "more advertising messages per capita," and the increase in number of advertisers and products advertised.

Just as people develop perceptual screens to advertising, so they can develop perceptual screens to creativity. As we said previously, they may be anxious about change or ignorant about what is involved in the utilization of a creative work. Some persons may even develop a resistance to producing anything new because it may mean expending additional effort to establish the new change. In one Research and Development organization we studied, we found that the group of research men who had been acknowledged as more creative than others was also not liked very much by their colleagues because they always tried to develop something new. Why did they do this, we were asked, because they only upset the apple cart. Didn't they know the company was making profits and that everyone was having a comfortable time? If the more creative men developed something new then their less creative colleagues had to "re-tool" and work harder.

Whatever the reason for the resistance, if change is to occur and creative works are to be accepted, then the resistance must be made salient and dealt with or else no change, no forward movement is possible. In what follows we shall discuss the use of benefit segmentation in the field of market research as a means of overcoming the effects of perceptual screens in the field of advertising. Then we shall turn to some classic studies in the field of social psychology that were specifically designed to overcome resistances to change.

Benefit Segmentation

To see if he could pierce existing perceptual barriers in the field of advertising, Haley (1971) undertook a series of laboratory and nonlaboratory studies based on benefit segmentation. Benefit segmentation is a technique that focuses on the benefits that people say they derive from using a product. A questionnaire is composed consisting of different benefits and people are asked which reflects their experience. Different subgroups can then be identified based on the kind of benefits that they have in common. Thus, one group of persons might say that use of a product improves their appearance, helps them make social contacts with others, etc. Another subgroup might say that use of the same product makes them feel personally more comfortable, they feel they have a better attitude toward themselves, etc. These different benefit profiles or constellations would lead to different advertising copy. Then to test whether an advertisement was getting through existing perceptual screens it could be presented to various groups, and especially a target group for whom the message was written specifically. One measure of effectiveness of the advertisement would be the extent to which it was recalled by different subgroups after they were exposed to it. Hence, if an advertisement based on benefit segmentation were presented to a target group, it would be expected that this group would recall the advertisement better or that the advertisement would have more attention value for this group than for other subgroups who did not receive the same benefits from the product. If this were so, then it would mean that the message was getting through, that the target audience was not blocking or screening out the message.

In one laboratory study Haley reports that a segment or subgroup of the population was first identified and then six advertisements with alternative themes were presented to it. One of the six ads was designed to focus on the benefits desired by the population segment, in this case, concern for their children's welfare. Testing the ads under laboratory conditions, it was found that the one with the child-oriented theme had an attention value score of 205. The next closest had a score of 103 and the lowest score in the group was 64.

Another example is a nonlaboratory instance in which effects of an advertising campaign on a fashion-oriented population were studied. Within this group a segment was selected as a target for an advertisement. The effects of the advertisement were measured by studying "top-of-mind awareness" of the client's brand and the industry leader, for both the target segment and other segments, before exposure to the ad and again after exposure.

The results of this study indicated that among the people in the target segment, awareness of the target brand increased from a score of 77 to 86, whereas among other segments it dropped slightly from a score of 67 to 66.

One of the elements involved in the effectiveness of a benefit segmentation study is the ability to generate a number of benefits that are appropriate to a product. Indeed, when a product is already on the market and numerous individuals have had an opportunity to use it, awareness of the kinds of benefits possible can be extensive; respondents can be equally aware of which benefits they do or do not associate with a product.

With a new product, however, this matter of highlighting appropriate benefits may not be as simple as it is with existing products. However, if careful checks and balances are provided for, appropriate corrections can be made. Haley discusses an experience that falls into this category. A new product was to be introduced into the market. On the basis of previous consumer research studies, one segment was selected as the target segment, and effectiveness of the advertising was tracked for both the market segment and the nonmarket segment. Preliminary results of this study indicated that *attention* scores were indeed highest for the market segment. The ad was reaching its target. However, when the criterion was *actual product purchase,* it was found that another segment of the population, not the target segment, bought at the highest rate "because of some specific product advantage which hadn't been fully appreciated until sales began to develop in unexpected ways [p. 8] ."

Two factors need to be underscored in the study just presented. First, as indicated previously, when new products are considered, we must be aware that all possible benefits may not be known. Second, we must be aware of the differences between such variables as attention value and actual purchase of a new product. Both attention value and actual purchase are not necessarily correlated for existing products, so they may not be for new products. If nothing else, if the product is really new, people will not have had a chance to learn of its values and uses. This is not a determining limitation, for (as in the Haley study just reported) if the effectiveness of the advertising campaign is followed up, such omissions can be rectified.

Benefit segmentation is only one of the audience or public segmentation techniques that may be used to determine which subgroups exist in the larger population that may be particularly acceptant of a creative work or who might be particularly resistant to it. Three of these other techniques were discussed previously—adopter categories (page 304), typologies (page 305), and life-style (page 307). Still another approach to overcoming resistance to change involves participation.

Social Psychological Studies of Group Participation in Making for Change

Lewin, the social psychologist, his students, and those he influenced under-took several studies designed to study the most effective ways through which groups of individuals can arrive at and accept change. The studies are by now classics in the field. They were carried out during World War II to investigate the possibility of changing housewives' meat-buying habits. The housewife was selected as the person to be changed because, if she could be changed, then through her the eating habits of the rest of the family could be changed. The housewife was the change agent, or "gatekeeper" in Lewin's terminology. Speci-fically, the goal was to get housewives to increase their use of beef hearts, sweetbreads, and kidneys.

One study by Lewin and his co-workers (Lewin, 1958) concerned the relative effectiveness of lectures and group discussions in achieving the desired change. The women participating in the study were Red Cross volunteers who partici-pated in a program of home nursing. Three groups of them listened to lectures for 45 minutes, and three groups participated in group discussions.

The (female) lecturers linked nutrition to the war effort and emphasized the vitamin and mineral value of the three meats that it was hoped the housewives would buy. The lectures were made interesting, and charts were used for illustra-tive purposes. Stress was placed on the health and economic aspects of the meats and means of preparing them so that the consumers would not be negatively affected by the meats' odor, texture, or appearance. Recipes were distributed. The lecturer also presented her own hints for preparing the various new foods and described her own success in serving them.

The other three groups were led by a male, who started the group discussion by linking nutrition to the war and general health. Then a discussion was begun to determine whether the housewives' attitudes and behavior could be changed. The discussion revolved about "housewives like themselves" and the problems they might encounter in trying to change. As with the lecture groups, recipes and solutions to problems were offered by the nutrition expert. But in this case, the recipes and solutions were offered only after the groups became so involved in the discussion that they wanted to know that they could actually do.

Prior to the group discussions and lecture sessions, which were the experi-mental variables, the women were asked how many of them had ever previously served beef hearts, sweetbreads, and kidneys. Then at the end of the sessions, to test the effects of the experimental variables, the women were asked to indicate, by a show of hands, how many of them were willing to try one of the meats within the next week. In the group discussion period the women were told that there would be a checkup on what they did. Women in the lecture sessions were not told this.

When the follow-up was conducted, it was found that among the women who heard the lectures, only 3% tried one of the foods they had never tried before.

On the other hand, among those who participated in the group discussions, 32% had done so.

These results are quite impressive, but there are a number of aspects in which the experiment was not clear-cut and which required further elaboration and clarification in other studies. One such study, conducted by Radke and Klisurich (1947), also compared the group process with the lecture method, but in addition it controlled for the possible effects of the leader's personality by holding this factor constant in both conditions. In this study the goal was to increase home consumption of milk, whether fresh or evaporated.

Again, there was group discussion that focused on "what housewives in general might do" and the lecture was kept "interesting." The same information was transmitted in both situations and a checkup of the milk-buying behavior of all the individuals studied was conducted two weeks and four weeks after their participation in the study.

The following results were obtained. (1) The group discussion meetings were more effective than the lectures. (2) The results were not affected by the personality or training of the leader, since the same leader was used in both lectures and discussions. (3) Since milk was involved in this study and meat in the previous one, the effectiveness of the group discussion procedure was not influenced by the type of food involved. (4) The effects were found to last a while—the greater effectiveness of the group procedure over the lecture method was observable after two and four weeks. (5) There was some concern that in the previous study (the one involving meat) the effects might be attributed to the fact that the women in the group discussion procedure knew that they would be contacted during the follow-up period. The same was true in this experiment, but after the second week, neither the discussion nor the lecture groups knew that there would be another check on their behavior. Still the group discussion procedure maintained its effectiveness. (6) The women in the second study were not part of a closely knit group, as were those in the first study who met periodically in Red Cross meetings. Thus, group meetings are effective regardless of how well organized the individual participants were.

In still another study by Radke and Klisurich (1947) a comparison was made between the effectiveness of group procedures and individual instruction in getting mothers, after having their first child, to give their children orange juice and cod liver oil. During the individual instruction period, which lasted from 20 to 25 minutes, the mother met with a nutritionist and was instructed in the importance of orange juice and cod liver oil. For the group procedure the mothers were divided into groups of six and the process was the same as that used with the groups in the previous studies.

A check was made after two weeks and after four weeks to determine whether the mother had followed the advice she had been given. The results of this experiment were as follows:

(1)   The group procedure was again more effective than the individual instruction period. The effectiveness for both procedures varied with whether cod liver oil or orange juice was involved. For cod liver oil, after two weeks between 40% and 50% of the group-process mothers gave their children cod liver oil, but among those who had individual instruction, only from 10% to 20% did so. After four weeks between 80% and 90% of the group-process and 50% to 60% of the individual-instruction mothers gave their children cod liver oil.

For orange juice, after two weeks from 80% to 90% of the mothers in the group process, and 30% to 40% in the individual-instruction procedure, gave their children orange juice, but after four weeks all of the mothers (100%) in the group process and between 50% and 60% of the individual-instruction mothers gave their children orange juice.

(2)   The group procedure in the previous study (Radke and Klisurich, 1947) had been shown to be effective with groups that were not well established. In this experiment, we find that the group experience was effective with mothers who had no contact with one another prior to the group experience and no contact after the experience.

(3)   Comparing the effects of lecture and group discussions on all foods involved, Lewin (1958) points out that lectures produce less change than group discussion. However, the rank order of the percentage of change for different foods after lectures follows the rank order after group discussion, namely (from low to high), glandular meat, fresh milk, cod liver oil for the baby, evaporated milk, orange juice for the baby. "Each of these foods—under the given circumstances and for these particular populations—[had] a specific degree of 'resistance to change' [p. 207]."

The last study to be considered in this area is one conducted by Bennett (1955). In it, four factors were isolated as critical to the obtained results: group discussion; the effects of decision to perform an action; the individual's commitment to "the degree to which the decision is indicated publicly [quoted in Maccoby *et al.*, 1958, p. 213]"; and the consensus in the group in arriving at the decision. In addition, this study included a more objective measure of whether an individual actually took the action he said he would. It did not concern itself with the effects of a specific time limit or the effects of knowing that the experimenter would conduct a follow-up study.

The goal of this study was to get beginning psychology students to volunteer as subjects in behavioral science experiments. Toward this goal 36 groups of 8-16 students each were studied under various experimental conditions. The possible effects of the group leaders or lecturers were held constant, for the same leaders participated in all major experimental conditions. In each of the experimental conditions the students were invited several days after the experiment to appear at a certain place during a specified time interval and to make their names, phone numbers, etc., available to experimenters. Students who did so were regarded as having taken action. Then, one week after they had had the opportunity to volunteer, the students were given a questionnaire and asked (a) such questions as whether they had decided to volunteer for the psychological experiments and (b) to estimate how many in their group had also signed up to do so.

The results of this study were as follows:

(1) There were no differences between the discussion, lecture, and a "no attempt to influence" variable in the proportion of students who signed up to be volunteers. A study of the discrepancy between the proportion of students who *did* volunteer and the proportion who *said* they did (which was lower in all three conditions), revealed that the greatest discrepancy was in the group discussion condition and the smallest in the control condition.

(2) When students were asked to make a decision to participate in an experiment, a larger proportion did so than was the case if they had not been asked to make a decision.

(3) Further, some subjects who were asked to make a decision to volunteer did decide not to volunteer. None of these students changed his mind.

Thus, considering points (2) and (3) together, it was found that "coming to a decision on future action" raised the "probability that such a decision would be executed [Bennett, 1955, quoted in Maccoby *et al.*, 1958, p. 215]."

(4) A more public commitment to an action was no more effective than a less public one.

(5) In each group where individuals were asked to make a decision, the proportion of those deciding favorably was calculated, and the groups were separated into high and low groups on the basis of "objective consensus." For each high and low group the proportion of those taking action was calculated. It was found that a higher proportion of those in the high groups tended to take action, but not significantly more so, than those in the low groups.

(6) A second measure of consensus was also employed—individuals' perceptions of whether a consensus existed or not. This was in contrast to the objective consensus just reported. The subjective measure of the consensus was obtained by asking each student after the experiment to estimate how many in his group signed up. Objective and subjective estimates were related significantly.

A test was then made of the effects of perceived consensus on an individual's tendency to act. It was found that when the request for a decision yielded a high proportion of positive decisions, the students carried out the action or reported having done so—only 10 students who *said* they had signed up had actually *not* done so. A large proportion of these came from groups that had a high objective consensus.

In short, this study disclosed that group discussion by itself as a means of influencing public commitment was not found to be crucial for the obtained results. However, a combination of the process of making a decision and the extent to which group consensus in the decision was actually obtained or perceived was the crucial factor. In other words, where a group makes a decision about individual goals, and where it is perceived that the group actually shares a norm, under those conditions, there is influence of "group decision" on the behavior of the group members.

There is still another study (Coch & French, 1948), much too long to cite at length, in which management and labor in a pajama factory worked together to overcome group resistance to change in methods of work and the piece rates involved. Change was achieved through the use of group meetings, at which management communicated the need for change. The group participated actively in planning the changes that would be involved in their work. Not only did the workers make important changes in their methods of work, but participation in effecting these changes also resulted in high production, higher morale, and better labor–management relations.

The difference between the studies just cited on overcoming the resistance to change and the material presented earlier (on the mass media and other communication or critical individuals involved in the communication process) is that in all of the latter communication procedures the individual's participation is held to a minimum. Indeed, the public's role in most of the communication procedures is very much like what it is in the lecture parts of the studies just described: essentially passive, with the individual limited to what the media wish to communicate. In studies oriented to overcoming resistance to change, the individuals participate actively and feel they have a significant role to play. Is it not conceivable that some such procedure if used with creative works might do much to reduce the time involved in their adoption and possibly also increase the number of individuals who make up the early adopter categories? One of the most immediate criticisms of this approach is that it might be costly in time and money. This may be so. But would they be so costly if the works were accepted and adopted rather than not? Is not the time, effort, and money involved in these works lost when they are not adopted? The crucial question is, in a sense, whether more people would not adopt creative works and establish a better environment for creativity if they were allowed to participate as partners in the communication stage of the creative process than if they were limited to being lectured to—passive participation.

SUMMARY

In this chapter attention was focused on the different kinds of intermediaries who play critical roles in the communication stage of the creative process, the flow of the communication process, characteristics of media and messages that need to be considered for effective communication, and the adoption process and characteristics of persons who are differentially responsive to creative works. Our intention was to make salient both the persons and processes involved so that the creative person will be aware of what confronts him as he presents his works to others. Lack of knowledge in this area and lack of knowledge of the resistances that might be involved and means of overcoming them can only result in wasting creative energies, in frustrations for the creative individual and in irritations for the misused intermediaries, audience, or public. On the other hand, knowledge of others who are involved in the communication stage and what processes they may go through in the adoption of a creative work may not only free the creative person from difficulties and problems, but also make the audience or public receptive to current creative works and encourage them to develop a positive environment for future creative works.

Author's Note

Close to the time when this chapter was nearing completion, we became aware of the fact that there was a second edition of Rogers (1962) *Diffusion of Innovations:* Rogers and Shoemaker (1971) *Communication of Innovations.* Try as we might we could not obtain a copy of the more recent work before this chapter was set in type. When we did obtain a copy and when we compared the two editions we found that there were some differences, although not very critical, between the two on several of the points for which the first edition served as the source for the material in this book. Two of them do require specific mention; in addition we do want to call attention to the second edition and recommend it most highly for those interested in this area.

Characteristics of Innovation*

In 1962 Rogers used the following terms to characterize the factors that affect an innovation's diffusion: Relative advantage, compatibility, complexity, divisibility, and communicability.

In the 1971 edition the first three terms are the same. But there are substitutes for the fourth and fifth terms—*trialibility* and *observability,* respectively. Rogers and Shoemaker (1971, p. 23) regard trialibility as implying "a somewhat broader meaning" than does divisibility. The new term also includes "the notion of psychological trial." The new term "observability" is regarded as "more precise" [Rogers and Shoemaker, 1971; p. 23] than the older term, communicability.

In the new edition the characteristics of the innovation are discussed at length in Chapter 4, pp. 137-157.

---

*Discussed on pages 295–297 of this volume.

The Adoption Process*

In the 1962 edition Rogers used the following steps for the adoption process: awareness, interest, evaluation, trial, and adoption. In the 1971 (Rogers and Shoemaker, p. 25) edition these five steps were shortened to four steps or functions as follows: (1) *"knowledge function"* which refers to a person's exposure to and understanding of an innovation; (2) *"persuasion function"* which refers to a person's attitude (positive or negative) to the innovation; (3) *"decision function"* which refers to a person's engaging in activities that led to the adoption or rejection of an innovation; and (4) *"confirmation function"* which refers to the reinforcement a person seeks for his decision. If he receives a conflicting message he may reverse a previous positive decision.

The adoption process is discussed by Rogers and Shoemaker (1971) at length on pp. 100–115.

*Discussed on pages 290–291 of this volume.

References

Numbers in brackets indicate chapters in which references are cited.

Adamson, R. E. Functional fixedness as related to problem solving. *Journal of Experimental Psychology*, **44**, 288-291.

Adler, D. An analysis of quality in the associated public school systems through a study of the patterns of diffusion of selected educational practices. Unpublished doctoral dissertation, Columbia University, Teachers College, New York, 1955. [11]

Aldrich, C. K. The effect of a synthetic marihuana-like compound on musical talent as measured by the Seashore Test. *Public Health Reports, 1944,* **59**, 431-433. [7]

Allen, M. S. *Morphological creativity*. Englewood Cliffs, New Jersey: Prentice-Hall, 1962. (a) [9]

Allen, M. S. *The Allen Morphologizer*. Englewood Cliffs, New Jersey: Prentice-Hall, 1962. (b) [9]

Allport, G. W., Vernon, P. E., & Lindzey, G. *Study of Values* (Rev. ed.). Boston, Massachusetts: Houghton, 1951. [10]

American Medical Association. Council on Mental Health and Committee on Alcoholism and Drug Dependence. "Dependence on Cannabis (Marihuana)." *Journal of the American Medical Association*, 1967, **201**, 368-371. [7]

Anonymous. The effects of marijuana on consciousness. In C. T. Tart (Ed.), *Altered states of consciousness*. New York: Wiley, 1969. [7]

Barber, T. The effects of "hypnosis" on learning and recall: A methodological critique. *Journal of Clinical Psychology*, 1965, **21**, 19-25. [5]

Barber, T., & Calverley, D. Toward a theory of "hypnotic" behavior. *Archives of General Psychiatry*, 1964, **10**, 209-216. [5]

321

Barkan, M. T. *Through art to creativity*. Rockleigh, New Jersey: Allyn and Bacon, 1960. [8]

Barnett, H. G. *Innovation: The basis of cultural change*. New York: McGraw-Hill, 1953. [11]

Barron, F. Threshold for the perception of human movement in inkblots. *Journal of Consulting Psychology*, 1955, **19**, 33-38. [4]

Barron, F. Originality in relation to personality and intellect. *Journal of Personality*, 1957, **25**, 730-742. [4]

Barron, F. The needs for order and for disorder as motives in creative activity. In C. W. Taylor (Ed.), *The 1957 research conference on the identification of creative scientific talent*. Salt Lake City: Univ. of Utah Press, 1958. [4, 10]

Barron, F. Creative vision and expression in writing and painting. In *Proceedings of "The creative person."* Conference presented at The Tahoe Alumni Center, October 13-17, 1968. Berkeley: University of California, Institute of Personality Assessment and Research and Liberal Arts Department. [5, 7]

Barron, F., & Leary, T. *To find and foster creativity*. A report of the Rhode Island School of Design. Providence, Rhode Island: 1961. [5]

Barron, F., Jarvik, M. E., & Bunnell, S., Jr. The hallucinogenic drugs. *Scientific American*, April 1964, **210**, 29-37. [7]

Barzun, J. Each age picks its literary greats. *The New York Times Book Review*, March 6, 1955. [11]

Beal, G. M., & Rogers, E. M. Informational sources in the adoption process of new fabrics. *Journal of Home Economics*, 1957, **49**, 630-634. [11]

Beal, G. M., & Rogers, E. M. *The adoption of two farm practices in a Central Iowa community*. Ames: Iowa Agricultural and Home Economics Experiment Station Special Report 26, 1960. [11]

Behrman, S. N. The days of Duveen. *The New Yorker*, 1951, **27**, 33-55; Published as *Duveen*. New York: Random House, 1952. [11]

Bender, M. Market research: Specialists moving to the fore. *The New York Times*, August 29, 1971, Section 3, Pg. 1. [11]

Bennett, E. B. Discussion, decision, commitment and consensus in "group dicision." *Human Relations*, 1955, **8**, 251-274. [11]

Berlin, L., Guthrie, T., Weider, A., Goodell, H., & Wolff, H. Studies in human cerebral function: The effects of mescaline and lysergic acid on cerebral process pertinent to creative activity. *Journal of Nervous Mental Disorders*, 1955, **122**, 487-491. [7]

Bertalanffy, L. von. *General system theory*. New York: George Braziller, 1968. [10]

Birch, H. G. The role of motivational factors in insightful problem solving. *Journal of Comparative and Physiological Psychology*, 1945, **38**, 295-317. [10]

Blatt, S. J. Experimental evidence of preconscious functioning in efficient problem solving. Paper presented at the Eastern Psychological Association meetings, New York, 1960. [10]

Blatt, S. J. Patterns of cardiac arousal during complex mental activity. *Journal of Abnormal and Social Psychology*, 1961, **63**, 272-282. [10]

Blatt, S. J. An attempt to define mental health. *Journal of Consulting Psychology*, 1964, **28**, 146-153. [4]

Blatt, S. J., & Stein, M. I. Some personality, value, and cognitive characteristics of the creative person. *American Psychologist*, 1957, **12**, 406. (Abstract) [4, 10]

Blatt, S. J., & Stein, M. I. Efficiency in problem solving. *Journal of Psychology*, 1959, **48**, 193-213. [10]

Bloom, B. S. Report on creativity research at the University of Chicago. In C. W. Taylor (Ed.), *The 1955 University of Utah research conference on the identification of creative scientific talent*. Salt Lake City: Univ. of Utah Press, 1956. [4]

Bloomquist, E. R. *Marijuana*. Beverly Hills, California: Glencoe Press, 1968. [7]
Bonnardel, R., & Lavoegie, M. S. Recherche sur la caractérisation des chercheurs scienti-fiques. *Journal de Psychologie Normale et Pathologique*, 1965, **62**, 333-349. [10]
Bonnardel, R., & Lavoegie, M. S. Préférences et attitudes de divers groupes de chercheurs relativement aux differents aspects et activites des travaux de recherche. *Le Travail Humain*, 1966, **29**, 199-223. [10]
Bowers, P. G. Effect of hypnosis and suggestions of reduced defensiveness on creativity test performance. Unpublished doctoral dissertation, University of Wisconsin, 1965.
[5]
Bowers, P. G. Effect of hypnosis and suggestions of reduced defensiveness on creativity test performance. *Journal of Personality*, 1967, **35**, 311-322. [5]
Brandwein, P. F. *The gifted student as future scientist*. New York: Harcourt, 1955. [8]
Brill, A. A. (Ed.). *The basic writings of Sigmund Freud*. New York: Random House, 1938. [2]
Brill, N. Q., Crumpton, E., & Grayson, H. M. Personality factors in marihuana use. *Archives of General Psychiatry*, 1971, **24**, 163-165. [7]
Brown, G. I. A second study in the teaching of creativity. *Harvard Educational Review*, 1965, **35**, 39-54. [5]
Bruner, J. S. The conditions of creativity. In H. E. Gruber, G. Terrell, & M. Wertheimer (Eds.), *Contemporary approaches to creative thinking*. New York: Atherton Press, 1962. [2]
Bruner, J. S. *The process of education*. New York: Vantage Books, 1963. [9]
Buhl, H. R. *Understanding the creative engineer*. New York: American Society of Mechanical Engineers, 1961. [8]
Burroughs, W. Points of distinction between sedative and consciousness-expanding drugs. *Evergreen Review*, December 1964. [7]
Castle, C. S. A statistical study of eminent women. *Columbia University contributions to philosophy and psychology*, Vol. 22, No. 1. New York: Science Press, 1913. [3]
Cattell, J. McK. A statistical study of eminent men. *Popular Science Monthly*, 1903, **62**, 359-377. [3]
Cattell, J. McK. A statistical study of American men of science: The selection of a group of one thousand scientific men. *Science*, New Series, 1906, **24**, 658-665. [3]
Cattell, R. B., & Drevdahl, J. E. A comparison of the personality profile (16 P.F.) of eminent researchers with that of eminent teachers and administrators, and of the general population. *British Journal of Psychology*, 1955, **46**, 248-261. [4]
Chein, I. Psychological functions of drug use. Paper presented at a *Symposium on the Scientific Basis of Drug Dependence*, under the auspices of the Biological Council Coordinating Committee for Symposia on Drug Action. London: April 8-9, 1968.
[7]
Clark, C. H. *Brainstorming*. Garden City, New York: Doubleday, 1958. [9]
Coch, L., & French, J. R. P., Jr. Overcoming resistance to change. *Human Relations*, 1948, **1**, 512-532. [11]
Cohen, S. *The beyond within: The LSD story*. New York: Atheneum, 1964. [7]
Coleman, J., Katz, E., & Menzel, H. The diffusion of an innovation. *Sociometry*, 1957, **20**, 253-270. [11]
Coleridge, S. T. Prefatory note to Kubla Khan. In B. Ghiselin, *The creative process*. Berkeley: Univ. of California Press, 1952. [2]
Cooper, L., & Erickson, M. *Time distortion in hypnosis: An experimental and clincial investigation*. Baltimore, Maryland: Williams & Wilkins, 1954. [5]
Covington, M. V. A childhood attitude inventory for problem solving. *Journal of Educational Measurement*, 1966, **3**, 234. [8]

Covington, M. V. Promoting creative thinking in the classroom. *Journal of Experimental Education*, 1968, **37**, (No. 1), 22-30. [8]

Covington, M. V. Personal communication, 1969. [8]

Covington, M. V., & Crutchfield, R. S. Facilitation of creative problem solving. *Programmed Instruction*, 1965, **4**, 3-5; 10. [8]

Covington, M. V., Crutchfield, R. S., & Davies, L. B. *The productive thinking program.* Series One: General problem solving. Berkeley, California: Brazelton Printing Co., 1966. [8]

Cramer, P. *Word association.* New York: Academic Press, 1968. [6]

Crawford, R. P. *How to get ideas.* Lincoln, Nebraska: University Associates, 1950. [9]

Crawford, R. P. *Techniques of creative thinking.* New York: Hawthorn, 1954. [9]

Crutchfield, R. S., & Covington, M. V. Programmed instruction and creativity. *Programmed Instruction*, 1965, **4**, 1-2; 9-10. [8]

Dahlberg, E. Dahlberg on Dreiser, Anderson and Dahlberg. *The New York Times Book Review*, January 31, 1971. [11]

DeBono, E. *New think.* New York: Basic Books, 1967. [9]

DeHaan, R. F., & Havighurst, R. J. *Educating gifted children.* Chicago: Univ. of Chicago Press, 1957. [8]

Deikman, C. J. Experimental meditation. In C. T. Tart (Ed.), *Altered states of consciousness.* New York: Wiley, 1969. [7]

Demby, E. H. Going beyond the demographics to find the creative consumer. A Motivational Programmers, Inc. Project presented to the Market Research Section, American Marketing Association, June 15, 1967. [11]

Demby, E. H. Psychographics: Who, what, why, when, where & how. Paper read at Third Annual Attitude Research Conference, American Marketing Association, Mexico City, March 3, 1970. [11]

Demby, E., & Cohen, L. The creative consumer: A report on Psychographics. Paper delivered to Market Research Section, American Marketing Association, November 7, 1968. [11]

Demby, E., & Cohen, L. Consumer life style more vital to marketing than income level. *Direct Marketing*, June 1969. [11]

Dichter, E. How word-of-mouth advertising works. *Harvard Business Review*, November-December 1966, 147-166. [11]

Drevdahl, J. E. Factors of importance for creativity. *Journal of Clinical Psychology*, 1956, **12**, 21-26. [4]

Drews, E. M. A critical evaluation of approaches to the identification of gifted students. In A. Traxler (Ed.), *Measurement and evaluation in today's schools.* Washington, D. C.: American Council on Education, 1961. [8]

Duncker, K. On problem solving. (Translated by L. S. Lees). *Psychological Monographs*, 1945, **58**, No. 5. [10]

Ellis, W. D. The man who said he invented the automobile. *True's Automobile Yearbook*, 1954, 3. [11]

Emery, F. E., & Oeser, O. A. *Information, decision and action: A study of the psychological determinants of changes in farming techniques.* New York: Cambridge University Press, 1958. [11]

Erickson, M. H. A special inquiry with Aldous Huxley into the nature and character of various states of consciousness. In C. T. Tart (Ed.), *Altered states of consciousness.* New York: Wiley, 1969; originally published in American Journal of Clinical Hypnosis, 1965, 8, 17-33. [7]

Erikson, E. H. *Childhood and society*, (2nd ed.) New York: Norton, 1963. [5]

Evans, W. D. & Smith, R. P. Some effects of morphine and amphetamine on intellectual functions and mood. *Psychopharmacology*, 1964, **6**, 49-56. [7]

Fearing, F. An examination of the conceptions of Benjamin Whorf in the light of theories of perception and cognition. In H. Hoijer (Ed.), *Language in culture*. Chicago, Illinois: Univ. of Chicago Press, 1954. [6]

Ferber, R., & Wales, H. G. *The effectiveness of pharmaceutical promotion*. Urbana: Univ. of Illinois, 1958. [11]

Foley, C. The legend of Rachmaninoff. *Music Guide*, 1963. [5]

Freeman, H. J. The development of a test for the measure of anxiety: A study of its reliability and validity. *Psychological Monographs*, 1953, **67**, No. 3. [10]

Freeman, L. *Farewell to fear*. New York: Ballantine Books, 1969. [5]

Freeman, L. (Ed.) *Celebrities on the couch*. New York: Pocket Books, 1971. [5]

Freud, S. Preface. In T. Reik (Ed.), *Ritual: Psycho-analytic studies*. London: Hogarth Press, 1931. [2]

Freud, S. *Leonardo da Vinci*. (Translated by A. A. Brill) London: Routledge & Kegan, 1948. [3]

Freud, S. *The origins of psycho-analysis*. (Translated by E. Mosbacher & J. Strachey) New York: Basic Books, 1954. [11]

Frost, R. Between prose and verse. *Atlantic Monthly*, April 1962. [10]

Gaines, R. LSD: Hollywood's status symbol drug. *Cosmopolitan*, 1963. [7]

Galton, F. *Hereditary genius*. New York: Appleton, 1870. [3]

Gardner, R. W., Holzman, P. S., Klein, G. S., Linton, H. B., & Spence, D. P. Cognitive control: A study of individual consistencies in cognitive behavior. *Psychological Issues*, 1959, **1**, No. 4. [9]

Gendlin, E. T., Beebe, J. III, Cassens, J., Klein, M., & Oberlander, M. Focusing ability in psychotherapy, personality, and creativity. In J. M. Shlien (Ed.), *Research in psychotherapy, Vol. 3*. Washington, D. C.: American Psychological Association, 1968. [5]

Getzels, J. W., & Jackson, P. W. *Creativity and intelligence*. New York: Wiley, 1962. [8]

Ghiselin, B. *The creative process*. Berkeley: Univ. of California Press, 1952. [10]

Ghiselin, B. Ultimate criteria for two levels of creativity. In C. W. Taylor & F. Barron (Eds.), *Scientific creativity: Its recognition and development*. New York: Wiley, 1963.
[2, 3]

Ghiselin, B., Rompel, R., & Taylor, C. W. A creative process check list: Its development and validation. In C. W. Taylor (Ed.), *Widening horizons in creativity*. New York: Wiley, 1964. [3]

Giarman, N., & Freedman, D. Biochemical aspects of the actions of psychotomimetic drugs. *Pharmacological Review*, 1965, **17**, 1-25. [7]

Giscard, P. H. L'étude des comportements dans la recherche scientifique: Adaptation du questionnaire R.S.Q.D. de H. G. Gough et D. G. Woodworth. *Le Travail Humain*, 1966, **29**, 89-94. [10]

Goldberger, L. Cognitive test performance under LSD-25, placebo and isolation. *The Journal of Nervous and Mental Disease*, 1966, **142**, 4-9. [7]

Goldner, B. B. *The strategy of creative thinking*. Englewood Cliffs, New Jersey: Prentice-Hall, 1962. [9]

Gordon, W. J. J. *Synectics*. New York: Harper, 1961. [2, 5, 8, 9, 10]

Gough, H. G. Techniques for identifying the creative research scientist. In *Proceedings of "The creative person."* Conference presented at The Tahoe Alumni Center, October 13-17, 1961. Berkeley: University of California, Institute of Personality Assessment and Research, and Liberal Arts Department. [4]

Gough, H. G. Identifying the creative man. *Journal of Value Engineering*, 1964, **2**, 5-12.
[4]

Gough, H. G., & Woodworth, D. G. Stylistic variations among professional research scientists. *Journal of Psychology*, 1960, **49**, 87-98. [10]

Grinspoon, L. *Marihuana reconsidered*. Cambridge, Massachusetts: Harvard University Press, 1971. [7]

Grossman, J. C., Goldstein, R., & Eisenman, R. Openness to experience and marijuana use: An initial investigation. In *Proceedings 79th Annual Convention*, American Psychological Association, 1971. [7]

Guilford, J. P. Creativity. *American Psychologist*, 1950, **5**, 444-454. [5]

Guilford, J. P. The structure of intellect. *Psychological Bulletin*, 1956, **53**, 267-293. [9]

Guilford, J. P. What to do about creativity in education. Paper presented at the Western Regional Conference on Testing Problems of the Educational Testing Service, Los Angeles, California, May 4, 1962. [1]

Guilford, J. P. Intellectual factors in productive thinking. Paper presented at the Second Conference on Productive Thinking, conducted by the Project on the Academically Talented Student, of the National Educational Association, Washington, D. C., May 2-4, 1963. [6]

Guilford, J. P. *The nature of human intelligence*. New York: McGraw-Hill, 1967.
[3, 5, 6, 7, 8, 9]

Guilford, J. P., & Hoepfner, R. Structure-of-intellect factors and their tests, 1966. Studies of aptitudes of high-level personnel. *Report No. 36*. Los Angeles: Psychological Laboratory, University of Southern California, June 1966. [6]

Haley, R. I. Beyond benefit segmentation. *Journal of Advertising Research*, 1971, 11 (No. 4), 3-8. [11]

Hall, C. S., & Lindzey, G. *Theories of personality*. New York: Wiley, 1970. [4]

Harman, W. W., McKim, R. H., Mogar, R. E., Fadiman, J., & Stolaroff, M. J. Psychedilic agents in creative problem solving: A pilot study. In C. T. Tart (Ed.), *Altered states of consciousness*. New York: Wiley, 1969. [7]

Harmon, L. R. The development of a criterion of scientific competence. In C. W. Taylor (Ed.), *The second (1957) University of Utah research conference on the identification of creative scientific talent*. Salt Lake City: Univ. of Utah Press, 1958. [3]

Hartmann, H. *Essays on Ego Psychology*. New York: International Universities Press, Inc., 1964. [9]

Havens, A. E. Social psychological factors associated with differential adoption of new technologies by milk producers. Unpublished doctoral dissertation, Ohio State University, Columbus, 1962. [11]

Hawkins, N. G. The detailman and preference behavior. *Southwestern Social Science Quarterly*, 1959, **40**, 213-224. [11]

Hess, R. D., & Tenezakis, M. The computer as a socializing agent: Some socioaffective outcomes of CAI. *Technical Report No. 13*. Stanford, California: Stanford Center for Research and Development in Teaching, October 1970. [8]

Hobelman, L. Three creative teachers. *Clearing House*, 1957, **32**, 161-162. [8]

Hogan, R., Mankin, D., Conway, J., & Fox, S. Personality correlates of undergraduate marijuana use. *Journal of Consulting and Clinical Psychology*, 1970, **35**, 58-63.
[7]

Hoijer, H. The Sapir-Whorf hypothesis. In H. Hoijer (Ed.), *Language in culture*. Chicago: Univ. of Chicago Press, 1954. [6]

Holland, J. L. The prediction of college grades from personality and aptitude variables. *Journal of Educational Psychology*, 1960, **51**, 245-254. [8]

Holton, G. On the duality and growth of physical science. *American Scientist*, 1953, **41**, 89-99. [2]

Horovitz, Z. P., Mulroy, M. I., Waldron, T., & Leaf, R. Behavioral and encephalographic effects of LSD. *Journal of Pharmaceutical Science*, 1965, **54**, 108-110.   [7]

Hughes, E. C. Psychology: Science and/or profession. *American Psychologist*, 1952, **7**, 441-443.   [11]

Huxley, A. *The doors of perception*. New York: Harper, 1963.   [7]

Hyman, R. Some experiments in creativity. New York: General Electric, 1960.   [8, 10]

Hyman, R. On prior information and creativity. *Psychological Reports*, 1961, **9**, 151-161.   [8]

Hyman, R. Creativity and the prepared mind: The role of information and induced attitudes. In C. W. Taylor (Ed.), *Widening horizons in creativity*. New York: Wiley, 1964.   [8]

James, B. J., Guetzkow, H., Forehand, G. A., & Libby, W. L. *Education for innovative behavior in executives*. Cooperative Research Project No. 975. Washington, D. C.: Office of Education, U. S. Department of Health, Education and Welfare, August 1962.   [3]

Jarvik, M. E., Abramson, H. A., & Hirsch, M. W. Lysergic Acid Diethylamide (LSD-25): IV. Effect on attention span and concentration. *Journal of Psychology*, 1955, **39**, 373-383. (a)   [7]

Jarvik, M. E., Abramson, H. A., & Hirsch, M. W. Lysergic Acid Diethylamide (LSD-25): VI. Effect upon recall and recognition of various stimuli. *Journal of Psychology*, 1955, **39**, 443-454. (b)   [7]

Jarvik, M. E., Abramson, H. A., Hirsch, M. W., & Ewald, A. T. Lysergic Acid Diethylamide (LSD-25): VIII. Effect on arithmetic test performance. *Journal of Psychology*, 1955, **39**, 465-473. (c)   [7]

John, E. R. Contributions to the study of the problem-solving process. *Psychological Monographs*, 1957, **71**, No. 18 (Whole No. 447).   [10]

Jones, E. *The life and work of Sigmund Freud, Vol. 1*. New York: Basic Books, 1953.   [9]

Kaplan, A. Freud and modern philosophy. In B. Nelson (Ed.), *Freud and the 20th century*. New York: Meridian, 1957.   [2]

Katz, E. The two-step flow of communication: An up-to-date report on an hypothesis. *Public Opinion Quarterly*, 1957, **21**, 61-78.   [11]

Katz, E., & Lazarsfeld, P. F. *Personal influence*. New York: Free Press, 1955.   [11]

Kerr, W. Pity the "almost-there" playwright. *The New York Times*, Section 2, Arts and Leisure, February 13, 1972.   [11]

Kivlin, J. E. Characteristics of farm practices associated with rate of adoption. Unpublished doctoral dissertation, Pennsylvania State University, University Park, 1960.   [11]

Klonglan, G., *et al*. The role of a free sample in the adoption process. Paper presented at the Midwest Sociological Society, St. Louis, Missouri, 1960.   [11]

Knight, K. E. Effect of effort on behavior rigidity in a Luchins water jar task. *Journal of Abnormal and Social Psychology*, 1963, **66**, 190-192.   [10]

Koffka, K. *Principles of Gestalt psychology*. New York: Harcourt, 1935.   [6]

Korzybski. A. *Science and sanity*. (2nd ed.) Lancaster, Pennsylvania: Science Press, 1941.   [6, 9]

Krauss, R. *A Hole is to dig: A first book of first definition* New York: Harper, 1952.   [9]

Krech, D., Crutchfield, R. S., & Livson, N. *Elements of psychology*. New York: Knopf, 1969.   [10]

Krippner, S. The psychedelic state, the hypnotic trance, and the creative act. In C. T. Tart (Ed.), *Altered states of consciousness*. New York: Wiley, 1969.   [5, 7]

Kris, E. *Psychoanalytic explorations in art*. New York: International Univ. Press, 1952.
[2, 11]

Kris, E. Psychoanalysis and the study of creative imagination. *Bulletin of the New York Academy of Medicine*, 1953, **29**, 334-351. [2]

Kubie, L. S. *Neurotic distortion of the creative process*. Lawrence: Univ. of Kansas Press. 1958. [7]

Lacklen, R., & Harmon, L. R. Criterion Committee report. In C. W. Taylor (Ed.), *The second (1957) University of Utah research conference on the identification of creative scientific talent*. Salt Lake City: Univ. of Utah Press, 1958. [2]

Lawshe, C., & Harris, D. *Purdue Creativity Test*. West Lafayette, Indiana: Purdue Research Foundation, 1960. [7]

Lazarsfeld, P. F., Berelson, B., & Gaudet, H. *The people's choice*. New York: Duell, Sloan & Pearce, 1944. [11]

Leary, T. The effects of test score feedback on creative performance and of drugs on creative experience. In C. W. Taylor (Ed.), *Widening horizons in creativity*. New York: Wiley, 1964. [5]

Lee, H. B. On the esthetic states of the mind. *Psychiatry*, 1947, **10**, 281-306. [9, 11]

Legon, E. M. *The growth and development of Christian personality*. Schenectady, New York: The Union College Character Research Project, 1957. [8]

Lehman, H. C. *Age and achievement*. Princeton, New Jersey: Princeton Univ. Press, 1953. [3]

Levey, H. B. A theory concerning free creation in the inventive arts. *Psychiatry*, 1940, **3**, 229-293. [2]

Levine, E., Abramson, H. S., Kaufman, M. R., & Markham, S. Lysergic Acid Diethylamide (LSD-25): XVI. The effect on intellectual functioning as measured by the Wechsler-Bellevue Intelligence Scale. *Journal of Psychology*, 1955, **40**, 385-395. [7]

Levinson, D. J., & Huffman, P. E. Traditional family ideology and its relation to personality. *Journal of Personality*, 1955, **23**, 251-273. [10]

Lewin, K. *A dynamic theory of personality*. New York: McGraw-Hill, 1935. [11]

Lewin, K. Group decision and social change. In E. E. Maccoby, T. M. Newcomb, & E. L. Hartley (Eds.), *Readings in social psychology*. (3rd ed.) New York: Holt, 1958. [11]

Linton, R. Cultural and personality factors affecting economic growth. In B. F. Hoselitz (Ed.), *The progress of underdeveloped areas*. Chicago: Univ. of Chicago Press, 1952. [11]

Lionberger, H. F. Some characteristics of farm operators sought as sources of farm information in a Missouri community. *Rural Sociology*, 1953, **18**, 327-338. [11]

Lionberger, H. F. *Information seeking habits and characteristics of farm operators*. Columbia: Missouri Agricultural Experiment Station Bulletin 581, 1955. [11]

Lionberger, H. F. Community prestige and the choice of sources of farm information. *Public Opinion Quarterly*, 1959, **23**, 111-118. [11]

Lionberger, H. F. *Adoption of new ideas and practices: A summary of the research dealing with the acceptance of technological change in agriculture, and implications for action in facilitating social change*. Ames: Iowa State Univ. Press, 1960. [11]

Luchins, A. S. Mechanization in problem-solving: The effect of einstellung. *Psychological Monographs*, 1942, **54**, No. 248. [10]

McAree, C. P., Steffenhagen, R. A., & Zheutlin, L. S. Personality factors in college drug use. *International Journal of Social Psychiatry*, 1969, **15**, 102-106. [7]

McCardle, H. J. An investigation of the relationship between pupil achievement in first-year algebra and some teacher characteristics. Unpublished doctoral dissertation, University of Minnesota, 1959. [8]

McClelland, D. C. On the psychodynamics of creative physical scientists. In H. E. Gruber, G. Terrell, & M. Wertheimer (Eds.), *Contemporary approaches to creative thinking.* New York: Atherton Press, 1962. [4]

Maccoby, E. E., Newcomb, T. M., & Hartley, E. L. (Eds.) *Readings in Social Psychology.* (3rd ed.) New York: Holt, 1958. [11]

McCord, H., & Sherrill, C. A. A note on increased ability to do calculus post-hypnotically. *American Journal of Clinical Hypnosis*, 1961, 4, 20. [5]

MacCurdy, E. *The notebooks of Leonardo da Vinci.* New York: Harcourt, 1956. [9]

McGlothlin, W., Cohen, S., & McGlothlin, M. *Long-lasting effects of LSD on normals.* Los Angeles: Institute of Government and Public Affairs, 1967. [7]

MacKinnon, D. W. The creative worker in engineering. Paper read at Eleventh Annual Industrial Engineering Institute, University of California at Los Angeles and at Berkeley, February 6-7, 1959. (a) [4]

MacKinnon, D. W. On becoming an architect. *Architectural Record*, 1959, 126, (No. 2.), 64-6 to 64-6 Western Section. (b) [4]

MacKinnon, D. W. The highly effective individual. *Teachers College Record*, 1960, 61, 367-378. [3, 8]

MacKinnon, D. W. Fostering creativity in students of engineering. *Journal of Engineering Education*, 1961, 52, 129-142. [8]

MacKinnon, D. W. The nature and nurture of creative talent. *American Psychologist*, 1962, 17 484-495. [4]

MacKinnon, D. W. The identification and development of creative potential. Paper read at Bowdoin College, Brunswick, Maine, May 2, 1964. [1, 2]

McLuhan, M. *Understanding media: The extensions of man.* New York: Signet, 1964. [11]

McPherson, J. H. *The people, the problems and the problem-solving* methods. Midland, Michigan: Pendell, 1967. [9]

Maddi, S. R. Activation and the need for variety. Paper delivered at Knox College and Galesburg State Hospital, Galesburg, Illinois, April, 1963. [4]

Maddi, S. R. *Personality theories: A comparative analysis.* Homewood, Illinois: Dorsey Press, 1968. [4]

Maddi, S. R., & Berne, N. Novelty of productions and desire for novelty as active and passive forms of the need for variety. *Journal of Personality*, 1964, 32, 270-277. [4]

Maddi, S. R., Andrews, S. L., & Hovey, R. D. Some structured self-report correlates of fantasy measures of the need for variety. *Research Bulletin 64-21.* Princeton, New Jersey: Educational Testing Service, 1964. [4]

Maddi, S. R., Propst, B. S., & Feldinger, I. Three expressions of the need for variety. *Journal of Personality*, 1965, 33, 82-98. [4]

Maier, N. R. F. An aspect of human reasoning. *British Journal of Psychology*, 1933, 24, 144-155. [10]

Maier, N. R. F. *Problem solving and creativity in individuals and groups.* Belmont, California: Wadsworth, 1969. [10]

Mandelbaum, D. G. *Edward Sapir: Culture, language and personality.* Berkeley: Univ. of California Press, 1962. [2]

Marsh, C. P., & Coleman, A. L. Farmers' practice-adoption rates in relation to adoption rates of "leaders." *Rural Sociology*, 1954, **19**, 180-181.   [11]

Martineau, P. *Motivation in advertising; motives that make people buy*. New York: McGraw-Hill, 1957.   [11]

Maslow, A. H. Creativity in self-actualizing people. In H. H. Anderson (Ed.), *Creativity and its cultivation*. New York: Harper, 1959.   [1, 4]

Mayor's Committee on Marihuana. *The marihuana problem in the City of New York: Sociological, medical, psychological, and pharmacological studies*. Lancaster, Pennsylvania: Jacques Cattell Press, 1944.   [7]

Meadow, A., & Parnes, S. J. Evaluation of training in creative problem-solving. *Journal of Applied Psychology*, 1959, **43**, 189-194.   [8]

Mednick, S. A. The associative basis of the creative process. *Psychological Review*, 1962, **69**, 220-232.   [10]

Mednick, S. A., & Mednick, M. T. An associative interpretation of the creative process. In C. W. Taylor (Ed.), *Widening horizons in creativity*. New York: Wiley, 1964.   [10]

Menzel, H. Public and private conformity under different conditions of acceptance in groups. *Journal of Abnormal and Social Psychology*, 1957, **55**, 398-402.   [11]

Menzel, H., & Katz, E. Social relations and innovation in the medical profession: The epidemiology of a new drug. In E. E. Maccoby, T. M. Newcomb, & E. L. Hartley (Eds.), *Readings in social psychology*. (3rd ed.) New York: Holt, 1958   [11]

Merton, R. K. *Social theory and social structure*. New York: Free Press, 1957.   [11]

Meyer, E. H. Is the golden goose beginning to lay leaden eggs? A.N.A. Seminar on TV Advertising Management, April 1970.   [11]

Miller Analogies Test Manual. New York: The Psychological Corp., 1970 revision.   [10]

Miller, D. *Survey of object visualization*. Monterey, California: California Test Bureau, 1955.   [7]

Milman, D. H. An untoward reaction to accidental ingestion of LSD in a 5-year-old girl. *Journal of the American Medical Association*, 1967, **201**, 143-146.   [7]

Mogar, R. E. Current status and future trends in psychedelic (LSD) research. In C. T. Tart (Ed.), *Altered states of consciousness*. New York: Wiley, 1969.   [7]

Moore, O. K. *Autotelic responsive environments and exceptional children*. Hamden, Connecticut: Responsive Environments Foundation, 1963.   [8]

Munsterberg, E., & Mussen, P. H. The personality structures of art students. *Journal of Personality*, 1953, **21**, 457-466.   [4]

Murray, H. A., *et al. Explorations in personality*. New York: Oxford Univ. Press, 1938.
                                                                                        [11]

Nash, H. *Alcohol and caffeine*. Springfield, Illinois: Thomas, 1962.   [7]

New York Times. Psychiatrists testify marijuana harms adolescents. May 18, 1971. (a)   [7]

New York Times. More states ease marijuana curbs. August 8, 1971. (b)   [7]

Nielsen, W. A. *The big foundations. A twentieth century fund study*. New York: Columbia Univ. Press, 1972.   [11]

Norton, W. A. The marijuana habit: Some observations of a small group of users. *Canadian Psychiatric Association Journal*, 1968, **13**, 163-173.   [7]

Nye, I. *The relationship of certain factors to county agent success*. Columbia: Missouri Agricultural Experiment Station Research Bulletin 498, 1952.   [11]

Ogilvy, D. *Confessions of an advertising man*. New York: Atheneum, 1963.   [11]

Opinion Research Corporation. America's tastemakers: A new strategy for predicting change in consumer behavior. Princeton, New Jersey, 1959.   [11]

Osborn, A. F. *Applied imagination*. (3rd ed.) New York: Scribner's, 1963.   [9]

Papini, G. *Michelanglo his life and his era*. Translated by L. Murnane. New York: Dutton, 1952.   [11]

Parloff, M. F. Myths in research on creativity. *Review of Existential Psychology and Psychiatry*, 1967, 7, 18-29. [2]

Parloff, M. B. Creativity research program: A review. In C. W. Taylor (Ed.), *Climate for creativity*. Elmsford, New York: Pergamon Press, 1972. [5, 7]

Parnes, S. J. *Programming creative behavior*. Title VII Project Number 5-0716, National Defense Education Act. Buffalo: State University of New York, and Albany: Research Foundation of State University of New York, 1966. [8]

Parnes, S. J. *Creative behavior guidebook*. New York: Scribner's, 1967. [9]

Parnes, S. J., & Harding, H. F. (Eds.) *A source book for creative thinking*. New York: Scribner's, 1962. [9]

Peck, R. F. What makes a man creative? *Personnel*, 1958, 35, 18-23. [4]

Pfeiffer, C. C., Goldstein, L., Murphree, H. B., & Sugarman, A. A. Times-series, frequency analysis and electrogenesis of the EEG's of normals and psychotics before and after drugs. *American Journal of Psychiatry*, 1965, 121, 1147-1155. [7]

Poincaré, H. Mathematical creation. In B. Ghiselin (Ed.), *The creative process*. Berkeley: University of California Press, 1952. [2]

Polya, G. *How to solve it*. Princeton, New Jersey: Princeton Univ. Press, 1946. [10]

Preiss, J. J. Functions of relevant power and authority groups in the evaluation of county agent performance. Unpublished doctoral dissertation, Michigan State University, 1954. [11]

Prince, G. M. *The practice of creativity*. New York: Harper, 1970. [11]

Radke, M., & Klisurich, D. Experiments in changing food habits. *Journal of American Dietetic Association*, 1947, 24, 403-409. [11]

Rahudkar, W. B. Impact of fertilizer extension programme on the minds of the farmers and their reactions to different extension methods. *Indian Journal of Agronomy*, 1958, 3, 119-136. [11]

Read, H. *Art now*. New York: Pitman, 1948. [2]

Reichenbach, H. *Experience and prediction*. Chicago: Univ. of Chicago Press, 1938. [2]

Rodin, E., & Luby, E. Effects of LSD-25 on the EEG and photic evoked responses. *Archives of General Psychiatry*, 1966, 14, 435-441. [7]

Roe, A. Artists and their work. *Journal of Personality*, 1946, 15, 1-40. (a) [4]

Roe, A. Painting and personality. *Rorschach Research Exchange and Journal of Projective Techniques*, 1946, 10, 86-100. (b) [4]

Roe, A. The personality of artists. *Educational and Psychological Measurement*, 1946, 6, 401-408. (c) [4]

Roe, A. Alcohol and creative work. *Quarterly Journal of Studies of Alcohol*, 1946, 6, 415-467. (d) [7]

Roe, A. Psychological examinations of eminent biologists. *Journal of Consulting Psychology*, 1949, 13, 225-246. [4]

Roe, A. A psychological study of eminent biologists. *Psychological Monographs*, 1951, 65, No. 14. [3]

Roe, A. A psychological study of eminent psychologists and anthropologists, and a comparison with biological and physical scientists. *Psychological Monographs*, 1953, 67, No. 2, (Whole No. 352). [4]

Rogers, E. M. Personal communication from A. W. van den Ban, 1961. (a) [11]

Rogers, E. M. *Characteristics of agricultural innovators and other adopter categories*. Wooster: Ohio Agricultural Experiment Station Research Bulletin 882, 1961. (b) [11]

Rogers, E. M. *Diffusion of innovations*. New York: Free Press, 1962. [11]

Rogers, E. M., & Leuthold, F. O. *Demonstrators and the diffusion of fertilizer practices.* Wooster: Ohio Agricultural Experiment Station Research Bulletin 908, 1962.   [11]

Rogers, E. M., & Shoemaker, F. F. *Communication of Innovations.* (2nd ed.) New York: Free Press, 1971.   [11]

Rosenfeld, A., & Farrell, B. The spread and perils of LSD. *Life*, 1966, **60**, 28-33.   [7]

Rosett, H. L., Robbins, H., & Watson, W. S. Standardization and construct validity of the Physiognomic Cue Test. *Perceptual & Motor Skills*, 1967, **24**, 403-420.   [9]

Rossman, J. *The psychology of the inventor.* Washington, D. C.: Inventors Publishing Co., 1931.   [3, 4, 11]

Rusch, R. R., Denny, D. A., & Ives, S. Fostering creativity in sixth grade. *Elementary School Journal*, 1965, **65**, 262-268.   [8]

Ryan, B. *Social and ecological patterns in the farm leadership of four Iowa townships.* Ames: Iowa Agricultural Experiment Station Bulletin 306, 1942.   [11]

Ryan, B., & Gross, N. C. The diffusion of hybrid seed corn in two Iowa communities. *Rural Sociology*, 1943, **8**, 15-24.   [11]

Sachs, H. *The creative unconscious.* (2nd ed.) Cambridge, Massachusetts: Sci-Art, 1951.   [11]

Sanford, N., Webster, H., & Freedman, M. Impulse expression as a variable of personality. *Psychological Monographs*, 1957, **71**, No. 11, (Whole No. 440).   [9]

Scheerer, M. Problem-solving. *Scientific American*, April 1963, **208**, 118-128.   [10]

Shannon, J. R. Traits of research workers. *Journal of Educational Research*, 1947, **40**, 513-521.   [4]

Sherif, M. *The psychology of social norms.* New York: Harper, 1936.   [11]

Simon, J. Critical prognosis: New chaps and old boys. *New York*, September 20, 1971, pg. 54.   [11]

Skinner, B. F. Teaching machines. *Scientific American*, Nov. 1961, **205**, 90-102.   [8]

Slotkin, J. S. *Menomini Peyotism.* Transactions of the American Philosophical Society. December 1952. Monograph.   [7]

Stein, M. I. *Individual qualification form.* New York: Abacus, 1959. (a)   [8]

Stein, M. I. *Personal data form for scientific, engineering, and technical personnel.* New York: Abacus, 1959. (b)   [8]

Stein, M. I. *Research personnel review form.* New York: Abacus, 1959. (c)   [8]

Stein, M. I. *Stein research environment survey.* New York: Abacus, 1959. (d)   [8, 11]

Stein, M. I. *Stein survey for administrators.* New York: Abacus, 1959. (e)   [8]

Stein, M. I. (Ed.) *Contemporary psychotherapies.* New York: Free Press, 1961.   [5]

Stein, M. I. Creativity and the scientist. In B. Barber & W. Hirsch (Eds.), *The sociology of science.* New York: Free Press, 1962.   [4, 11]

Stein, M. I. Creativity in a free society. *Educational Horizons*, 1963, **41**, 115-130.   [11]

Stein, M. I. Explorations in typology. In C. S. Hall and G. Lindzey (Eds.), *Theories of personality.* New York: Wiley, 1965.   [4, 11]

Stein, M. I. *Volunteers for peace.* New York: Wiley, 1966.   [10, 11]

Stein, M. I. Creativity and culture. In R. L. Mooney & T. A. Razik (Eds.), *Explorations in creativity.* New York: Harper, 1967.   [1, 2]

Stein, M. I. Creativity. In E. F. Borgatta & W. W. Lambert (Eds.), *Handbook of personality theory and research.* Chicago: Rand McNally, 1968.   [4, 6]

Stein, M. I. *Physiognomic cue test*, New York: Behavioral Publications, 1974.   [9]

Stein, M. I., & Heinze, S. J. *Creativity and the individual.* New York: Free Press, 1960.   [1, 4]

Stein, M. I., & Neulinger, J. A typology of self-descriptions. In M. M. Katz, J. O. Cole, & W. E. Barton (Eds.), *The role and methodology of classification in psychiatry and psychopathology*. Washington, D. C.: Government Printing Office, Public Health Service Publication No. 1584, 1968. [10, 11]

Stein, M. I., Heinze, S. J., Rodgers, R. R. Creativity and/or success. In C. W. Taylor (Ed.), *The second (1957) University of Utah research conference on the identification of creative scientific talent*. Salt Lake City: Univ. of Utah Press, 1958. [3]

Steinbeck, J. Critics—from a writer's viewpoint. *Saturday Review*, August 27, 1955, pg. 20. [11]

Stern, B. J. Social factors in medical progress. In Faculty of Political Science of Columbia University (Eds.), *Studies in History, Economics, and Public Law, No. 287*. New York: Columbia Univ. Press, 1927. [11]

Stern, G. G. *High School Characteristics Index*. Syracuse, New York: Syracuse University, Psychological Research Center, 1958. [8]

Stern, G. G., & Pace, C. R. *College Characteristics Index*. Syracuse, New York: Syracuse University, Psychological Research Center, 1958. [8]

Stern, G. G., Stein, M. I., & Bloom, B. S. *Methods in personality assessment*. New York: Free Press, 1956. [9]

Stern, G. G., Winters, C. L., Jr., Archer, N. W., & Meyer, D. L. *Evening College Characteristics Index*. Syracuse, New York: Syracuse University, Psychological Research Center, 1961. [8]

Stevens, E. The artist as an affluent man. *The Wall Street Journal*, February 4, 1971, pg. 12. [11]

Stewart, F. A. A sociometric study of influence in Southtown. *Sociometry*, 1947, **10**, 11-31. [11]

Stewart, K. Dream theory in Malaya. In C. T. Tart (Ed.), *Altered states of consciousness*. New York: Wiley, 1969. [7]

Stone, J. T. *How county agricultural agents teach*. East Lansing: Michigan Agricultural Extension Service Mimeo Bulletin, 1952. [11]

Strother, R. The concentrations of Isaac Newton. *Saturday Review*, July 23, 1955, pp. 7, 25, 26. [11]

Suchman, J. R. Inquiry training: Building skills for autonomous discovery. *Merrill-Palmer Quarterly*, 1961, 7, 147-169. [8]

Sullivan, H. S. *Interpersonal theory of psychology*. New York: Norton, 1953. [8]

Tart, C. T. (Ed.) *Altered states of consciousness*. New York: Wiley, 1969. (a) [7]

Tart, C. T. Introduction to Section 6. Minor psychedelic drugs. In C. T. Tart (Ed.), *Altered states of consciousness*. New York: Wiley, 1969. (b) [7]

Taylor, C. W. A search for a creative climate. Paper presented at Seventeenth National Conference on the Administration of Research, Estes Park, Colorado, September 11-13, 1963. [4, 8]

Taylor, J. W. *How to create new ideas*. Englewood Cliffs, New Jersey: Prentice-Hall, 1961. [9]

Taylor, J. A personality scale of manifest anxiety. *Journal of Abnormal and Social Psychology*, 1953, **48**, 285-290. [9, 10]

Time, November 16, 1953, pp. 20, 27. [11]

Tinnin, L. Cognitive activity without awareness. *American Journal of Clinical Hypnosis*, 1963, 6, 37-39. [5]

Torrance, E. P. Explorations in creative thinking in mental hygiene: III. Effects of induced evaluative sets on the development of new ideas. *Research Memo BER-59-15*. Minneapolis: Bureau of Educational Research, Univ. of Minnesota, 1959. [8]

Torrance, E. P. The creative teacher and the school team: Problems and pleasures of the principal. In *Professional growth for principals*. New London, Connecticut: Arthur C.

Croft Publishing, April 1961. (a)   [8]

Torrance, E. P. The teacher as a team member: Team leadership through creative administration. In *Professional growth for administrators*. New London, Connecticut: Arthur C. Croft Publishing, April 1961. (b)   [8]

Torrance, E. P. *Guiding creative talent*. Englewood Cliffs, New Jersey: Prentice-Hall, 1962. (a)   [8]

Torrance, E. P. Cultural discontinuities and the development of originality in thinking. *Exceptional Children*, 1962, **29**, 2-13. (b)   [8]

Torrance, E. P. *Rewarding creative behavior*. Englewood Cliffs, New Jersey: Prentice-Hall, 1965.   [8]

Torrance, E. P., & Gupta, R. *Programmed experiences in creative thinking: Development and evaluation of recorded programmed experiences in creative thinking in the fourth grade*. Minneapolis: Bureau of Educational Research, University of Minnesota, 1964.
                                                                               [8]

Torrance, E. P., *et al. Role of evaluation in creative thinking, revised summary report*. U. S. Office of Education, Department of Health, Education, and Welfare, Cooperative Research Project No. 725. Minneapolis: Bureau of Educational Research, University of Minnesota, 1964.   [8]

Trent, W. The demented world of KY Izumi. *Weekend Magazine*, February 1966.   [7]

Uhr, L. Learning under hypnosis: What do we know? What should we know? *Journal of Clinical and Experimental Hypnosis*, 1958, **6**, 121-135.   [5]

Usher, A. P. *A history of mechanical inventions*. Cambridge, Massachusetts: Harvard University Press, 1954.   [11]

Van Zelst, R. H., & Kerr, W. A. Some correlates of technical and scientific productivity. *Journal of Abnormal and Social Psychology*, 1951, **46**, 470-475.   [4]

Von Fange, E. K. *Professional creativity*. Englewood Cliffs, New Jersey: Prentice-Hall, 1959.
                                                                               [9]

Walker, D. E. The relationship between creativity and selected test behavior for chemists and mathematicians. Unpublished doctoral dissertation, University of Chicago, 1955.
                                                                               [9]

Wall Street Journal. Business Bulletin: New products continue to be risky undertakings. June 17, 1971, pg. 1.   [11]

Wallach, M. A., & Kogan, N. *Modes of thinking in young children*. New York: Holt, 1965.
                                                                               [8]

Wallas, G. *The art of thought*. New York: Harcourt, 1926.   [2]

Warner, W. L., & Lunt, P. S. *The social life of a modern community, Vol. 1*. New Haven: Yale Univ. Press, 1941.   [11]

Weil, A. T., Zinberg, N. E., & Nielsen, J. M. Clinical and psychological effects of marihuana in man. *Science*, 1968, **162**, 1234-1242.   [7]

Weissman, P. *Creativity in the theater—A psychoanalytic study*. New York: Dell Publ., 1965.   [11]

Wells, W. D., & Tigert, D. Activities, interests and opinions. *Journal of Advertising Research*, 1971, **11**, No. 4, 27-35.   [11]

Werner, H. *Comparative psychology of mental development*. New York: International Univ. Press, 1957.   [2, 9]

Werre, P. F. Electroencephalographic effects of LSD and some psychiatric implications. *Journal of Neuropsychiatry*, 1964, **5**, 516-524.   [7]

Wertheimer, M. *Productive thinking*. New York: Harper, 1945.   [2, 3, 9, 10]

Wessel, H. M. Four teachers I have known. *Saturday Review*, June 17, 1961, pp. 70 ff.
                                                                               [8]

Westcott, M. R. On the measurement of intuitive leaps. *Psychological Reports*, 1961, **9**, 267-274. [9]

Westcott, M. R. Empirical studies of intuition. In C. W. Taylor (Ed.), *Widening horizons in creativity*. New York: Wiley, 1964. [9]

Westcott, M. R. A note on the stability of intuitive thinking. *Psychological Reports*, 1966, **19**, 194. [9]

Westcott, M. R. *Toward a contemporary psychology of intuition*. New York: Holt, 1968. [9]

Westcott, M. R., & Ranzoni, J. H. Correlates of intuitive thinking. *Psychological Reports*, 1963, **12**, 595-613. [9]

Westcott, M. R., & Tolchin, M. Individual and age-related differences in perceptual inference behavior. *Perceptual & Motor Skills*, 1968, **26**, 683-697. [9]

White, R. K. The versatility of genius. *Journal of Social Psychology*, 1931, **2**, 460-489. [4]

Whiting, C. S. *Creative thinking*. New York: Reinhold, 1958. [2, 9]

Wild, K. *Intuition*. New York: Macmillan, 1938. [9]

Wilkening, E. A. consensus in role definition of county extension agents between the agents and local sponsoring committee members. *Rural Sociology*, 1958, **23**, 184-197. [11]

Winick, C. The use of drugs by jazz musicians. *Social Problems*, 1960, **7**, 240-253. [7]

Wispé, L. G., & Parloff, M. B. Impact of psychotherapy on the productivity of psychologists. *Journal of Abnormal Psychology*, 1965, **70**, 188-193. [5]

Witkin, H., Dyk, R., Faterson, H., Goodenough, D., & Karp, S. *Psychological differentiation: studies of development*. New York: Wiley, 1962. [7]

Witkin, H. A., Oltman, P. K., Raskin, E., & Karp, S. A. *A manual for the Embedded Figures Tests*. Palo Alto, California: Consulting Psychologists Press, 1971. [7, 10]

Wollman, L. Influence of hypnosis on the learning process. *Journal of the American Society of Psychosomatic Dentistry and Medicine*, 1965, **12**, 79-99. [5]

Zegans, L., Pollard, J., & Brown, D. The effects of LSD-25 on creativity and tolerance to regression. *Archives of General Psychiatry*, 1967, **16**, 740-749. [7]

Zinberg, N. E., & Weil, A. T. A comparison of marijuana users and non-users. *Nature*, 1970, **226**, 119-123. [7]

Zwicky, F. *Morphological astronomy*. Berlin and New York: Springer-Verlag Press, 1957. [9]

Zwicky, F. *Discovery, invention, research*. New York: Macmillan, 1969. [9]

Subject Index

A 4
B 5
C 6
D 7
E 8
F 9
G 0
H 1
I 2
J 3